EPICUREANISM AND SCIENTIFIC DEBATES:
EPICUREAN TRADITION AND ITS ANCIENT RECEPTION

VOLUME II. EPISTEMOLOGY AND ETHICS

ANCIENT AND MEDIEVAL PHILOSOPHY

DE WULF-MANSION CENTRE
Series I

LXIV, 2

Editorial Coordinator

Russell Friedman

Editorial Board

Lisa Devriese
Pieter d'Hoine
Jan Opsomer
Andrea Robiglio
Carlos Steel
Gerd Van Riel

Advisory Board

Brad Inwood, Yale University, USA
Jill Kraye, The Warburg Institute, London, United Kingdom
John Marenbon, University of Cambridge, United Kingdom
Lodi Nauta, University of Groningen, The Netherlands
Timothy Noone, The Catholic University of America, USA
Robert Pasnau, University of Colorado at Boulder, USA
Martin Pickavé, University of Toronto, Canada
Pasquale Porro, Università di Torino, Italy
Geert Roskam, KU Leuven, Belgium

The "De Wulf-Mansion Centre" is a research centre for Ancient, Medieval, and Renaissance philosophy at the Institute of Philosophy of the KU Leuven, Kardinaal Mercierplein, 2, B-3000 Leuven (Belgium).
It hosts the international project "Aristoteles Latinus" and
publishes the "Opera omnia" of Henry of Ghent and the "Opera Philosophica et Theologica" of Francis of Marchia.

EPICUREANISM AND SCIENTIFIC DEBATES: EPICUREAN TRADITION AND ITS ANCIENT RECEPTION

Volume II. Epistemology and Ethics

Edited by
Francesca Masi, Pierre-Marie Morel and Francesco Verde

LEUVEN UNIVERSITY PRESS

This book is published in Open Access thanks to support by the Open Book Collective.

For details on the supporting institutions, participating in the Open Book Collective, see www.lup.be/obc.

Published in 2024 by the De Wulf-Mansioncentrum – De Wulf-Mansion Centre
Leuven University Press / Presses Universitaires de Louvain/ Universitaire Pers Leuven
Minderbroedersstraat 4, B-3000 Leuven / Louvain (Belgium)

Selection and editorial matter © 2024, Francesca Masi, Pierre-Marie Morel and Francesco Verde
Individual chapters © 2024, the respective authors

This book is published under a Creative Commons Attribution Non-Commercial Non-Derivative 4.0 License. For more information, please visit https://creativecommons.org/share-your-work/cclicenses/

Attribution should include the following information:
Francesca Masi, Pierre-Marie Morel and Francesco Verde (eds.), *Epicureanism and Scientific Debates. Epicurean Tradition and its Ancient Reception. Volume II. Epistemology and Ethics*. Leuven: Leuven University Press, 2024. (CC BY-NC-ND 4.0)

ISBN 978 94 6270 437 4 (hardcover)
eISBN 978 94 6166 604 8 (ePDF)
eISBN 978 94 6166 605 5 (ePUB)
https://doi.org/10.11116/9789461666048
D/2024/1869/46
NUR: 732

Cover: Geert de Koning
Typesetting: Crius Group

In memory of David Konstan (1940-2024)

CONTENTS

Introduction   1
    Francesca Masi, Pierre-Marie Morel, and Francesco Verde

PART I   EPISTEMOLOGY   9

The Scientific Lexicon in Epicurus, *On Nature* XI: Some Observations   11
    Giuliana Leone

Epicurean *akribeia*   25
    Pierre-Marie Morel

Epicurus on the Arts and Sciences: A Reappraisal   47
    Geert Roskam

Τὸ προσμένον: Epicurus' *Propositional* Theory of Truth   67
    Francesco Verde

The Elaboration of *Prolepsis* between Epicurus and the Stoics: A Common Challenge to Innatism?   83
    Jean-Baptiste Gourinat

Science, Ethics, and ἀνάγκη in Epicurean Thought   119
    Phillip Mitsis

PART II   ETHICS AND ITS SCIENTIFIC BACKGROUND   139

Medicina ancilla philosophiae: The Epicurean Remedy for the Fear of a Childless Life   141
    Wim Nijs

Plutarch on Epicurus on Wine   167
    Mauro Bonazzi

Diogenes of Oinoanda and the Epicurean Epistolary Tradition   177
    Attila Németh

PART III ANCIENT RECEPTION OF EPICUREAN ETHICS AND EPISTEMOLOGY — 191

Epicurean Translations/Interpretations by Cicero and Seneca — 193
  Stefano Maso

"To inquire implies to know": Epicurus and Sextus on the Possibility of Knowledge — 217
  Stéphane Marchand

Alexander of Aphrodisias and the Naturalness of Justice (*Mantissa* 19): An Attack Against Epicurus? — 245
  Maddalena Bonelli

About the Contributors — 259

Index of Ancient Names — 263

Index of Modern Names — 267

INTRODUCTION

Francesca Masi, Pierre-Marie Morel, and Francesco Verde

The present work collects the final results of *Science and Philosophical Debates: A New Approach Towards Ancient Epicureanism*, a project devoted to Epicurean science and led by F. Masi (PI), P.-M. Morel, and F. Verde. The volume follows the publication of the first work within the same series, titled *Epicureanism and Scientific Debates. Antiquity and Late Reception*. The research conducted in the present volume, therefore, also concerns the study of several areas of Epicurean philosophy, namely: physiology, understood as an atomistic set of doctrines about nature capable of accounting for the most complex aspects of reality; epistemology, understood as a theory of knowledge capable of precisely distinguishing the various degrees and forms of knowledge, as well as of providing criteria to verify the truth value of opinions and to formulate true and consistent judgments; and finally ethics, understood as the philosophical field concerned with the realization of the ultimate human good, in which scientific and epistemological assumptions find their fullest expression and application.

As already explained in the introduction to the first volume,[1] the investigation has been carried out from several perspectives: the reconstruction and analysis of primary sources, including ones less widely known even among specialists, such as Epicurus' work *On Nature* and Diogenes of Oinoanda's inscription; an examination of the debates and controversies in which Epicurus' school was engaged at various stages during its historical development; and a review of how Epicurean philosophy was received in later eras. The purpose of this study was to paint a new picture of Epicureanism by challenging the widespread stereotype of Epicurus' philosophy as a dogmatic, closed system of thought, resistant to any internal evolution or cultural stimuli. The philosophy of Epicurus and his heirs is actually the result of the constant reworking and deepening of doctrines through close dialectical exchanges with other currents of thought. Throughout its long history, Epicureanism proved capable of dealing with the most pressing philosophical questions and of refining its theoretical solutions in light of the main scientific orientations of its day, as well as the most advanced and up-to-date research in medicine, music, mathematics, and astronomy.

Like the previous volume, therefore, this one does not have a thematic or monographic slant. Its aim is not to deal with a specific aspect of Epicureanism or to propose an exegetical line with respect to a particular issue, but to promote a new approach to the study of Epicureanism, that is, through a rigorous multidisciplinary,

---

[1] F. Masi, P.-M. Morel, F. Verde (edd), *Epicureanism and Scientific Debates. Antiquity and Late Reception*, Volume 1: *Language, Medicine, Meteorology*, Leuven, 2023: Leuven University Press, 1-7.

namely, historical, philological, literary, philosophical, and scientific study based on a global approach to the sources. It thus examines certain themes from the epistemological, physiological, and ethical spheres, so as to outline the working methodology of Epicurus and the Epicureans; the dialectic underlying the elaboration of certain specific doctrines; the developments of their philosophy in the context of the debate with other schools; the deep interconnections between its constituent parts and the relation with other scientific disciplines; and the impact of Epicureanism on other philosophies.

*
* *

In particular, this volume collects the proceedings of two international conferences attended by a number of distinguished scholars. The first workshop, entitled *Theory of Language and Scientific Lexicon in Epicureanism – Théorie du langage et lexique scientifique dans l'épicurisme*, was held online on May 25-27, 2021, and organized for Université Paris 1 – Panthéon-Sorbonne, in collaboration with the research team Gramata (UMR 7219 Sphere), by F. Masi, P.-M. Morel, F. Verde, and S. Marchand. The second conference, which marked the official end of the project, was entitled *Science, Epistemology, and Ethics* and was held in Venice from May 30 to June 1, 2022. It was attended not only by the scientific board of the project, but also by all those who had contributed to it over the years: F. Bakker, M. Bonazzi, M. Cassan, F. Cacciabaudo, F. G. Corsi, D. De Sanctis, T. Dorandi, J. Giovacchini, M. Erbì, M. Erler, J.-B. Gourinat, J. Hammerstaedt, J. E. Heßler, D. Konstan, G. Leone, S. Marchand, S. Maso, P. Mitsis, A. Németh, W. Nijs, A. Peralta, E. Piergiacomi, G. Roskam, C. Rover, E. Spinelli, and V. Tsouna, in addition to F. Forcignanò, G. Mingucci, F. Trabattoni, and D. Zucca.

This second volume, like the first, is divided into three parts. The first part, "Epistemology", focuses on issues related to the scientific vocabulary used by Epicurus in his major work *On Nature*, the exegesis of technical terms, epistemological criteria along with the theory of truth, scientific research methodology, and the attitude toward science and art adopted by Epicurus and the Epicureans in general. This first section includes five contributions.

G. Leone's article, titled "The Scientific Lexicon in Epicurus, *On Nature* XI: Some Observations", outlines an exegetical method applicable to the technical-scientific language employed in Epicurus' *On Nature*. The author addresses the question of the "immobility" (*mone*) of the earth, a doctrine found in Scolium 74 on the *Letter to Herodotus* and taken up in Book V of Lucretius' *De rerum natura*, yet never mentioned in the *Letter to Pythocles*. She does so in light of a passage from Book XI of *On Nature* devoted to the study of celestial and meteorological phenomena. In this passage, a key term used by Epicurus is *pyknotes*, "density". Leone reconstructs the meaning of this and related words through a detailed examination of the various contexts in which they occur within Epicurus' corpus. Proceeding to comment on the passage in which the notion of *pyknotes* appears to be associated with the doctrine of the Earth's *mone*, Leone first lays out her main criticisms of current translations; then, based on Brunschwig-Monet-Sedley's translation, she explains how the density of air is to be understood in relation to the immobility of the Earth, the most critical point for the demonstration of the Earth's *mone*.

In his contribution, "Epicurean *akribeia*", P.-M. Morel begins with the well-known distinction between general and particular knowledge of nature outlined by Epicurus at the beginning of his *Letter to Herodotus*. This distinction has traditionally been taken to establish a hierarchy between the two forms of knowledge, so as to identify two categories of pupils who differ in terms of their level of preparedness, ensuring that both may attain tranquillity. Morel instead suggests we interpret the difference between these two forms of knowledge in terms of an epistemological circuit, from the general to the particular and from the particular to the general – a circuit necessary for a comprehensive and continuous understanding of the science of nature. Within this virtuous circle, a key role is played by *akribeia*, or precision. Morel then analyzes the meanings and epistemological function of *akribeia*, showing that, due to its transversal function, *akribeia* is an epistemological operator that powerfully contributes to preserving, if not ensuring, the continuity of the scientific περιοδεία. The distinction between general and particular knowledge – understood in terms of circularity and the precision applied to various stages of the epistemological circuit – together with other epistemological tools, contributes to both happiness and the fulfilment of the scientific programme itself, which Epicurus has set.

G. Roskam's article, "Epicurus on the Arts", analyzes the attitude of Epicurus and the Epicureans towards the arts. It is divided into two parts. In the first, the essay addresses Epicurus and the Epicureans' critique of the traditional arts and sciences, as well as education more generally. In the second, in light of Plutarch's polemic against Epicurus and the Epicureans, the author highlights some of the limitations of their position. The contention is that Epicurus and the Epicureans' attitude towards art should be understood in light of the criterion of *utilitas*: only what is instrumental and functional to pleasure can be integrated into Epicurean science. Plutarch, however, makes it clear that Epicurean hedonism risks being too reductive to be able to consistently include pleasures of a merely intellectual kind.

F. Verde's article, "Τὸ προσμένον: Epicurus' *Propositional* Theory of Truth", sets out from a recent essay by Andree Hahmann and Jan Maximilian Robitzsch, *Epicurus' Non-Propositional Theory of Truth*, in which the notion of τὸ προσμένον – translated as "that which awaits confirmation", an essentially correct yet only partial translation – is analyzed within a broader argumentative context aimed at demonstrating that Epicurus upheld a non-propositional theory of truth. Hahmann and Robitzsch's work provides Verde with an opportunity to reflect on τὸ προσμένον, one of the least studied concepts, but one fundamental to the Epicurean Canonic. The aim of his paper is twofold: first, Verde shows that τὸ προσμένον requires a propositional theory of truth; second, he investigates the function and role of τὸ προσμένον in Epicurean epistemology by referring especially to the relationship between the acquisition of truth/knowledge and time. On the basis of the occurrences of the term in the *Letter to Herodotus* and the *Capital Maxims*, Verde argues that "what awaits confirmation" is a notion that was introduced by Epicurus himself and which must be identified with the content of the opinion formed in the subject through the processing of sensory experience.

In "The Elaboration of *prolepsis* between Epicurus and the Stoics: A Common Challenge to Innatism?", J.-B. Gourinat begins by noting that, despite their numerous and irreducible doctrinal differences, Stoics and Epicureans share certain patterns of thought, primarily in the domains of physics and epistemology. As the title suggests, this contribution focuses especially on the notion of *prolepsis*: the author examines its origin, function, and development in Epicurean and Stoic epistemology, highlighting similarities and differences between the two schools. Through a rigorous chronological study, Gourinat first shows how the notion, introduced by Epicurus, was later used in Stoic philosophy, beginning with Chrysippus. By analyzing the sources, the author then highlights how for both philosophers a *prolepsis* is a stored notion, a universal thought derived from sense-perception or, more precisely, arising from a memory formed by sense impressions. Moreover, every *prolepsis* is 'engraved' in our minds by nature and is in some way 'innate', insofar as it is common to all human beings; precisely for this reason, preconceptions constitute excellent criteria of truth. For the Epicureans, all perceptions are true and, as such, constitute the basis for the formation of *prolepseis*. For the Stoics, however, only some perceptions are true, and they alone form *prolepseis*. Moreover, for both schools *prolepseis* constitute a useful research tool, and both would appear to have used *prolepseis* to solve the *Meno*'s problem of knowledge and offer an alternative solution to the doctrine of reminiscence and innatism.

The second part of the volume, "Ethics and Its Scientific Background", generally investigates the relationship between the scientific-epistemological realm and the practical one, explaining how the physical structure of Epicurus' atomistic world is compatible with human *praxis* and how scientific research can help ensure the realization of the ultimate human good. More specifically, this second part also includes contributions focusing on generally seldom studied sources for the reconstruction of Epicurean ethical doctrine, its development and reception, such as the fragments of Epicurus' *Symposium* transmitted by Plutarch and Diogenes of Oinoanda's letters. This section consists of four papers.

In his "Science, Ethics, and ἀνάγκη in Epicurean Thought", P. Mitsis discusses a 1952 work by C. Diano, *Form and Event. Principles for an Interpretation of the Greek World*.

On the basis of a specific textual reconstruction and interpretation of paragraph 133 of the *Letter to Menoeceus*, Diano had envisaged the coexistence of necessity, chance, and the *eventum* of human freedom in the Epicurean world. Mitsis addresses some of the tensions that may arise from this reading, asking how it is possible for freedom to be supported by necessity while at the same time requiring the breakdown of natural laws as a condition of possibility. More generally, Mitsis asks how we are to understand the status of *ananke*, which on the one hand guarantees the operative structure of the world, but on the other must be abolished in order to ensure freedom.

By adopting a different textual reconstruction of the *Letter to Menoeceus*, based on Dorandi's edition of Diogenes Laertius, and by reconsidering the notions of necessity and natural laws in Epicureanism, Mitsis challenges the assumption that necessity is somehow still required in the Epicurean world. Mitsis' thesis is that the *eventum* of free human action is not sustained by necessity in some unclear way, but rather depends on the very elimination of necessity. Freedom exists against the backdrop of chance, which provides us with opportunities within a world structured by variable limits.

In *"Medicina ancilla philosophiae.* The Epicurean Remedy for the Fear of a Childless Life", W. Nijs investigates the relationship between science and ethics, starting with the analysis of one particular fear, namely the fear of being childless because of infertility. As is widely known, Epicurus believed that the science of nature serves to remove the causes of major fears. Particularly emblematic in this regard is the case of the study of *meteora*, which is necessary to remove the fear of natural phenomena due to a misunderstanding of their origin and essence. In his article, W. Nijs tries to determine whether and how medical insights were combined with ethical precepts in the pursuit of Epicureanism's overarching objectives. In particular, Nijs discusses the arguments which the Epicureans used to help people get rid of their fear of childlessness. The author also reconstructs and assesses the different aspects of the Epicurean therapy for the fear of a childless life.

M. Bonazzi's article, "Plutarch on Epicurus on Wine", analyzes the surviving fragments and evidence from Epicurus' *Symposium*, a dialogue that, by its very title, invites comparison with Plato and Aristotle. Unlike his predecessors, Epicurus does not seem to show particular interest in the stylistic aspects of texts. Nevertheless, the passages handed down to us – especially those related to the topics of wine and sex and their possible interrelation – show an attention to the structure and order of the arguments. Bonazzi focuses on some fragments of the *Symposium* – especially those which are transmitted by Plutarch – that touch upon the nature of sensible qualities and the reliability of the senses. These passages turn out to be relevant from a methodological perspective, insofar as they clarify how Plutarch himself transmitted and analyzed the sources. Bonazzi's thesis is that, far from reconstructing the Epicurean position in all of its complexity, Plutarch ends up dealing with the question of the truth of sensations based on his own assumptions and prejudices.

A. Németh's paper, "Diogenes of Oinoanda and the Epicurean Epistolary Tradition", aims to investigate how Diogenes used the epistolary genre in his inscription. To this end, Németh first presents an overview of the Epicurean epistolary tradition and then scrutinizes, on the one hand, how Diogenes' letters fit into this tradition and, on the other, what function his epistles serve in the overall context of the inscription. This research concludes that Diogenes shows a considerable degree of originality in his use of letters as a means of communication compared to the earlier Epicurean tradition. Diogenes stands out on account of his rhetorical inventiveness, deep knowledge of Epicureanism, and literary skills and erudition, all of which contribute to outlining a philosophical method of teaching through texts inscribed on stone. Finally, Németh argues that Diogenes constructed his philosophical discourse – based on his knowledge of the science of nature – by paying close attention to those forms of exposition most suitable for the attainment of salvation, that is "according to art".

Finally, the third section, "Ancient Reception of Epicurean Ethics and Epistemology", focuses on the reception of Epicurus' philosophy by later authors. It illustrates how in some cases these authors understood, disseminated, and drew upon Epicurean doctrines to substantiate, supplement, and improve their own theory, while in other cases they criticized – or even misunderstood and distorted – certain aspects of the Epicurean system because of certain assumptions and prejudices that influenced their interpretation of it. The aim of this final section of the volume, comprising three chapters, is to carefully reconstruct the historical and theoretical contexts in which Epicurus' theories were taken up – often by exponents of opposing schools – and to clarify the hermeneutical perspectives and aims of the various authors.

S. Maso's article, "Epicurean Translations / Interpretations by Cicero and Seneca", provides a comparative analysis of these two authors' works and original Epicurean sources, with the aim of assessing how Cicero and Seneca contributed to the accurate and correct Latin translation and interpretation of the Epicurean scientific lexicon. The former author could rely on his knowledge of Epicurus' fundamental doctrines, perhaps based on first-hand knowledge of some of the texts. While highly critical of such doctrines, he always pays close attention to the context and displays considerable philosophical sensitivity in dealing with the issues touched upon by his opponent. In certain cases, Cicero endeavors to coin new terms (the emblematic case being *atomos*); in others, he seeks to diversify the translation of the same term to reflect its different meanings (e.g., *sophrosyne* or *prolepsis*). Seneca instead frequently uses and quotes Epicurus to address and sometimes substantiate his own Stoic ethical and physical doctrines. In doing so, he approaches Epicurean texts without biases or assumptions, showing respect for Epicurean writings from both a conceptual and stylistic perspective. As proof of this, Maso refers to certain passages from Seneca's letters that are particularly revealing of the Latin author's philological *akribeia*.

In "'To Inquire Implies to Know': Epicurus and Sextus on the Possibility of Knowledge", S. Marchand focuses on the argument that inquiring necessarily implies knowing or having a notion of the object of inquiry (Us. 255). More generally, he assesses the importance of the problem of the possibility of knowledge in Epicurus' time. Sextus Empiricus is one of the sources for this fragment; but he cites this argument in different and apparently contradictory ways, either to confirm his own skeptical method or as an anti-skeptical argument. The primary objective of Marchand's article is to assess the divergence between the two positions as regards two crucial issues at stake in this argument: the nature of inquiry and the function of preconception. This comparison makes it possible to highlight the radical conflict between the two positions in relation to the function of language and concepts. The essay is divided into two parts. In the first, Marchand establishes the significance of this argument in the Epicurean context; in the second, he analyzes Sextus' strategy in using this argument to show that – despite the apparent convergence between the two positions on this topic – this common usage is based on a fundamental disagreement about the nature and function of concepts and, more specifically, of *prolepsis* or preconception.

Finally, in her contribution "Alexander of Aphrodisias and the Naturalness of Justice (*Mantissa* 19): An Attack against Epicurus?", M. Bonelli examines a text by Alexander of Aphrodisias, *Mantissa* 19, which addresses the issue of the existence or non-existence of natural justice. Alexander of Aphrodisias approaches the question from an Aristotelian perspective, criticizing the Stoics, who like Aristotle hold that justice is by nature, but argue that positive laws derive their force and efficacy from a single eternal law, identifiable with divine rationality. Bonelli seeks to show that in *Mantissa* 19, Alexander is not only criticizing the Stoics, but also attacking the Epicurean thesis of social coexistence as purely conventional. Moreover, she identifies an Epicurean influence in Alexander's own treatment of justice.

*
* *

With these two volumes devoted to Epicurus' science, the debates in which his school was involved at various historical stages, and the later reception of his philosophy in subsequent, intellectually varied, lively, and stimulating epochs, we have offered fresh research perspectives on Epicureanism. In particular, it seems to us that the working methodology adopted – attentive both to the comparison of the various sources available (even the most difficult ones, such as the Epicurus' *On Nature*, the Diogenes' Inscriptions, the more hostile testimonies) and to the dialectical dimension of Epicurean philosophy – has allowed us to better delineate certain technical aspects of the vocabulary used by Epicurus and his followers; their linguistic theory; the communicative strategy of their works; many fundamental aspects of epistemology, physiology, and ethics; as well as the relationship between philosophy and sciences (such as astronomy and medicine) or *techne*.

This perspective is less stereotypical and more respectful of a tradition that – despite the scarcity and fragmentary nature of its primary sources, as well as the discredit cast upon it by rival schools – continued to flourish for centuries, to the point of influencing the origin and development of modern science, as the contributions on Gassendi's philosophy in the first volume sought to establish. The very foundations of modern science, which is rooted in Epicurean philosophy, disproves historiographical attempts to reduce Epicureanism to ethics: even if the sole *telos* of Epicurus' philosophy is the concrete attainment of happiness, its theoretical core and the only possible paths to achieve lie in the knowledge and study of nature.[2]

Venice, Paris, Rome, March 2024

Francesca Masi
Pierre-Marie Morel
Francesco Verde

---

[2] We would like to sincerely thank Chiara Rover for the care she took in preparing the indexes of names.

Part I

Epistemology

THE SCIENTIFIC LEXICON IN EPICURUS, *ON NATURE* XI: SOME OBSERVATIONS

Giuliana Leone

Whoever regularly works on new editions of the books of Epicurus' *On Nature* contained in the Herculaneum papyri knows that recourse to all the available sources is nearly a categorical imperative in the attempt, at times desperate, to decipher and interpret the carbonized and lacunose papyrus fragments. As our editions continue to improve, however, it is also true that the books of *On Nature* restore to us important doctrinal particularities as well as lively sparks of polemic, which are absent or only implied in the indirect tradition and *testimonia* about Epicurean doctrine. They are therefore essential for any attempt to reconstruct in all its complexity the philosophy of the Founder of the Garden.

One of the most fascinating aspects of research on our papyri is the possibility of increasing, or at least better understanding, Epicurus' scientific lexicon through the rich harvest of terms that are new or only used in unusual contexts, which the books of his *magnum opus* restore to us. The great philologist Hermann Usener was aware of this richness when he included the words that he could track down in the editions of his day in his *Glossarium Epicureum*,[1] occasionally offering illuminating explanations of them. Not rarely is it a question of an extremely technical lexicon that Epicurus always used with full control, one which reveals the rich tapestry of connections binding the philosopher to the background of his thought, against which we see that his doctrine has the originality that he claims for it.

It is appropriate to repeat Epicurus' recommendations to his students about the suitable and consistent use of language in scientific research, language which, by relying on the very words of things and fleeing from artificial usages,[2] is freed from all ambiguity and avoids the false interpretations of bad-faith detractors. The consistency that Epicurus invokes and pursues imposes on us the necessity, in our work as interpreters and translators of his words, of grasping the force of the words and translating each individual term satisfactorily while keeping their meanings constant to the extent possible in every single occurrence, as my teacher, Marcello Gigante, the unsurpassed interpreter and translator of Diogenes Laertius, recommended.

If our goal is to understand the exact valence of Epicurus' terms as best we can, it is useful in many cases to extend our research into their meanings to the latest Epicurean writers as well as to study particular cases in which Latin authors grappled with the task of rendering the Greek technical terms found especially in texts

---
[1] Usener 1977.
[2] On this topic, see my Leone 2020a.

on Epicurean physics into their *sermo patrius*. If in so doing we can maintain a certain balance in order to avoid the risk of what Walter Lapini has defined as "confrontazionismo" or "locosimilismo"[3] (i.e., the excessive attempt to explain lexical occurrences or unusual grammatical constructions through *loci similes* or comparisons with other authors), we nonetheless cannot give up the attempt to understand passages that, considered in isolation, do not always *speak* to the modern reader.

In the work of translation and exegesis, it is not always easy to understand and render the shades of meaning of terms that belong to a single semantic field, in addition to these terms' contexts, which determined Epicurus' usage, that must occasionally be taken into account. It seems to me that book XI of *On Nature*, of which I am preparing a new edition, could be an interesting starting-point for this kind of study.

In my chapter in the commemorative *Festschrift* for the late Enrico Flores, titled "La stabilità della terra nella dottrina di Epicuro: Lucrezio lettore dell'XI libro *Sulla natura*",[4] I dealt with a passage from the final section of that book[5] about the question of the μονή, "stability", of the Earth. Ever since the *accademico ercolanese* Carlo Maria Rosini published the first edition of *PHerc*. 1042 in 1809,[6] this subject has been known to be one of the principal themes that Epicurus treated in book XI[7] which was dedicated, as Epicurus says in its conclusion, to celestial phenomena.[8] There is a reference to this doctrine in a scholium to *Letter to Herodotus* (74)[9] and Lucretius dedicated a passage in *On Nature* V to it (534-549), but it is completely absent from the *Letter to Pythocles*.[10]

In the passage in question, Epicurus focuses on the term πυκνότης, "density", which is accompanied by numerous other terms formed by the same root. Used in various contexts, they deserve, I think, some consideration.

The examination of these Epicurean texts brings out that the notion of "density" is, in the first place, strictly connected to the fundamental notions of atoms and void and of the larger or smaller proportions of them present in compound bodies. The idea is not only applied, as expected, to entities, phenomena, and both physical and, in particular, meteorological processes but also, more surprisingly, to intellectual

---

[3] Cf. Lapini 2015: 202.
[4] Leone 2021.
[5] [26.42] 9-18 Arr.
[6] *HV* 1809: 30-78.
[7] *Ibid.*: 78, *In caput IV. Cur terra stet immobilis, neque a Solis rotatione adficiatur.*
[8] Regarding this conclusion and, more generally, on the conclusions of the books in Epicurus' *magnum opus*, cf. De Sanctis 2015: 179-186.
[9] = fr. 348 Us. καὶ ἐν ἄλλοις τὴν γῆν τῷ ἀέρι ἐποχεῖσθαι.
[10] Arrighetti 1967 explained the absence of the theme of the Earth's μονή in the *Letter to Pythocles* by the fact that "per questo problema . . . Epicuro non ammetteva il metodo delle molteplici spiegazioni, per cui non si presentava in armonia col tono generale della lettera che di quel metodo è praticamente una celebrazione." On the other hand, for Verde 2022: 61, "È probabile . . . che la *mone* della terra non fosse un fenomeno così rilevante nell'economia di un compendio come la lettera a Pitocle, forse perché non era così immediatamente/direttamente orientato e connesso al fine etico che regge la scienza dei *meteora* e che l'epistola esibisce di continuo."

operations in a unified vision. From that perspective, it clearly emerges that Epicurus wants to highlight that this "dense", material nature associates the individual and everything related to him to the world that surrounds him.

That emphasis is evident in the exordium of the *Letter to Herodotus*:[11] here Epicurus indicates with τὸ πύκνωμα "the dense nucleus" of the research – in Italian there would be the expression "nocciolo" or "sodo" of a question –, in particular "of the continuous circuit of research that embraces everything", τῆς συνεχοῦς τῶν ὅλων περιοδείας. In other words, τὸ πύκνωμα is the fulcrum of the research that, though aimed at a deep, exact, and detailed knowledge of the totality of things, should satisfy our need "in an intense way", πυκνόν, "for the comprehensive application of the doctrine", τῆς ... ἀθρόας ἐπιβολῆς,[12] in a "continuous", συνεχῶς, and "swift", ὀξέως, way.[13]

It should be said that the perfect circularity and, above all, the pregnant sense of the adverbial neuter accusative πυκνόν and the substantive πύκνωμα (at the beginning and end of Epicurus' methodological indications at §§ 35-36) have not escaped several of the translators and commentators on the *Letter*, from Bollack-Bollack-Wismann[14] to Morel.[15] Particular attention to the use – never accidental – of the terms that belong to this same semantic field made these translators attribute a pregnant sense to the adverb πυκνῶς at its sole attestation in the *Letter to Herodotus*[16] as well. There, in the expression πᾶσαν σύγκρισιν πεπερασμένην τὸ ὁμοειδὲς τοῖς θεωρουμένοις πυκνῶς ἔχουσαν, in reference to worlds similar to ours, these interpreters preferred associating the adverb with the participle ἔχουσαν. Thus, they translated τὸ ὁμοειδὲς ... πυκνῶς ἔχουσαν as "doués d'une ressemblance compacte" (Bollack-Bollack-Wismann[17]), or "ayant une étroite similitude de forme" (Delattre[18]), or even "étroitement similaire, ressemblants" (Morel[19]), instead of taking it, rather banally, with τοῖς θεωρουμένοις and translating "ciò che frequentemente osserviamo".[20]

Both the adverbial neuter πυκνόν and the substantive πύκνωμα are used by Epicurus in his teachings about the εἴδωλα and perception as well. In *Nat.* II, col. 94, 12 Leone,[21] μὴ πυκνόν refers to the "non-intense, non-frequent way" in which the

---

[11] Epicur. *Hrdt.* 36.
[12] Epicur. *Hrdt.* 35.
[13] Epicur. *Hrdt.* 36.
[14] Bollack-Bollack-Wismann 1971.
[15] Morel 2011.
[16] Epicur. *Hrdt.* 73.
[17] Bollack-Bollack-Wismann 1971: 145. In their commentary (233), the translators explain: "L'adverbe, portant sur ἔχουσαν et non sur θεωρουμένοις, révèle que la ressemblance ne se situe pas dans l'aspect extérieur seulement, mais dans la profondeur des corps."
[18] Delattre 2010: 27.
[19] Morel 2011: 75, 140.
[20] Verde 2010: 57.
[21] Leone 2012 = [24.37] 12 Arr.

εἴδωλα return to their places of departure – something that happens, e.g., in the case of reflection in a mirror– to guarantee the continuity of their flow. On the other hand, in *Hrdt.* 62, the same word means the "intense, frequent way" in which the atoms included in compounds strike against each other until the continuity of the movement reaches the domain of sensation. In this way, we observe the connection between the notions of "density" and "continuity" on the physical-epistemological level, which we gathered from the methodological indications that Epicurus furnished in the proem to the *Letter to Herodotus*. Incidentally, this connection is confirmed, *inter alia*, by ancient lexicography as well.[22]

The connection between the notions of "density" and "continuity" is also confirmed for the substantive πύκνωμα, which appears in the same letter at § 50. There, in the problematic and frequently discussed expression κατὰ τὸ ἑξῆς πύκνωμα ἢ ἐγκατάλειμμα τοῦ εἰδώλου,[23] it indicates, as Francesco Verde has recently written,[24] "una massa densa, una concentrazione compatta che è anche ἑξῆς, ossia continua, non intervallata". In this connection, we should remember that in the *Glossarium Epicureum s.v.* συνεχής, Usener explained κατὰ τὸ συνεχές, which occurs in fr. 293 Us., as synonymous with ἐφεξῆς.

As I maintained in my edition of *On Nature* II,[25] it is probably due to the cohesion that connects the atoms constituting an image among themselves (ἀλληλουχία) and to the possibility of resistance to external blows (ἀντικοπαί), however few they be. Accordingly, this cohesion gives assurance that the εἴδωλον can, at the end of its route to the sense organs, appear as a "continuously dense mass", τὸ ἑξῆς πύκνωμα, with a guarantee of consistent ὁμοιομορφία with respect to the solid object from which it detached.[26] On this interpretation, which finds illustrious precedents,[27] the ἐγκατάλειμμα τοῦ εἰδώλου is the "residue, that which remains of the εἴδωλον", in case it undergoes atom losses along its route to the sense organs. However, Verde's recent proposal cannot be ruled out: he takes up clues offered by a different interpretative tradition that began with Bailey[28] and hypothesized that the πύκνωμα of the image can be "l'oggetto dell'ἐπιβολή degli organi sensoriali, mentre l'ἐγκατάλειμμα lo sarebbe di quella della διάνοια (ossia della mente/pensiero)".[29]

---

[22] Cf., e.g., Phot. 79, 14.
[23] Cf. Leone 2012: 108 n. 319.
[24] Verde 2016: 57.
[25] Leone 2012: 108-110. Verde 2016: 57 n. 57 agrees on this point.
[26] For further discussion of this aspect, cf. Corti 2015.
[27] For related bibliography, see Verde 2016: 58 n. 63. Verde 2010: 135 shared this explanation.
[28] Bailey 1926: 197. Various other scholars have views along this interpretive path; cf. Verde 2016: 59 n. 67.
[29] Verde 2016: 57. This position was held by Masi 2016 as well, who tried to reconcile it with the thesis of Lapini 2015: 53, according to whom πύκνωμα would indicate the condition of the complete εἴδωλον and ἐγκατάλειμμα that of its remains, or rather "il simulacro che ha percorso dello spazio, subendo una perdita di atomi ma non una perdita sfigurante o deformante."

That the term πύκνωμα, like many other technical terms ending in -μα in the Epicurean lexicon,[30] indicates "something in a certain state," specifically "something that is dense" is certain from two passages in the *Letter to Pythocles* (105 and 115). There, it designates "compact masses" of land and "thickenings" of fog in respectively meteorological contexts. Yet particularly interesting, especially in comparison with the expression τὸ ἑξῆς πύκνωμα which we just examined, is *Ep. Pyth.* § 103, in which the adjective πυκνός[31] is used with reference to τοὺς ἑξῆς τόπους πυκνοτέρους in a discussion of the multiple explanations of the formation of lightening. These are locations where the clouds become more dense,[32] which causes a rupture and consequently a downwards fall of their inflamed part, and this is the origin of bolts of lightning. Again, the connection between our previously emphasized notions of "density" and "continuity" is confirmed.

In several passages of *On Nature* XIV,[33] the noun πύκνωσις, "condensation," and the verb πυκνοῦσθαι, "to become condensed", are used as technical terms to designate this *process* within Epicurus' polemic against those who support monistic doctrines of the elements, especially those who hold that the ἀρχή is ἀήρ.[34] These thinkers hold that precisely through the processes of condensation and rarefaction (ἀραίωσις,[35] ἀραιοῦσθαι) air's transformations into other elements come about in a series of changes of state which leads to the generation of all things that exist in nature. In particular, the formation of clouds represents one of these changes of state *via* the condensation of air, according to Anaximenes,[36] and it leads immediately to the formation of water, just as in Epicurus.

Bignone[37] noted that Epicurus can be shown to be an expert connoisseur of his opponents' Ionic lexicon because he opposes πύκνωσις to ἀραίωσις rather than μάνωσις, which Aristotle had preferred in the same context.[38]

Although the verb ἀραιοῦσθαι is not attested in the surviving Epicurean texts, Epicurus constantly contrasts the noun ἀραιότης and the adjective ἀραιός with πυκνότης and πυκνός, so as to designate the qualities of "thinness" and "density", respectively, and their corresponding adjectives. In *Ep. Pyth.* § 88, we read that "un cosmo è una porzione di cielo ... terminante in un confine di costituzione rada o

---

30   Cf. Todd 1974: 211 n. 15.
31   The adjective πυκνός has a different use in Epicur. SV 29, in which it connotes ἔπαινος, the "loud applause", of the crowd, which can be easily gained by agreeing with their opinions, but which Epicurus declares that he wants to renounce in favour of offering instead that which is useful to everyone.
32   Cf. Verde 2022: 205.
33   Epicur. *Nat.* XIV, coll. XXVII 2f., 7f., XXXIII 1, 10; frr. 59, 2 and 60, 3 Leone 1984.
34   Cf. Leone 1984: 79f.
35   Epicur. *Nat.* XIV, coll. XXVII 8, XXXI 8, XXXIII 2 Leone 1984.
36   Cf. esp. Simpl. *in Aristot. Phys.* 24 (Thphr. *Phys. Opin.* fr. 2 = *Dox.* 476): Ἀναξιμένης ... μίαν μὲν ... τὴν ὑποκειμένην φύσιν ... φησιν ... ἀέρα λέγων αὐτήν· ... καὶ ἀραιούμενον μὲν πῦρ γίνεσθαι, πυκνούμενον δὲ ἄνεμον, εἶτα νέφος, ἔτι δὲ μᾶλλον ὕδωρ, εἶτα γῆν, εἶτα λίθους, τὰ δὲ ἄλλα ἐκ τούτων.
37   Cf. Bignone 1933: 82.
38   Cf., e.g., Aristot. *GC* 330b10.

densa, ἐν πέρατι ἢ ἀραιῷ ἢ πυκνῷ". In *Nat.* XI, col. [26.17], 1-4 Arr., the opposition between the "density or thinness of the environment" – again emphasized by a disjunctive ἤ – occurs again: διὰ τὴν | τοῦ περιέχοντος πυ|κνότητα ἢ ἀραιότη|τα. Note that in the same book, the adjective ἀραιός occurs at least two more times, namely, in the phrase ἀραιὰ φύσις, "thin nature", which seems to refer to the element of air.[39] In that case, as we will see in a passage examined later, πυκνότης appears to be a quality of the Earth. In a different context, in a difficult passage of the *Letter to Pythocles* (107)[40] on the formation of snow, a "uniform thinness", ὁμαλὴς ἀραιότης, is said to be a property of the frozen clouds from which snow falls.

Lastly, it is appropriate to cite a passage from *On Nature* XXXIV, in *PHerc.* 1431, in which I read the term πυκνότης for the first time.[41] There, Epicurus affirms that the proportionality of pores allows images that originate outside the body to pass into the mind, although πυκνότης does not help them to do so (πυκ]νότης κᾶ[ν μὴ σ[υ]γ[ῆι]). On the basis of Theophrastus' report that Democritus attributed πυκνότης both to the external membrane of the eyes as well as to the air,[42] I hypothesized, in my edition of 2012,[43] that Epicurus transferred this quality of "compactness" from the eyes to the images themselves. I put it in relation to the notion of ἀλληλουχία, which Epicurus insists on for the εἴδωλα in book II, and compared the expression τὸ ἑξῆς πύκνωμα (discussed above), in clear reference to the εἴδωλον. Further, in support of this hypothesis, I cited, in my edition of 2002,[44] the presence of the term πυκνότης in *PHerc.* 1055, col. XXII 5 (apparently a work "On the Shape of God", attributed to Demetrius Laco), where πυκνότης is mentioned in reference to the density of the bodies that we perceive via αἴσθησις as a cause of their disintegration.[45] This πυκνότης could allude to a density that is only mental, νοητή,[46] which belongs to the imperceptible, divine, immortal εἴδωλα as a part of the particular subtlety of their structure.[47] However, in a 2015 paper titled "Dagli occhi alla mente. Il cammino tortuoso degli eidola", Francesca Masi[48] proposed connecting the πυκνότης that Epicurus invokes in book XXXIV to the extreme "density" of the porous structure of the perceiving subject. As a result, along the crooked road to the mind, the images suffer an inevitable reduction by contraction (cυνίζησις)[49] and become that

---

[39] Cf. *infra*.
[40] On which cf. Verde 2022: 221f., whom I follow in the reconstruction of the text (with a conjecture by Meibom) and in the exegesis of the passage.
[41] Epicur. *Nat.* XXXIV, col. XXIV 2 Leone 2002.
[42] Thphr. *Sens.* 50 (68 A 135 D.-K.)
[43] Leone 2012: 94-96. Cf. Leone 2002: 130f. as well.
[44] Leone 2002: 131.
[45] Cf. Santoro 2000: 175f.
[46] Cf. Phld. *Di* XI 18-20 in Arrighetti 1958.
[47] Cf. Piergiacomi 2017: 177f. On the exegetical difficulties of this column, see also Verde 2017.
[48] Masi 2015: 117-119.
[49] For this idea, which appears in several passages of Epicur. *Nat.* II, cf. Leone 2012: 148-151.

which is called ἐγκατάλειμμα in *Hrdt.* 50.[50] This change would not impede them from transporting the permanent characteristics of the object or from forming a corresponding φαντασία in the mind.

Finally, we come to the passage of Epicurus in *Nat.* XI in which we find the term πυκνότης.[51] It immediately follows Epicurus' affirmation of the μονή, "stability", of the Earth: he claims that, due to his doctrine, "the mind will comprehend (this notion) in a more firm manner ... and in a manner more in line with the phenomena that are present to our senses."[52]

The passage was notably improved over Rosini's version by Achille Vogliano in the edition of the book that he published in Cairo in 1940,[53] after Theodor Gomperz identified *PHerc.* 154 as a second copy of the book in 1867.[54] Vogliano reconsidered and further supplemented the text in an article published in *Athenaeum* in 1941;[55] later, in a lengthy study dedicated to the question of Earth's stability in *On Nat.* XI, published in 1950, Adelmo Barigazzi offered a different interpretation.[56] Graziano Arighetti also advanced a new proposal for explaining the passage in his edition of the book that appeared in his *Epicuro. Opere* of 1973.[57] I report his version here, which mostly follows that of Vogliano, with the exception of the punctuation in lines 12 and 14:

```
        πυκνότητα [δ]ὲ
τὴν κάτω [π]αρὰ [συνέ-           10
χειαν αὐτῆι νοητ[έ-
ον τῆς ἄνωθ[ε]ν, ἵν[α
ἐσθλαὶ πρὸς τὴν ἀ[ν-
τ[έ]ρεισιν τοῦ μὴ φ[έ-
ρ[ε]σθαι τὴν γῆν τὴν             15
π[ρέπ]ουσαν ἀναλ[ογί-
αν [ὦσι]ν κεκτημ[έ-
ναι].
```

Vogliano limited himself to giving the following paraphrase of the passage:[58]

e la densità, quella in basso, va pensata in rapporto di continuità con quella che le sta al di sopra, perché esse si trovino nella condizione necessaria per stabilire la resistenza, in modo che la terra non si muova.

---

50 Cf. Masi 2015: 129 n. 70; cf. Masi 2016 as well.
51 [26.42] 9-18 Arr.
52 [26.42] 1-9 Arr.
53 Vogliano 1940, Fr. K col. II 9-18.
54 Gomperz 1867.
55 Vogliano 1941.
56 Barigazzi 1950.
57 Arrighetti 1973², [26].
58 Vogliano 1941: 142.

In turn, this is Barigazzi's translation:[59]

> La densità poi sottostante dev'esser pensata per la terra in rapporto di continuità con quella di sopra, affinché esse abbiano la conveniente proporzione per sostenere l'appoggiarsi della terra per il fatto che non si muove.

Here, lastly, is Arrighetti's:[60]

> la densità poi della parte inferiore deve essere pensata in rapporto di continuità con quella superiore, affinché (i sostegni), capaci di opporre resistenza (al peso della terra), posseggano la proporzione adatta a che la terra non si muova.

As is already clear from the translations on offer, this passage of Epicurus has provoked rather diverse proposal for interpretation on the part of the critics, though they all compare it with a passage from Lucretius (V 534ff.), which I give here in the edition and translation of Enrico Flores:[61]

Terraque ut in media mundi regione quiescat,	
euanescere paulatim et decrescere pondus	535
conuenit atque aliam naturam supter habere	
ex ineunte aeuo coniunctam atque uniter aptam	
partibus aeriis mundi quibus insita uiuit.	
propterea non est oneri neque deprimit auras;	
ut sua cuique homini nullo sunt pondere membra	540
nec caput est oneri collo nec denique totum	
corporis in pedibus pondus sentimus inesse	
...	
sic igitur tellus non est aliena repente	546
allata atque auris aliunde obiecta alienis,	
sed pariter prima concepta ab origine mundi	
certaque pars eius, quasi nobis membra videntur.	

E come la terra proprio al centro dell'universo sia immobile,	
conviene che il suo peso svanisca a poco a poco	535
e vada perdendosi, e un'altra natura al di sotto abbia,	
fin dall'iniziale tempo congiunta, e in modo stretto unita	
alle parti aeree del mondo, nelle quali inserita vive.	
Perciò non è di peso sull'aria e non la preme in basso;	
come per ogni uomo di nessun peso son le sue membra	540
e il capo non è di peso al collo, e infine non avvertiamo	
che tutto quanto del corpo il peso sui piedi gravare;	
...	

---

[59] Barigazzi 1950: 4.
[60] Arrighetti 1973²: 247.
[61] Flores 2009.

così dunque la terra non è stata come aliena d'un tratto   546
aggiunta, e in arie straniere d'altro luogo scagliata,
ma in pari tempo concepita dalla prima origine del mondo,
e definita parte di esso, come in noi le membra si scorgono.

I will try to summarize the points that strike me as problematic in the proposals that are the bases of the translations above, and I will add some considerations of my own.[62]

1. With Barigazzi, I hold that the dative αὐτῆι, taken with νοητέον, should refer to the Earth, the μονή, "stability", of which was affirmed shortly before this passage in the text. Vogliano and perhaps Arrighetti connect it to [συνέ]χειαν.

2. Like Barigazzi, I hold that Epicurus established the connection of συνέχεια that consists between two πυκνότητες, which both refer to the Earth, and that the syntax does not allow us to refer the notion of "the density below" to the element of air – as Vogliano tried to do in his commentary – because there is no mention of it in the substantially well-preserved text.

It is a question, in particular, of "the density below" – τὴν κάτω, which confines the air that holds it up – and of that "which proceeds from above", τῆς ἄνωθεν. Especially in the phrase παρὰ συνέχειαν – which, as we have seen, refers to continuity as well as to the step-by-step succession of one thing followed by another – but also in the use of the adverb ἄνωθ[ε]ν due to the particular suffix that distinguishes it from the preceding κάτω, I would find the traces of the notion which Lucretius rendered as *euanescere paulatim et descrescere* – two verbs in which, it should be noted, the suffix -θεν in the Greek became a prefix. Indeed, if it is true that Lucretius refers this notion to the weight of the Earth, *pondus*, it is not impossible that he assimilated *pondus* to πυκνότης, because just this assimilation finds an exact comparison in Greek as well. Particularly interesting, in my opinion, is a passage in Plutarch's *Quaestiones Convivales* (701 E 11), in which the notions of "dense" and "continuous" are closely associated with "weight": τὸ δὲ πυκνὸν καὶ συνεχὲς διὰ βάρος ὑφίσταται τῷ λεπτῷ.

3. The notion of συνέχεια between the zones of the Earth in our passage cannot be the one on which "Lucrezio insiste illustrandola col paragone del corpo umano", as Barigazzi wrote.[63] Indeed, the analogy with the limbs of the human body is clearly deployed by the poet for the relationship that binds Earth and air and, in particular, to demonstrate that the Earth is not a weight on the air. Barigazzi's affirmation that the Earth, resting on the air, exerts a pressure, a weight, therefore remains questionable, because exactly the opposite conception is the one that Lucretius insists on (*propterea non est oneri neque deprimit auras*).

---

[62] For more details, see my Leone 2021.
[63] Barigazzi 1950: 5.

4. Next, Barigazzi's assimilation of the expression *alia natura supter*, which Lucretius clearly attributes to the Earth, to the Epicurean notion of ἀραιὰ φύσις is also uncertain.[64] Previously,[65] Epicurus referred explicitly this notion to the supports positioned below the Earth, the ὑπερείσεις. In particular, according to Barigazzi,[66] "per Epicuro la terra sta sospesa, nonostante il principio del peso dei corpi, perché il suo peso diminuisce gradatamente e svanisce in una ἀραιὰ φύσις che è congiunta strettamente con l'aria del mondo." In short, the πυκνότης ἡ κάτω would be assimilated to the ἀραιὰ φύσις,[67] whereas, as we have seen, in Epicurean texts and in *Nat.* XI itself, the notions of πυκνότης and ἀραιότης are clearly distinct and even opposed to each other. It is therefore difficult to think that the former could "disappear" into the latter. Additionally, a little further on in the book, just before the conclusion, the ὑπερείσεις are explicitly defined as αἱ τῶν ἀέρων ὑπερείσεις.[68] It is therefore plausible to see a reference to air in ἀραιὰ φύσις, as Vogliano hypothesized.[69]

5. Although Vogliano and Barigazzi made the articular infinitive τοῦ μὴ φ[έ]|ρ[ε]-σθαι τὴν γῆν (ll. 14f.) depend on the substantive ἀντέρεισιν which precedes it – the former interprets the infinitive as indicating purpose; the latter, cause – I nonetheless find the syntax that Arrighetti established by punctuating after ἵνα (l. 12) and after πρὸς ἀντέρεισιν (l. 14) far more convincing than the previous proposals. In this way, the phrase πρὸς ἀντέρεισιν is connected to the adjective ἐσθλαί (l. 13) – absent, clearly, in Vogliano's paraphrase and Barigazzi's translation – while the articular infinitive is connected to the substantive ἀναλογίαν (l. 16).

6. However, I do not believe in Arrighetti's hypothesis, that "the supports" of the air (ὑπερείσεις), which were not mentioned in the preceding lines, should be taken as the subject of the purpose clause in ll. 12ff. Instead, that clause finds its natural subject in the πυκνότητες that were discussed just before, as Vogliano and Barigazzi held. Therefore, ἀντέρεισις cannot be the "resistenza (al peso della terra)", as Arrighetti translates (that the airy supports exert), but should refer to the Earth itself, as Barigazzi saw.

Evidence in favour of this hypothesis, it seems to me, comes from a papyrus in Florence, *PSI* 3192, which contains an interesting anonymous Epicurean treatise on physics, and which was published for the first time by Manfredo Manfredi[70] and

---

[64] Barigazzi 1950: 6. This assimilation is presupposed by Gale 2008: 47 as well; her comment on Lucr. V 534-563 affirms that fragments [26.22] and [26.41] Arr. – these are the passages in which the term ἀραιὰ φύσις appears – "show traces of the slightly more sophisticated theory of the 'other substance' here elaborated by L.".

[65] Cf. [26.41] 21-24 Arr.

[66] Barigazzi 1950: 6.

[67] With reference to Barigazzi's thesis, Isnardi Parente 1983²: 221 n. 1 clarifies that "anche la 'natura rada' nella sua gran massa raggiunge una densità, πυκνότης".

[68] [26.44] 13f. Arr. On the final columns of the book, cf. Leone 2020b as well.

[69] Vogliano 1940: 59.

[70] Manfredi 1996.

re-edited recently by Giulio Iovine in the *Corpus dei papiri filosofici*.[71] The author, perhaps Epicurus himself, explains clearly that "la natura dell'aria è rarefatta e non può opporre resistenza", π[ολ]υκένου οὔ[σης] | τῆς φύσεω[ς] τῆς τοῦ ἀέρος | καὶ ἀντέρει[σι]ν οὐκ ἐχούσης (col. II 3-5). Further, a passage of Aristotle's *De Caelo*[72] should be kept in mind, in which Aristotle reports that for Anaximenes, Anaxagoras, and Democritus, the Earth owes its μονή to its flat shape, since it acts against the air underneath it, πρὸς τὸν ὑποκείμενον ἀέρα, like all flat bodies do against the wind, "on account of their resistance to it", διὰ τὴν ἀντέρεισιν. Although – as Frederik Bakker tried to show in his book on Epicurean meteorology[73] – there is no proof that Epicurus adopted this solution for the shape of the earth, the terminology proper to the Presocratics that appears in *Nat.* XI in the discussion of the earth's stability is certainly striking.

Barigazzi, who explained ἀντέρεισις as "la resistenza d'una cosa appoggiata su un'altra",[74] wrote "La terra s'appoggia sull'aria per una speciale connessione *in quanto non si muove* ed esercita una pressione, un peso, termini a cui sembra equivalere qui il senso di ἀντέρεισις". For Isnardi Parente,[75] on the other hand, ἀντέρεισις would be the "resistenza reciproca delle due zone, l'inferiore e la superiore, di cui il testo ha sottolineato la continuità, cυνέχεια". I consider it more plausible to understand ἀντέρεισις as the "resistance" or "counter-force" with which the Earth, with its own πυκνότητες above and below, opposes, primarily, the ὑπερείσεις of the air beneath itself in an equilibrium of forces that assures that the Earth has μονή. It cannot be without meaning, I believe, that the terms ἀντέρεισις and ὑπέρεισις – which Epicurus uses here in reference to the Earth and air and to the rapport which exists between the two – are clearly constructed from the same root.

7. Lastly, it seems to me more coherent with Epicurus' texts to understand the term ἀναλογία not in the sense of "proportion", as Barigazzi and Arrighetti do – a meaning which I would attribute instead to the Epicurean technical term συμμετρία – but rather in its customary, equally technical meaning of "analogy", which, in this case, can be worked out between the two πυκνότητες of the Earth in a way that produces its μονή.

Therefore the translation that Brunschwig-Monet-Sedley offered of our passage in 2010 in *Les Épicuriens* seems appropriate:[76]

> Quant à la densité qu'elle a en bas, il faut la concevoir dans sa continuité avec celle qu'elle a en haut, afin que ces densités, qui sont bonnes pour fournir un contre-appui, maintiennent le modèle analogique approprié pour l'immobilité de la Terre.

---

[71] Iovine 2019.
[72] Aristot. *Cael.* 294b17.
[73] Bakker 2016: 162ff.
[74] Barigazzi 1950: 5.
[75] Isnardi Parente 1983²: 221 n. 1.
[76] Brunschwig-Monet-Sedley 2010: 89.

These translators do not comment on the passage, but it seems clear to me that they take the articular infinitive τοῦ μὴ φ[έ]|ρ[ε]σθαι τὴν γῆν as final.

I believe that the dependence of the articular infinitive on ἀναλογίαν allows the translation "the analogy *of* the immobility of the Earth", from which I deduce that here Epicurus – after reiterating that both the πυκνότητες of the Earth, those above and below, have the capacity of causing a counter-force continuously and reciprocally – affirms by analogy the immobility of the earth not only *below* – surely the most critical point for the demonstration of μονή, for the force of gravity that carries heavy bodies downwards – but also *above*. For the rest, as Epicurus specifies a little further on,[77] air surrounds the Earth equally on all sides, and it is not an accident that Lucretius, in the passage V 550ff. which follows immediately on the one cited above, reaffirms the intimate union of the Earth "to the airy parts of the world and to the sky", *partibus aeriis mundi caeloque* (n.b. the addition here of *caelo*, which I cannot believe is accidental, in reference to the things that are *above* the earth, *super quae se sunt*). The rereading of *Nat.* XI will furnish more certain responses to this question.

Even though, as I have stated in the beginning of this paper, I have chosen to limit myself just to some aspects of Epicurus' usage of scientific lexicon – this is not even the right place to propose a more comprehensive study – I do hope that this paper shows how complex it is to understand Epicurus' terminology in context, above all in his books *On Nature* and such a difficult book like *On Nature* XI. This demonstration is in any case worth the effort, since to enlighten his terminology it also means to be able to grasp the contents, and in order to do so – especially when it comes to meteorology, astronomy, and physics in a broader sense – his *opus magnum* is for obvious reasons the most important source we must rely on.

REFERENCES

Arrighetti, G., 1958, "Filodemo, De dis III, col. X-XI", *Studi Classici e Orientali* 7: 83-99.
Arrighetti, G., 1967, "La struttura dell'epistola di Epicuro a Pitocle", *Studi Classici e Orientali* 16: 117-128 = Idem, 1969, "La structure de la lettre d'Epicure à Pythoclès", Actes VIIIᵉ Congrès Ass. G. Budé 1968, Paris: Les Belles Lettres, 236-252 = Idem 1973², "Appendice I", in Arrighetti 1973²: 691-705.
Arrighetti, G. (ed.), 1973², *Epicuro. Opere*, Turin: Einaudi.
Bailey, C., 1926, *Epicurus: The Extant Remains, with Short Critical Apparatus, Translation and Notes*, Oxford: Clarendon Press.
Bakker, F.A., 2016, *Epicurean Meteorology: Sources, Method, Scope and Organization*, Leiden-Boston: Brill.

---

[77] [26.43] Arr.

Barigazzi, A., 1950, "La μονή della terra nei frammenti ercolanesi del libro XI del περὶ φύcεωc di Epicuro", *Studi Italiani di Filologia Classica* N.S. 24: 3-19.

Bignone, E., 1933, "Studi critici sul testo di Epicuro", *Studi Italiani di Filologia Classica* 10: 71-118.

Bollack, J., – Bollack, M., – Wismann, H., 1971, *La Lettre d'Épicure*, Paris: Éditions de Minuit.

Brunschwig, J., – Monet, A., – Sedley, D.N., 2010, "Épicure, La Nature", in D. Delattre – J. Pigeaud (eds.), *Les Épicuriens*, Paris: Les Belles Lettres: 79-117.

Corti, A., 2015, "'Ὁμοιοcχήμων e ὁμοιόμορφοc. Alcune riflessioni sulle proprietà degli εἴδωλα", in F. G. Masi – S. Maso (eds.), *Epicurus on Eidola. Peri Phuseos Book II: Update, Proposals, and Discussions*, Amsterdam: Hakkert: 83-105.

Delattre, D., 2010, "Épicure, Lettre à Hérodote", in D. Delattre – J. Pigeaud (eds.), *Les Épicuriens*, Paris: Les Belles Lettres: 14-31.

De Sanctis, D., 2015, "Strategie della comunicazione di Epicuro nell'epilogo delle sue opere", in F. G. Masi – S. Maso (eds.), *Epicurus on Eidola. Peri Phuseos Book II: Update, Proposals, and Discussions*, Amsterdam: Hakkert: 172-190.

Flores, E., 2009, *Titus Lucretius Carus, De rerum natura*, vol. III, edizione critica con introduzione e versione, Quinto Supplemento a La Scuola di Epicuro, Collezione di testi ercolanesi fondata da M. Gigante e diretta da G. Arrighetti e F. Longo Auricchio, Naples: Bibliopolis.

Gale, M.R., 2008, *Lucretius, De Rerum Natura Book V*, Liverpool: Liverpool University Press.

Gomperz, T., 1867, "Neue Bruchstücke Epikur's "über die Natur". Herculanensium voluminum collectio altera. Tom. VI, Fasciculus 1. (Neapel 1866)", *Zeitschrift für die Oesterreichischen Gymnasien* 18: 207-213 = Dorandi, T. (ed.), 1993, *Theodor Gomperz. Eine Auswahl Herkulanischer Kleiner Schriften (1864-1909)*, Leiden-New York: Brill: 45-51.

HV 1809 = *Herculanensium voluminum quae supersunt*, Tomus II, Naples: 30-78.

Iovine, G., 2019, "PSI inv. 3192. Trattato di fisica epicurea", in *CPF* II.1* *(Frammenti Adespoti)*, Florence: L.S. Olschki: 217-227.

Isnardi Parente, M., 1983², *Opere di Epicuro*, Turin: UTET.

Lapini, W., 2015, *L'Epistola a Erodoto e il Bios di Epicuro in Diogene Laerzio. Note testuali, esegetiche e metodologiche*, Rome: Edizioni di Storia e Letteratura.

Leone, G., 1984, "Epicuro, *Della natura*, libro XIV", *Cronache Ercolanesi* 14: 17-107.

Leone, G., 2002, "Epicuro, *Della natura*, libro XXXIV (PHerc. 1431)", *Cronache Ercolanesi* 32: 7-135.

Leone, G., 2012, *Epicuro, Sulla natura, Libro II*, edizione, traduzione e commento a cura di G. Leone, La Scuola di Epicuro, Collezione di testi ercolanesi fondata da M. Gigante e diretta da G. Arrighetti e F. Longo Auricchio, 18, Naples: Bibliopolis.

Leone, G., 2020a, "Epicuro e 'le voci delle cose'", in G. Leone – F. G. Masi – F. Verde (eds.), *'Vedere' l'invisibile. Rileggendo il XXXIV libro Sulla natura di Epicuro*, Sesto Supplemento a *Cronache Ercolanesi*, Naples: Centro Internazionale per lo Studio dei Papiri Ercolanesi Editore: 71-83.

Leone, G., 2020b, "'Connessioni' scorrette e 'connessioni' insospettate nell'XI libro *Sulla natura* di Epicuro", *Cronache Ercolanesi* 50: 15-25.

Leone, G., 2021, "La stabilità della terra nella dottrina di Epicuro: Lucrezio lettore dell'XI libro *Sulla natura*", in M. Paladini (ed.), *Templa serena. Studi in onore di Enrico Flores*, Naples: Federico II Open Access University Press: 59-73.

Manfredi, M., 1996, "Un inedito frammento di fisica (*PSI* inv. CNR 81)", in M. S. Funghi (ed.), ΟΔΟΙ ΔΙΖΗΣΙΟΣ. *Le vie della ricerca. Studi in onore di Francesco Adorno*, Florence: Olschki: 31-40.

Masi, F. G., 2015, "Dagli occhi alla mente: il cammino tortuoso degli εἴδωλα", in F. G. Masi – S. Maso (ed.), *Epicurus on Eidola. Peri Phuseos Book II: Update, Proposals, and Discussions*, Amsterdam: Hakkert: 107-134.

Masi, F. G., 2016, "'A mutual horizon of events'. Epicurus' *Letter to Herodotus* between philology and philosophy", *Eirene* 52: 485-500.

Morel, P.-M. (tr.), 2011, *Épicure. Lettres, maximes et autres textes*, Paris: Editions Flammarion.

Piergiacomi, E., 2017, *Storia delle antiche teologie atomiste*, Rome: Sapienza Università Editrice.

Santoro, M., 2000, *[Demetrio Lacone]: [La forma del dio]* (PHerc. 1055), edizione, traduzione e commento a cura di M. Santoro, La Scuola di Epicuro, Collezione di testi ercolanesi diretta da M. Gigante, 17, Naples: Bibliopolis.

Todd, R. B., 1974, "Lexicographical Notes on Alexander of Aphrodisias' Philosophical Terminology", *Glotta* 52: 207-215.

Usener, H., 1977, *Glossarium Epicureum, edendum curaverunt M. Gigante et W. Schmid*, Rome: Edizioni dell'Ateneo & Bizzarri.

Verde, F. (ed.), 2010, *Epicuro, Epistola a Erodoto*, introd. di E. Spinelli, Rome: Carocci Editore.

Verde, F., 2016, "Percezione, errore e residuo percettivo in Aristotele, Epicuro e Alessandro di Afrodisia", *Giornale Critico della Filosofia Italiana* 1: 44-62.

Verde, F., 2017, "Οὐδὲν διφυὲς αἰσθητόν ([Dem. Lac.] [*De forma dei*] PHerc. 1055, col. XXII 9-10 Santoro)", *Vichiana* 54/2: 163-167.

Verde, F. (ed.), 2022, *Epicuro: Epistola a Pitocle*, in collaborazione con M. Tulli, D. De Sanctis, F. G. Masi, Baden-Baden: Academia.

Vogliano, A., 1940, *I resti dell'XI libro del Περὶ φύσεως di Epicuro*, Le Caire: Imprimerie de l'Institut Français d'Archéologie Orientale.

Vogliano, A., 1941, "Un passo dell'XI libro del ΠΕΡΙ ΦΥΣΕΩC di Epicuro", *Athenaeum* 19: 141-143.

EPICUREAN *AKRIBEIA*

Pierre-Marie Morel

The first paragraphs of the *Letter to Herodotus* – Epicurus' Physics Compendium – oppose the knowledge of the doctrine taken as a whole to the knowledge of the parts; in other words, on the one hand, the general or comprehensive knowledge of nature and the main lines of the doctrine and, on the other, the knowledge of the particular and of the detail. Both types of knowledge are legitimate. In the case of things whose knowledge is necessary – that is, necessary for happiness – it is legitimate not only to grasp them in their totality, but also to apprehend them in their detail or in their parts.

This double approach is justified first of all, as we can see from the very first lines of the *Letter*, by the need to address different audiences, by virtue of what might be called a 'principle of multiple addressees'. The Physics Compendium is intended not only for those who have attained a proven expertise and a complete understanding of the system, both in its entirety and in detail, but also for those who have not been able to "examine with precision (ἐξακριβοῦν) each of the points" of the science of nature. These people must favour a global approach, either because they are still beginners or because they lack time, for example, because of their practical occupations:

[T 1]
For those who are unable, Herodotus, to make a detailed study (ἐξακριβοῦν) of all my works on nature, or to examine my longer treatises, I have myself prepared a summary of the whole system as an aid to preserving in memory enough of the principal doctrines (…).[1]

This theme is in line with one of the best-known features – also one of the most flattering for modern minds – of the Epicurean conception of science: the idea of open scientific knowledge, accessible to different audiences and not reserved for a learned elite. More generally, in ethics, the search for happiness is accessible to everyone. The *Letter to Menoeceus* is addressed to all, young and old, because the search for happiness is everyone's business, at any age.[2] We might thus have the impression

---

[1] Epicur. *Hrdt.* 35 (ed. Dorandi 2013; transl. Mensch 2018, here and below). I would like to thank the participants at the Venice symposium – in particular Voula Tsouna, Wim Nijs, Emidio Spinelli, Franco Trabattoni, Maddalena Bonelli, Francesco Verde and Stéphane Marchand – for their valuable questions and remarks. A modified version of this text was also presented to the Faculty of Philosophy at Oxford, and I would like to thank the colleagues present for their helpful comments, in particular Alexander Bown, Luca Castagnoli, Terence Irwin, Anna Marmodoro. Finally, I would like to extend my warmest thanks to Philip Mitsis for his careful reading of this text.
[2] Epicur. *Men.* 122.

that the principle of multiple addressees is not a strictly scientific requirement, but, first and foremost, an ethical and pedagogical issue.

There is, however, another justification for the dual approach I have just mentioned, a justification which is properly epistemological and applies, as it were, within science itself: achieved knowledge, fully constituted *phusiologia*, requires that one moves from global knowledge to the knowledge of the particular and back again (*Hrdt.* 36). Epicurus' science not only requires different approaches for different audiences; it also requires a passage between these two levels, or rather two types[3] of knowledge, so that one can make a "circuit" that allows one to apprehend the totality continuously.[4] This epistemological circuit involves each of the two types of knowledge – the comprehensive grasp of the totality and the knowledge of detail – but is not reduced to either of them. It is necessary to be able to link them and to move from one to the other. All this is clearly evidenced by the texts, while the introductory and concluding paragraphs, not only of the *Letter to Herodotus*, but also of the *Letter to Pythocles*, make it easy to establish.

Nevertheless, this doctrine raises some difficulties. In the first place, the question might be asked whether the two types of knowledge have equal status. Do they have the same degree of practical necessity and the same scientific value? Epicurus explicitly favours a holistic conception of knowledge, not only to satisfy the synthetic requirements of writing in abridged form, but also to meet a properly *practical* need: we need, for life itself and for happiness, to grasp easily the totality of the basic elements or the overall theses. As he says in the first paragraph of the *Letter to Herodotus*, a few lines after [T 1], "a comprehensive view is often required, the details not in the same way" (τῆς γὰρ ἀθρόας ἐπιβολῆς πυκνὸν δεόμεθα, τῆς δὲ κατὰ μέρος οὐχ ὁμοίως; *Hrdt.* 35). Knowledge of detail, by contrast, remains secondary and optional. What, then, is the *epistemological* value of each of the two approaches and, in particular, of knowledge of detail? If the knowledge of detail seems less necessary, at least at first sight, does this mean that it is less reliable or less well-founded than the apprehension of the totality?

I believe that this is not the case and that the distinction between the two approaches should not be made in terms of epistemological value. What is at stake here is not a minor point: it is in fact the issue of the coherence and unity of scientific discourse. The comprehensive approach has some priority – an ethical one – but this does not mean that it has a higher degree of scientific reliability. In order to argue this point, I would like to focus the debate on a notion that applies equally to

---

[3] It is preferable, at this stage of the investigation, to use an expression ("two types of knowledge") that may appear somewhat imprecise, but which has the merit of avoiding two expressions that could be misleading: the idea of "levels" of knowledge, on the one hand, if this were to suggest a form of discontinuity between knowledge of the general and that of the particular; and the idea of "kinds" of knowledge in the strict sense, for reasons to which I will return later.

[4] See the terms περιοδεία, in Epicur. *Hrdt.* 36; 83; περίοδος, in *Hrdt.* 83; περιοδεύω, in *Letter to Pythocles* (*Pyth.*) 85.

the knowledge of detail and to the global approach of the doctrine. It is the notion of *akribeia*, "exactness", "precision", "accuracy", or "rigour". It appears repeatedly, in various forms (*akribeia, akribôma, akribôs, exakriboun, epakriboun*), in the passages of the *Letters* that reveal the Epicurean conception of science. It therefore deserves *a priori* special attention, if we are to resolve the difficulties I have just mentioned.

It seems to me that this attention is too rarely given to it.[5] This relative neglect can probably be explained by two types of factors. The first one is semantic; the second one is properly philosophical.

Firstly, on the semantic level, the term *akribeia* has its own weaknesses. In Greek, it can have an ironic connotation and designate either an excess of meticulousness or the laborious character of an awkward approach. It can also mean a form of excessive harshness, as opposed to moderation and balance in behaviour or in the judgment of others.[6] In a more positive sense, it can refer to the precision with which one practises an art or observation, or with which one takes measurements. One can also speak of the *akribeia* either of sensation or of a particular sense, as Aristotle often does.[7] As we shall see, it can also have a more general meaning than just "precision" and can refer to the "rigour" with which one follows principles or applies a rule – the distinction between these two meanings being sometimes difficult to establish.[8] It is therefore clear that the vocabulary of exactness belongs to a common register of expression and is not limited to philosophical usage.[9] Even Epicurean texts give a good idea of this diversity of meanings and degrees of philosophical technicality, sometimes evoking in a very common way the "literal" meaning of a term, as the fragment 72 Smith of Diogenes of Oinoanda:

[T 2]
Well, he regained consciousness and, during those times when the assaults of the waves were intermittent, came little by little out of the danger, barely making it safely to dry land, literally flayed all over.

διένηψε δ' οὖν καὶ κα-   MFS: διένηψε δ' οὖν καὶ κατὰ μεικρὸν ἐκ τ[ο]ῦ δεῖν[οῦ],
ἐν οἷς δὴ χρόν[ο]ις α[ἱ] τῷ[ν]

---

[5] Among the exceptions, see Spinelli in Verde 2010; Verde 2010: 70, 223, 225; Angeli 1985.

[6] See, e.g., Thucydides, *Hist. of the Peloponnesian War*, III 46: the Athenian orator Diodotus takes a stand against the application of the death penalty to the inhabitants of Mytilene, who had revolted against Athens in 428, and warns against an excess of *akribeia* by the Athenians.

[7] Arist. *De an.* II 7, 419a16: "Democritus is wrong to think that if the intervening medium were a void, even an ant in heaven would be seen clearly (ἀκριβῶς)" (transl. C. Shields); *Hist. An.* I 15, 494b16: "the most precise (ἀκριβεστάτην) sense in humans is touch; taste comes second"; see also *Parv. nat. De sens.* 4, 441a2.

[8] Lloyd 1982: 130 n. 3.

[9] As Kurz 1970 has shown, it originally belonged to the field of *technai* – to signify that one object "sits" firmly on another – especially in medicine and in the field of law.

κυμάτων ἐπεμπτῴςει[c]
διελίμπανον, εἰς τὸ ξη-
ρὸν ἐςώθη μόγις ἐγδε-
δαρμένος ἀκρειβῶς
(col. III)
ὅλος.[10]

In the same vein, about the skill of the letter engraver, see Diogenes' New Fragment 215:

[T 3]
for, some accurate shorthand-writers having made a record of the address, I made a copy of this (MFS: I made this copy) for myself and [took it] away.

cημειογράφων γὰρ
ἀκρειβῶν τινων ἐγλαβόντων
τὴν ἀκρόαcιν ἀντίγραφον τ[ού]-   MFS: τὴν ἀκρόαcιν ἀντίγραφον
του ν ἐποιηcάμην καὶ ἀπ[ῆρα.]   τοῦτ' ἐποιηcάμην καὶ ἀπ[ῆρα.][11]

It is therefore not always easy to determine the exact meaning of the term and the philosophical issues it may cover, even within the Epicurean corpus.

Secondly, from the strict point of view of Epicureanism, one may wonder whether the appeal to knowledge of detail is in any way compatible with the texts that criticize excessive erudition in the sciences, notably in the *Letter to Pythocles*, where Epicurus invites us to turn away from specialized inquiries,[12] because they would lead us away from what is truly essential for the pursuit of happiness. From this point of view, one could have the impression that the relative valorization of *akribeia* indicates a kind of concession to positive knowledge, a partial retreat from global knowledge before specialized investigations. It would, however, be a tactical retreat, essentially intended to establish the superiority of the former over the latter. The quality of *akribeia*, if it is true that it applies exclusively to knowledge of detail, – that is, to the one of the two approaches that is in principle the least valued – would therefore be secondary.

I believe, however, that the notion plays a decisive role, as suggested by its repeated appearance at the beginning and end of the *Letter to Herodotus*, and that it reveals fundamental features of *phusiologia*, that is, of science itself as Epicurus conceives it: a rational empiricism, which connects continuously particular facts and explanations to general views. To this end, I would like to show not only that

---

[10] Diog. of Oinoanda, fr. 72 II 14 (ed. Hammerstaedt-Smith 2018, with 'MFS' for M.F. Smith).
[11] Diog. of Oinoanda, NF 215 II (ed. Hammerstaedt-Smith 2018, with 'MFS' for M.F. Smith).
[12] See Epicur. *Pyth.* 85-86.

this notion cannot be reduced to the knowledge of detail, but also that it occupies a function that is central within the "path" that constitutes *phusiologia*.

To clarify my position, I will start from Anna Angeli's valuable study, published in *Cronache Ercolanesi* in 1985, "L'esattezza scientifica in Epicuro e Filodemo". Angeli has usefully reacted against the idea, shared and defended in particular by Kurz 1970, according to which the notion of *akribeia* would experience a kind of decline after Aristotle and Plato. Among the most notable results of Angeli's study, I will mention five points: (i) the association of *akribeia* and *aisthêsis*, attested by a testimony of Olympiodorus;[13] (ii) the idea of exhaustive knowledge; (iii) the very importance of the knowledge of detail; and (iv) the identification of a diversified skill: for Epicurus, *akribeia* is not limited to unchangeable realities, as in Plato, because it is applied diversely according to the requirements of the type of knowledge considered. From this point of view – again, according to Angeli – Epicurus would be much closer to Aristotle. The latter, as we know, defends a nuanced conception of the requirement of *akribeia*, in which I have proposed to see a "principle of relative rigour".[14] One should not, says Aristotle, seek the same accuracy everywhere. It is normal and even the sign of a cultured mind not to demand that the carpenter knows the right angle with the same accuracy as the geometer. I will come back to this point. Finally (v), Angeli insists on the relationship between *akribeia* and the preservation of *ataraxia*, thus on the practical purposes of the requirement of precision or rigour. She also cites numerous texts by Philodemus that provide valuable support for her rehabilitation effort.

I am in general agreement with these observations, which are in accordance with textual evidence. However, I would like to propose a different approach to the notion in Epicurus and to ask myself, as I said at the beginning, about its meaning for the "science" that the Garden intends to define, that is, for *phusiologia*. In other words, I propose to clarify the epistemological function of *akribeia* in the Epicurean construction of science. Angeli believes that it is above all the preservation of the soul that constitutes the exactitude of philosophy. This exactitude, according to her, is "no longer absolute but essential, no longer abstract but concretely operative in view of the happy life".[15] This is true, but this very general observation gives absolute priority to the ethical end over scientific goals. For my part, I would like to propose an alternative to this line of interpretation since it may obscure the properly epistemological role of exactitude for Epicurus. From a general point of view, it is undoubtedly true that ethical goals take precedence over acquisition of knowledge as such, but this priority does not mean that these goals are, for Epicurus, the only justification for his methodological and epistemological theses. I am not convinced, in this case, by this sort of 'ethical escape' precisely because I think that *akribeia*,

---

[13] Olympiod. *In Plat. Phaed.* 80.1 (Us. 247, p. 183, 1).
[14] Morel 2003: 57-58.
[15] Angeli 1985: 70. In the same line, see Bénatouïl 2003.

for Epicurus, belongs above all to epistemological terminology, and that invoking the practical goal does not permit us to reach the core of the notion.

Let me start from a less optimistic point of view than that of Angeli. While it is true that the notion is central, it is not, however, the subject of a perfectly systematic treatment. It even seems to lead to a certain dispersion, because of the diversity of its applications.[16] In particular, how can we reconcile the two main meanings of the idea of *akribeia*, namely, precision of detail, on the one hand, and rigour of the highest and most general knowledge, on the other? It seems to me, however, that Epicurus' text provides a means of resolving this difficulty.

To indicate the direction of my investigation now, it seems to me that the notion of *akribeia* does not correspond to a type of reality or a class of objects, nor even to a single point of view on the objects of knowledge – for example, that of detail – but rather that it designates a quality of knowledge or of the one who knows – perhaps an intellectual or epistemic virtue – which must be exercised at several steps of the scientific circuit. It thus gives empirical knowledge of detail a value of its own, which is not inferior, in its order, to comprehensive and more abstract knowledge. More importantly, it brings together a set of qualities, which attest to the genuinely scientific nature of the investigation as a whole. I would even be tempted to put forward the supposition that the *akribeia* of the discourse on nature attests to the fact that the latter truly has the status of a science.

I will therefore consider the notion of *akribeia* through its different features. I will mainly identify four of them, which alternately appear in the texts: clarity in the knowledge of detail; the firmness and certainty of the knowledge; the distinctive or discriminating function of *akribeia*, through which it acquires a critical and polemical dimension; and finally, its variability and transversality – the idea of a global demand for accuracy, which is operative in the two approaches I mentioned at the beginning.

1. CLARITY AND DETAILED KNOWLEDGE

Let us start with the idea of clarity in grasping the detail or in knowing the "parts".[17] By clarity, here, I mean the fact of relating assertions to elementary entities and unequivocal terms. This idea appears in particular in the preamble of the *Letter to Herodotus*. The end of paragraph 35 contrasts two types of apprehensions, or "mental projections" (*epibolai*): that which concerns the totality of the doctrine and that which concerns the detail. We constantly "need" (δεόμεθα) the former, not the latter. The rest of the passage in § 36, shows that the first *epibolē* is truly "principal", or "of

---

[16] I see confirmation of this in the texts of Diogenes of Oinoanda [T 2] and [T 3] above – which could not be examined by Angeli as we can today thanks to the work of M.F. Smith and J. Hammerstaedt.

[17] See the expression τὸ κατὰ μέρος ἀκρίβωμα in *Hrdt.* 36; 83.

major importance" (κυριωτάτη) in relation to the things we are studying. However, it does not exclude the "precise knowledge of detail" (τὸ κατὰ μέρος ἀκρίβωμα); this is added to it (καὶ δὴ καὶ). This relationship between global grasp and particular knowledge is reflected in the very form of the abstract that constitutes the *Letter to Herodotus*. As D. Delattre has shown,[18] the paragraphs of the *Letter* generally begin by stating the overall thesis, the chapter heading, and then give detailed arguments or explanations and possibly more precise information, especially that which is derived from – or inferentially related to – sensible observation. We may assume that we can know, at the level of the main theses, that "the soul is a body composed of subtle parts disseminated throughout the aggregate" (*Hrdt.* 63), and further learn, at the level of detailed knowledge, that it is similar to a breath containing a certain mixture of heat, that it also contains a particularly subtle element, and so forth, as Epicurus then explains.

In any case, the preamble to the *Letter to Herodotus* does not aim to define the level of precision designated by the expression κατὰ μέρος, but to articulate the two approaches. The global approach seems to determine in some ways the particular knowledge and regulate its use:

[T 4]
We must return constantly to those main points and commit to memory an amount of doctrine sufficient to secure a reliable conception of the facts; furthermore, all the details will be discovered accurately if the general outlines are well understood and remembered, since even for the advanced student the chief condition of accurate knowledge is the ability to make ready use of his conceptions by referring each of them to fundamental facts and simple terms. For it is not possible to obtain the results of a continuous diligent study of the universe unless we can embrace in brief terms everything that could have been accurately known down to the smallest detail.

βαδιστέον μὲν οὖν καὶ ἐπ' ἐκεῖνα συνεχῶς, ἐν τῇ μνήμῃ τὸ τοσοῦτο ποιητέον, ἀφ' οὗ ἥ τε κυριωτάτη ἐπιβολὴ ἐπὶ τὰ πράγματα ἔσται καὶ δὴ καὶ τὸ κατὰ μέρος ἀκρίβωμα πᾶν ἐξευρήσεται, τῶν ὁλοσχερωτάτων τύπων εὖ περιειλημμένων καὶ μνημονευομένων· ἐπεὶ καὶ τοῦ τετελεσιουργημένου τοῦτο κυριώτατον τοῦ παντὸς ἀκριβώματος γίνεται, τὸ ταῖς ἐπιβολαῖς ὀξέως δύνασθαι χρῆσθαι, καὶ πρὸς ἁπλᾶ στοιχειώματα καὶ φωνὰς συναγομένων. οὐ γὰρ οἷόν τε τὸ πύκνωμα τῆς συνεχοῦς τῶν ὅλων περιοδείας εἰ<δέ>ναι μὴ δυναμένον διὰ βραχεῶν φωνῶν ἅπαν ἐμπεριλαβεῖν ἐν αὑτῷ τὸ καὶ κατὰ μέρος ἂν ἐξακριβωθέν.[19]

The "precise knowledge of the detail" (τὸ κατὰ μέρος ἀκρίβωμα) becomes possible "if the general outlines are well understood and remembered" (τῶν ὁλοσχερωτάτων τῶν τύπων εὖ περιειλημμένων καὶ μνημονευομένων). The participial proposition, even if it

---

[18] Delattre 2004.
[19] Epicur. *Hrdt.* 36.

is not considered to have an exactly conditional value, at least has a circumstantial meaning. It shows that, in order to be able to reach the desired precision, it is necessary to have well understood and remembered the general schemes, achieving this by quickly using the *epibolai*, relating them to the elementary data of the doctrine and to simple, unequivocal expressions.[20] It is on this condition that one will grasp, not precision for its own sake – which would undoubtedly be a vain search for erudition – but what is essential or fundamental: "the chief condition of accurate knowledge" (τοῦτο κυριώτατον τοῦ παντὸς ἀκριβώματος). The end of the paragraph confirms this condition with the proposition "that could have been accurately known down to the smallest detail" (τὸ καὶ κατὰ μέρος ἂν ἐξακριβωθέν). In order to be able to carry out in a continuous way the "journey" – both scientific and therapeutic – of *phusiologia*, one must "embrace within oneself" (ἐμπεριλαβεῖν ἐν αὐτῷ) in a synthetic way the particular knowledge one has acquired. I suppose the implicit idea is that if we were not able to do this, the plurality of this knowledge would end up fragmenting knowledge and introducing a discontinuity between psychic states, whereas we need to achieve a global psychic serenity through a "continuous activity in the science of nature" (τὸ συνεχὲς ἐνέργημα ἐν φυσιολογίᾳ; *Hrdt.* 37).

From this point of view, for Epicurus, we should not simply refer to *akribeia*, pure and simple, for two reasons. First, exactness is accepted, even recommended, but it carries with it the risk of fragmentation and must therefore be seriously monitored. Second, the valorization of *akribeia* calls for specifications, and this demand contrasts with the sometimes emphatic character of its evocations in Epicurus' predecessors. The break with Plato, and to a lesser extent with Aristotle, is very clear here. In the Platonic dialogues, one of the most remarkable texts on *akribeia*[21] reserves it for the highest and clearest knowledge, the one obtained by the long way that leads to dialectic. Here, we are far from precision in the grasp of particularities: *akribeia* applies primarily to an eminent knowledge that prepares, even constitutes, the dialectic proper, and which is based on the anhypothetical principle of the idea of the Good.[22] In Aristotle, the situation is contrasted. In some texts, he indirectly joins the Platonic position by reserving the highest degree of *akribeia* for sciences that do not admit deliberation, because their objects are universal and necessary, whereas the objects of deliberation are particular and contingent. The latter are

---

[20] The recommendation to use clear and unambiguous terms is one of the fundamental requirements of Epicurus' epistemology and his conception of the proper use of language. See in particular *Hrdt.* 37-38; 72-73. On linguistic controversies and scientific terminology in Epicurus' *Peri phuseôs*, see Masi 2023.

[21] Plat. *Resp.* VI 504b-e.

[22] Plat. *Resp.* VI 505a-b. In contrast, the shorter route, earlier taken by Socrates (IV 435d), though "demonstrative", was still hypothetical. On this point, see Scott 2015: 51. On "eminent" *akribeia*, see also Plat. *Phileb.* 56b f., where techniques are distinguished according to their degree of precision, the most precise being also the most "scientific". Significantly, in *Phil.* 57b-c, the most precise sciences "reach the higher degree of clearness" (σαφεστέραν).

not always the same and are true only for the most part. Such sciences are said to be "exact and fully sufficient" (ἀκριβεῖς καὶ αὐτάρκεις).[23] It also happens to coincide with the idea of clarity, the most exact knowledge being also the clearest[24] and, in the most favourable cases, the clearest in itself and not only for us. At the end of the *Posterior analytics*, Aristotle reminds us that there is no knowledge "truer" (ἀληθέστερον) than science or intellection, and that only the latter is "more exact" (ἀκριβέστερον) than science. This is why it is in a sense the "principle" of science.[25] Thus, it is not impossible that by granting *akribeia* to particular knowledge, mainly graspable through sensible experience, Epicurus wants to oppose the idea – shared by Plato and, at least partly, by Aristotle – of a restricted conception of *akribeia*, that is, of the accuracy inherent in the most general objects of knowledge. It is possible, rather, that Epicurus does so in the name of an other conception of knowledge, a knowledge that is more diversified and more attentive to particular explanations.[26] I will return to the implicitly polemical dimension of the Epicurean valorization of *akribeia* below.

In certain texts, however, as I mentioned at the beginning, Aristotle urges to take into account different levels of *akribeia* according to the subject matter – that of practical thought is variable and particular, whereas that of theoretical sciences like geometry is eternal and universal – and according to the ends sought. Thus, the enlightened politician will investigate the soul, because he must make citizens virtuous, but he will do so without excessive scientific precision and only up to the degree of precision necessary for his activity, because "to push the examination of detail too far would undoubtedly be too burdensome a task compared to what he proposes to achieve" (τὸ γὰρ ἐπὶ πλεῖον ἐξακριβοῦν ἐργωδέστερον ἴσως ἐστὶ τῶν προκειμένων).[27] This reasoning is precisely the same as saying that specialists in ethics and politics must also demonstrate accuracy, but in their own field, as well as by aiming for the degree of accuracy that is appropriate to that field. On this particular point, it is not impossible that Epicurus endorses Aristotle's views, at least partly.

We have another indication of this contrasting heritage in the relevant texts of Aristotle's *Nicomachean Ethics*. In the passage just quoted, *akribeia* is opposed to the approximate or sketched conception, which we have to be content with, if we consider the theoretical limits inherent in practical knowledge. Indeed it is obvious that, for Aristotle, a sketched representation *(tupos)* of the good is more appropriate

---

[23] Arist. *Nic. Eth.* III 5, 1112b1.
[24] Lesher 2010.
[25] Arist. *Post. an.* II 19, 100b5-17. See also *Post. an.* I 24, 86a16-17: "the demonstration which starts from the principles is more exact (ἀκριβεστέρα) than the one which does not start from them, and the one which starts more directly from the principle <i.e.: the universal demonstration> is more exact than the one which starts less directly from it". On *akribeia* in sciences, see also *Post. an.* I 27.
[26] Angeli 1985.
[27] Arist. *Nic. Eth.* I 13, 1102a25-26.

in this particular context than a demonstrative or purely scientific approach.[28] In contrast, the opposition between *akribeia* and "sketch" *(hupographê)* also appears in Plato, but in this case in favour of the *akribeia* of the "longer route" – that is, the dialectical foundation of the discourse on the best *polis*.[29] In [T 4] above, like Aristotle in several places, Epicurus does not oppose *tupos* to *akribeia*, since there is no conflict for him between exactness, on the one hand, and a sketch of the whole system, on the other. I think that all this is very significant. These overlaps of semantic fields – like the link 'precision-clearness' – and oppositions – such as the contrast between *akribeia* and *tupos* – clearly show that Epicurus builds his own conception of *akribeia* from a pre-existing debate. The confrontation between Plato and Aristotle on the question of the highest knowledge and the highest degree of exactness is probably in the background of his own conception of *akribeia*.

The preamble of the *Letter to Herodotus*, in any case, explicitly justifies the acquisition of particular knowledge and thus the search for *akribeia* understood as a clear representation of the details, while at the same time subjecting the latter to two fundamental conditions: (a) that it can be constantly related to the global grasp through the work of memory; (b) that it is subordinated to the practical and therapeutic purpose of the Garden doctrine. The search for precision is thus subject to a doubly conditional justification. It is clear that Epicurus closely links the two main meanings of the idea of *akribeia*, namely, precision of detail and general rigour.

2. CERTAINTY

Let us consider the second feature of the notion: the firmness of precision and the certainty it implies.

> [T 5]
> Accordingly, when we refer all these arguments about the soul to our feelings and sensations, bearing in mind the premises stated at the outset, we will see that they have been adequately comprehended in the outlines, and hence we will be able, on this basis, to work out the details with accuracy and firmness (ἐξακριβοῦσθαι βεβαίως).[30]

Epicurus draws the conclusion of the development on the soul (*Hrdt.* 63-67) and considers that he has reached a satisfactory examination, because the arguments are sufficiently "comprehended in the outlines" (τοῖς τύποις ἐμπεριειλημμένα) that

---

[28] On the principle of just measure in *akribeia*, see Arist. *Nic. Eth.* I 1, 1094b13; 24; I 7, 1098a27; II 2, 1103b24-1104a10; X 8, 1178a20-3. For an analysis of these texts, see Scott 2015: 123-141. On the opposition of precision and sketch in Aristotle, see Lesher 2010.

[29] Plat. *Resp.* VI 504d.

[30] Epicur. *Hrdt.* 68. Mensch translates the last expression as "confidence".

have been traced out and because, as a result, they allow us "to work out the details with accuracy and firmness" (τὸ κατὰ μέρος ἀπὸ τούτων ἐξακριβοῦσθαι βεβαίως). We find here the principle mentioned above of the conditional justification of the examination of detail: overall knowledge must be well constituted and well memorized "so that" (εἰς) the precise examination has all the required firmness.

The notion of "firmness", in this context, is twofold: it is at the same time psychological and epistemological. It applies, concomitantly, to the mental state of certainty and to the status of the propositions or knowledge which serve as principles or starting points for research. In *Pyth.* 85, it qualifies the "confidence" (*pistis*) provided by *ataraxia*; in *Key Doctrine* XL, the "assurance" (*pistôma*) provided by living together; in *Hrdt.* 63, the "confidence" (*pistis*), this time epistemic, provided by the criteria of truth (in this case sensations and affections). In other words, the firmness of a knowledge or a disposition denotes its indisputable character and assigns it a function as a secure starting point, whether in the theoretical or practical order. Thus, to return to *Hrdt.* 68, although the *akribeia* may not be, *in itself*, a guarantee of firmness – insofar as it needs to be related to the knowledge as a whole – it participates directly in the definition of scientific principles, that is, in the establishment of points that will no longer have to be demonstrated.

In this way, it is implicitly included in the rules of method stated in *Hrdt.* 37-38: the immediate meaning of the simple terms, to which we must refer, must not be further demonstrated; we must, in general, avoid demonstrative regression *ad infinitum* and not question the evidence of the criteria – especially sensation and the "natural notions", or preconceptions,[31] which derive from it – in order to be able to carry out our research. Similarly, our inferences should be based on mental apprehensions, of "focusings" whose validity is deemed to be firmly established (see *Hrdt.* 38, last sentence).

Generally speaking, it can be assumed that the "parts" that constitute the detail of the explanation are indivisible terms for research. They are definitively assured points whereby it is no longer a question of subdividing or justifying, but of integrating into the correctly unified totality of knowledge. In this sense, from the methodological point of view, the requirement of *akribeia* has an essential function: it coincides with the need to have non-demonstrable stopping points in order to make the search for inference possible.[32]

---

[31] In this regard, see Gourinat, same volume.
[32] On the epistemological necessity of positing indemonstrable terms and on the possibility, under this condition, of a genuine "demonstration", see Morel 2015.

3. CRITICAL FUNCTION

I now come to the third aspect that I have been able to identify: the distinctive or discriminating character of *akribeia*, through which it also functions as a critical, even polemical concept.

This notion, in the first place, can be applied to a correct way of expressing oneself, to speaking 'accurately' as opposed to a misleading or imprecise use of terms, or to reading and understanding. Fragment 72 of Diogenes of Oinoanda, text [T 2] above, is perhaps an indirect illustration of this meaning. It is possible that it is an echo of Epicurus' criticism of rhetoric. Epicurus believed that rhetoric need not have any other purpose than "clarity of expression", *saphêneia*.[33]

More generally, *akribeia* is found in the ability to refute an error or an unfounded opinion, as in Philodemus' *De ira*, where the *spoudaios* is said to practise a "rigorous refutation in his writings and discussions" (ἔλεγχος ἀκριβὴς ἔν τε γραφαῖς καὶ διατριβαῖς) of those who have committed errors.[34] This text poses a difficulty, because it is not certain that the Epicurean assumes the statement and takes it on board: this passage seems to describe, in the attitude of the Epicurean sage, excessive fits of anger. Conversely, if this use of the phrase is positive,[35] it suggests that the rigour of refutation goes hand in hand with frankness or freedom of speech (*parrhêsia*); *akribeia* seems to apply not only to the technique of refutation itself, but also to the moral qualities of the wise person who practises it.

Significantly and convergently, what is "more exact" is also what is less general and closer to experience. This indirect property may have no critical dimension, as in *Hrdt.* 75:

[T 6]
Furthermore, one must suppose that human nature has received all sorts of lessons from the facts themselves, and has been compelled to learn them, and that reason later refined (ἐπακριβοῦν) what it thus received and made additional discoveries, among some peoples more swiftly, among others more slowly, progress being greater at certain seasons and times, at others less.[36]

Epicurus states, about the formation of language, that nature was instructed by the facts themselves and that reason later "refined" nature's prescriptions. We

---

[33] See Diog. Laert. X 13-4.
[34] Philod. *De ira*, col. 35.33-34. In Armstrong-McOsker 2020: 271: "a severe style of refutation, in both writing and lecturing". Erler has drawn attention to a passage in Philodemus where he demands absolute precision in reading in order to respect the orthodoxy of the Garden. See Erler 2003: 227, referring to Philod, *PHerc.* 1005, col. XII.
[35] In fact, even if it is about an excess of rigour, it is nevertheless positive: we admit that the Epicurean sage is "fallible and, above all, deeply human", in contrast to the Stoic sage, as shown by Nijs 2024: 215 (for this reading of the passage, see 211-215).
[36] Epicur. *Hrdt.* 75.

can assume here that the first signifying sounds were given by nature, under the constraint of facts and circumstances, such as need or necessity, but that these linguistic designations still lacked the semantic precision that human reasoning later brings. In contrast to universal circumstances, common to all human beings, reasoning leads to the use of more precise terms, dictated by the particular circumstances of each people. It is for this reason that linguistic designations, originally natural, have gradually become conventional terms.[37]

By extension, and this time in a clearly polemical manner, *akribeia* is opposed – at least indirectly – to baseless and empty opinions, such as those rejected at the beginning of the *Letter to Pythocles*: the study of nature must be practised, not by referring to empty and arbitrary opinions, but to apparent facts and, if necessary, to multiple explanations, which is precisely the case in the study of meteors.[38] If the opposition with the *kenodoxia* seems to be at stake here – whereas the terms of the semantic family of *akribeia* are not present in this context – it is because Epicurus has just announced, in terms parallel to those of the *Letter to Herodotus*, arguments that will have to be kept in mind and that the addressee of the letter will also have to "go through with acuity" (ὀξέως αὐτὰ περιόδευε).[39] We find here not only the theme of circular knowledge, of the *periodos*, but also an adverb, ὀξέως, which qualifies a sharp, pointed, or precise knowledge. Now Epicurus uses this same adverb at the beginning of the *Letter to Herodotus*, in a context strongly marked by the requirement of *akribeia*.[40] We are called to "be able to make use of apprehensions with acuity" (τὸ ταῖς ἐπιβολαῖς ὀξέως δύνασθαι χρῆσθαι). It therefore seems to me very likely that the presence of the adverb ὀξέως in the particularly polemical context of the beginning of the *Letter to Pythocles* refers to the requirement of *akribeia* and thus gives it a clear critical connotation.

Let us note in passing that the possibility of an allusion to *akribeia* in the context of the *Letter to Pythocles* is all the more likely since Epicurus is careful to specify that accuracy is not incompatible with the method of multiple explanations:[41]

[T 7]
Accordingly, if we discover multiple causes for solstices, risings, settings, eclipses, and the like, as we did in matters of detail, we must not suppose that our treatment of these matters fails to achieve a degree of accuracy (ἀκρίβειαν) sufficient to ensure our undisturbed and happy state.[42]

---

[37] This process is described in the rest of paragraph 75. On the anthropological and in some way 'political' conditions for language development, see Giovacchini 2023.
[38] Epicur. *Pyth.* 86-87.
[39] Epicur. *Pyth.* 85.
[40] Epicur. *Hrdt.* 36.
[41] See in this sense the observations of Bénatouïl 2003: 46; Verde 2013; Verde 2022: 62; Tsouna 2023: 238-239.
[42] Epicur. *Hrdt.* 79-80.

Moreover, it is likely that this only apparent paradox is justified by the two main meanings of the idea of *akribeia*, namely, precision of detail and general rigour. On the one hand, the fact that there is a multiplicity of explanations for the same phenomenon in no way prevents each of them from being sufficiently precise in itself; on the other hand, from the global point of view, the fact of resorting to the method of multiple explanations is probably, in the cases concerned, more rigorous than wanting to give a single explanation.

This negative, critical and polemical dimension of the demand for *akribeia* is also apparent in the following passage:

[T 8]
Furthermore, we must hold that arriving at precise (ἐξακριβῶσαι) knowledge of the cause of the most important things is the work of natural science, and that our happiness depends on this, and upon understanding what the heavenly bodies actually are, and everything related to them that contributes to the accuracy (ἀκρίβειαν) of our knowledge.

Moreover, on such questions we must admit no plurality of causes or alternative explanations, but must simply assume that nothing suggestive of conflict or confusion is compatible with a nature that is immortal and blessed; and the mind is capable of grasping the absolute truth of this.[43]

In this text, to which I will return, the call for precise knowledge of the true "causes" clearly contrasts – as the immediate context makes clear – with unfounded opinions and superstitious fears. It also arguably contrasts with false explanations of celestial phenomena, such as those of Platonically inspired astral theology, to which this section no doubt alludes in several places. In other words, to exercise *akribeia* is not only to be able to identify particular causes with certainty, but also, more generally, to choose resolutely the etiological survey, the rational knowledge of causes, as opposed to empty opinions, superstition, and other irrational beliefs.

4. VARIABILITY AND TRANSVERSALITY

This observation leads me to the fourth feature of Epicurean *akribeia*: its variability and its application, not only to detailed knowledge, but also at a general level, to that of scientific knowledge as a whole. The confidence that *akribeia* can inspire is indeed a transversal quality, which is neither limited to the knowledge of detail – i.e., to the case of *akribeia* κατὰ μέρος – nor to the synthetic and global approach, but which leads and helps to move from one level to another. This is what we shall now see.

---

[43] Epicur. *Hrdt.* 78.

Let us first look at a passage taken from book XXVIII of *Peri phuseôs*:

[T 9]
... the nature [of void is] here, according to the opinion of the first man to think of void in terms of immediacy and time and place. Consequently void too is given this meaning in those expressions which we have written in our work concerning the men who first had knowledge of them. We subsequently resumed that book and made a study of (εἶ]τα δ' ἀναλαβόντες αὖ[θις τ]ὸ [β]ιβλίον ἠκριβ[ώσαμεν])...[44]

It is impossible to confirm that the verbal form ἠκριβ[ώσαμεν] refers exclusively to an examination of detail; Epicurus may just as well mean that he has, in the book that has been "resumed", proceeded to a *complete* examination of his subject.

Furthermore, in the text of *Hrdt.* 36 ([T 4] above), it is not clear that the second occurrence of ἀκρίβωμα is specifically about detail: it is about "total accuracy", without explicit restriction to the parts. In this case, one could just as easily speak of *akribeia* in relation to global knowledge. This point is perhaps difficult to decide from *Hrdt.* 36 alone, but other texts show that the Epicureans do not limit *akribeia* to the details of doctrine.

An other example is to be found in Fragment 63 of Diogenes of Oinoanda:

[T 10]
(...) And this doctrine came to be better articulated as a result of being turned over between the two of us face to face; for our agreements and disagreements with one another, and also our questionings, rendered the inquiry into the object of our search more precise (ἀκρειβεστέραν).[45]

Diogenes speaks of the utmost precision in the *search* (ἔρε[υν]αν) of the object of inquiry. This fragment refers to the reflection on the infinity of worlds (col. II) and the improvements that were made to the argument through contradictory discussions and mutual questioning. There is no indication that it is solely about the *akribeia* κατὰ μέρος; rather, *akribeia* appears in the context of a *dialegesthai* and is justified by a *zêtêsis* regarding a large issue. Similarly, see fr. 119:

[T 11]
(...) And being perfectly (ἀκρειβῶς) aware that it is through knowledge of the matters, concerning both physics and the emotions, which I explained in the places below, that [tranquillity of mind comes about, I know well that I have advertised the remedies that bring salvation].[46]

---

[44] Epicur. *Nat.* XXVIII, *PHerc.* 1479, fr. 1 col. IV; cf. Sedley 1973.
[45] Diog. of Oinoanda, fr. 63 III 2-12, ed. and transl. Smith 1993.
[46] Diog. of Oinoanda, 119 III 4-12, ed. and transl. Smith 1993.

Here, the adverb ἀκρειβῶς refers to the participle ἐπιστάμενος (i.e., to 'knowing'), in a very general sense, since it is about relying on "knowledge of the matters" (τῇ γνώσει τῶν πραγμάτων), both those of physics and those of our affections.

Other texts of Epicurus confirm that the notion applies beyond detail. See for example *Hrdt.* 78, text [T 8] above, which is very clear on this point. Epicurus establishes that the very task of *phusiologia* is "to arrive at the precise knowledge of the reason for the main facts" (τὴν ὑπὲρ τῶν κυριωτάτων αἰτίαν ἐξακριβῶσαι). This time, the *akribeia* refers to the main facts, those that must be mentioned at the level of global knowledge, as the preamble of the *Letter* indicated. Accordingly, the occurrence of ἀκριβεία appearing in the rest of the text clearly concerns global knowledge, since it is not an optional knowledge, but the essential knowledge to which the investigation of celestial phenomena and related facts can eventually contribute.

Similarly, in *Hrdt.* 83, accuracy refers to the way in which we remember the "most crucial statements about nature taken as a whole" (κεφαλαιωδέστατα ὑπὲρ τῆς τῶν ὅλων φύσεως). To appreciate the importance of the notion of *akribeia* in this particular context, it is worth quoting the entire passage:

[T 12]
Accordingly, if this statement is accurately retained and takes effect, a man will, I presume, be far better prepared than others, even if he does not go into all the exact details. For he will himself elucidate many of the points I have worked out in detail in my complete treatise; and this summary, if retained in memory, will be of constant use to him.

Its character is such that those who are already adequately, or even perfectly, acquainted with the details can, by distilling their observations into such fundamental concepts as these, best pursue their diligent study of nature as a whole; those, on the other hand, who have not fully mastered the material, will be able to review, silently and with the speed of thought, the doctrines most likely to ensure peace of mind.

ὥστ' ἂν γένοιτο οὗτος ὁ λόγος δυνατὸς κατασχεθεὶς μετ' ἀκριβείας, οἶμαι, ἐὰν μὴ καὶ πρὸς ἅπαντα βαδίσῃ τις τῶν κατὰ μέρος ἀκριβωμάτων, ἀσύμβλητον αὐτὸν πρὸς τοὺς λοιποὺς ἀνθρώπους ἁδρότητα λήψεσθαι. καὶ γὰρ καὶ καθαρὰ ἀφ' ἑαυτοῦ ποιήσει πολλὰ τῶν κατὰ μέρος ἐξακριβουμένων κατὰ τὴν ὅλην πραγματείαν ἡμῖν, καὶ αὐτὰ ταῦτα ἐν μνήμῃ τιθέμενα συνεχῶς βοηθήσει.

τοιαῦτα γάρ ἐστιν, ὥστε καὶ τοὺς κατὰ μέρος ἤδη ἐξακριβοῦντας ἱκανῶς ἢ καὶ τελείως, εἰς τὰς τοιαύτας ἀναλύοντας ἐπιβολὰς τὰς πλείστας τῶν περιοδειῶν ὑπὲρ τῆς ὅλης φύσεως ποιεῖσθαι· ὅσοι δὲ μὴ παντελῶς αὐτῶν τῶν ἀποτελουμένων εἰσίν, ἐκ τούτων καὶ κατὰ τὸν ἄνευ φθόγγων τρόπον τὴν ἅμα νοήματι περίοδον τῶν κυριωτάτων γαληνισμὸν ποιοῦνται.

Thus, in the rest of the paragraph, when the idea of accuracy is accompanied by the "κατὰ μέρος" clause, it plays the role of a distinctive qualification, a specification, as opposed to the *akribeia* that applies to global knowledge.

One cannot exclude, moreover, that the expression κατὰ μέρος applies to different levels of explanation. After all, even when Epicurus gives details in the *Letter to Herodotus*, we are still in the context of an abridgement; it is, however, well established that the corresponding developments in the *Peri phuseôs* represent an even higher level of understanding. In other words, it can be assumed that, while the *Letter to Herodotus* goes into the "detail" of the explanations with precision, it does not do so in such a developed way as in the *Peri phuseôs*.

All this leads us to believe that we are dealing not with a single standard of excellence in *akribeia* – as, to put it schematically, in Plato – but with different ways of applying the demand for accuracy, from the closest scrutiny to the most general form of *akribeia*, understood in the sense of "rigour". The latter is achieved when scientific discourse conforms to the ultimate requirements and ends of philosophy, namely, happiness. From this point of view, it would make no sense to try to define a single level of absolute rigour or an invariable standard of accuracy. Rather, for Epicurus, it is a matter of formulating a general requirement, which is in fact a relative or variable standard.

I see at least three clues to this idea. First, in *Hrdt*. 80, [T 7] above, Epicurus states, as we have seen, that multiple explanations allow us to reach an explanation sufficient for the "use" (χρείαν) we have to make of them. In so doing, he makes it clear that the degree of exactness of an explanation is relative to the ethical and therapeutic purpose to which all scientific discourse must be subordinated. Here, "similarity" (τὸ ὅμοιον) with nearby phenomena allows us to formulate a discourse about distant phenomena which provides "the same freedom from trouble" as if we had a single particular explanation. Secondly, according to *Hrdt*. 83, [T 12] above, it will be possible to achieve the absence of trouble, even in the absence of the explanation of the detail, which means that the same *overall* rigour can be achieved as if we also possessed the precise knowledge of the details. Finally, the third clue, again in *Hrdt*. 83, is that the precise examination of detail can be either "completely" (τελείως) accomplished or "sufficiently" (ἱκανῶς) accomplished. This alternative suggests that the variations in *akribeia* are also justified by what I have called the 'principle of multiple adressees', the diversity of recipients of the *Letter*.

Does Epicurus agree with Aristotle on this point, when the latter invites us not to demand the same *akribeia* in all circumstances, in accordance with a sort of principle of relative rigour? In a sense, yes – whether or not this is a deliberate rapprochement – especially if we contrast this approach with the Platonic idea of an absolute *akribeia*, and if we consider the necessities of ethical ends, which in both cases require the adaptation of the standard. However, Aristotle's relative rigour should also be understood in relation to the issue about scientific "kinds" *(genê)*, which must remain distinct, even if, in a sense, a common requirement links them.

More generally, it has something to do with the order of questions in a given survey. See for example the following passages:

[T 14]
The minute accuracy of mathematics (τὴν δ' ἀκριβολογίαν τὴν μαθηματικὴν) is not to be demanded in all cases, but only in the case of things which have no matter.[47]

[T 15]
This then is one way of solving the difficulty. Another consists in pointing out that the same things can be spoken of in terms of potentiality and actuality. But this has been done with greater precision (διώρισται δι' ἀκριβείας) elsewhere.[48]

In the first case, it is important not to confuse two types of *akribeia*, because they belong to different scientific kinds. In the second text, Aristotle is not exactly appealing to a distinct scientific kind, but to another research, the results of which have been achieved, and in which it would not be relevant to engage at this precise moment. However, let us focus on the issue of scientific kinds in Aristotle. Scientific kinds, according to him, are incommunicable,[49] except when it is about common principles – like the principle of non-contradiction – and for some particular situations, like subordination of one science to another.[50] As a general rule, kind-crossing is forbidden, because each science has its proper principles; it is impossible to demonstrate geometric properties from principles which belong *properly* to arithmetic. In Epicurus, on the contrary, philosophers move continuously from one point of the scientific circuit to another, but they do not move from one *kind* to another – either because of the subordination of scientific kinds to a higher one, or because of a derogation from the negative principle of kind-crossing prohibition, as in Aristotle. The explanation for this move is quite simple, if not radical, and can be summed up in two points. First, if one admits that there are no scientific *kinds* properly speaking, moving (for instance) from the study of meteors to physiology or to the most general knowledge of nature cannot be considered as a sort of kind-crossing. This shift is simply about adopting a different *way* of considering different facts, explanations, or issues which belong to the *same* science. To put it differently, there is a single science, *phusiologia*, which both rules on the relevance of specialized positive knowledge – such as the study of meteors or physiology – and on the general knowledge of the doctrine as a whole. Secondly, this science is at one with ethics, which determines the ultimate *telos*. It is at the same time theoretical and practical. In several texts from Aristotle, conversely, the need to adapt the

---

[47] Arist., *Metaph.* α 3, 995a15 (transl. B. Jowett, in J. Barnes (ed.), *The Complete Works of Aristotle. The Revised Oxford Translation*).
[48] Arist., *Phys.* I 8, 191b29 (transl. B. Jowett, in J. Barnes (ed.), *The Complete Works of Aristotle. The Revised Oxford Translation*).
[49] Arist. *Post. An.* I 7-9.
[50] Arist. *Post. An.* I 13.

search for precision to the subject under consideration is directly linked to the distinction between theoretical knowledge and practical wisdom.[51]

*
* *

To conclude, the Epicurean conception of *akribeia* as a transversal notion justifies the possibility of moving from the knowledge of details and parts to the perception of the whole, and vice versa, without ever losing the rigour required to exercise properly scientific knowledge. From this point of view, the notion of *akribeia* is a secret operator of the epistemological circularity I mentioned at the beginning, and which marks *phusiologia* for Epicurus.

Is precision an objective property of things, an ontological quality? Is it, rather, a safe disposition of the mind, a sort of epistemic virtue? I think I have shown that the first hypothesis must be rejected. The second is much easier to defend, provided that *akribeia* is also conceived as a certain activity, linked to the achievement of knowledge. This is particularly the case when Epicurus uses the verbal forms (*exakriboun, epakriboun*) associated with the idea of accuracy. We could then say that *akribeia* is this: it is the activity of the subject that attests the validity and firmness of his knowledge at different stages of the epistemological circle, in order to go through these different stages in a continuous manner.

To sum up, the texts we have just considered lead to a double result: (i) there is no epistemological hierarchy between two levels of knowledge but, rather, the same requirement of precision, variously applied to the different points of the epistemological circle; (ii) the notion of *akribeia*, thanks to its transversal function, is an epistemological operator that contributes powerfully to preserving – if not to ensuring – the continuity of the scientific περιοδεία.

This does not mean, of course, that the scientific path is purely circular, in the weak sense. The Epicurean sage does not retrace his steps, but makes real progress towards a better constituted scientific discourse and a more complete knowledge which are more appropriate to the happy life.[52] Most important, this progress cannot be achieved without a circulation between the two types of knowledge and, correlatively, between the different fields of application of *akribeia*.

Lastly, I think that all this confirms that Epicurus, in accordance with his rational empiricism, has real and consistent scientific commitments, whose immediate

---

[51] We might add that this demarcation is partly explained by the distinction, in Aristotle's universe, between the necessity of the supralunar world and the relative contingency of the sublunar world. For Epicurus – and this perspective is a major difference between the two philosophers – physics leaves no room for differences in modality. From this point of view, there is no objective difference between celestial phenomena and the phenomena of our world. All are, in the same way, movements or aggregates of atoms. See Bénatouïl 2003:18-19 and 46-47.
[52] I owe this important remark to Voula Tsouna.

justifications are above all epistemological, and that these commitments are not entirely reducible to the search for happiness and the preservation of *ataraxia*, even though this goal is the ultimate *telos*.

If we keep in mind that, for Plato as for Aristotle, the requirement for *akribeia* is a distinctive criterion of scientific knowledge as such – that is, knowledge of the highest causes – we could even make the following assumption: by describing *phusiologia* as "precise", "rigorous", or "accurate" (*akribes*), Epicurus wanted to emphasize its status as a genuine science. In so doing, he may be preserving a legacy of earlier doctrines, even when he wants to distance himself from them.

REFERENCES

Angeli, A., 1985, "L'esattezza scientifica in Epicuro e Filodemo", *Cronache Ercolanesi* 15: 63-84.

Armstrong, D., – McOsker, M., 2020, *Philodemus, On Anger*, Introduction, Greek Text and Translation, Atlanta: SBL Press.

Bénatouïl, T., 2003, "La méthode épicurienne des explications multiples", *Cahiers Philosophiques de Strasbourg* 15: 15-47.

Delattre, D., 2004, "Un modèle magistral d'écriture didactique: la *Lettre à Hérodote* d'Épicure", in S. Cerasuolo (ed.), *Mathesis e Mneme. Studi in memoria di Marcello Gigante*, Naples: Pubblicazioni del Dipartimento di Filologia Classica 'Francesco Arnaldi' dell'Università degli Studi di Napoli Federico II (25): 149-169.

Dorandi, T. (ed.), 2013, *Diogenes Laertius: Lives of Eminent Philosophers*, Cambridge: Cambridge University Press.

Erler, M., 2003, "*Philologia medicans*. Comment les épicuriens lisaient les textes de leur maître ?", *Cahiers Philosophiques de Strasbourg* 15: 217-253.

Giovacchini, J., 2023, "Thinking or speaking: the paradoxes of the Epicurean theory of language", in F. Masi – P.-M. Morel – F. Verde (eds.), *Epicureanism and Scientific Debates. Antiquity and Late Reception, Volume I: Language, Medicine, Meteorology*, Leuven: Leuven University Press: 15-37.

Hammerstaedt, J., – Smith, M. F. (eds.), 2018, "Diogenes of Oinoanda: The new and unexpected discoveries of 2017 (NF 214-219), with a re-edition of Fr. 70-72", *Epigraphica Anatolica* 51: 43-79.

Kurz, D., 1970, Ἀκρίβεια. *Das Ideal der Exaktheit bei den Griechen bis Aristoteles*, Göppingen: "Göppinger Akademische Beiträge" 8.

Lesher, J. H., 2010, "*Saphêneia* in Aristotle: 'Clarity', 'Precision', and 'Knowledge'", *Apeiron*: 143-156.

Loyd, G. E. R., 1982, "Observational Error in Later Greek Science", in J. Barnes – J. Brunschwig – M. Burnyeat – M. Schofield (eds.), *Science and Speculation. Studies in Hellenistic Theory and Practice*, Cambridge: Cambridge University Press / Paris: Éditions de la Maison des Sciences de l'Homme: 128-164.

Masi, F., 2023, "Language theory, scientific terminology, and linguistic controversies in Epicurus' *On Nature*", in F. Masi – P.-M. Morel – F. Verde (eds.), *Epicureanism and Scientific Debates. Antiquity and Late Reception, Volume I: Language, Medicine, Meteorology*, Leuven: Leuven University Press: 39-63.

Morel, P.-M., 2003, *Aristote. Une philosophie de l'activité*, Paris: GF-Flammarion.

Morel, P.-M., 2015, "Esperienza e dimostrazione in Epicuro", in D. De Sanctis – E. Spinelli – M. Tulli – F. Verde (eds.), *Questioni Epicuree*, Sankt Augustin: Academia Verlag: 132-147.

Nijs, W., 2024, *The Epicurean Sage in the Ethics of Philodemus*, Leiden-Boston: Brill.

Scott, D., 2015, *Levels of Arguments. A Comparative Study of Plato's* Republic *and Aristotle's* Nicomachean Ethics, Oxford: Oxford University Press.

Sedley, D., 1973, "Epicurus, *On Nature* Book XXVIII", *Cronache Ercolanesi* 3: 5-83.

Smith, M.F., 1993, *Diogenes of Oinoanda. The Epicurean Inscription*, Naples: Bibliopolis.

Tsouna, V., 2023, "The Method of Multiple Explanations Revisited", in F. Masi – P.-M. Morel – F. Verde (eds.), *Epicureanism and Scientific Debates. Antiquity and Late Reception, Volume I: Language, Medicine, Meteorology*, Leuven: Leuven University Press: 221-255.

Verde, F., 2010, *Epicuro. Epistola a Erodoto*, Traduzione e commento, Introduzione di Emidio Spinelli, Rome: Carocci.

Verde, F., 2013, "Cause epicuree", *Antiquorum Philosophia* 7: 127-142.

Verde, F. (ed.), 2022, *Epicuro: Epistola a Pitocle*, In collaborazione con M. Tulli – D. De Sanctis – F. G. Masi, Baden-Baden: Akademia Verlag.

EPICURUS ON THE ARTS AND SCIENCES: A REAPPRAISAL

Geert Roskam

1. THE BIRTH OF EPICURUS' PHILOSOPHY

This chapter opens with a crucial moment in the life of the young Epicurus. As a fourteen-year-old boy, Epicurus read Hesiod's verse that Chaos was created first of all (*Theog.* 116). When Epicurus asked his schoolteacher what was Chaos created from, the latter had no answer ready and could only refer him to the philosophers. Epicurus took the obvious consequence: if these are the people who know the truth of things (αὐτοὶ τὴν τῶν ὄντων ἀλήθειαν ἴσασιν), I should go off to them.[1] Thus, a new philosopher was born. This charming anecdote (whether or not historical) contains several interesting elements. To begin with, it shows the sharp, inquiring, and critical mind of the young Epicurus, who eagerly pursued insight and thus wanted to listen to those people who knew the truth. Secondly, it illustrates the ambivalent role of poetry, which sets people thinking but which also contains problematic statements that are self-contradictory (thus Sextus, *M.* 10.18). Finally, it lays bare the limitations of traditional education, since the poor schoolmaster is unable to come up with a satisfactory answer to his pupil's pertinent question. He was not supposed to be an expert in metaphysics or cosmology, to be sure, but his expertise nevertheless proved worthless when it came to serious and important questions.

This anecdote, then, is interesting because it contains precious information about the labour pains of Epicurus' philosophical thinking. More precisely, its birth is traced back here to a confrontation with the limitations of traditional education. Epicurus' notorious rejection of all liberal education thus deserves careful attention. It does not merely throw light on the negative, polemical aspect of his thinking but also reveals his own philosophical ideals and the possible pitfalls he wants to avoid. Epicurean φυσιολογία has indeed been regarded as an anti-*paideia*.[2] A better insight in Epicurus' rejection of traditional παιδεία thus reveals the aims and focus of Epicurean φυσιολογία and philosophy in general (sections 2 and 3) as well as their limits and problems (section 4).

---

[1] The anecdote is told in Sextus Empiricus, *M.* 10.18-19. Its source was probably the first book of Apollodorus' *Life of Epicurus* (Diog. Laert. X 2).

[2] According to Parisi 2017: 44.

2. WHY DID EPICURUS REJECT THE TRADITIONAL ARTS AND SCIENCES?

Epicurus' rejection of traditional παιδεία is often mentioned in ancient sources.[3] In a prized passage at the very outset of his *Adversus mathematicos*, Sextus Empiricus also speculates on Epicurus' motivations:

> The case against the Mathematici (or Professors of Arts and Sciences) has been set forth in a general way, it would seem, both by Epicurus and by the School of Pyrrho, although the standpoints they adopt are different. Epicurus took the ground that the subjects taught are of no help in perfecting wisdom (ὡς τῶν μαθημάτων μηδὲν συνεργούντων πρὸς σοφίας τελείωσιν); and he did this, as some conjecture, [1] because he saw in it a way of covering up his own lack of culture (ἀπαιδευσίας) (for in many matters Epicurus stands convicted of ignorance, and even in ordinary converse his speech was not correct). [2] Another reason may have been his hostility towards Plato and Aristotle and their like who were men of wide learning. [3] It is not unlikely, too, that he was moved by his enmity against Nausiphanes, the disciple of Pyrrho, who kept his hold on many of the young men and devoted himself earnestly to the Arts and Sciences, especially Rhetoric. Epicurus, then, though he had been one of this man's disciples, did his best to deny the fact in order that he might be thought to be a self-taught and original philosopher, and tried hard to blot out the reputation of Nausiphanes and became a violent opponent of the Arts and Sciences wherein Nausiphanes prided himself. (...) Such, in fact, – as we may conjecture – were the sort of motives which decided Epicurus to make war on the Arts and Sciences.[4]

In this famous passage, Sextus brings forward three possible reasons that may explain Epicurus' criticism of the arts and sciences. Firstly, it may mask his own lack of education, an argument that often returns in ancient sources. Athenaeus also says that Epicurus was "uninitiated in general education" (ἐγκυκλίου παιδείας ἀμύητος, 588a), and Timon even calls him "the most uneducated man alive" (ἀναγωγότατος ζωόντων, *SH* 825).[5] Secondly, Epicurus' attitude may also reveal his hostility to Plato and Aristotle, who were men of great learning. This adds a further dimension to the first argument: Epicurus' own rudeness is not merely a personal shortcoming but also mars his feelings towards other, well-educated people. Thirdly, Epicurus' rejection of traditional παιδεία should be understood against the background of his animosity towards his former teacher Nausiphanes. Teacher and pupil were on bad terms indeed, and here Sextus connects their quarrel with Epicurus' wish to appear as self-taught.[6] Quite remarkably, the three motivations brought forward

---

[3] Good recent discussions include Clay 2004; Blank 2009; Verde 2013a: 251-266.
[4] Sextus Empiricus, *M.* 1.1-5. All translations, unless otherwise indicated, are taken from the Loeb Classical Library.
[5] Cf. Plutarch, *Non posse* 1095A on the Epicureans' want of learning (ἀνηκοΐα).
[6] On Epicurus' polemics against Nausiphanes, see, e.g., Longo Auricchio – Tepedino Guerra 1980 and Verde 2013a: 253-266. On Epicurus' claim to be autodidact, cf. Diog. Laert. X 8 and X 12; Cicero, *ND* 1.72-73 and 1.92; Freeman 1938: 158-160; Laks 1976: 68-69; Erler 2011.

by Sextus all presuppose that Epicurus' rejection of the arts and sciences stems from his own intellectual and/or moral shortcomings. It is a rationalization of his own lack of culture (1), of feelings of envy (2), or of rivalry and vain ambitions (3). Needless to say, this picture is based on a biased polemical point of view. What Sextus, strikingly enough, completely ignores as a possible motivation are Epicurus' philosophical arguments. He only in passing mentions that Epicurus was convinced that the arts and sciences do not contribute anything at all to the completion of wisdom (μηδὲν συνεργούντων πρὸς σοφίας τελείωσιν). This, no doubt, is a strong and straightforward claim, and it is a far more reliable path to a correct understanding of Epicurus' philosophical view and its motivations.

Epicurus' attitude towards the arts and sciences rests on a thoroughly utilitarian outlook: all the erudition provided in the common school curriculum is utterly worthless as far as wisdom is concerned. We should note how radical the phrase μηδὲν συνεργούντων actually is. Epicurus does not merely deny that the arts and sciences by themselves lead to wisdom but even that they contribute anything at all to the completion of wisdom. This disavowal shows Epicurus' sober-mindedness vis-à-vis the exaggerated claims of different specialists who unduly overemphasized the importance of their disciplines. In his view, geometrical demonstrations, for instance, are entirely useless. Euclid's theorem that in any triangle, two sides taken together are greater than the remaining side is evident even to an ass; it needs no proof (Proclus, *In Eucl.* 322.1-14), and, we may add, it certainly does not make you a better man.

Such a down-to-earth view should be seen against the background of Epicurus' philosophy of desires and pleasures. All intellectual pleasures, for Epicurus, supervene on prior experiences of the body,[7] and all our natural and necessary desires are limited and can easily be satisfied.[8] If we are neither hungry nor thirsty nor cold, we can contend with Zeus in happiness (*SV* 33; cf. also the passages collected in fr. 602 Us.). If that is true, it is difficult to see indeed why we should still take the trouble to become familiar with all the specialized knowledge provided by general education. This position is the core of Epicurus' view, and it is consistent and based on good arguments. At the same time, it yields a normative criterion for the role of φυσιολογία in Epicurean philosophy. Such φυσιολογία only makes sense if and to the extent that it contributes to the completion of wisdom.[9] Finally, it is important to note that Epicurus' utilitarian argument focuses on wisdom. What it does not

---

[7] See, e.g., *KD* XVIII; Athenaeus, 546f (= fr. 409 Us., with Gargiulo 1982); Clement of Alexandria, *Strom.* 2.21.130-131 (= fr. 451 Us.); Plutarch, *Non posse* 1088E; Cicero, *fin.* 2.98.

[8] *KD* XV and XXI; *SV* 68; *Men.* 130; Porphyry, *Ad Marc.* 30 = fr. 200 Us.; Stobaeus, 3.17.22 = fr. 469 Us.

[9] *Hdt.* 37; *Pyth.* 85 and 116; *RS* 11 and 12. See also Porph., *Ad Marc.* 31 = fr. 221 Us. on the λόγος of the philosopher.

discuss is the relevance of the arts for pleasure. The importance of this focus and the problems it may entail will become clear in due course (see section 4).

Epicurus' rejection of the arts, however, was not merely motivated by utilitarian concerns. It also had to do with truth claims. This concern already appears from the anecdote with which we began: the young Epicurus was looking for insight and eager to join those who know the truth of things. Apparently, the specialists of the different arts and sciences lacked such knowledge. The many erroneous statements of the poets had already been criticized by the Presocratics (see, e.g., Xenophanes fr. 11 B 11 D.-K.; Heraclitus fr. 12 A 22 and 12 B 42 D.-K.) and had been attacked at length by Plato. Other domains of knowledge were no less problematic. The principles of geometry, for instance, were rejected by Epicurus (Proclus, *In Eucl.* 199.10-12).[10] In *Epist. ad Pyth.* 86-87, Epicurus stipulates that φυσιολογία should not rest on empty postulates and laws, but on the phenomena (ὡς τὰ φαινόμενα ἐκκαλεῖται; cf. also 96). This basis shatters the vain pretensions of the specialists who claim to offer the definitive explanation of heavenly phenomena. Reality indeed refutes such unjustified claims. The appeal to look at the facts is a recurrent motif in the *Epist. ad Pyth.* (86, 87, 93, 96) and proves relevant for other domains, too. Philodemus argues his view of music with a reference to concrete life (*De mus.* 4, fr. 61.7-8: τοῖς λεγομένοις ὁ βίος μαρτυρεῖ) and his view of rhetoric by pointing to the evidence of history (*Rhet.* II, 209, col. 6.28-30 S.). Here too, the Epicurean position stands out in its sober-minded realism.

Furthermore, in Epicurus' view, traditional education aims at wrong ideals. It is a direct preparation of a political career and as such is obviously at odds with the Epicurean ideal of an unnoticed life.[11] In this respect, Sextus Empiricus probably has it right that Epicurus' rejection of the arts and sciences also entails polemics against Plato, Aristotle, and Nausiphanes. The latter indeed regarded φυσιολογία as an ideal foundation for a political career.[12] For Epicurus, on the other hand, traditional education is the *via regia* to unhappiness. It is not a useful preparation to later life, and certainly not to philosophy, but rather forces us into the straitjacket of useless erudition. Like politics, general education is a prison from which we should free ourselves (*SV* 58). Demetrius Laco likewise refers to the adamant chains of traditional education,[13] and Epicurus refers to the slavish artifices (ἀνδραποδώδεις τεχνιτείας) of the astronomers (*Pyth.* 93). It is clear, then, that such studies are no liberal studies, no ἐλευθέριος παιδεία at all. In opposition, Epicurean φυσιολογία

---

[10] Zeno of Sidon admitted the principles but questioned the propositions that followed from them (Proclus, *In Eucl.* 199.12-200.1). For the Epicurean criticism of geometry, see, e.g., White 1989; Bénatouïl 2010; Verde 2013a: 249-308.

[11] See Roskam 2007a and 2007b: 17-41 for further details.

[12] Nausiphanes' view was attacked by Metrodorus; see Roskam 2007a: 71-72; Verde 2013a: 259-266.

[13] *PHerc.* 831, col. 12.2-3, with Parisi 2017: 46-47.

does not create self-conceited persons who display their empty knowledge (cf. *SV* 45) but really frees us from our fears.[14]

Finally, the obvious implication of Epicurus' position is that wisdom need no longer be the privilege of the well-educated upper class. Epicurus underlines that everybody, young and old, should philosophize (*Epist. ad Men.* 122), and the Garden was open to women[15] and slaves. In short, even those who had not passed through the elitist curriculum of traditional παιδεία were welcome in Epicurus' philosophical community. This acceptance raises the question as to whether we discover another motivation for Epicurus' rejection of traditional education here. Did Epicurus want to "break down the social barriers maintained in large part by the ability to parade one's cultural credentials"?[16] This question, I think, calls for a nuanced answer. On the one hand, Epicurus never intended to convince the great multitude (*SV* 29; fr. 187 Us.), and even if he addressed everybody,[17] he addressed everyone as an individual (Seneca, *epist.* 7.11-12 = fr. 208 Us.: *haec ego non multis, sed tibi*). On the other hand, Epicurus had an eye for the needs of less gifted students (*Epist. ad Hdt.* 35 and 83). No ancient source, however, suggests that Epicurus had in mind a radical revolution in the widespread educational system. His ambitions clearly lay elsewhere and focused on the interests of his own community rather than on the well-being of the polis.[18] His criticism of the arts and sciences obviously had implications for the social context and presuppositions of traditional παιδεία, but it should be seen as a tangential aspect of his thinking rather than as part of a militant project of educational reform.

3. HOW RADICAL WAS EPICURUS' REJECTION OF THE TRADITIONAL ARTS AND SCIENCES?

3.1. A massive attack…

The above discussion not only lays bare the motivations behind Epicurus' rejection of traditional παιδεία but also shows how massive this rejection actually was. All these arts and sciences contributed nothing at all to the completion of wisdom. This radical judgement gains further confirmation from several other testimonia and fragments.

---

[14] Thus, Epicurus developed an alternative παιδεία, in line with his philosophical insights; see on this esp. Asmis 2001.
[15] On the presence of women in the Garden, see Gordon 2004 and 2012; Di Fabio 2017.
[16] According to Sider 1995: 39.
[17] Plutarch, *Adv. Colot.* 1126F (πρὸς πάντας ἐγράφετο καὶ πάσας); *De lat. viv.* 1129A (πᾶσι καὶ πάσαις); Seneca, *epist.* 14.18 (*omnibus dixit*). Cf. also the position of Diogenes of Oinoanda, fr. 3.I.11-13; 32.II.9-III.1; 29.III + NF 207.I.13 – NF 207.III.13, with Roskam 2015.
[18] Cf. Roskam 2007b: 40.

According to Heraclitus the grammarian, Epicurus purified himself indiscriminately from all poetry (ἅπασαν ὁμοῦ ποιητικὴν ... ἀφοσιούμενος; *Hom. All.* 4). The emphatic combination of ἅπασαν and ὁμοῦ again suggests a complete rejection, which is further underscored by the strong term ἀφοσιούμενος: Epicurus purified himself from poetry as from pollution, and such pollution, of course, should be cleansed entirely, not partly. Heraclitus, though, is a later, non-Epicurean source, and this posteriority may have influenced his presentation of Epicurus' view. Yet there are also fragments from Epicurus and Metrodorus that point in the same direction.

Metrodorus tells us not to be dismayed when we do not even know on which side Hector fought or if we cannot quote the first line of Homer's *Iliad* (Plutarch, *Non posse* 1094E = fr. 24 K.). We may presume that many ordinary Greeks had at least heard of Hector, but even the most uncultivated fool need not worry. Metrodorus points to the radical consequences of Epicurus' position, with the frankness for which he was known (cf. Philodemus, *De lib. dic.* fr. 15.6-10 and col. 5b.1-6). Once again, the conclusion is clear: we are indeed dealing with a radical and complete rejection of traditional παιδεία.

In his *Letter to Apelles*, Epicurus congratulated his addressee for having come to philosophy while being pure from all education (καθαρὸς πάσης παιδείας) (Athenaeus, 588ab = fr. 117 Us.). It is not immediately clear how this statement should be understood. Is Epicurus merely congratulating Apelles because he (for whatever reason) did not have to take the trouble to master the different domains of knowledge? Or is his point rather that Apelles, in spite of his familiarity with this knowledge, has not become corrupted and has remained pure (καθαρός)? In any case, Epicurus' statement should be traced back to the context of a one-to-one communication. Epicurus presumably takes into account Apelles' past history and (re)interprets it in a positive sense. It cannot be excluded that the letter forms part of a psychotherapeutic correspondence in which Epicurus is confirming and encouraging Apelles. Yet even in that case, the quotation appears to confirm the picture above that Epicurus radically rejected every (πάσης) traditional education.

Finally, Epicurus advised Pythocles to hoist all sail and flee from all παιδεία (Diogenes Laertius, X 6 = fr. 163 Us.). This text is a famous passage that is often quoted in ancient authors,[19] and this observation already provides ground for caution. It is remarkable indeed that Epicurus' rejection of the arts and sciences is time and again illustrated with this same quotation, also in erudite authors. Should we conclude that there were no other relevant passages in Epicurus' works? Neither the Κύριαι δόξαι nor the extant *Letters* contain statements about this issue. Is Epicurus' notorious advice to Pythocles more than an unparalleled passage isolated from its

---

[19] See, apart from Diogenes Laertius, also Plutarch, *De aud. poet.* 15D; *Quaest. conv.* 662CD; *Non posse* 1094D; Quintilian, 12.2.24. On Virgil, *Catalept.* 5, see Clay 2004.

original context? It is difficult to say, of course, but in view of the above-mentioned fragments, it is not unreasonable to presume that the popularity of this passage (both in ancient sources and in modern scholarly research) especially rests on the fact that it is a particularly telling illustration of Epicurus' general position. Unlike the fragment from the *Letter to Apelles*, this one contains no evaluation of the addressee's past history but the downright advice to flee education, even under full sail. We again cannot but conclude that Epicurus' rejection of the arts and sciences was total.

3.2. ... with some qualifications
a) And yet, there was probably room for some nuance. An interesting text in this respect is the end of Cicero's *De finibus* 1. In it, Torquatus defends Epicurus against the reproach of being uneducated (1.71-72):

> You are pleased to think him uneducated (*parum ... eruditus*). The reason is that he refused to consider any education worth the name that did not help to school us in happiness (*nullam eruditionem esse duxit nisi quae beatae vitae disciplinam iuvaret*). Was he to spend his time, as you encourage Triarius and me to do, in perusing poets, who give us nothing solid and useful (*nulla solida ... utilitas*), but merely childish amusement (*puerilis ... delectatio*)? Was he to occupy himself like Plato with music and geometry, arithmetic and astronomy, which starting from false premises cannot be true, and which moreover if they were true would contribute nothing to make our lives pleasanter (*nihil afferent quo iucundius ... viveremus*) and therefore better? Was he, I say, to study arts like these, and neglect the master art, so difficult and correspondingly so fruitful (*tamque operosam et perinde fructuosam*), the art of living? No! Epicurus was not uneducated: the real philistines are those who ask us to go on studying till old age the subjects that we ought to be ashamed not to have learnt in boyhood.

Torquatus' presentation of Epicurus' view in this passage bears close similarity to that of Sextus Empiricus discussed in section 2. The radical claim of μηδὲν συνεργούντων in Sextus is paralleled by Torquatus' *nullam ... iuvaret*, and the focus on the completion of wisdom (σοφίας τελείωσιν) in Sextus is echoed by Torquatus' focus on the *disciplina beatae vitae*. Thus we also encounter basically the same utilitarian point of view: Torquatus' criterion is *solida utilitas*. Moreover, this utilitarian view is also coupled here with a concern for the truth. Torquatus indeed emphasizes that the different arts and sciences start from false premises and thus cannot be true. Even the polemical attack against Plato returns in both Sextus and Cicero. Torquatus, however, does not consider this polemic as a rationalization of Epicurus' hidden envy but as part and parcel of a philosophical argument. Finally, he concludes that it is not Epicurus who should be blamed, but rather those who never go beyond the elementary stage of general education. This answer is an example *sui generis* of what Plutarch calls an ἀντεπιστρέφουσα ἀπάντησις (*Praec. ger. reip.* 810E): a retort that throws back a speaker's own words upon himself. Such retorts, as Plutarch explains, have a powerful rhetorical effect and that helps to explain why Cicero placed this passage at the very end of book 1. Moreover, Torquatus' argument is philosophically interesting as well. He seems to suggest indeed that Epicurus' rejection is not so radical and that such general studies are acceptable in one's youth.[20] We only should leave them behind at the threshold of adulthood.

The question of course remains whether Torquatus' argument accurately represents that of Epicurus or whether it rather reflects the point of view of an erudite Epicurean like Philodemus. The latter likewise refutes in detail the traditional attack on the Epicureans' supposed lack of erudition (*De mus.* 4, 140.14-144.6), and he even argues that philosophical authors need a thorough Greek education and a familiarity with the arts and sciences (Πρὸς τοὺς – col. 16.1-6). Such a view, however, may well result from a later evolution in the Epicurean school, when Epicurus' radical and provocative statements were somewhat mitigated.[21] If true, then Torquatus is an unreliable guide in this matter.

Even apart from that, Torquatus' position poses three other problems which I merely mention here, but the relevance of which will become clear in due course. (1) His opposition of *utilitas* and *delectatio* seems odd from an Epicurean point of view. The addition of the adjective *puerilis* helps a lot in making the clash palatable,[22] but it also masks a difficult problem. It remains to be seen indeed how *puerilis* this kind of pleasure really is. (2) Torquatus' statement that the arts do not contribute anything at all to one's pleasure (*nihil afferent quo iucundius ... viveremus*) is a rash claim that is made without further argument. (3) His characterization of the art of life as both *operosam* and *fructuosam* is not without problems, either, as it may partly undermine Epicurus' view. We shall come back to these three problems in section 4.

b) Torquatus, however, is not the only one who has defended Epicurus against the reproach of being utterly ignorant. Modern scholars have also tried to nuance the radicalness of Epicurus' rejection of the arts and sciences and have demonstrated that many of them can even be useful from an Epicurean point of view. Epicurus, for instance, castigates the madness of the astronomers (*Epist. ad Pyth.* 113) and regards their study as useless and even harmful (*Epist. ad Hdt.* 79). Yet that position does not imply that he ignores the field altogether. His *Letter to Pythocles*, indeed, is devoted to celestial phenomena. Epicurus does not elaborate a systematic and mathematically based theory but rather focuses on specific problems and provides satisfactory solutions for them.[23] An analogous conclusion may hold true for the

---

[20] Epicurus, after all, did not recommend illiteracy (Sextus Empiricus, *M.* 1.49 = fr. 22 Us.).
[21] Cf. Erler 2020: 105.
[22] Cf. Asmis 1995: 23, who points to a parallel with Plato's *Republic* (608a: παιδικὸν ἔρωτα).
[23] Parisi 2014: 50.

domain of geometry. Again, Epicurus proved critical and rejected the principles of Euclidean geometry, but a few indications suggest that the Epicureans may have explored an alternative geometrical system that could be reconciled with their physical doctrine of *minima*.[24] Epicurus' view of rhetoric was already controversial among later members of his own school, as the fragments from Philodemus' *Rhetoric* show.[25] It is clear that Epicurus had no ambitions as a professional orator or rhetorical teacher, and the Epicurean sage will neither make fine speeches (Diogenes Laertius X 118 = fr. 565 Us.) nor compose panegyric (Diogenes Laertius X 120a = fr. 566 Us.). Again, though, this stance does not mean that Epicurus entirely ignored rhetoric. A careful analysis of his *Letter to Menoeceus* rather shows that he was familiar with rhetorical devices and principles and that he did not hesitate to benefit from them.[26] A similar conclusion can be made regarding poetry. We have seen that Epicurus rejected poetry as a source of useless and erroneous ideas. He regarded it as a deadly allurement of myths (ὀλέθριον μύθων δέλεαρ, Heraclitus, *Hom. All.* 4 = fr. 229 Us.) and as confusion (Plutarch, *Non posse* 1087A = fr. 228 Us.). Nevertheless, Epicurus repeatedly used poetry to support or express his own philosophical doctrines.[27] This usage even led to the charge that he had stolen his views from the poets.[28] This criticism, of course, is uncharitable polemics, yet it cannot be doubted that Epicurus indeed saw no problem to benefit from the poets in the context of his own *philosophia medicans*,[29] and strikingly enough, even his above-mentioned advice to Pythocles to hoist all sail and flee from all education subtly alludes to a passage from Homer (*Od.* 12.39-54 and 158-200).[30] Finally, as far as music is concerned, Epicurus again emphasized that it is useless for reaching wisdom (Sextus Empiricus, *M.* 6.27) but of course he did not plug his followers' ears with wax in order to prevent them from listening to music. The Epicureans knew to enjoy music, as appears from several passages in the extant fourth book of Philodemus' *On Music*.

This short survey displays a general pattern that puts Epicurus' position towards traditional παιδεία in a new light. His critical attitude is coupled with a willingness to recover useful elements from the different arts and sciences and benefit from them. Yet whenever the Epicurean philosopher thus deals with these fields, he does so not as a specialist but as an outsider, on the basis of a reasonably well-informed but non-technical familiarity with them. This quality is confirmed by an interesting passage from Philodemus' *De oeconomia*, where he deals with the art of making

---

[24] See Verde 2013b and 2016 versus Netz 2015.
[25] For Epicurus' view of rhetoric, see, e.g., Blank 2001; Erbì 2011; Chandler 2020.
[26] Heßler 2016.
[27] Clay 1972: 60-62; Erler 2006: 245-246; 2020: 107-108.
[28] Sextus Empiricus, *M.* 1.273; Heraclitus, *Hom. All.* 4 and 79; the charge is refuted in Sextus Empiricus, *M.* 1.283-285.
[29] See esp. Erler 2006.
[30] Clay 2004: 26; Sider 1995: 39. Cf. Plutarch, *De aud. poet.* 15D.

money. He argues that the sage, though not an expert in financial matters, will nevertheless manage his property fairly well and that this feature also holds true in several other domains: although there exist specialists for each field, the non-expert often succeeds in obtaining satisfactory results as well (*De oec.* 17.2-40).[31] We may infer that this reasoning applies to the different domains of traditional παιδεία too.

If this is true, how should we understand Pythocles' flight from education? Is it the flight of the lover who runs away but deliberately slows down, just enough so that the pursuing girl can gain upon him? That is not what Epicurus intended: Pythocles should not slow down but hoist all sail. In that sense, Epicurus' rejection of the arts and sciences has a radical dimension that should not be too easily dismissed. His insight that traditional παιδεία is not useful at all for the completion of wisdom remains valid, and Metrodorus' frankness shows a clear, uncompromising, and straightforward attitude that should not be explained away. Pythocles has no need at all to become a geometer or grammarian in order to reach happiness. In other words, he need not lose his precious time in order to become a conceited and miserable specialist. His flight need not imply, though, that he is not even allowed to benefit from the fruits of this παιδεία; the advantage is only optional, and Apelles can be equally happy if he refuses to do so. Pythocles was especially gifted (Plutarch, *Adv. Colot.* 1124C; cf. Philodemus, *De mort.* col. 12.36-13.1) and seems to have cultivated a certain interest in celestial phenomena.[32] Epicurus' φυσιολογία gave him all he needed, of course, yet he might have derived some additional pleasures from his non-expert knowledge of traditional astronomy (and its shortcomings). That is fine, but if Mys or Mammarion preferred to ignore the traditional arts altogether, they could live just as well as gods among men.

4. CHALLENGING EPICURUS' POSITION

We may presume that Mammarion welcomed this message with open arms and pressed it to her bosom, but should we do the same? Epicurus' view is consistent and well argued, no doubt, and shows sensible and sober-minded realism, but it also raises several questions that will be dealt with in the remainder of this chapter.

As our point of departure, we may turn to Plutarch's criticism of Epicurus' position in his *Non posse suaviter vivi secundum Epicurum*. In this dialogue, Plutarch develops a clever and original polemical argument. Rather than repeating the traditional attack that the Epicureans do not lead an honourable life (καλῶς ζῆν), he

---

[31] Cf. Blank 2009: 219. Furthermore, Philodemus actually thinks that being an expert in *oikonomia* will *wreck* your happiness, because the expert money-maker will harbour destructive attitudes towards money; cf. O'Keefe 2016. On Epicurus' view of art and the arts, see esp. Tsouna 2021.

[32] This is suggested by the extant *Letter to Pythocles* (84). On the problem of the letter's authenticity, see the recent discussion of Podolak 2010.

prefers to start from the Epicurean doctrines in order to show that these do not lead to a pleasurable life. The Epicureans, in other words, cannot reach their own τέλος when they follow their own principles.[33] Plutarch first draws attention to several problems caused by Epicurus' idiosyncratic understanding of pleasure (*Non posse* 1087D-1092D). Epicurus is wrong to characterize pleasure as mere absence of pain, and by focusing on corporeal pleasures, he builds his ethics on a shaky basis, for it is impossible to be sure that our flesh will continuously retain its stable and painless condition.[34] Then, Plutarch underlines that intellectual pleasures far surpass those of the body. This section (1092D-1096E) is of particular interest for our purposes, as Plutarch explicitly connects his argument with Epicurus' rejection of traditional education and actually quotes both Epicurus' famous advice to Pythocles and the *Letter to Apelles* (1094D), as well as Metrodorus' radical statement regarding Hector and the first verse of Homer's *Iliad* (1094E).

4.1. Geometry and mathematics

Plutarch's general claim in this section, as said, is that the intellectual pleasures of the soul far surpass those of the body. This contention, indeed, is evident from different domains. In the field of astronomy and geometry, for instance, men like Euclid, Philip of Opus, and Archimedes derived many exquisite pleasures from their discoveries, pleasures which cannot be compared to the gastronomical pleasures of the Epicureans (1093E-1094A). No one, Plutarch argues, has ever sacrificed an ox for having won the woman he loved; no one has ever prayed to die on the spot if he could eat some royal meat or cakes. Eudoxus, though, prayed to be consumed in flames if he could stand next to the sun, and Pythagoras sacrificed an ox after having discovered his theorem (1094AB). As to Archimedes (1094C),

> at the bath, as the story goes, when he discovered from the overflow how to measure the crown, as if possessed or inspired, he leapt out shouting 'I have it' and went off saying this over and over. But of no glutton have we ever heard that he shouted with similar rapture 'I ate it' and of no gallant that he shouted 'I kissed her,' though sensualists unnumbered have existed in the past and are with us now.

This passage is not merely attractive, entertaining, and well written, but it is also a clever philosophical argument. We have seen that Epicurus rejects traditional παιδεία because he considers it to be useless for the completion of wisdom. We should not master Euclid's theorems in order to be happy. That point is taken indeed. What if we now introduce the criterion of pleasure into our discussion, however? This move is valid, for Epicurus himself, after all, underlined that all our decisions

---

[33] I deal with the programmatic introduction of this work in Roskam 2017.
[34] See the short discussion in Adam 1974; much useful material can also be found in Zacher 1982 and Albini 1993.

should be assessed according to the standard of our own pleasure (*RS* 25; Diogenes Laertius X 34). We have seen that Torquatus opposed usefulness to pleasure in his defence of Epicurus. In light of Plutarch's argument, this is no longer self-evident. Should we say that Epicurus has made the wrong calculus?

Of course Epicurus is not without reply. He could argue that the study of astronomy and geometry requires many efforts and that we can always, if we really desire so, derive some intellectual pleasures from Archimedes' discoveries as non-specialists (or, of course, refute Euclid's discoveries, since they rest on erroneous principles). Moreover, he could stress, like Torquatus, that we should give far more attention to the art of life. These serious, weighty arguments are probably convincing for Mammarion. Are they also convincing for Euclid and Archimedes? We should not accept Plutarch's polemical argument too readily, but we should not dismiss it all too easily either. We are all familiar with the intense intellectual pleasures that scholarly discoveries can yield. Is it naïve to suppose that some people would argue that these indeed contribute to their happiness?

Moreover, Plutarch also introduces the criterion of time. Corporeal pleasures decrease when growing older. An old man, so he argues, derives more pleasures from history, poetry, music, and geometry than from touching a fair young boy. Old impotent Epicureans who still pursue the pleasures of their belly are miserable indeed (1094E-1095B). This argument is worthy of serious consideration, too: apparently, a careful calculus shows that general knowledge yields more pleasure in the long run. Epicurus, of course, could easily dispute this point and rather regard Plutarch's argument as a typical example of a bad calculus. It is unwise to delay our pleasure, since we have no control over what tomorrow will bring (SV 14). We cannot be certain of ever reaching old age, so why dissipate precious time and waste so much energy on the study of useless erudition? Moreover, Plutarch's argument reflects a typically Platonic outlook,[35] one that regards the desires of the flesh as leaden weights (1096C) and the Epicureans as swineherds of the soul (1096D). Yet Plutarch does raise pertinent questions. What may be convincing for Pythocles and Mammarion need not be convincing for Euclid and Archimedes. And if that is true, Epicurus' overall rejection of the arts and sciences is no longer unproblematic as such.

4.2. Music

Similar questions may be raised regarding the domain of music. In a famous passage, Plutarch points to the absurdity of Epicurus' view (1095CD):

> no one could forget even if he wished their rejection and avoidance of music with the great pleasures and exquisite delight it brings; the absurd discrepancy (ἀτοπίαν) of Epicurus' statements sees to that. On the one hand he says in the *Disputed Questions* that the sage is a lover of spectacles and yields to none in the enjoyment

---

[35] Cf. Warren 2011.

of theatrical recitals and shows; but on the other he allows no place, even over the wine, for questions about music and the enquiries of critics and scholars and actually advises a cultivated monarch to put up with recitals of stratagems and with vulgar buffooneries at his drinking parties sooner than with the discussion of problems in music and poetry.

The details of Epicurus' position have been explained with admirable acumen by Asmis.[36] She has argued that Epicurus' view was not inconsistent at all. He states that the sage enjoys listening to music but rejects listening to the discussions of the specialists of music, since such discussions contribute nothing to wisdom or happiness. Asmis' interpretation has been accepted by many scholars,[37] and she has indeed correctly shown that Epicurus cannot be blamed for inconsistency. It is now time for the next step, that is, for carefully assessing the value of Plutarch's argument. In this passage, Plutarch does not point to the inconsistency (ἐναντίωμα) of Epicurus' position but to its absurdity (ἀτοπία). In order to know what absurdity Plutarch has in mind, we should place this passage back into its broader context. What Plutarch finds absurd is that Epicurus systematically prefers corporeal pleasures to intellectual ones. In this case, Epicurus prefers the corporeal pleasure of listening to music to the intellectual pleasures of reflecting on music. This is Plutarch's point (not a supposed inconsistency; cf. 1095EF), and a correct understanding of his argument throws light on the value and the blind spots of the positions of both Epicurus and Plutarch.

To begin with Epicurus: he regarded music as useless for reaching happiness (Sextus Empiricus, M. 6.27) but saw no problem in enjoying listening to it. In one of his notorious fragments, he even states that he cannot conceive of the good if he eliminates the pleasures of music.[38] This statement is corroborated by Plutarch's testimony in this passage and by a few passages in later Epicureans.[39] Still, theoretical discussions about music during a drinking party are of no avail. Epicurus, in short, prefers the position of the melomaniac to that of the musicologist.

Plutarch challenges this view. For him, the intellectual discussions among musicologists yield more pleasure, and he adds a whole list of such intriguing musical problems (Non posse 1096AB). This position is the direct consequence of his general polemical argument that intellectual pleasures surpass corporeal ones, and it characterizes Plutarch as an erudite intellectualist, but the argument obviously has its limitations. Most people probably derive more pleasure from a nice performance

---

[36] Asmis 1995.
[37] See, e.g., Erler 2006: 245; 2020: 105; Blank 2009: 222; Celkyte 2016: 59-61; McOsker 2020: 351.
[38] Athenaeus, 280ab and 546ef; Diog. Laert. X 6; Cicero, Tusc. 3.41 and other passages collected in fr. 67 Us.
[39] See, e.g., Lucretius 5.1390-1391 on the music of primitive people; Philodemus, De mus. 4, 150.24-25. See on Philodemus' position Verde 2021.

of Beethoven's fifth piano concerto than from a detailed analysis of it by a learned musicologist.

Plutarch's argument, however, gains power if we only recall that the musicologist is not the only specialist. What about the concert pianist? He/She seems to be unduly ignored by both Epicurus and Plutarch. Will (s)he not derive more pleasures from playing Beethoven than the melomaniac from listening to the performance or the musicologist from discussing it? In some sources, this is simply denied. Sextus Empiricus points out that children and even animals also enjoy music without understanding it and that the expert – either the musicologist or the musician – even if (s)he can better assess the artistical performance than ordinary people, gets no greater feeling of pleasure because of that (*M.* 6.31-34). The problem, however, is that the latter is a mere statement, no argument, so it should not be taken for granted.

More helpful is *SV* 27:

> In other activities, the rewards come only when people have become, with great difficulty, complete [masters of the activity]; but in philosophy the pleasure accompanies the knowledge. For the enjoyment does not come after the learning but the learning and the enjoyment are simultaneous.

This point is a more interesting and more nuanced position, which at least acknowledges that rewards may come from music (as from other activities) in the long run and after many efforts, while underlining that the pleasures that come from philosophy are far easier to obtain. Here, the hedonistic calculus is relevant of course. Yet on closer inspection, this argument is less evident than it seems, for philosophy requires efforts, too. We should at this point recall Torquatus' characterization of the art of living as both *operosam* and *fructuosam*. Philosophy is apparently not only a pleasurable business. If the combination of pleasure and efforts also applies to philosophy, it is no longer a priori clear why we should always prefer philosophy to music *in this respect*.[40]

The most detailed argument can be found in Philodemus' fourth book *On music*. Philodemus also points to the hedonistic calculus: it takes great efforts to become a skilled musician (col. 151.15 and 33-34), and there are many recitals where we can enjoy musical performances for free (col. 151.16-22). Philodemus, then, like Epicurus, clearly opts for the position of the melomaniac. Moreover, specialists like our concert pianist act like striplings (μειρακιωδῶς, col. 151.37-38) – an argument that recalls Torquatus' view that the arts and sciences only yield *puerilis delectatio*. Yet Philodemus' argument suffers from the same weakness as those of Epicurus and Plutarch: it reflects the calculus of an outsider. The question remains as to whether

---

[40] The Epicurean, of course, will argue that you need philosophy to gain happiness, insofar as it includes both practical wisdom (understanding what our ultimate good is and how to obtain it) and theoretical wisdom (needed to dispel our fears), while you do not need music.

this argument would convince a concert pianist. Perhaps the latter would agree that practising five hours every day requires, indeed, quite an effort, but (s)he would certainly not consider this as a merely negative duty. On the contrary, (s)he would, at least to a certain extent, even enjoy going through the most difficult passages and regard it, in Euripides' celebrated words, as a πόνον ἡδύν and a κάματον εὐκάματον (*Ba.* 66-67). In the end, it is not unreasonable to presume that the pianist's pleasures surpass those of the audience. In that sense, we should not too easily ignore the pleasures of the pianist (or the composer). Again, we can thus think of cases where technical expertise, in spite of Epicurus' radical denial, indeed contributes to happiness. Would Beethoven be happier without music?

Interesting in this respect is the position of Lucretius. His decision to compose poetry seems diametrically opposed to Epicurus' position. Here is not the place to enter at length into this frequently discussed problem.[41] In this context, we may briefly wonder whether Lucretius adopts the position of the concert pianist. Surprisingly enough, the answer seems to be no. He motivates his decision to write poetry with the famous imagery of honey on the cup (1.935-950). His poetry, then, is a useful means that helps to swallow his philosophical message, clearly reflecting a utilitarian perspective in which poetry is used in the context of a *philosophia medicans*. So far so good, but we keep wondering whether that is all. Should we conclude indeed that Lucretius derived no pleasure at all from the creative process of writing and from all his felicitous phrases? I find this assessment difficult to believe.

4.3. Scholarship

A last domain that we would like to discuss in this chapter is the scholarship of ancient grammarians. They were convinced of the usefulness of their field and argued that poetry provides many starting-points (ἀφορμάς) to wisdom and happiness, which cannot be discerned without the expertise of the grammarians (Sextus Empiricus, *M.* 1.270-276). Epicurus countered their claims by emphasizing that poetry contains a wealth of erroneous ideas as well. Moreover, he insisted that it is the work of the philosophers, not of the grammarians, to distinguish between correct and wrong views (*M.* 1.279-280). This is a pertinent point indeed and many will presumably side with Epicurus against the exaggerated claims of the grammarians.

Yet here, too, possible objections can be raised against Epicurus' radical rejection of the scholarship of the grammarians. Heraclitus, for instance, argues that Epicurus has borrowed his doctrine of pleasure from a few verses in the *Odyssey* (9.6-7 and 11), without realizing that Odysseus says these verses because he wants to adapt his speech to the customs of the Phaeacians (*Hom. All.* 79). Epicurus, in other words, wrongly turns Odysseus' hypocritical words into a principle of the good

---

[41] It is an issue that is obscured by the textual problems in Diog. Laert. X 121b = fr. 568 Us. (ποιήματα τε ἐνεργείᾳ οὐκ ἂν ποιῆσαι); cf., e.g., Sider 1995: 36-37; Arrighetti 1998: 16-17; McOsker 2020: 352-353.

life. Heraclitus' argument can easily be refuted, of course: Epicurus simply did not derive his hedonistic philosophy from Homer and thus did not make this mistake. Yet Heraclitus' attack does reveal a potential problem. As long as the Epicureans stay far away from poetry, they will commit no silly mistakes, but when they try to recover it in their own philosophy – as, indeed, Epicurus himself repeatedly did, and as Philodemus did even more elaborately in his *De bono rege* – they run the risk of misunderstanding it. Non-expert knowledge can always lead to dilettantism. In such contexts, the expertise of the grammarians can indeed be helpful as *ancilla philosophiae*.

Moreover, Epicurus' schoolmaster lacked the erudition to solve his pupil's problem and wisely referred to the philosophers, but it should not be excluded a priori that more learned colleagues would be able to come up with interesting material from the poetic tradition. That impression may be gained, at least, from Plutarch's *Table Talks*, where different grammarians take part in the discussions and repeatedly come up with relevant answers – though usually not the best ones.[42]

Finally, here we may come back to Plutarch's general argument in *Non posse*. Even if discussions about grammatical problems are not directly useful to reach wisdom, they may still yield considerable intellectual pleasures. In the *Table Talks*, the company discusses the intriguing question which of Aphrodite's hands did Diomedes wound (739BD). This conversation is an example of a clever and entertaining question[43] that receives an ingenious answer. For Torquatus, it is no doubt a typical example of *puerilis delectatio*. Granted, it hardly contributes to wisdom, but *puerilis* is no more than a label. For an erudite company like that of Plutarch's friends, such discussions were probably a most agreeable pastime. They yielded pleasures that had little to do with the belly but that no doubt seasoned their lives. The same holds true for all the interesting papers presented at international conferences. Is all this just *puerilis delectatio*?

5. CONCLUSION

Epicurus' philosophy is imbued with a consequently utilitarian perspective. Everything that is not directly useful for the completion of wisdom is rejected, and traditional παιδεία is among the first victims. For it indeed, in Epicurus' eyes, did not contribute to happiness and wisdom, it did not open a reliable path to the truth, and it incarcerates us in erroneous convictions and ideals. The implication is obvious: we should hoist all sail and flee from it, towards the safe haven of philosophy.

---

[42] See esp. Eshleman 2013, who argues that grammarians usually appear as problem symposiasts. This point is generally true, although there are some notable exceptions, like Theon (626E-627F).

[43] Or, in Plutarch's own terms, a 'fluid' question (*Quaest. conv.* 614D) which easily spreads over the company; Vamvouri Ruffy 2012: 67-75.

This view does not imply, of course, that we cannot occasionally benefit from all the fields of traditional education. Indeed, the tree of παιδεία does not bear forbidden fruits. We should not take the trouble to cultivate the tree but can certainly eat from it. Diogenes the Epicurean aptly characterizes education (ἀγωγή) as διαγωγή (Diogenes Laertius X 138). This estimation is an excellent crystallization of Epicurus' view. In a negative sense, διαγωγή denotes the mere passing of time. Education proves useless and our well-educated life simply passes by. In a positive sense, διαγωγή points to amusement, and indeed, non-experts can likewise enjoy the fruits produced by general knowledge.

Epicurus' view of the arts and sciences, then, was nuanced and intelligent. He was a particularly sober-minded thinker who did not lose himself in the siren song of the different arts but had only eye for their real value. Yet his view also had its blind spots, and Plutarch's attack in *Non posse* is helpful to reveal them (although Plutarch's Platonic position has its blind spots, too). Epicurus' calculus regarding purely intellectual pleasures is not self-evident for everyone. Did all experts and artists indeed enjoy merely an empty, *puerilis delectatio* that contributed nothing to their happiness? Euclid, Beethoven, and scholars probably came to a different conclusion, and it is far too easy to reject their view as silly.

Epicurus had a point, no doubt, but Plutarch also raises intelligent and pertinent objections in his *Non posse*, and it is unwise to ignore them. It is with one such challenging question that I would like to conclude this chapter (*Non posse* 1093C):

> Who would take greater pleasure in stilling his hunger or quenching his thirst with Phaeacian good cheer than in following Odysseus' tale of his wanderings? Who would find greater pleasure in going to bed with the most beautiful of women than in sitting up with Xenophon's story of Pantheia, Aristobulus' of Timocleia, or Theopompus' of Thebê?

I leave the answer to the reader.

REFERENCES

Adam, H., 1974, *Plutarchs Schrift* Non posse suaviter vivi secundum Epicurum. *Eine Interpretation*, Amsterdam: Grüner.

Albini, F., 1993, *Plutarco.* Non posse suaviter vivi secundum Epicurum. *Introduzione, Traduzione, Commento*, Genoa: Università di Genova, Facoltà di Lettere e Filosofia.

Arrighetti, G., 1998, "Gli epicurei, la poesia e Lucrezio", *Athenaeum* 86: 13-33.

Asmis, E., 1995, "Epicurean Poetics", in D. Obbink (ed.), *Philodemus and Poetry. Poetic Theory and Practice in Lucretius, Philodemus, and Horace*, New York-Oxford: Oxford University Press: 15-34.

Asmis, E., 2001, "Basic Education in Epicureanism", in Y. L. Too (ed.), *Education in Greek and Roman Antiquity*, Leiden-Boston-Cologne: Brill: 209-239.

Bénatouïl, T., 2010, "Les critiques épicuriennes de la géométrie", in P. E. Bour – M. Rebuschi – L. Rollet (eds.), *Construction. Festschrift for Gerhard Heinzmann*, London: College Publications: 151-162.

Blank, D., 2001, "La philologie comme arme philosophique: la connaissance technique de la rhétorique dans l'épicurisme", in C. Auvray-Assayas – D. Delattre (eds.), *Cicéron et Philodème. La polémique en philosophie*, Paris: ENS, Editions Rue d'Ulm: 241-257.

Blank, D., 2009, "'Philosophia' and 'technē': Epicureans on the Arts", in J. Warren (ed.), *The Cambridge Companion to Epicureanism*, Cambridge: Cambridge University Press: 216-233.

Celkyte, A., 2016, "Epicurus and Aesthetic Disinterestedness", *Mare Nostrum* 7: 56-74.

Chandler, C., 2020, "Rhetoric", in P. Mitsis (ed.), *The Oxford Handbook of Epicurus and Epicureanism*, Oxford: Oxford University Press: 333-346.

Clay, D., 1972, "Epicurus' Κυρία δόξα XVII", *GRBS* 13: 59-66.

Clay, D., 2004, "Vergil's Farewell to Education ('Catalepton' 5) and Epicurus' Letter to Pythocles", in D. Armstrong et al. (eds.), *Vergil, Philodemus, and the Augustans*, Austin: University of Texas Press: 25-36.

Di Fabio, T., 2017, "Donne epicuree: cortigiane, filosofe o entrambe?", *Bollettino della Società Filosofica Italiana* 221/2: 19-36.

Erbì, M., 2011, "La retorica nell'epicureismo: una riflessione", *CErc* 41: 189-205.

Erler, M., 2006, "*Interpretatio medicans*. Zur epikureischen Rückgewinnung der Literatur im philosophischen Kontext", in M. van Ackeren – J. Müller (eds.), *Antike Philosophie verstehen – Understanding Ancient Philosophy*, Darmstadt: Wissenschaftliche Buchgesellschaft: 243-256.

Erler, M., 2011, "Autodidact and Student: On the Relationship of Authority and Autonomy in Epicurus and the Epicurean Tradition", in J. Fish – K. R. Sanders (eds.), *Epicurus and the Epicurean Tradition*, Cambridge: Cambridge University Press: 9-28.

Erler, M., 2020, *Epicurus. An Introduction to His Practical Ethics and Politics*, Basel: Schwabe Verlag.

Eshleman, K., 2013, "'Then our Symposium becomes a Grammar School': Grammarians in Plutarch's *Table Talks*", *SyllClass* 24: 145-171.

Freeman, K., 1938, "Epicurus – A Social Experiment", *G&R* 7: 156-168.

Gargiulo, T., 1982, "Epicuro e 'il piacere del ventre' (fr. 409 Us. = [227] Arr.)", *Elenchos* 3: 153-158.

Gordon, P., 2004, "Remembering the Garden: The Trouble with Women in the School of Epicurus", in J. T. Fitzgerald – D. Obbink – G.S. Holland (eds.), *Philodemus and the New Testament World*, Leiden-Boston: Brill: 221-243.

Gordon, P., 2012, *The Invention and Gendering of Epicurus*, Ann Arbor: University of Michigan Press.

Heßler, J. E., 2016, "τὸν σοφὸν οὐ δοκεῖ ῥητορεύσειν καλῶς? Rhetorik in Texten Epikurs", in I. Männlein-Robert et al. (eds.), *Philosophus Orator. Rhetorische Strategien und Strukturen in Philosophischer Literatur. Michael Erler zum 60. Geburtstag*, Basel: Schwabe Verlag: 161-179.

Laks, A., 1976, "Édition critique et commentée de la 'Vie d'Épicure' dans Diogène Laërce (X, 1-34)", in J. Bollack – A. Laks (eds.), *Études sur l'Épicurisme antique*, Lille: Publications de l'Université de Lille III: 1-118.

Longo Auricchio, F., – Tepedino Guerra, A., 1980, "Per un riesame della polemica epicurea contro Nausifane", *SicGymn* NS 33: 467-477.

McOsker, M., 2020, "Poetics", in P. Mitsis (ed.), *The Oxford Handbook of Epicurus and Epicureanism*, Oxford: Oxford University Press: 347-376.

Netz, R., 2015, "Were there Epicurean Mathematicians?", *OSAPh* 49: 283-319.

O'Keefe, T., 2016, "The Epicureans on Happiness, Wealth, and the Deviant Craft of Property Management", in J. A. Baker – M. D. White (eds.), *Economics and the Virtues. Building a New Moral Foundation*, Oxford: Oxford University Press: 37-52.

Parisi, A., 2014, "Le forme del sapere astronomico nell'epicureismo: un saggio di lettura di 'PHerc.' 831, IX-XI Körte", *CErc* 44: 49-64.

Parisi, A., 2017, "Laus physiologiae, παιδεία e parenesi: Una proposta di lettura (*PHerc.* 831, VII-XV Körte)", *CErc* 47: 41-53.

Podolak, P., 2010, "Questioni Pitoclee", *WJA* 34: 39-80.

Roskam, G., 2007a, *Live Unnoticed (Λάθε βιώσας). On the Vicissitudes of an Epicurean Doctrine*, Leiden-Boston: Brill.

Roskam, G., 2007b, *A Commentary on Plutarch's* De latenter vivendo, Leuven: Leuven University Press.

Roskam, G., 2015, "Epicurean Philosophy in Open Access. The Intended Reader and the Authorial Approach of Diogenes of Oenoanda", *EA* 48: 151-174.

Roskam, G., 2017, "Considering Tit for Tat: The Programmatic Introduction to *Non posse suaviter vivi secundum Epicurum*", in M. Sanz Morales *et al.* (eds.), *La (inter)textualidad en Plutarco*, Cáceres-Coimbra: Universidad de Extremadura: 345-356.

Sider, D., 1995, "Epicurean Poetics: Response and Dialogue", in D. Obbink (ed.), *Philodemus and Poetry. Poetic Theory and Practice in Lucretius, Philodemus, and Horace*, New York-Oxford: Oxford University Press: 35-41.

Tsouna, V., 2021, "The Epicureans on *Technê* and the *Technai*", in T. K. Johansen (ed.), *Productive Knowledge in Ancient Philosophy. The Concept of Technê*, Cambridge: Cambridge University Press: 191-225.

Vamvouri Ruffy, M., 2012, *Les vertus thérapeutiques du banquet. Médecine et idéologie dans les Propos de Table de Plutarque*, Paris: Les Belles Lettres.

Verde, F., 2013a, *'Elachista'. La dottrina dei minimi nell'epicureismo*, Leuven: Leuven University Press.

Verde, F., 2013b, "Epicurean Attitude Towards Geometry. The Sceptical Account", in S. Marchand – F. Verde (eds.), *Épicurisme et Scepticisme*, Rome: Sapienza Università Editrice: 131-150.

Verde, F., 2016, "Ancora sulla matematica epicurea", *CErc* 46: 21-37.

Verde, F., 2021, "Il piacere della musica nell'Epicureismo", *La cultura* 59: 45-71.

Warren, J., 2011, "Pleasure, Plutarch's *Non posse* and Plato's *Republic*", *CQ* 61: 278-293.

White, M. J., 1989, "What to Say to a Geometer", *GRBS* 30: 297-311.

Zacher, K.-D., 1982, *Plutarchs Kritik an der Lustlehre Epikurs. Ein Kommentar zu* Non posse suaviter vivi secundum Epicurum: *Kap. 1-8*, Königstein: Anton Hain.

Τὸ προσμένον: EPICURUS' *PROPOSITIONAL* THEORY OF TRUTH[1]

Francesco Verde

1. FOREWORD

There seem to be few doubts that in recent years research on Epicurean epistemology has made significant progress. It has contributed to clarifying many notions of canonic, as well as delving into its possible doctrinal background in classical philosophy (Plato and Aristotle), which Epicurus likely knew. In other words, not only for Stoicism but also for Epicureanism, the idea that Hellenistic philosophy was not a rupture with the great philosophical systems of the fifth and fourth centuries BC is gaining ground: although actual evidence is scarce, it is highly probable that Epicurus engaged in a simultaneously critical and fruitful dialogue with Plato and Aristotle. This point does not at all diminish the originality of Hellenistic philosophies; rather, it suggests that to understand the innovative features of these philosophies, one cannot avoid comparing them with earlier systems of thought. Among these concepts, in my opinion, one of the most original in Epicurean epistemology is τὸ προσμένον; despite scarce direct textual references to it, it seems to me that this notion has not been adequately explored, although it is one of the most significant in Epicurean canonic.

My main reason for proposing this topic lies in a stimulating article published in the prestigious journal *Mnemosyne* entitled *Epicurus' Non-Propositional Theory of Truth* by Andree Hahmann and Jan Maximilian Robitzsch.[2] This essay is not entirely devoted to the analysis of τὸ προσμένον, an expression generally translated with "that which awaits confirmation", an essentially correct but *partial* translation, as we shall see. Τὸ προσμένον is studied within a broader argumentative context aimed at demonstrating that Epicurus theorized a *non*-propositional theory of truth not limited to *aisthesis* alone, which is *alogos* (non-rational). Moreover, as I have already pointed out, this article has also reminded me that the 'device' of τὸ προσμένον is surprisingly one of those aspects of Epicurean epistemology that has been less studied: to my knowledge, there is no study entirely devoted to "what awaits", which is, on the contrary, one of the most important and original notions of Epicurus' canonic.

---

[1] I would like to thank Frederik A. Bakker, Tiziano Dorandi, and Margherita Erbì for their valuable comments and suggestions on an earlier version of this article. As is always said in these cases, the only person responsible for the claims made here is the author. My gratitude also goes to all those who took part in the discussion at the Venice Conference that concluded the rich and fruitful experience of the Spider Project I shared with Francesca G. Masi and Pierre-Marie Morel to whom goes my gratitdine.

[2] Hahmann–Robitzśch 2021.

The aim of this paper is, therefore, twofold: on the one hand, I will try to show that τὸ προσμένον requires a *propositional* theory of truth; on the other hand, I will attempt to investigate the function and role of τὸ προσμένον in Epicurean epistemology by referring above all to the relationship between the acquisition of truth/knowledge and time, which are central (and often neglected) elements in Epicurus' epistemological theory.

2. THE TRUTH OF SENSE–PERCEPTIONS AND *PROLEPSEIS*

In their article, Hahmann and Robitzsch argue that it is possible "to characterize the Epicurean theory of truth as a theory that can be understood by referring to images and visual metaphors".[3] In other words, the self-evident truth of *Canon*'s criteria (sense-perceptions, *prolepseis*, affections) can easily be explained without appealing to the propositional nature of truth.[4] The truth of the criteria is the same as the truth of the images (i.e., the *eidola*), which are continuously detached from *steremnia*, the solid objects (i.e., formed of atoms and void). *Eidola* must be considered as the objects themselves and not as their independent parts.[5] In my opinion, this assumption is correct for the first criterion, sense-perception (*aisthesis*). In his report on Epicurus' canonic (X 31), Diogenes Laertius states that every *aisthesis* is *alogos* and devoid of any memory (μνήμης οὐδεμιᾶς δεκτική); sense-perception is true and self-evident because it presents only itself (Diog. Laert. X 31: "for neither is it induced by itself, nor when induced by something else is it able to add or subtract anything"[6]). Diogenes (X 32) adds, "The real occurrence of sensations also confirms the truth of sense-perceptions" (καὶ τὸ τὰ ἐπαισθήματα[7] δ' ὑφεστάναι πιστοῦται τὴν τῶν αἰσθήσεων ἀλήθειαν).

Thus: when a sense-perception is given, it is always true. The truth of *aisthesis* is in its concrete existence: since each sense-perception 'records' *only* the collision of *eidola* with the sensory organs of the perceiving 'subject', without *eidola* there is no perceptive act. Accordingly: *aisthesis* is true because *eidola* are actually real and existent. Here there is no need to invoke the propositional theory of truth because this notion of truth coincides with the physical/material existence of *eidola* or *simulacra*.

---

[3] Hahmann–Robitzsch 2021: 740.
[4] For a similar approach on the criterion of *pathe* in Epicurus' epistemology, see the recent Robitzsch 2022. For a different view on the same topic, see Verde 2018b.
[5] See Verde 2018a: 100–101.
[6] All translations of Diogenes Laertius' *Lives* are by White 2020.
[7] *Epaisthema* is a term clearly connected to *epaisthesis* (a sort of 'attentive' perception). On the meaning of the latter notion, see Cavalli 2012; some short remarks in Verde 2022: 53–54; and the very recent and close examination offered by Blank 2023: 99ff.

According to the two scholars, the same can be said of the self-evident truth of *prolepseis*: "Preconceptions as such do not have to have a propositional structure, although they might serve as a foundation for judgements [...] Accordingly, preconceptions are forms and imprints, which are not linguistic".[8] Diogenes Laertius (X 33) states that *prolepsis* is "a memory of something that has often appeared outside us. For example, a human is such and such" (μνήμην τοῦ πολλάκις ἔξωθεν φανέντος, οἷον τὸ Τοιοῦτόν ἐστιν ἄνθρωπος·). There is no doubt that every *prolepsis* is a *typos*, a physical (i.e., atomic) mould formed on the *dianoia* (or *mens*) dependent on the confluence of several *eidola* from outside. This material unification is guaranteed by *mneme*, which is a rational capacity/faculty: *aisthesis*, being devoid of memory, is completely incapable of 'storing' information except the pure physical existence of *simulacra*. This feature means that *prolepsis* is a rational criterion: it is necessarily provided with *logos*. It is no coincidence that in Diogenes Laertius the first example of *prolepsis* is ἄνθρωπος: it is a 'concept' identified with a name. The name itself immediately recalls the fundamental features that are exactly those included in the *prolepsis*. From this point of view, *prolepsis* is a *linguistic* entity because it identifies itself with a name.[9] One must ask whether the linguistic truth of *prolepsis* is also propositional. Although the question is controversial, my opinion is that the truth of *prolepsis* is *also* propositional. One of the distinctive elements of being human is that of being bipedal; the character 'bipedal' is included in the *prolepsis* of being 'human'. But: how? In my view, the connection is propositional: 'humans are bipedal'. It is possible to recognize a human being or think of them (without them being present) or to linguistically formulate a proposition because *prolepsis* is structured in propositional terms.

On this we have to read again Diogenes Laertius (X 33):

For example, whether the thing standing far away is a horse or an ox; for we must have some prior cognizance of the shape of a horse or ox in line with a preconception (δεῖ γὰρ κατὰ πρόληψιν ἐγνωκέναι ποτὲ ἵππου καὶ βοὸς μορφήν·). Nor would we have applied any names to something if we had not previously learned its mould in line with a preconception (οὐδ' ἂν ὠνομάσαμεν τι μὴ πρότερον αὐτοῦ κατὰ πρόληψιν τὸν τύπον μαθόντες). (White's translation, slightly modified)

Depending either directly on Epicurus' *Canon* or more likely on a kind of Epicurean philosophy 'handbook', Diogenes links *prolepsis* to *morphe*, the shape that immediately recalls the essential features of an object. This form is the *typos*, the physical mould that allows the attribution of a name: *typos* precedes the name, though only logically and physiologically.[10] Each *typos* is identified with its name: distinguishing clearly between the *typos* and the name can be misleading. It is true

---

[8] Hahmann–Robitzsch 2021: 746.
[9] See Long 1971.
[10] See on this point Németh 2021: 104–105.

that the Laertian text emphasizes the priority (πρότερον) of *typos* over the name, but this emphasis is only to indicate that each name has at its roots a *prolepsis*, i.e., an atomic *typos* that, thanks to the *selective* memory of the external *eidola*,[11] unified the essential information about the *morphe* of the object. If the structure of *typos* were not also linguistic and propositional, it would be difficult to understand the role of memory and the close relationship of *prolepseis* with *onomata*.[12]

3. Τὰ προσμένοντα: WHAT ARE "THE THINGS THAT AWAIT"?

I do not think it is by chance that Diogenes Laertius (or his Epicurean source) deals with *doxa* or *hypolepsis* immediately after discussing *prolepsis*. This order shows how *prolepsis* is essential for the formation of opinion. It is in the context of *doxa* or *hypolepsis* that Diogenes introduces τὸ προσμένον, which also cannot be a coincidence. Before examining the Laertian text in detail, it is worth considering the exegesis of τὸ προσμένον that Hahmann and Robitzsch offer in their article. According to the scholars, "Under this heading [*scil.* the objects that await further confirmation], the Epicureans discuss optical illusions such as that of the square tower that looks round from a distance or the straight stick that submerged in water looks bent [...]."[13] Thus, τὰ προσμένοντα would concern optical illusions that the Epicureans would not explain/solve by appealing to opinions but, if I correctly understand, by consistently composing images together: "[...] the perceiver is not entitled to the opinion that the stick is bent, since the stick is actually straight, as the sense of touch and other observations of a stick (that is, outside of the water) clearly tell her. Note again that propositions are unnecessary to explain this. One might imagine that the way that the Epicureans think of προσμένοντα is in terms of puzzle pieces that have to be appropriately integrated into a consistent picture. [...] In fact, we suggested in this paper that the Epicureans explain all sorts of truths with the help of images and their combination, which of course includes the explanation of optical illusions."[14]

---

[11] See Masi 2014.
[12] See Striker 2020: 46 and especially Tsouna 2016: 170–172. I fully agree with what Tsouna writes: "Presumably, we may 'refer' to our preconceptions either in the weaker sense of entertaining our *prolēpsis* of an object when the latter gets problematised, or in the stronger sense of *deducing* from the proposition entailed by the preconception other truths. In either case, in such contexts the preconceptions must be understood as entailing true and indemonstrable *propositions* which serve as premises in scientific proofs. And, as argued above, they derive their epistemic legitimacy from their origin in sensation, not the mental act of association of the preconception with its corresponding word and the object that that word names" (2016: 172; emphasis my own). Tsouna very rightly underlines the propositional feature of *prolepsis*: in the specific field of the nature of *prolepsis* the difference between what is merely linguistic and what is propositional does not seem very plausible.
[13] Hahmann–Robitzsch 2021: 753.
[14] Hahmann–Robitzsch 2021: 754.

At this point we can examine § 34 of the 'canonic section' of Book 10 of Diogenes' *Lives* devoted to opinion and "what awaits":

τὴν δὲ δόξαν καὶ ὑπόληψιν λέγουσιν, ἀληθῆ τέ φασι καὶ ψευδῆ· ἂν μὲν γὰρ ἐπιμαρτυρῆται ἢ μὴ ἀντιμαρτυρῆται, ἀληθῆ εἶναι· ἐὰν δὲ μὴ ἐπιμαρτυρῆται ἢ ἀντιμαρτυρῆται, ψευδῆ τυγχάνειν. ὅθεν τὸ προσμένον εἰσήχθη· οἷον τὸ προσμεῖναι καὶ ἐγγὺς γενέσθαι τῷ πύργῳ καὶ μαθεῖν ὁποῖος ἐγγὺς φαίνεται.

Beliefs they also call judgments, and they say some are true and some are false: if a belief is attested or not contested, it is true; but if it is contested or not attested, it is false. That is why they introduced deferral; for example, deferring until you get near to the tower and learn how it appears from nearby.

Opinion or, as the Epicureans call it, *hypolepsis* is the domain of truth or falsity understood as correspondence or non-correspondence of the content of *doxa* to reality. Therefore, an opinion can be true or false: opinion when it is true has no different status from truth or *episteme* (as in Plato)[15] but coincides directly with truth. Diogenes Laertius adds the necessary conditions of the truth and falsity of *doxa*: when the content of opinion is confirmed or not rejected by *enargeia* (or perceptual self-evidence: this term is not made explicit but is implied, as we know, from other sources, primarily Sextus Empiricus[16]), it will be true; when it is not confirmed or rejected it will be false.

It is only *after* shortly describing the conditions of truth and falsity of *doxai* that Diogenes speaks of τὸ προσμένον (I only point out that the addition of the article <τὸ> – in my view, with Bailey,[17] necessary – is by Gassendi). It is important to note that the brief section on τὸ προσμένον is opened by ὅθεν (= whence), an adverb that immediately connects what is said after with what is said before. Τὸ προσμένον is introduced in relation to *doxai* and their conditions of truth and falsity (i.e., *epimartyresis* and *antimartyresis*): if this were not so, the use of ὅθεν would make no sense. If τὸ προσμένον is literally "the thing that awaits" one must ask what awaits and what is awaited. Diogenes does not say it explicitly but only implicitly. In my opinion, the answer lies precisely in the adverb ὅθεν that links τὸ προσμένον to the two 'criteria' of the truth or falsity of *doxai*, namely *epimartyresis* and *antimartyresis*. If this hypothesis is plausible, τὸ προσμένον is what awaits confirmation (*epimartyresis*) or refutation (*antimartyresis*).

At this point another question arises: what are τὰ προσμένοντα? Hahmann and Robitzsch have little doubt and answer that τὰ προσμένοντα are basically optical illusions and therefore perceptual objects: "[…] different conflicting perceptions are made consistent with each other by indexing them to the circumstances, in

---

[15] For a first overview on the topic, see Trabattoni 2018: CII–CIX.
[16] Sext. Emp. *M* VII 211–212. See also below, 75–77.
[17] Bailey 1926: 416.

which they were observed. All of these cases can be described without reference to propositions."[18] I do not agree with this exegesis, which does not seem to me to be grounded in the texts, in particular the account of Diogenes Laertius.

If τὸ προσμένον is that which awaits confirmation (*epimartyresis*) or refutation (*antimartyresis*), it is inevitable that it is identified with *doxa* or *hypolepsis*. Indeed, only opinion is subject to confirmation and refutation. To sum up: if τὸ προσμένον is what awaits confirmation or refutation by *enargeia*, and if confirmation and refutation are 'criteria' applicable exclusively to opinions, τὸ προσμένον is necessarily a *doxa* or *hypolepsis* that must be verified to establish its truth or falsity. *Epimartyresis* and *antimartyresis* do not concern objects but *only doxai*.

4. FURTHER EPICUREAN ACCOUNTS OF τὸ προσμένον

In the *Letter to Herodotus*, τὸ προσμένον appears twice. In § 38 we read that it is necessary to start from sense-perceptions, from *epibolai tes dianoias* and *pathe*, in order to make semiotic inferences (σημειωσόμεθα) about both τὸ προσμένον and τὸ ἄδηλον. The latter term refers to *objects* (not to the content of *doxa*)[19] that are non-evident and therefore escape perceptual self-evidence (for example: void). Epicurus makes a very interesting point here: semiotic inference is an epistemological procedure valid both for both non-evident objects and the content of those opinions that are to be verified by *enargeia* and for evident phenomena taken as signs for further inferences. Bear in mind that Epicurus does *not* identify τὸ προσμένον and τὸ ἄδηλον.

The other extremely problematic occurrence is in the tormented § 50 of the letter: it is an addition (<ἐπὶ τοῦ προσμένοντος>) proposed by Schneider[20] and later also accepted by Usener. It is not possible here to go into the philological details of this text; anyway, whether it is the *ipsissima verba Epicuri* (as, for example, Usener believes) or an *additamentum* and interpolation (Von der Mühll),[21] one needs to understand the reasons that led Usener to accept Schneider's τὸ προσμένον. It seems to me that the main motivation is the fact that falsehood and error lie in the opinion *added* to the perceptual object (ἐν τῷ προσδοξαζομένῳ, emphasis my own).[22] The content of an opinion, as we know, can be true or false, and truth and falsity depend on the

---

[18] Hahmann–Robitzsch 2021: 755.
[19] Even if *to prosmenon* is juxtaposed with *to adelon*, and if the latter refers to objects, according to my hypothesis, it is not necessary that *to prosmenon* is an object too.
[20] Schneider 1813.
[21] See also Natorp 1884: 227 n. 1 and Long–Sedley 1987: II 78.
[22] On the genesis of epistemological error in Epicurus' philosophy, crucial information comes from *Peri physeos*. See, e.g., *Nat*. XXXIV (*PHerc*. 1431) col. XV Leone and XXVIII (*PHerc*. 1479/1417) fr. 12 col. III 6–12 Sedley.

comparison with *enargeia* and, therefore, on *epimartyresis* and *antimartyresis* that apply to the opinion waiting to be confirmed or rejected.

The other text that cannot be overlooked in the Epicurean dossier on τὸ προσμένον is the difficult *Capital Maxim* 24. Again, I cannot go into too much philological details on this controversial text, but I will limit myself to examining the presence of τὸ προσμένον in it. In this maxim, Epicurus states that if one rejects a single sense-perception (*aisthesis*) one also rejects all criteria of knowledge (τὸ κριτήριον ἅπαν ἐκβαλεῖς). One must not only not reject a single sense-perception but also distinguish (διαιρήσεις) – i.e., not confuse – τὸ δοξαζόμενον κατὰ τὸ προσμένον. While Usener, Arrighetti, and Isnardi Parente here read τὸ δοξαζόμενον καὶ τὸ προσμένον (emphasis my own), I believe that, at least from the historical-philosophical point of view, it is more plausible to read, with Bignone, Von der Mühll and Bailey, τὸ δοξαζόμενον κατὰ τὸ προσμένον (emphasis my own). Moreover, this reading in all likelihood is to be preferred also from the very philological point of view because of the subsequent κατὰ τὴν αἴσθησιν: κατὰ τὸ προσμένον and κατὰ τὴν αἴσθησιν form a completely symmetrical construction. Now, κατὰ appears in BP¹ manuscripts while καὶ in F;[23] moreover, while τὸ προσμένον appears in F,[24] in BP one reads τὸ προσμενόμενον. In his edition of Diogenes Laertius,[25] Dorandi follows the BP tradition and consistently prints κατὰ τὸ προσμενόμενον in both *RS* XXIV and § 38 of the *Letter to Herodotus*. The same is done by Long and Sedley,[26] who recommend printing τὸ προσμενόμενον not only in *RS* XXIV and *Hrdt*. 38 but also in the Laertian report (X 34), although in the latter text "the active form is found in all MSS".[27] In Diog. Laert. X 34, Dorandi[28] consistently prints τὸ προσμένον and in the apparatus mentions Sedley's conjecture τὸ προσμενόμενον, which he considers "*fortasse recte*".[29] The translation that Long and Sedley offer of τὸ προσμενόμενον, thus of the passive form with respect to τὸ προσμένον, is "evidence yet awaited";[30] White, in his recent English translation of Diogenes Laertius, following Dorandi's

---

[23] See Dorandi 2013: 60 for dating Laertian codices.

[24] Manuscript F generally aims to correct BP's text and improve it linguistically and not in terms of philosophical content. I sincerely thank Tiziano Dorandi again for helping me to untangle the difficulties of the manuscript tradition of Diogenes Laertius.

[25] As is well known, Dorandi's 2013 edition of Diogenes Laertius' *Lives*, with regard to the works contained in Book 10, is not a critical edition of those writings by Epicurus but is aimed at presenting the state of Epicurus' text known to Diogenes Laertius (see Dorandi 2013: 49–52).

[26] Long–Sedley 1987: II 91.

[27] Long–Sedley 1987: II 91.

[28] Dorandi 2013: 755.

[29] Frederik A. Bakker *per litteras electronicas* points out that "exactly the same solution (i.e., reading *prosmenomenon* in *RS* XXIV, *Hrdt*. 38 and Diog. Laert. X 34) was already proposed by P. Gassendi, *Animadversiones* (1649) p. 28 (edition) and p. 156 (commentary)". This fact is generally neglected by the scholars.

[30] Long–Sedley 1987: II 91 ("that which is awaited" is Long–Sedley 1987: I 91's translation of Diog. Laert. X 34).

critical text, translates "beliefs about anything deferred".[31] According to Sedley,[32] the passive form is preferable because the idea that the expression means – i.e., "waiting to get near the tower and find out what it looks like from close to" – is quite inappropriate to the active form τὸ προσμένον which, according to the traditional interpretation, concerns the opinion and not the observer that does the waiting.

According to this interpretation, in *RS* XXIV τὸ δοξαζόμενον κατὰ τὸ προσμενόμενον should be translated as "opinions reliant on evidence yet awaited":[33] τὸ προσμενόμενον would indicate the awaited evidence (by the observer) that makes it possible to establish, in the example of the tower, whether it is round or square. In the passive form it is the evidence (i.e., approaching the tower and seeing what its concrete shape is) that is expected; in the active form it is the opinion that awaits confirmation or refutation by the evidence. Even if τὸ προσμενόμενον is adopted, it is in any case necessary to clarify better from whom or what the evidence is expected: the observer or the opinion?[34] As I have tried to show, I believe it is the opinion.

On the difficult problem of choosing here the active form or the passive form of *prosmeno*, I merely note that the active form does not seem to me so implausible but perhaps it is even preferable after an already passive form (τὸ δοξαζόμενον). Κατὰ τὸ προσμένον essentially refers to the content of the opinion awaiting verification: which is opined in relation to which awaits (confirmation or refutation). I consider Von der Mühll's text (τὸ δοξαζόμενον κατὰ τὸ προσμένον) to be the most plausible one, although τὸ δοξαζόμενον κατὰ τὸ προσμενόμενον (the opinion concerning the awaited evidence or refutation) is not necessarily incorrect, either. On the other hand, Usener's text (τὸ δοξαζόμενον καὶ τὸ προσμένον) seems much less plausible to me because it presupposes the distinction between opinion and τὸ προσμένον, which in my view makes no sense. If I correctly understand the text of *RS* XXIV, Epicurus exhorts not to reject the criterion of sense-perception and not to confuse opinion with what awaits from what is already present in sense-perception or affections or any presentational application of thought (τὸ παρὸν ἤδη κατὰ τὴν αἴσθησιν καὶ τὰ πάθη καὶ πᾶσαν φανταστικὴν ἐπιβολὴν τῆς διανοίας). The point seems to me the following one: to confuse what is waiting to be verified (and is therefore not yet self-evident, i.e., neither true nor false) and what is already self-evident (i.e., true) is to confuse truth with uncertainty and thus to lose any actual criterion of knowledge able to distinguish the true from the false.

Again at the end of *KD* XXIV appears another occurrence of τὸ προσμένον/τὸ προσμενόμενον which is specular to the opening one; at the same time, the general meaning of the final part of the maxim seems to me essentially specular to the opening part. To sum up, although the text is very uncertain, Epicurus, according

---

[31] White 2020: 460.
[32] Long–Sedley 1987: II 91.
[33] Long–Sedley 1987: I 87.
[34] See Asmis 2009: 96.

to White's translation, states that "if you're going to affirm (βεβαιώσεις) not only whatever is deferred in your concepts and beliefs (τὸ προσμενόμενον ἅπαν ἐν ταῖς δοξαστικαῖς ἐννοίαις) but also what <has> no attestation, then you will not evade falsehood, and you will find yourself upholding every challenge on every decision about what is correct or incorrect (πᾶσαν ἀμφισβήτησιν κατὰ πᾶσαν κρίσιν τοῦ ὀρθῶς ἢ μὴ ὀρθῶς)." The expression ἐν ταῖς δοξαστικαῖς ἐννοίαις is not immediately clear; White, incorrectly in my view, translates it with two terms ('concepts and beliefs'), Gigante with "giudizi basati sull'opinione", Arrighetti with "pensieri che riguardano le opinioni",[35] and Long and Sedley with "conjectural conceptions". First, for the purposes of this paper, it is interesting that τὸ προσμένον (*lectio* which, by following Von der Mühll, I prefer) is clearly related to *doxai*. I do not think that *ennoiai* here is a reference to *prolepseis*:[36] as canons/criteria of truth *prolepseis* are always true whereas *doxai* are not necessarily so. I think that Gigante's translation (and to some extent those by Arrighetti and by Long and Sedley) is plausible: *ennoia* is to be understood as a thought content based on (mere) opinion. Epicurus argues against taking for certain what awaits to be verified in opinions; it should be noticed that τὸ προσμένον is ἐν ταῖς δοξαστικαῖς ἐννοίαις (emphasis my own): what awaits is included in the thoughts expressed (in propositional terms) in opinions. In short: taking τὸ προσμένον as true means not verifying it and so confusing truth with uncertainty.

5. Τὸ προσμένον IN SEXTUS EMPIRICUS?

Leaving aside the texts of Epicurus and the testimony of Diogenes Laertius, while delaying for another occasion the examination of this concept in the Herculaneum works,[37] there is not much evidence on τὸ προσμένον. This lack is problematic because it is not only an original epistemological device in the ancient theory of knowledge, but also a truly crucial one in the Epicurean canonic. Unfortunately, our ancient texts for knowledge of canonic are poor, and very often they are hostile sources. In my opinion, this situation is one of the reasons why there are so few testimonies on this concept: τὸ προσμένον is an extremely refined epistemological notion that, since it safeguards the truth of sensible knowledge, was necessary to pass over in silence in order to reject Epicurus' philosophy. According to these hostile sources, if all sense-perceptions are true, then the sense-perception (and the opinion) about the round tower and the following sense-perception (and opinion) about the actually square tower cannot be true at the same time. This reasoning is enough for the critics of Epicureanism (like Plutarch)[38] to show how this philosophy

---

[35] See Morel 2011: 110 ("les pensées relevant de l'opinion").
[36] See Diog. Laert. X 33.
[37] For a first overview see Asmis 1984: 191 n. 50.
[38] See e.g. Plutarch. *Adv. Col.* 1121C–E.

is false and contradictory. On the other hand, τὸ προσμένον means that the opinion at first expressed about the round tower (which later turns out to be square) is neither true nor false before direct and close verification.[39] This means:
1. that the truth of an opinion must be carefully verified by *enargeia*;
2. that there can be no precipitancy in the truth or falsity of an opinion, but both are to be scrutinized by *enargeia*.

A very important and well-known source on the 'criteria' of verification (*epimartyresis* and *antimartyresis*) is a long passage from Book I of Sextus Empiricus' *Against the Logicians*.[40] Sextus – who usually depends on reliable Epicurean sources[41] – does not explicitly mention τὸ προσμένον, but I think it is possible to find an implicit reference to it. Sextus' evidence cannot be analyzed in full. Here I will only examine § 212 on ἐπιμαρτύρησις:

> ἔστι δὲ ἐπιμαρτύρησις μὲν κατάληψις δι' ἐναργείας τοῦ τὸ δοξαζόμενον τοιοῦτον εἶναι ὁποῖόν ποτε ἐδοξάζετο, οἷον Πλάτωνος μακρόθεν προσιόντος <u>εἰκάζω μὲν καὶ δοξάζω</u> παρὰ τὸ διάστημα ὅτι Πλάτων ἐστί, προσπελάσαντος δὲ αὐτοῦ προσεμαρτυρήθη ὅτι ὁ Πλάτων ἐστί, συναιρεθέντος τοῦ διαστήματος, καὶ ἐπεμαρτυρήθη δι' αὐτῆς τῆς ἐναργείας.

"Testimony in favor" is an apprehension through plain experience of the fact that the thing on which the opinion is held is such as the opinion held it to be. For example, when Plato is approaching from a long way away, <u>I conjecture and hold the opinion</u> (given the distance) that it is Plato, but when he comes near there is additional testimony that it is Plato, now that the distance has been shortened, and there is testimony in favor of it through plain experience itself. (transl. Bett; emphasis my own)

---

[39] In reference to this last sentence, one of the anonymous reviewers of this article writes: "I don't think that this is correct. Now, Epicurus *does* believe in "truth value gaps" for statements regarding future contingents, e.g., "there will be a sea battle tomorrow," according to Cicero's testimony in *De Fato*. But when I have the opinion that the tower is round, Epicurus (I would think) should say that that opinion is simply false when I make it, because it says of the square tower something that contradicts what is the case. My direct and close verification *reveals* that that opinion is false, and I come to *know* that it is false at this time, but it's not the case that a previously "neutral" statement acquires a definite truth value upon confirmation or disconfirmation." It is naturally correct what the reviewer writes regarding future contingents according to Cicero's testimony in the *De fato* (on this topic see Bown 2016); however, I do not believe that *to prosmenon* concerns future contingents. The point is this: when I express the opinion that the tower is round, I do so because I genuinely believe the tower is round. Obviously, this opinion *in itself* is always either true or false, yet the perceiving subject is not, so to speak, conscious until the expressed opinion is confirmed or refuted by reality/*enargeia*. I would object to the reviewer: 1. If the subject is already aware of the falsehood of the expressed opinion, why should he/she express it?; 2. There may be cases in which opinions are formed without being fully certain of the truth (or falsehood) of their content, for example, due to the distance of the tower and poor perceptual conditions related to the subject and/or the object. In these cases, it is possible to express an opinion that will only be proven true or false after confirmation or refutation by reality/*enargeia*: in my interpretation, *to prosmenon* is precisely this type of opinion that requires confirmation to be true or refutation to be false.

[40] Sext. Emp. *M* VII 203–216 = 247 Usener.

[41] See Spinelli 1991.

Sextus is describing the confirmation: to explain what the ἐπιμαρτύρησις is he gives the example, so to speak, of an 'optical illusion'. If Plato is approaching me from afar, because of the distance, I conjecture and hold the opinion that he is Plato, and only when he has approached me I will have confirmation that it was indeed Plato. The verbs εἰκάζω and δοξάζω are somehow a reference to τὸ προσμένον; these are verbs indicating the formation of an opinion. Since Plato is distant, I do not know whether he is Plato or Socrates; for this reason, in genuinely propositional terms, I conjecture and opine that it is Plato. The content of my opinion (τὸ δοξαζόμενον) is exactly τὸ προσμένον; if this hypothesis is plausible, Sextus, while not explicitly mentioning this concept, shows how what is waiting to be verified is exclusively expressed by opinion.

6. CONCLUSIONS: TIME, VERIFICATION, KNOWLEDGE

In this paper I have stressed the importance of τὸ προσμένον for Epicurean epistemology, a concept frequently neglected by scholars. Given the use of this notion in the *Letter to Herodotus* and the *Capital Maxims*, it is very likely that it was theorized directly by Epicurus. The main reason for Epicurus to conceive this notion seems to me the defence of his rational empiricism: thanks to *to prosmenon* the truth of knowledge (= correspondence of the content of *doxa* with reality) was the outcome of meticulous verification in close contact with the investigated phenomenon.

Contrary to the hypothesis of Andree Hahmann and Jan Maximilian Robitzsch who reduce the προσμένοντα to merely optical illusions and interpret what awaits in non-propositional terms, I have attempted to show how τὸ προσμένον is identified with the content of opinion (τὸ δοξαζόμενον) and with opinion itself formulated on the basis of the elaboration of external *simulacra*.

If one assumes that τὸ προσμένον is the content of the image (= *eidolon*) coming from outside (as these scholars seem to claim), this same image, after verification, may turn out to be true or false. If it is true, the truth of sense-perception (the cornerstone of Epicurean canonic) is saved; if it is false, the truth of sense-perception fails, and so the entire Epicurean epistemology is ultimately doomed to collapse.[42] By identifying τὸ προσμένον with opinion, Epicurus can attribute falsity

---

[42] It is not possible to delve into this issue in this article, but I believe that the propositional level plays an essential role in Stoic epistemology as well. The cataleptic representation (which occurs on the *hegemonikon*) has (also) linguistic-propositional content, meaning it contains an *axioma* that likely condenses the essential characteristics of the externally present object no differently from Epicurean *prolepsis*: the rational subject that, so to speak, 'undergoes/suffers' the representation of the external object processes the immediate perceptual data, and such processing can only occur in propositional terms. Therefore, assent is given by the subject to the propositional content of the *phantasia*; it goes without saying that each *axioma* can be either true or false. For proper bibliographic references, I would like to refer to Verde 2024.

to *doxa* and not to *aisthesis*: by doing so, the truth of *aisthesis* is guaranteed. In the example of the tower, the critics of Epicureanism (i.e., all those who do not believe that sense-perceptions are able to attain the truth of things)[43] claim that sense-perceptions are not all true: the sense-perception of the distant round tower is false, while the sense-perception of the close square tower is true. If this is so, the critics of Epicureanism can only condemn the reliability of sense-perceptions and the consistency of the Epicurean canonic. Instead, Epicurus argues that the round *eidolon* of the tower (from a distance) is also true because it really exists (see Lucret. IV 353–363); what is false *is* the content of the opinion that requires an additional interpretation of the pure *eidolon*. This interpretation is the *doxa* or *hypolepsis*, which certainly has to do with the *eidolon* but which interprets and elaborates it: this interpretation/elaboration can be true or false. If it is false, this does not affect the truth of sense-perception, which remains irrefutable.[44]

This interpretation of τὸ προσμένον emphasizes the double concept of truth in Epicureanism: truth as the material existence of external *eidola* and truth as the correspondence of the content of *doxa* to concrete reality. In this (and not in anything else) Epicurus shares Aristotle's view – as we read, for example, in Book III of the *De anima* – that the true and the false are in the connection of notions (III 8, 432a 11–12: συμπλοκὴ γὰρ νοημάτων ἐστὶ τὸ ἀληθὲς ἢ ψεῦδος; see too *e.g. Cat.* 10, 13b 10–12).[45]

---

[43] If *to prosmenon* is a concept invented by Epicurus, it is possible that these critics of his philosophy are contemporary to Epicurus himself: on the topic of the anti-sceptical attitude of some famous texts by Epicurus and Lucretius, Corradi 2021 – rightly observing that the Epicurean anti-sceptical polemic has similarities with Aristotle's *Metaphysics* Book Γ – argues that the targets could be identified with "posizioni scettiche o proto-scettiche, coeve o anteriori al filosofo di Samo, sviluppatesi probabilmente in ambito democriteo o derivate dal magistero socratico." (313; see too Mensch–Miller 2018: 507 n. 23). See especially Spinelli 2020 on the strong possibility that Timon of Phlius was a likely target of some specific arguments presented by Epicurus in *On Nature* Book 34.

[44] See on this point Striker 2020: 45. In the book that still remains unsurpassed on Epicurean epistemology, *Epicurus' Scientific Method*, Elizabeth Asmis wrote that the προσμένοντα "are not objects that already exist and remain to be recognized; instead, they are expected entities, existing as expectations and "waiting" to come into existence by becoming evident" (Asmis 1984: 191). She added: "I understand τὸ προσμένον as an object that is expected to be perceived in the future; and I agree with Bignone (*Epicuro*, 74 n. 1) that it is an object of opinion added to a present perception" (191 n. 51). Despite the quotation by Bignone's *Epicuro*, the latter's position and Asmis's are different. Asmis interprets τὸ προσμένον as an object waiting to be perceived; Bignone (1920: 74 n. 1) writes that τὸ προσμένον "è l'opinamento che noi aggiungiamo ad una percezione avuta dal senso, opinamento che può essere vero o falso, secondo che l'esperienza lo confermi o no" (see also Bignone 1920: 63 n. 2). I believe that one cannot be clearer than Bignone and that what the Italian scholar writes is extremely correct: τὸ προσμένον is not an object but is the opinion itself waiting to be verified or refuted.

[45] See too Plat. *Theaet.* 179c 1–7 with Ioppolo 1999: 241 n. 114 and Trabattoni 2018: 210 n. 214. According to Hahmann–Robitzsch 2021: 741 Epicurus would follow Aristotle not so much in the *symploke* but in the fact that "Aristotle claims that what is simple is always true and that all falsity is found in combination". The authors (2021: 741 n. 6) refer to the famous beginning of *De an.* III 6, 430a 26–28 on the so-called intellection (*noesis*) of the *adiaireta* to which the false does not belong. Leaving aside the nature of these *adiaireta* (see at least Berti 1978 and Movia 1991: 384–385), Aristotle states that a single (= indivisible) notion cannot be false and stresses that the true and the false (and *not* only the

Finally, one must ask whether this original Epicurean doctrine of τὸ προσμένον is somehow consistent with certain attitudes typical of Hellenistic epistemologies. Τὸ προσμένον entails that truth (of *doxai*) is not something intuitive or immediate but needs time, attention to be verified. Now, the relationship between time and truth, for instance, is briefly suggested by a passage of Plato's *Theaetetus* (158d),[46] but it is above all in the Hellenistic philosophies that time, attention, and non-rashness become necessary conditions for the achievement of knowledge. This qualification is evident in ancient Stoicism: the Stoics (in all likelihood especially Chrysippus) called ἀπροπτωσία (Diog. Laert. VII 46) – i.e., literally, "freedom from precipitancy", "pondering" – the science of the opportune moment in which one should assent or not. They defined ἀνεικαιότης (Diog. Laert. VII 47) as caution, "reason firm in regard to what is merely likely, so as not to succumb to it" (transl. White), προπέτεια (Diog. Laert. VII 48) as rashness in making statements based on uncertain representations. In this context, one cannot avoid a reference to Chrysippus' ἡσυχάζειν, the state of tranquillity in the face of paradoxes such as the sorites (Cic. *Lucull*. 93 = *SVF* II 277).

It is well known that Carneades distinguished between different degrees of persuasive representations (Sext. Emp. *PH* I 227–229; *M* VII 185–189): circumstances and time are essential factors that determine the higher degree of persuasiveness of these representations.[47] Just think of the 'well-pondered' persuasive representation: one follows "the one that is persuasive and explored all round in cases where time is available for employing one's judgment, on the matter that confronts one, with care and by going over it in detail (τῇ δὲ πιθανῇ καὶ περιωδευμένῃ ἕπονται ἐφ' ὧν χρόνος δίδοται εἰς τὸ μετὰ ἐπιστάσεως καὶ διεξόδου χρῆσθαι τῇ κρίσει τοῦ προσπίπτοντος πράγματος). For example, someone observing a coil of rope in an unlit room immediately jumps over it, supposing it to be in fact a snake. But after this he turns round and examines what is true, and finding it motionless he already has in his thinking an inclination towards its not being a snake." (Sext. Emp. *M* VII 187; transl. Bett; emphasis my own).[48]

The Stoic and Academic testimonies just quoted show how the Hellenistic philosophers attached much importance to time as a necessary condition for the attainment of knowledge. Truth (or, as in the case of Carneades, a more persuasive representation than others) is achieved by time and the careful attention one puts

---

false) is only in the *synthesis noematon*. It seems to me that Epicurus shares with Aristotle the view that it is only in the connection of notions or of a subject and a predicate that the true and the false lie. The *adiaireta* of *De an*. III 6 are always true but have nothing to do with the truth/existence of *simulacra*, like in the Epicurean canonic.

[46] In all likelihood a not unfamiliar dialogue to Epicurus: for a first overview on the point, see Verde 2020.

[47] See Ioppolo 1986: 206–207.

[48] See too Sext. Emp. *M* VII 189: "[…] so that because of these things the appearance is trustworthy, since we have had sufficient time for going over in detail the things observed at its location. (transl. Bett)

into verifying the opinions formulated, leaving aside rashness and precipitancy that lead directly to falsehood. I believe that in this context there is also room for τὸ προσμένον, a notion that compellingly shows how refined Epicurean canonic is, far from the self-contradictory nature that the critics of Epicureanism of all times have superficially attributed to it.

REFERENCES

Asmis, E., 1984, *Epicurus' Scientific Method*, Ithaca-London: Cornell University Press.
Asmis, E., 2009, "Epicurean Empiricism", in J. Warren (ed.), *The Cambridge Companion to Epicureanism*, Cambridge: Cambridge University Press: 84-104.
Bailey, C. (ed.), 1926, *Epicurus: The Extant Remains*, Oxford: Clarendon Press.
Berti, E., 1978, "The Intellection of 'Indivisibles' according to Aristotle *De Anima* III 6", in G. E. R. Lloyd – G. E. L. Owen (eds.), *Aristotle on Mind and the Senses*, Proceedings of the Seventh Symposium Aristotelicum, Cambridge: Cambridge University Press: 141-163.
Bignone, E. (ed.), 1920, *Epicuro: Opere, frammenti, testimonianze sulla sua vita*, Bari: Laterza (repr. 1964: Rome: L'Erma di Bretschneider).
Blank, D., 2023, "Do You Hear What I Hear? Philodemus on Diogenes of Babylon's «Scientific Perception»", *Cronache Ercolanesi* 53: 81-146.
Bown, A., 2016, "Epicurus on Bivalence and the Excluded Middle", *Archiv für Geschichte der Philosophie* 98: 239-271.
Cavalli, R., 2012, "Il processo di ἐπαίσθησις presso gli Epicurei", *Würzburger Jahrbücher für die Altertumswissenschaft* 36: 157-167.
Corradi, M., 2021, "*Qui capite ipse sua in statuit uestigia sese*: Lucrezio e lo scetticismo nel libro IV del *De rerum natura*", *Elenchos* 42: 291-319.
Dorandi, T. (ed.), 2013, *Diogenes Laertius: Lives of Eminent Philosophers*, Cambridge: Cambridge University Press.
Hahmann, A., – Robitzsch, J. M., 2021, "Epicurus' Non-Propositional Theory of Truth", *Mnemosyne* 75: 739-758.
Ioppolo, A. M., 1986, *Opinione e scienza: Il dibattito tra Stoici e Accademici nel III e nel II secolo a.C.*, Naples: Bibliopolis.
Ioppolo, A. M. (ed.), 1999, *Platone: Teeteto*, Trad. e note di M. Valgimigli, Introd. e note aggiornate di A. M. Ioppolo, Rome-Bari: Laterza.
Long, A. A., 1971, "*Aisthesis, Prolepsis* and Linguistic Theory in Epicurus", *Bulletin of the Institute of Classical Studies* 18: 114-133.
Long, A. A., – Sedley, D. N. (eds.), 1987, *The Hellenistic Philosophers*, 2 vols., Cambridge: Cambridge University Press.
Masi, F. G., 2014, "Gli atomi ricordano? Fisicalismo e memoria nella psicologia di Epicuro", *Antiquorum Philosophia* 8: 121-141.
Mensch, P., – Miller, J. (eds.), 2018, *Diogenes Laertius. Lives of the Eminent Philosophers*, Oxford: Oxford University Press.
Morel, P.-M. (ed.), 2011, *Épicure: Lettres, maximes et autres textes*, Paris: Flammarion.

Movia, G. (ed.), 1991, *Aristotele: L'anima*, Naples: Loffredo.
Natorp, P., 1884, *Forschungen zur Geschichte des Erkenntnisproblem im Altertum: Protagoras, Demokrit, Epikur und die Skepsis*, Berlin: Wilhelm Hertz.
Németh, A., 2021, "Atoms and Universals in Epicurus", in U. Zilioli (ed.), *Atomism in Philosophy*, London-New York: Bloomsbury: 93-112.
Robitzsch, J. M., 2022, "Epicurean Feelings (*pathē*) as Criteria", *Archiv für Geschichte der Philosophie*: Ahead of Print.
Schneider, J. G. (ed.), 1813, *Epicuri physica et meteorologica duabus epistolis eiusdem comprehensa*, Lipsiae [i.e.: Leipzig]: F. C. G. Vogelii.
Spinelli, E., 1991, "Sesto, Epicuro e gli epicurei", *Studi Italiani di Filologia Classica* 9: 219-229.
Spinelli, E., 2020, "Un ginepraio scettico nel XXXIV libro 'Sulla natura' di Epicuro? Fra ipotesi esegetiche e polemica filosofica", *Cronache Ercolanesi* Sesto Supplemento (G. Leone – F. G. Masi – F. Verde (eds.), *'Vedere' l'invisibile: Rileggendo il XXXIV libro* Sulla natura *di Epicuro (PHerc. 1431)*), 95-105.
Striker, G., 2020, "Epistemology", in P. Mitsis (ed.), *The Oxford Handbook of Epicurus and Epicureanism*, Oxford: Oxford University Press: 43-58 (repr. in G. Striker, 2022, *From Aristotle to Cicero: Essays on Ancient Philosophy*, Oxford: Oxford University Press: Ch. 14).
Trabattoni, F. (ed.), 2018, *Platone: Teeteto*, Trad. di A. Capra, Turin: Einaudi.
Tsouna, V., 2016, "Epicurean Preconceptions", *Phronesis* 61: 160-221.
Verde, F., 2018a, "Ancora sullo statuto veritativo della sensazione in Epicuro", *Lexicon Philosophicum: International Journal for the History of Texts and Ideas* Special Issue: F. Verde – M. Catapano (eds.), *Hellenistic Theories of Knowledge*: 79-104.
Verde, F., 2018b, "I *pathe* di Epicuro tra epistemologia ed etica", *Elenchos* 39 (Special Section: F. G. Masi – S. Maso – F. Verde (eds.), *Materialistic Pathe*): 205-230.
Verde, F., 2020, "L'epistemologia di Epicuro e il *Teeteto* di Platone", *Historia Philosophica* 18: 13-44.
Verde, F., 2022, *Peripatetic Philosophy in Context: Knowledge, Time, and Soul from Theophrastus to Cratippus*, Berlin-Boston: De Gruyter.
Verde, F., 2024, "Arcesilao e la teoria stoica dell'azione", *forthcoming*.
White, S. (ed.), 2021, *Diogenes Laertius: Lives of Eminent Philosophers, An Edited Translation*, Cambridge: Cambridge University Press.

THE ELABORATION OF *PROLEPSIS* BETWEEN EPICURUS AND THE STOICS: A COMMON CHALLENGE TO INNATISM?

Jean-Baptiste Gourinat

In spite of the rivalry between the Stoics and the Epicureans, who were in strong opposition on many matters, both schools shared some common patterns of thought, notably the endorsement of a materialistic physics. In epistemology, they similarly had common views on the empiricist origins of knowledge, in tune with their materialism, and they shared some epistemological notions, including the celebrated *prolepsis*. Against the Sceptics, both Epicurus and the founder of the Stoic school, Zeno of Citium, firmly believed in the possibility of attaining secure knowledge.[1] There is no doubt that Epicurus was the first philosopher to introduce the notion of *prolepsis*, but it seems that Zeno, who was his junior, did not introduce the *prolepsis* in his epistemology. However, in two generations, significant moves were made, and Chrysippus recognized *prolepsis* as a criterion of truth, in terms evocative of Epicurus' position. In his *On Reason*, Chrysippus is reputed to have listed two criteria, sense-perception and preconception,[2] as Epicurus did before him, only omitting Epicurus' third criterion, namely, "feelings" (πάθη).[3] In fr. 215f Sandbach, Plutarch considers the "natural conceptions" of the Stoics and the *prolepseis* of the Epicureans as similar responses to the '*Meno* problem', "namely whether search and discovery are possible" – and precisely Stoic *prolepseis* are "natural conceptions",[4] so that Plutarch is coupling the *prolepseis* of both schools as similar if not identical responses to the problem of knowledge. Plutarch presents natural conceptions and preconceptions, in an association with the Peripatetic notion of "potential intellect" (δυνάμει νοῦς), as alternatives to the Platonic doctrine of recollection. The situation is complicated by the fact that *prolepseis* are sometimes presented as ἔμφυτοι, *insita*, or *innata*, in a sense that some scholars take to mean "inborn" "inbred", or "innate" in the sense of "literal innateness",[5] so that one may wonder whether Epicurean and Stoic *prolepseis* are empiricist alternatives to the doctrine of recollection or just rival alternatives, sharing with the Platonists a non-empiricist view of notions naturally inborn in us before any experience. Whatever may be the case (and I will try to disentangle this), it is striking that the Epicureans and the Stoics did not content themselves with the reliability of sense-perception but felt the need of having preconception as an additional criterion of truth. Why is it that, two generations

---
[1] See Angeli 1993: 19.
[2] Diog. Laert. VII 54.
[3] Diog. Laert. X 31.
[4] See Diog. Laert. VII 54 and [Plutarch], *Plac.* IV 11, 900C.
[5] The strongest advocates of 'literal innateness' in recent scholarship are Sedley 2011 for Epicureanism, and Hadot 2014: 373-414 for Stoicism.

after the founders of the schools, the two schools shared a major epistemological notion, and what are the similarities and the differences between the two schools on this issue? To answer these questions, I will proceed chronologically, trying to follow step by step the elaboration and the evolution of the notion of *prolepsis*, between Epicurus and the Stoa, inside their respective epistemological frameworks.[6]

1. THE CHRONOLOGICAL AND EPISTEMOLOGICAL FRAMEWORKS

The first thing to take into account are the chronological data. The chronology of Zeno and Cleanthes are difficult matters, subject to some uncertainty, since there exist alternative dates for the birth of Zeno, with a difference of a quarter of a century (between 361/360 and 334/333), but all chronologies have him die between 264 and 262/261.[7] As a consequence, it is certain that Epicurus and Zeno were contemporaries, since Epicurus died a decade before Zeno, in 271/270.[8] It is attested by Aulus Gellius, *N. A.* XVII 21, 37-39, that in the year 470 of the foundation of Rome – namely, in 280 BC – Zeno and Epicurus were the two most famous philosophers in Athens. Since Epicurus – born in 341/340 and dead in 271/270 – is probably eight years older than Zeno (if he was born in 334/333), they belonged to the same generation. And if Cleanthes – who died in 230/229 after a very long life, at the age of 100 – was born in 331/330, he was their contemporary, though, as a scholarch, he represented the second generation. When Chrysippus, born in 280/276, succeeded to Cleanthes at the head of the Stoa, Epicurus was dead for more than forty years and Zeno for thirty years, and, born in Soli, Chrysippus never had had the chance to know Epicurus or Zeno in person. In sum, while Epicurus, Zeno, and Cleanthes were contemporaries, Chrysippus was of a completely different generation. Whatever may have been Chrysippus' motivations, this generational distance may have made things easier for him when adopting Epicurus' criterion of *prolepsis*. Meanwhile, as I shall try to demonstrate, Cleanthes had already adopted some of Epicurus' views on concept formation, and it may have paved the way for Chrysippus' integration of the *prolepsis* in his epistemology.

It is quite obvious that the Epicurean and Stoic schools, over the centuries of their existence, were rival schools, in opposition on many issues, despite some affinities mentioned above. Yet was it already the case with Epicurus and Zeno? As the two most famous philosophers of their time in Athens, Epicurus and Zeno could hardly

---

[6] The Epicurean origins of the Stoic *prolepsis* is examined in the ground-breaking and now classic paper by Goldschmidt 1978/2006, which remains the reference work on the topic. While Goldschmidt does a structuralist comparison of the concept between the two schools in an invaluable way, I shall adopt a different method by trying to explore its historical development in the successive generations of philosophers. An intermediate method is followed by Dyson 2009.

[7] On the chronology of Zeno, see Gourinat 2018a: 376-378.

[8] On the chronology of Epicurus, see Goulet 2000: 160-162.

have ignored the existence of each other, and we know, thanks to Diog. Laert. VII 5 and VII 9, that Epicurus mentioned Zeno and his school in his letters. Still, there is no clear evidence of any dispute between Epicurus and Zeno. Specialists are divided on the existence of a dispute or a more friendly collaboration between the schools at this early stage of their development, since the evidence is lacking.[9] On the issues on which an explicit Stoic criticism targeting Epicurus and his school is recorded in our sources, the evidence points to later generations: for instance, when Diogenes Laertius – in his exposition of the celebrated Stoic argument of *oikeiosis* – says that "the claim, made by some, that the first impulse of animals is for pleasure, is false" (VII 85), obviously targeting the Epicureans, the most probable source is Chrysippus' *On Ends*, quoted just before. Similarly, the rejection of Epicurean atomism is attributed by Plutarch (*Stoic. Repugn.* 44, 1054B) to Chrysippus, not to Zeno. And it is Chrysippus, not Zeno or Cleanthes, who is said by Œnomaus to have uttered numerous imprecations against Epicurus.[10] Stoic attacks on Epicurus' theology, going to the point of accusation of atheism, may be traced back to Aristo,[11] Chrysippus,[12] and Posidonius,[13] but not to Zeno. Conversely, evidence of early Epicurean polemics against the Stoics is not conclusive. It is well known that Polyaenus, Epicurus' disciple and contemporary, wrote a treatise *Against Aristo*,[14] and what we know about it is that Polyaenus responded to Aristo's criticisms on Epicurean views on the gods, but Aristo was a dissident in the Stoic school.[15] In a fragment from an anonymous Epicurean, it is attested that Polyaenus and the members of the Stoic school were in good dispositions (εὐμενεῖς) towards each other.[16] A rare testimony of Epicurus' criticism of the Stoics is that they lack grief and emotion (in Plutarch, *Non posse* 1101A).[17] Thus Kechagia 2010, as already Angeli 1993: 24, convincingly argues that the evidence of Epicurean polemics against the Stoics in the early stages of the school is meagre and tends to be limited to ethical matters.

However, on epistemological matters, both Sextus and Cicero report a dissension on the truth of sense-perceptions between Zeno and Epicurus: while Epicurus maintained that all sense-perceptions were true, Zeno made a distinction between them. This difference seems not to have been taken into account by scholars interested in the relationship between Zeno and Epicurus, but it probably should not be neglected. Cicero presents Zeno as taking an intermediate position between Arc-

---

[9] Angeli 1993: 18-19 n. 100-101 recalls the opposite scholarly views on the issue and discusses the evidence (18-23). More recently see Kechagia 2010.
[10] Eusebius, *P. E.* VI 7.41 (Œnomaus, fr. 14 Mullach).
[11] See below.
[12] Plutarch, *Stoic. Repugn.* 38, 1051D-E.
[13] Cic. *DND* I 123.
[14] Philodemus, *Piet.* 1 col. 25.702-705 Obbink.
[15] Ioppolo 1980: 312-314, Angeli 1993: 18, Kechagia 2010: 141-143.
[16] PHerc 176 fr. 5 XXIV Vogliano. See again the comments of Kechagia 2010: 137-138.
[17] See the comments of Kechagia 2010: 139.

esilaus, who deemed all sense-perceptions to be false, and Epicurus, who deemed them all to be true; and, more importantly, he describes Epicurus as reacting to Arcesilaus' challenge to Zeno's epistemology:

> Arcesilaus attacked Zeno since, while he himself said that all that appears to the senses is false, Zeno said that some of the impressions were false, but not all. Epicurus feared that if a single impression were false, none would be true: he therefore said that all the senses were reporting the truth. (Cic. *DND* I 70)[18]

In Sextus, the disagreement is only between Zeno and Epicurus, and Epicurus is mentioned first, with Democritus endorsing a proto-sceptic position:

> And one may see some prominent men, the leaders of every school, in disagreement, since Democritus threw over every sensible reality, but Epicurus declared that every sensible thing is secure, while Zeno the Stoic made a distinction between them. (Sextus Emp. *AM* VIII 355)

Thus, according to both authors, who probably relied on an Academic or a Sceptic tradition, Zeno and Epicurus reacted in opposite ways to the challenges of Scepticism, but it is only Cicero who suggests that Epicurus wanted to elude Arcesilaus' challenge to Zeno. This story may be unlikely, and Epicurus may have had his own agenda to defend the truth of all impressions, more likely in reaction to Democritus, as Sextus attractively suggests. In any case, both stories are not incompatible, since Epicurus may have found in the dispute between Arcesilaus and Zeno an additional reason to endorse his views on the truth of all impressions, which he may have originally elaborated as a response to Democritus. Whatever may be true, it seems quite clear that Zeno and Epicurus were seen as taking opposite views on the reliability of the senses, and it is their major disagreement on epistemological issues. However, it does not seem to have been the object of a polemical dispute between them, comparable to the epic battle between Arcesilaus and Zeno on the *katalepsis*.[19] What is striking is that no other disagreement of importance is reported between Epicurus and Zeno on epistemological matters, and that, on such matters, the Stoics and the Epicureans shared a common vocabulary: *criterion, canon, prolepsis,* and *ennoia*. This shared terminology seems to emerge in the Stoa mainly with Chrysippus, but the notion of a criterion is likely to have been endorsed already by Zeno.

The first use of the word *criterion* in an epistemological context goes back to Plato's *Theaetetus* 178b, where Socrates explains that Protagoras' doctrine that "man is the measure of all things" means that humans have within themselves the *criterion* of sensible properties (i.e., the means to judge and discriminate them). However,

---

[18] Unless otherwise specified, translations are mine.
[19] On this dispute presented (with irony) as an epic battle see Numenius in Eusebius, *E. P.* XIV 6.7-14.

though it is very likely that this passage may have been an inspiration for using the word in epistemological contexts,[20] it is used in passing by Plato, it is not a technical word, and it has a rather different meaning.[21] The very notion of a criterion of truth was first introduced by Epicurus: it is attributed to him by Diog. Laert. X 31, but the term may be found in a passage of Epicurus himself, *Hrdt*. 38. There is no direct evidence that Zeno used the word: the notion of a *norma scientiae*, that is ascribed to him by Cicero,[22] is more likely a translation of *kanon* than of *kriterion*. However, since the word *criterion* was used by Arcesilaus in his attack against Zeno,[23] it is likely that Zeno himself used the word, otherwise Arcesilaus' criticism would make no sense. Diog. Laert. VII 54 attributes the notion of a criterion to Chrysippus' *Physics* and to his *On Reason*. The word *kanon*, also introduced by Epicurus, seems to have been used by Zeno, as attested in the passage of Cicero mentioned above, but there is no evidence that it was used by Chrysippus. Though the Stoics may rely on Plato for the use of the word *criterion*, in the case of Chrysippus it is obvious that the fact that he uses the same criteria as Epicurus (sense-perception and preconception) shows that his direct inspiration comes from him, not directly or not only from Plato.

Diog. Laert. X 31 ascribes to Epicurus three criteria: sense-perceptions (αἰσθήσεις), preconceptions (προλήψεις), and feelings (πάθη). Similarly, Diog. Laert. VII 54 says that Chrysippus recognized two criteria in his treatise *On Reason*, sense-perception (αἴσθησις) and preconception (πρόληψις). As a contrast, preconception does not seem to be ascribed in our sources to Zeno[24] nor to Cleanthes; and sense-perception, as mentioned above, is clearly denied the status of a criterion by Zeno. Zeno retrieved only a certain kind of impression as a criterion, namely, the "cognitive", "perceptive", or "comprehensive" impression – i.e., the καταληπτικὴ φαντασία or the "cognition", "comprehension", or "perception" (κατάληψις)[25] – as acknowledged both by Cicero (*Acad*. I 41-42) and by Numenius in Eusebius (*E. P.* XIV 6.13). Though Epicurus himself does not include κατάληψις as a criterion, it is one of the terms used by Diog. Laert. X 33 to describe the preconception. It is difficult to say if this

---

[20] It is virtually certain in the case of Zeno and the Stoics, given their description of sense-perceptions as impressions in the soul comparable to the imprint of seals in wax, inspired from the wax simile of the *Theaetetus*. See below.
[21] See Long 2006: 226, who argues that the Hellenistic philosophers who used the word were not relativists like Protagoras, but "rather they adapted his perceptual criterion, as described by Plato, to a non-relative concept of truth, claiming that a *determinable* set of our perceptions [...] is a criterial for true *objective* judgments".
[22] Cic. *Acad*. I 42.
[23] Sextus Emp. *AM* VII 150-153.
[24] Cic. *Acad*. I 42 leaves room for doubt. I shall discuss that passage later, but in any case, there is no mention of the *criterion* here, and no source says that Zeno admitted the *prolepsis* or the *ennoia* as a criterion.
[25] The various ways to translate κατάληψις all date back from Cicero's Latin, who acknowledges to use three alternative translations: *cognitio*, *perceptio*, and *comprehensio* (*Acad*. II 17; cf. *Fin*. III 17). See Gourinat 2012: 46-48.

a non-technical use of the term or an allusion to Zeno's criterion, but in any case Epicurus uses several times the verb καταλαμβάνειν in epistemological contexts to indicate a mental grasping.[26] Surprisingly enough, no ancient source attributes the κατάληψις to Cleanthes who, from the silence of our sources, does not seem to have shown any interest in his master's criterion. Even so, according to Diogenes Laertius, it reappears in the *Physics* by Chrysippus who, according to Diog. Laert. VII 54, "contradicts himself" (διαφερόμενος πρὸς αὑτόν) by adopting the cognitive impression as a criterion in his *Physics* and "sense-perception and preconception" in *On Reason*. Indeed, it gives the impression that in his *Physics*, Chrysippus endorsed Zeno's criterion of truth and that in *On Reason* he adopted Epicurus' criterion. At first sight, this move is certainly disconcerting.

Finally, the word *ennoia* is attributed in epistemological contexts both to the Epicureans and the Stoics: for instance, Diog. Laert. X 32 attributes it to the Epicureans, and it is found, among other sources, in a quotation of Chrysippus in Galen.[27] It seems quite clear that the word appears in Stoicism as early as Zeno, since Cicero (*Acad.* I 42) attributes to him the *notiones rerum*; he also attributes to Cleanthes the *notiones* of the gods,[28] and *notio* in Cicero is a translation of *ennoia*.[29] In addition, Diog. Laert. X 32 attributes to Epicurus three means of concept-formation (*epinoia*), by confrontation, analogy, similarity, and combination that Cic. *Fin.* III 33 attributes to the Stoics, while Diog. Laert. VII 52-53 attributes to the Stoics an expanded classification of seven modes of concept formation.[30]

All this can be summed up in the following table,[31] encapsulating how the epistemological concepts circulate between Epicurus and the three generations of Stoics:

	Epicurus	Zeno	Cleanthes	Chrysippus
Criterion	*Epicurus, Kanon* (Diog. Laert. X 31) *Ep. Hrdt.* 38	*Plausibly*	*No evidence*	*Chrysippus, On reason, Physics* (Diog. Laert. VII 54)

---

[26] Epicur. *Hrdt.* 78; *Pyth.* 88, 89.
[27] Galen, *PHP* V 3, p. 304, 34-35 De Lacy.
[28] Cic. *DND* II 13.
[29] Cic. *Top.* 7; *Fin.* III 6; *Tusc.* I 24. Note that in the first text, Cicero even presents it as a translation of *ennoia* or *prolepsis*.
[30] More on this below. See Gourinat 2005.
[31] See the useful tables in Dyson 2009: 153-162.

	Epicurus	Zeno	Cleanthes	Chrysippus
Prolepsis	*Epicurus, Kanon* (Diog. Laert. X 31; Cic. *DND* I 43 + S.E. *AM* I 57)	No evidence	No evidence	*Chrysippus, On reason* (Diog. Laert. VII 54)
Aisthesis	*Epicurus, Kanon* (Diog. Laert. X 31), *Ep. Hrdt.* 38	No: S.E. *AM* VIII 355 and Cic. *DND* I 70	No evidence (as a criterion)	*Chrysippus, On reason* Diog. Laert. VII 54
Katalepsis, phantasia kataleptike	Diog. Laert. X 33	Cic. *Acad.* I 41-42; Numenius in Eusebius, *E.P.* XIV 6.13	No evidence	*Chrysippus, Physics* (Diog. Laert. VII 54)
Classification of *epinoiai / noumena*	*Epicureans (Diog. Laert. X 32)*	*notiones rerum* (Cic. *Acad.* I 42)	*notiones* of the gods (Cic. *DND* II 13)	*Stoics (Cic., Fin.* III 33; Diog. Laert. VII 52-53)

2. THE GENERATION OF THE FOUNDERS: EPICURUS AND ZENO

2.1. The *prolepsis* as a criterion in Epicurus

Prolepsis is listed among Epicurus' criteria of truth in Diog. Laert. X 31, along with sense-perceptions and feelings (αἰσθήσεις καὶ πάθη), in a list attributed to Epicurus' *Kanon*:

> Ἐν τοίνυν τῷ Κανόνι λέγων ἐστὶν ὁ Ἐπίκουρος κριτήρια τῆς ἀληθείας εἶναι τὰς αἰσθήσεις καὶ προλήψεις καὶ τὰ πάθη. (Diog. Laert. X 31)

> Epicurus in the *Kanon*, says that sense-perceptions, preconceptions, and feelings are the criteria of truth.

Diogenes Laertius immediately adds that some later Epicureans added the "focusings of thought" (ἐπιβολαὶ τῆς διανοίας). I will not discuss those other criteria here.[32]

---

[32] On πάθη as criteria, see Robitzsch 2022. On sense-perceptions, see Verde 2018. I shall not discuss either the role of the "focusings of thought" in preconceptions, on which see Morel 2008.

Also quoting the same work – described as the *volumen de regula et iudicio*" of Epicurus[33] – Cicero defines *prolepsis* as follows:[34]

> Solus uidit primum esse deos quod in omnium animis eorum notionem inpressisset ipsa natura. Quae est enim gens aut quod genus hominum quod non habeat sine doctrina anticipationem quandam deorum, quam appellat *prolepsin* Epicurus, id est anteceptam animo quandam informationem sine qua nec intellegi quicquam nec quaeri nec disputari potest? Quoius rationis uim atque utilitatem ex illo caelesti Epicuri de regula et iudicio uolumine accepimus (Cic. *DND* I 43)

> He alone was the first to see that the gods exist, because nature itself has imprinted the notion of them in the minds of all. For which is the human nation or race that does not have, without any teaching, some preconception of the gods? This is what Epicurus calls a *prolepsis*, namely a delineation of a thing, preconceived by the mind, without which no one can understand, inquire about, nor discuss anything. The strength and utility of this process we have learnt from Epicurus' heavenly book on the rule and the judgment.

Later in the same passage Cicero acknowledges that the very word *prolepsis* is Epicurus' terminological innovation, applied to something that had not been thought before:

> Sunt enim rebus nouis noua ponenda nomina, ut Epicurus ipse *prolepsin* appellauit quam antea nemo eo uerbo nominarat (Cic. *DND* I 44)

> There are some new things that require new names, so that Epicurus himself gave the name *prolepsis*, which nobody had previously used.

A more detailed description of the *prolepsis* may be found in Diogenes Laertius, without any restriction to the notion of the gods, which seems to have been dictated by the context of the *De natura deorum*, where Cicero is not interested in Epicurus' epistemology (though he quotes the *Kanon*).

> Τὴν δὲ πρόληψιν λέγουσιν οἱονεὶ κατάληψιν ἢ δόξαν ὀρθὴν ἢ ἔννοιαν ἢ καθολικὴν νόησιν ἐναποκειμένην, τουτέστι μνήμην τοῦ πολλάκις ἔξωθεν φανέντος, οἷον τὸ "Τοιοῦτόν ἐστιν ἄνθρωπος·" ἅμα γὰρ τῷ ῥηθῆναι ἄνθρωπος εὐθὺς κατὰ πρόληψιν καὶ ὁ τύπος αὐτοῦ νοεῖται προηγουμένων τῶν αἰσθήσεων. Παντὶ οὖν ὀνόματι τὸ πρώτως ὑποτεταγμένον ἐναργές ἐστι· καὶ οὐκ ἂν ἐζητήσαμεν τὸ ζητούμενον εἰ μὴ πρότερον ἐγνώκειμεν αὐτό· οἷον Τὸ πόρρω ἐστὼς ἵππος ἐστὶν ἢ βοῦς; δεῖ γὰρ κατὰ πρόληψιν ἐγνωκέναι ποτὲ ἵππου

---

[33] In Diog. Laert. X 31, the title is given as *Kanon*, but in the list of Epicurus' works, in Diog. Laert. X 27, there is a double title, *On the criterion* or *Kanon* (Περὶ κριτηρίου ἢ Κανών), obviously corresponding to the description as a volume *de regula et iudicio* (namely, "on the *kanon* and the *criterion*") in Cicero, so that one may be confident that both Diogenes' list and Cicero's description come from the same work.

[34] See also Sextus Emp. *AM* I 57.

καὶ βοὸς μορφήν· οὐδ' ἂν ὠνομάσαμέν τι μὴ πρότερον αὐτοῦ κατὰ πρόληψιν τὸν τύπον μαθόντες. Ἐναργεῖς οὖν εἰσιν αἱ προλήψεις. (Diog. Laert. X 33)

Preconception, they say, is as it were a cognition, or correct opinion, or notion, or universal stored thought (i.e., memory) of that which has frequently become evident externally: for example, "Such and such a kind of thing is a human being." For as soon as "human being" is uttered, immediately its delineation also comes to mind by means of preconception, since the senses give the lead. Thus what primarily underlies each name is something self-evident. And what we inquire about we would not have inquired about if we had not had prior knowledge of it. For example: "Is what is standing over there a horse or a cow?" For one must at some time have come to know the form of a horse and that of a cow by means of preconception. Nor would we have named something if we had not previously learnt its delineation by means of a preconception. Thus preconceptions are self-evident. (Long & Sedley translation, slightly modified)

Thus some general features of the preconception appear both in Diogenes Laertius and in Cicero: the preconception is a notion (ἔννοια, *notio*, § 43) stored in the mind (ἐναποκειμένη, *insita*, § 43),[35] and it includes a sketch or delineation (τύπος, *informatio*, § 44).[36] That it is a "cognition, or correct opinion", and a "universal thought" is not explicitly stated by Cicero. However, it is obvious from the fact that Cicero talks about the notion of the gods that it is not a preconception of a particular god, but of gods in general, similar to the way Diogenes refers to the preconception of human being in the sense of a universal human being, not of a human being in particular.[37] The idea that a preconception is a "correct opinion" (δόξα ὀρθή) is not obvious in itself but seems to be illustrated by the example "such and such a kind of thing is a human being": one has a preconception of what a human being is if one has the correct opinion that "such and such a kind of thing is a human being". Thus, it seems that, up to a certain point, a preconception implies a certain kind of propositional content about the nature of the object of which we have a preconception. Even if it is not explicitly stated by Cicero, it seems to be what he has in mind when he says that in addition to the "delineation of the gods themselves, nature has also engraved in our minds the view of them as everlasting and blessed": this implies that the preconception of the gods includes a view that "such and such a kind of thing is a god", in

---

[35] Verde 2016a: 357, convincingly argues that Cicero's *insita* is the translation of ἐναποκειμένη.
[36] Sedley 2011: 36 n. 18, convincingly assumes that Cicero's *informatio* is the translation of τύπος – see also Long & Sedley 1987: 2; 148. Note that there is a debate in scholarship as to whether preconception and τύπος are identical as Tsouna 2016: 164 argues or distinct as Morel 2008: 41-42 argues. Diog. Laert. X 33 seems to imply a distinction, while Cic. *DND* I 43, seems to imply identity. What seems to be the case is that preconception includes a τύπος but is not reducible to it.
[37] In contrast, as we shall see in the case of the Stoics, a notion (ἔννοια) can be of an individual, for instance, of Socrates (Diog. Laert. VII 53). There is no clue, though, that such is the case of the *prolepsis* in Epicurus nor in the Stoics. In both schools, it is quite clear that a preconception has a universal content (see Diog. Laert. VII 54 for the Stoics).

similar terms to what is reported by Diogenes Laertius about the preconception of a human being.[38] Thus, it is quite clear that preconceptions include a mental image of what something is, described by Diogenes Laertius as a the 'shape' (μορφή) of a horse or a cow, and that it also includes a conceptual thought about what the object is.[39]

Cicero adds that a preconception is formed without being taught (*sine doctrina*, § 43), and though it is not explicitly stated by Diogenes Laertius, it is clear from the way he describes the empirical formation of a preconception that it is also what he has in mind. Finally, when Diogenes says that "what we inquire about (τὸ ζητούμενον) we would not have inquired about if we had not had prior knowledge of it" is echoed by Cicero when he says that "without" this delineation, "no one can understand, inquire about (*quaeri*) nor discuss anything".

In other words, preconceptions are mental images stored and engraved in the mind, but they also include a conception of what something is, they are the basis for human knowledge and recognition of universal objects, and they are *naturally* formed in the mind, without being taught.

However, there is a difference between the two accounts, since Diogenes Laertius gives examples of preconceptions of natural kinds (i.e., human, horse, or cow) and describes a concept formation that is the result of sense-perception and memory. Cicero by contrast does not refer to the preconceptions of natural kinds but to the preconceptions of the gods, and he does not say that we form this preconception by perception and memory, but that we have an "inborn" (*insita uel potius innata*) knowledge that nature has "engraved in our minds" (*inculpsit in mentibus*):

> Solus enim uidit primum esse deos quod in omnium animis eorum notionem inpressisset ipsa natura. [...] Cum enim non instituto aliquo aut more aut lege sit opinio constituta maneatque ad unum omnium firma consensio, intellegi necesse est esse deos quoniam insitas eorum uel potius innatas cognitiones habemus. [...] Quae enim nobis natura informationem ipsorum deorum dedit eadem inculpsit in mentibus ut eos aeternos et beatos haberemus. (Cic. *DND* I 43-45)

> For he alone saw, first, that the gods existed, because nature itself has imprinted the conceptions of them in all minds. [...] For since belief has not been established by any convention, custom or law, and retains unanimous consent, it must necessarily be understood that there are gods, given that we have implanted, or rather innate, knowledge[40] of them. [...] For as well as giving a delineation of the gods themselves, nature has also engraved in our minds the view of them as everlasting and blessed. (Long & Sedley translation, 23 E, slightly modified).

---

[38] See Sedley 2011: 32-33. As Konstan 2011: 63 notes, according to Philodemus (*Sign.* 52, 7-10 De Lacy), the *prolepsis* of a human being includes that it is a rational animal and this implies that our impressions of a human being do not only include its bodily shape, but also evidence of his rational behaviour.

[39] See Morel 2008, especially 41-42; and Tsouna 2016, especially 164.

[40] Note here that, consistently with Cicero's practice, *cognition* here could translate κατάληψις.

Here, Cicero does not explicitly attribute to Epicurus the claim that we are born and come to life with such a preconception of the gods already implanted in our minds at the very moment of our birth. However, he uses such words as *insitus* and *innatus* that point to an innate knowledge, not depending on any sense experience.[41] He also insists that nature engraves preconceptions in our mind, not memory. And indeed it is clear that, whatever maybe the process of formation of our notions of the gods, they cannot come from repeatedly seeing gods as we see humans, horses, and cows and by memorizing the impressions we have of such natural kinds. Thus with the description given by Cicero, it seems that the preconceptions of the gods is formed quite differently from the empiricist way by which we form a preconception of a cow. It is implanted by nature and does not seem to have an empirical origin. It is not the case in Cicero that the *prolepsis* is built on memory nor in such a way that "the senses give the lead" (προηγουμένων τῶν αἰσθήσεων). It remains that both kinds of preconceptions are sketches or delineation of things, engraved in the mind and preliminary to enquiry and discussion.

The process of the formation of the preconception as described in Diog. Laert. X 32, has a certain similarity with the process of concept formation described by Aristotle in the final chapter of the *Posterior Analytics* (II 19, 100a3-9), and it is not impossible that Epicurus may have had this passage in mind, maybe with a polemical intention, since he seems to have known Aristotle's *Analytics*.[42] Aristotle describes the formation of the "universal in the soul" (καθόλου ἐν τῇ ψυχῇ) as starting from the "memory of the sense impression" (αἰσθήσεως μνήμη): from repeated memories arises experience, and from experience and the universal "in rest in the soul" comes a principle of knowledge or of art. The passage is disputed among Aristotelian scholars,[43] but there are some similarities with the process attributed by Diogenes Laertius to Epicurus: sense-perception comes first, then the memory of several similar sense-perceptions, and from this a universal notion, which both in Aristotle and Epicurus is assimilated to a certain type of memory. The difference is of course that Aristotle does not use the word "preconception". He also refers to a certain connection between such a universal and a principle of knowledge, while Epicurus (perhaps polemically) describes such a preconception as a preliminary for enquiry, meaning that enquiry starts from here, not that it is a principle of knowledge. Yet there is of course some ambiguity because of the status of the preconception as a criterion of truth: preconceptions, like sense-perceptions and affections are true and for that reason they function as a criterion of truth; and

---

[41] See Sedley 2011: 36, 39.
[42] Philodemus, *PHerc.* 1005/862, fr. 111 Angeli (quoting a letter from Epicurus, fr. 127 Arrighetti). On Epicurus' knowledge of Aristotle, see Verde 2016b, and on this evidence 37-38. Striker 1996: 40-42 argues for a different parallel, with *APo* I 3, 72b5-25. She uses this parallel mainly to argue in favour of a propositional content of the *prolepsis*, something which seems to be derivable from Diogenes Laertius.
[43] See the classic discussion in Barnes 1993: 262-265.

the logical and epistemological function of the *prolepsis* being such, they are not only the starting point for enquiry, they also function as the warrant of truth. As Diog. Laert. X 33 argues, "opinion depends on something prior and self-evident, which is our point of reference (ἐφ' ὃ ἀναφέροντες) when we say, for example 'How do we know this is a human being?'" (Long and Sedley translation, slightly modified). The preconception is self-evident, its truth is warranted by its derivation from true sense-perceptions and, therefore, it is what we refer to as the criterion of truth. As Striker (1996, 42), convincingly puts it – though without a comparison to *APo* II 19 – "the difference lies in the conception of what a demonstration is: while for Aristotle the demonstration of a scientific proposition consists in its syllogistic derivation from first premises, Epicurus seems to think of a proof as the evaluation of an opinion with the help of criteria, whereby the opinion is shown to be true."[44] Any preconception is "both sufficiently imprecise and sufficiently constraining",[45] so as to function as a criterion of truth and as a starting point for enquiry rather than as a principle of demonstration.

Though Aristotle's views may have been at the background of the Hellenistic views of concept formation, another source seems to have been Plato's *Philebus*. Togni (2013) has argued that Plato's book simile in the *Philebus* 39a may be a source for the Stoics' analogy of the soul with a blank papyrus,[46] where notions are progressively imprinted, as reported in the *Placita* IV 11, 900B.[47] Though the Stoics are likely to have had Plato's simile in mind, it should be obvious here that there are even stronger analogies with what Epicurus had in mind according to Diogenes Laertius. For Plato describes in the *Philebus* 38b-39b a situation in which someone wonders what it is that someone sees "from far" (πόρρωθεν) "standing" (ἑστάναι) by a rock under a tree. In an inner dialogue, this person judges that what he sees is a human, confronting his present sense-perception with his memory. According to Diogenes Laertius' report, one of the roles of the preconception recalls the same kind of situation: we are wondering whether what we see "standing" (ἑστὼς) "from far" (πόρρω) is a horse or a cow: "Is what is standing over there a horse or a cow?" We confront what we know as "the form of a horse and that of a cow by means of preconception" with our present sense-perception, and then we form an opinion about it. Thus, it seems very likely that the situation described in this context by Plato, and which makes no use at all of the theory of recollection, is at the background of Epicurus' views here. Plato's empiricist views of concept formation in this context seems to be in the background for Epicurus, perhaps even more directly than Aristotle's views. In both texts, the being to be identified is seen from far (πόρρω, πόρρωθεν), and it is not a necessary circumstance if one wants to describe how we recognize a being

---

[44] See Morel 2008: 37-38, 44-45.
[45] Morel 2008: 43.
[46] See in particular Togni 2013: 166-168.
[47] See below, p. 106.

by comparing it to our memory of previously seen similar beings. This detail is a striking affinity between the two texts.

From Diogenes, it is also possible to gather some additional information on the role of preconception for Epicurus. First, it is a basis for language communication: we need to have a sketch, a *tupos* to put a name on something: "nor would we have named something if we had not previously learnt its delineation" (Diog. Laert. X 33). In other words, we must first form the preliminary notion of something in our minds, and we attach a word to this notion we have of it, stored in the mind. Conversely, we need to have a sketch of something to grasp the meaning of a word, and because of this association between the word and its preconception, as soon as we hear a word, it recalls its preconception: "for as soon as the word 'human' is uttered, immediately its delineation also comes to mind by means of preconception" (*ibid.*).

To sum up the nature and the role of preconception as it emerges from Diogenes and Cicero, it is a mental image associated to a conceptual content; it is a sketch and a "universal thought", formed by an individual, based on memory, but shared by many individuals if not by everyone, without being taught (*sine doctrina* according to Cicero) and coming from the senses and from memory (according to Diogenes). It is a basis for language: we need to have a *tupos* to put a name on something and to grasp the meaning of a word; it is a basis for perceptual recognition and opinion, and it is a basis for inquiry and a criterion of truth.

Finally, we must turn to the difference between the preconception of natural species, like animal, horse, and cow and the more specific preconception of the gods. It is clear that the *prolepsis* of the gods is a special case, but to what extent and how does this affect the Epicurean conception of the *prolepsis*? A passage from Sextus Empiricus seems to be quite illuminating. The passage belongs to the chapter "on the gods" of Sextus' *Against the Physicists* and describes how, according to Epicurus, "the gods were conceived" (ἐνοήθησαν οἱ θεοί) and men formed "a thought of the gods" (νόησις θεῶν).[48] Sextus does not mention the *prolepsis*, but there is no doubt that Epicurus admitted a *prolepsis* of the gods, since he mentions such a *prolepsis* in *Ep. Men.*, 123-124, so that Cicero is clearly not mistaken.[49] And yet, one may wonder whether everything that Sextus describes as a thought of the gods is a *prolepsis*.

Ἡ μὲν ἀρχὴ τῆς νοήσεως τοῦ εἶναι θεὸν γέγονεν ἀπὸ τῶν κατὰ τοὺς ὕπνους ἰνδαλλομένων ἢ ἀπὸ τῶν κατὰ τὸν κόσμον θεωρουμένων, τὸ δὲ ἀίδιον εἶναι τὸν θεὸν καὶ ἄφθαρτον καὶ τέλειον ἐν εὐδαιμονίᾳ παρῆλθε κατὰ τὴν ἀπὸ τῶν ἀνθρώπων μετάβασιν. Ὡς γὰρ τὸν κοινὸν ἄνθρωπον αὐξήσαντες τῇ φαντασίᾳ νόησιν ἔσχομεν Κύκλωπος, ὃς οὐκ ἐῴκει « ἀνδρί γε σιτοφάγῳ ἀλλὰ ῥίῳ ὑλήεντι ὑψηλῶν ὀρέων, ὅτε φαίνεται οἶον ἀπ᾽ ἄλλων », οὕτως ἄνθρωπον εὐδαίμονα νοήσαντες καὶ μακάριον καὶ συμπεπληρωμένον πᾶσι τοῖς ἀγαθοῖς, εἶτα ταῦτα ἐπιτείναντες τὸν ἐν αὐτοῖς ἐκείνοις ἄκρον ἐνοήσαμεν θεόν. (46) Καὶ πάλιν πολυχρόνιόν τινα φαντασιωθέντες ἄνθρωπον οἱ παλαιοὶ ἐπηύξησαν τὸν χρόνον

---

[48] Sextus Emp. *AM* IX 43.
[49] See Sedley 2011: 32.

εἰς ἄπειρον, προσσυνάψαντες τῷ ἐνεστῶτι καὶ τὸν παρῳχημενον καὶ τὸν μέλλοντα· εἶτα ἐντεῦθεν εἰς ἔννοιαν ἀιδίου παραγενόμενοι ἔφασαν καὶ ἀίδιον εἶναι τὸν θεόν. (Sextus Emp. *AM* IX 45-46)

The origin of the thought that god exists came from appearances in dreams, or from the phenomena of the world, but the thought that god is everlasting and imperishable and perfect in happiness arose through a process of transition from humans. For just as we acquired the thought of a Cyclops, who was not "like a corn-eating man, but rather a peak well-wooded High on the mountain-tops, when it loometh apart from its fellows"[50] by enlarging the common human being in imagination, so too having started to think of a happy human being, blessed with all the goods, then having intensified these, they thought of god as their highest point. (46) And again, having formed the impression of a long-lived human, the ancients increased their time-span to infinity by combining the past and future with the present; and then, having thus arrived at the notion of eternity, they said that god was eternal too.

Thus, according to Sextus' account, Epicurus considers that the notion of god includes two elements: (1) that god exists, and (2) what god is, namely, that god is everlasting and imperishable and perfect in happiness. Similarly, in Cicero, Epicurus considers that the *prolepsis* of the gods is not only that they exist but also that they are everlasting and blessed. Thus it seems that the content of what Sextus describes as our "thought" (νόησις, 43) or "notion" (ἔννοια, 46) of god is identical with the content of what Cicero describes as the *prolepsis* of the gods. The first aspect of our thought of the gods (i.e., that the gods exist) comes from dreams and observation of the world, according to Sextus. The second aspect (i.e., the eternity and blessedness of the gods) comes from "a process from transition from humans" (κατὰ τὴν ἀπὸ τῶν ἀνθρώπων μετάβασιν). This genealogy of the belief in the existence in the gods is not surprising in itself. It is a little more embarrassing if we try to combine it with Cicero's assertion that the notion that god exists is shared by all humans and then must be true on the basis of the universality of such notions.

The first origin of the notion of the existence of god is that humans received some images of the gods in their dreams. It is not strange as an argument, if we consider that it is an argument on the origin of our notion of the gods, but it is embarrassing if this is the origin of our preconception of the god that warrants the truthfulness of this preconception. That it is authentically Epicurean is confirmed by a similar passage in Lucret. V 1169-1182, who attributes to humans visions of the gods when they are awake and "even more so in their dreams". Two lines of interpretation may give consistency to such an origin of our notion of the gods. One is what Sedley (2011: 29) calls the "idealist interpretation" of Epicurean gods, – namely, that "gods are our own graphic idealization of the life to which we aspire" – and, according to this line of interpretation, then our *prolepsis* of the gods is formed from our dreams,

---

[50] Homer, *Odyss*. IX 191.

because it is just an idealization of our notion of a happy and long life.[51] The other is that the Lucretian passage "explains not so much the preconception of divinity as the acquisition by primitive human beings of a false conception of the gods".[52] Obviously, the same interpretation should apply to the Sextian counterpart of the Lucretian passage.

The same difficulty arises with the second origin of the thought of the existence of the gods, namely the observation of the world (τὰ κατὰ τὸν κόσμον θεωρούμενα). This is the idea, standard in Greek thought, that by contemplating the regularity of the heavens and the beauty and complexity of the world, we conceive that it is the work of a divinity. According to Cic. *DND* II 15, Cleanthes will ascribe a similar origin (among others) to our notions of the gods. Sextus describes it only as the "origin (ἀρχή) of the thought of the gods", so that in itself it is not particularly embarrassing since it does not mean that Epicurus thinks that it is correct to think that the gods are responsible for what we may contemplate in the world. If one argues, though, that such origins of our belief in the existence of the gods warrants the existence of the gods, then it is more embarrassing.

The second aspect of our thought of god – namely, that god is everlasting and imperishable and perfect in happiness – comes, according to Sextus, by *metabasis* from humans, and he explains it in comparison with the way we form the notion of a Cyclops by enlarging in imagination a common human being. Similarly, we enlarge our notion of the goods a happy human being enjoys to its peak and our notion of a long life to an eternal life, and we have the notion of the gods as perfectly happy and blessed and living forever. Sextus does not explain why he says that such a notion is formed by *metabasis*, but this is in fact a piece of technical terminology which one can find in three other passages (i.e., Sextus Emp. *AM* III 40-42, IX 393-395, and IX 250-251).[53] In all these passages, Sextus divides what is conceived in thought between what is formed by direct encounter with external objects (κατὰ περίπτωσιν) and what is formed by a transitional process (κατὰ τὴν μετάβασιν) from these encounters:

> Καθόλου τε πᾶν τὸ νοούμενον κατὰ δύο τοὺς πρώτους ἐπινοεῖται τρόπους· ἢ γὰρ κατὰ περίπτωσιν ἐναργῆ ἢ κατὰ τὴν ἀπὸ τῶν ἐναργῶν μετάβασιν καὶ ταύτην τρισσήν· ἢ γὰρ ὁμοιωτικῶς ἢ ἐπισυνθετικῶς ἢ ἀναλογιστικῶς. (Sextus Emp. *AM* III 40)

> In general, everything that is thought is conceived in two different ways: it is conceived by an evident encounter or by a transition from things evident, and thus in three ways: either by similarity, or by composition, or by analogy.

---

[51] Sedley 2011: 44-49.
[52] Tsouna 2018: 250.
[53] A parallel passage, *AM* VIII 56-60, does not include the word μετάβασις.

This classification echoes a division of 'notions' attributed to Epicurus by Diogenes Laertius which immediately precedes the description of the preconception in X 33:

> Καὶ γὰρ καὶ ἐπίνοιαι πᾶσαι ἀπὸ τῶν αἰσθήσεων γεγόνασι κατά τε περίπτωσιν καὶ ἀναλογίαν καὶ ὁμοιότητα καὶ σύνθεσιν, συμβαλλομένου τι καὶ τοῦ λογισμοῦ. (Diog. Laert. X 32)
>
> Also, all notions arise from the senses by means of encounter, analogy, similarity, and composition, with some contribution from reasoning, too.

All the passages in Sextus where this quadripartition of thought formation appears include under the category of analogy 'by increase' the example of the Cyclops conceived by increasing the normal size of a man, with the same Homeric quotation as in the theological passage of Sextus Emp. *AM* IX 45-47. There can be little doubt that the formation of the notion of a god by "transition from humans" in IX 45-47 belongs to the same piece of Epicurean doctrine that the exposition of concept formation in Diog. Laert. X 32. In Diog. Laert. X 32-33, ἐπίνοιαι and προλήψεις are treated separately and do not seem to be identical. According to the way Sextus describes the formation of the νόησις or the ἔννοια of the gods, however, it seems to be completed through a double process that seems similar to two of the processes of the formation of ἐπίνοιαι in Diog. Laert. X 32: the thought that the gods exist is formed through dreams and contemplation of the world and so it seems to be formed through περίπτωσις, while the conception that the gods are "everlasting and blessed" comes by μετάβασις, through an analogical enlargement of the happy and long life of humans. To be sure, one can even wonder if the conception of god from the contemplation of the world does not fall under the category of μετάβασις. In any case, if Sextus in IX 45-47 describes the way we form our preconceptions of the gods, then it is no exception to Epicurus' empiricism, since, ultimately, our preconceptions of the gods are formed from "transition" from sense-perception.

2.2. Zeno's epistemological agenda: The katalepsis

Zeno was apparently not concerned by Epicurus' agenda. As mentioned above, Cic. *DND* I 70 and Sextus Emp. *AM* VIII 355 both say that while Epicurus maintained that all sense-perceptions were true, Zeno said that some were true and some false. So obviously sense-perception without qualification was not a criterion for Zeno. Still, as he denied that all sense-perceptions were true, he had to isolate a certain kind of impression as trustworthy, and – according to Cic., *Acad.* I 41-42 and to Numenius in Eusebius, *E. P.* XIV 6.13 – this type was the φαντασία καταληπτική, an expression and a notion he invented:[54]

---

[54] See Cic. *Acad.* II 145.

Visis non omnibus adiungebat fidem sed is solum quae propriam quandam haberent declarationem earum rerum quae uiderentur; id autem uisum cum ipsum per se cerneretur comprehendibile [...] sed cum acceptum iam et approbatum esset, comprehensionem appellabat, similem is rebus quae manu prenderentur; ex quo etiam nomen hoc duxerat (at) cum eo uerbo antea nemo tali in re usus esset, plurimisque idem nouis uerbis (noua enim dicebat) usus est. (Cic. *Acad.* I 41)

[Zeno] held that not all impressions were trustworthy but only those that have a 'manifestation', peculiar to themselves, of the objects presented; and a trustworthy impression, being perceived as such by its own intrinsic nature, he termed "graspable" [...]. But after it had been received and accepted as true, he terms it a "grasp", resembling objects gripped in the hand – and in fact he had derived the actual term from manual prehension, nobody before having used the word in such a sense, and he also used a number of new terms (for he said new things). [Rackham translation, modified]

It is not the place here to give an account of Zeno's theory of the φαντασία καταληπτική.[55] However, it may be relevant to recall some elements of Zeno's views. Sextus and Cicero give us its definition, which Cic. *Acad.* II 77 attributes to Zeno:

Καταληπτικὴ δέ ἐστιν ἡ ἀπὸ ὑπάρχοντος καὶ κατ' αὐτὸ τὸ ὑπάρχον ἐναπομεμαγμένη καὶ ἐναπεσφραγισμένη, ὁποία οὐκ ἂν γένοιτο ἀπὸ μὴ ὑπάρχοντος. (Sextus Emp. *AM* VII 248)

A cognitive [impression] is one that arises from what is, and is stamped and impressed in accordance with what is, of such a kind as could not arise from what is not. (Long & Sedley translation, 40E).

The cognitive impression is a definite kind of φαντασία, which in turn Zeno defined as an impression (τύπωσις) in the soul.[56] This kind of impression one can trust,[57] and it indicates in which primary sense the cognitive impression is a criterion of truth: it is the kind of impression one can believe to be true and give assent to.[58] It is trustworthy in contrast to false impressions (the ones that do not arise from what is) and to impressions insufficiently precise (the ones that are not stamped and impressed in accordance with what is). The term "impression" was coined by reference to the impressions rings make in wax, with a probable inspiration from the wax simile in Plato's *Theaetetus* 191d-e, though Chrysippus rejected any literal interpretation

---

[55] For my views on this, see Gourinat 2012 and Gourinat 2018b: 131-137. In particular, I will not discuss here the question raised by Sedley 2005 about the possibility that Zeno's definition may have applied to impressions other than sense impressions.
[56] Sextus Emp. *AM* VII 230, 236.
[57] Cic. *Acad.* I 41.
[58] See Striker 1996: 51-57.

of the "impression" in wax.⁵⁹ Yet the metaphor is pursued in the definition of the cognitive impression, since it is "stamped and impressed in accordance with the object", meaning that the cognitive impression reproduces accurately every aspect of the object.⁶⁰ Cicero attributes to Zeno the idea that the cognitive impression has a proper way to "declare" (*propria declaratio*) itself and is identified as such by its own nature (*ipsum per se cerneretur*). Sextus Emp. *AM* VII 252 says similarly that the cognitive impression has some "proper feature" (ἰδίωμα) that distinguishes it from all other impressions, "like the horned snakes in comparison to all the other snakes".

It is difficult to say whether Zeno identified the criterion with the "cognitive impression" (καταληπτικὴ φαντασία) itself or with the "cognition" (κατάληψις), because the only testimony concerning Zeno (that of Cic. *Acad.* I 41) is rather imprecise. Still, it is very likely that Zeno introduced κατάληψις as the criterion, because Cicero's testimony goes in this direction and seems to be confirmed by Sextus: according to him, Arcesilaus criticized the Stoic claim that κατάληψις is the criterion (Sextus Emp. *AM* VII 150-153),⁶¹ and Arcesilaus could only be targeting his contemporary Zeno. Since in any case κατάληψις is an assent to καταληπτικὴ φαντασία – as Sextus Emp. *AM* VII 155 points out – the difference between the two theses is quite meagre. This also applies to the very notion of a criterion of truth: though there is no direct evidence that Zeno used the word, Arcesilaus' polemics against Zeno's identification of the κατάληψις as the criterion of truth seems to prove that he did. In that sense, it would be rather clear that Zeno's agenda was to replace Epicurus' three criteria of truth (sense-perception, preconception, and feelings) by a unique criterion (the cognition) that worked quite differently from Epicurus' criterion, even if the common ground was to rely on the senses, though not trusting them in the same way as Epicurus.

There is no evidence that Zeno mentioned or discussed the *prolepsis*. However, there is an isolated piece of evidence in Cic. *Acad.* I 42 that seems to indicate that Zeno conferred to the *katalepsis* a more complex role than just warranting the truth of an impression, since he would have made it the origin of 'notions' from which knowledge can be constructed. This passage almost immediately follows the passage of § 41 quoted above; it is quoted by von Arnim in the same fr. 60, but it is seldom commented:⁶²

> Inter scientiam et inscientiam comprehensionem illam, quam dixi, collocabat, eamque neque in rectis neque in pravis numerabat, sed soli credendum esse dicebat. E quo sensibus etiam fidem tribuebat, quod, ut supra dixi, comprehensio

---

[59] Diog. Laert. VII 50; Sextus Emp. *AM* VII 229.
[60] Sextus Emp. *AM* VII 249-251.
[61] See also Eusebius, *Prep. Evang.* XIV 6.13 (Numenius fr. 25 Des Places). Numenius says that in return Zeno criticized Plato, probably an allusion to Zeno's attacks on Plato's doctrine of ideas (see Stobaeus, *Eclog.* I 12.3, t. I, p. 136, 21-137, 6 Wachsmuth).
[62] Yet see Alesse 1989: 642, with references to previous discussions.

facta sensibus et vera esse illi et fidelis videbatur, non quod omnia, quae essent in re, comprehenderet, sed quia nihil quod cadere in eam posset relinqueret quodque natura quasi normam scientiae et principium sui dedisset, unde postea notiones rerum in animis imprimerentur, e quibus non principia solum, sed latiores quaedam ad rationem inveniendam viae reperiuntur. (Cic. *Acad.*, I 42)

Between knowledge and ignorance, he placed that "cognitio" I mentioned sooner, and he included it neither among correct nor incorrect impressions, but he said that it was the only one that ought to be believed. As a consequence, he deemed sense-perceptions also to be trustworthy, since, as I said before, he considered that a cognition performed by the senses was true and faithful, not because it could grasp everything that was in the thing itself, but because it did not bypass anything that could fall into that impression, and thus nature had bestowed him with a kind of rule of knowledge and a principle, from which later the notions of things would be impressed into the minds, out of which not only principles, but also some larger paths of discovery of reason would be found.

Cicero's spokesman here, Varro, assigns a highly articulated role to the κατάληψις as a criterion or a rule (canon), and it may explain why and in what sense it is κατάληψις and not καταληπτικὴ φαντασία that is the criterion. Κατάληψις does not only warrant that such and such an impression is trustworthy and therefore must be believed to correctly and precisely represent its object. It is also the case that a κατάληψις is a rule of knowledge, from which notions can be impressed in the mind, and from this, reason can discover new paths and new truths. This often neglected passage is important since, if it is faithful to Zeno's doctrine, then it gives to the Zenonian κατάληψις a more articulated role than is usually believed, and it also means that Zeno had a place in his epistemology for notions and that he considered them as trustworthy, inasmuch as they are derived from κατάληψις. It means that, though Zeno only recognized κατάληψις as a rule or a criterion, he would recognize the importance of notions used as rules or principles in the construction of knowledge and the discovery of truth. What, though, does Cicero translate by *notio*? There are two possibilities: *notio* in Cicero is a translation of *ennoia*,[63] but it is also a translation of *prolepsis*.[64] In the second case, then, Zeno would have fully integrated into his epistemology the Epicurean *prolepsis*, as Chrysippus would do later. If it is not the case, however, and if Cicero's *notio* translates *ennoia*, then it means that Zeno was very much aware of Epicurus' criteria and constructed an alternative but not completely alien system to them, in which cognitive impressions and cognitions played more or less the same criterial role as sense-perceptions (αἰσθήσεις) in Epicurus, while notions (ἔννοιαι) took the place of Epicureans preconceptions (προλήψεις), though not recognized as criteria, but rather as relying on cognitive impressions as criteria.

---

[63] Cic. *Fin.* III 6; *Tusc.* I 24.
[64] Cic. *Top.* 7.

3. THE SECOND AND THIRD GENERATIONS OF STOICS: CLEANTHES AND CHRYSIPPUS

3.1. The second Stoic generation: Cleanthes

Surprisingly enough, no ancient source attributes the κατάληψις to Cleanthes who, from the silence of our sources, does not seem to have shown any interest in his master's criterion. We do know that he commented on Zeno's definition of φαντασία as a τύπωσις, though, and gave a literal exegesis of Zeno's definition that was later criticized by Chrysippus.[65] There is no evidence that Cleanthes ever mentioned the *prolepsis*, but according to Cicero, he discussed at length the formation of the "notions of the gods" (*deorum notiones*),[66] an expression that is likely to translate the Greek ἔννοιαι.[67] Cicero (*De Natura deorum*, I 37) first seems to imply that Cleanthes had a confused vision of the nature of the gods and did not say anything about the way the notion of the gods arises. Cicero implies that Cleanthes derived his views on the gods from Zeno but was not particularly consistent, alternatively saying that the universe is god and that god is the soul of the universe.[68] Now, "in those books that he wrote against hedonism" (*in his libris quos scripsit contra uoluptatem*), says Cicero, he "errs like a madman" (*delirans*) and switches from anthropomorphic views on the gods to the views that they are pure reason or stars. The result is that the "notion" of the god has completely vanished. This judgment, put in the mouth of the Epicurean spokesman of the dialogue, makes a polemical charge against Cleanthes' views, trying to dissolve them by the charge of inconsistency and craziness. What is relevant, however, is that it refers to Cleanthes' book *On pleasure*, a treatise whose existence under this title is well attested[69] but is presented by Cicero as a book *against* pleasure, in other words against Epicurean views. Hence Velleius' aggressivity is probably the sign that Cleanthes, on theological issues, was not particularly well disposed towards Epicurus' views. When it turns to Balbus, the Stoic spokesman of book II, Cleanthes' views on the origins of the notions of the gods are presented with no charge of inconsistency and with more details:

> It is agreed among all nations, for that there are gods is inborn (*innatum*) in all and so to say engraved in the mind (*in animo quasi insculptum*). (13) Opinions vary about what they are like, but nobody denies that they are. Our Cleanthes said that the notions of the gods have been formed in the minds of humans from four causes (*quattuor de causis dixit in animis hominum informatas deorum esse*

---

[65] Diog. Laert. VII 50; Sextus Emp. *AM* VII 228-231.
[66] Cic. *DND* II 13.
[67] As mentioned above, it is explicitly stated by Cic. *Top.* 7; *Fin.* III 6; *Tusc.* I 24.
[68] This is not necessarily contradictory: god is frequently assimilated by the Stoics to the world itself (see, e.g., Diog. Laert. VII 138), but since it is a living being the name can also be applied "in a more differentiated way" (διαφορώτερον) to its soul (VII 139). In the same way, it is customary in Greek philosophy to say that the essence of a human being is either the whole compound of body and soul or their soul.
[69] Diog. Laert. VII 87; VII 175; Clemens Alex., *Strom.* II 22.

notiones). He stated that the first cause was the one I have just mentioned, the one that had arisen from the precognition of future events. The second was what we received from the magnitude of the benefits which we get from the temperateness of climate, the fertility of the earth, and the vast abundance of other advantages. (14) The third was what terrified the mind by lightning, storms, rains, snow, hail, floods, pestilences, earthquakes, and occasionally subterranean rumblings, showers of stones and raindrops the colour of blood, also landslides and chasms suddenly opening the grounds, also unnatural monstrosities human and animal, and also the appearance of meteoric lights and what are called by the Greek "comets"[...] all things through the terror of which human beings have suspected the existence of some divine celestial force. (15) The fourth and main cause was the regularity of the motion, the revolution of the heavens, and the individuality, usefulness, beauty and order of the sun, the moon, and all the stars. The mere sight of these things, he said, was proof enough that they are not products of accident. (Cic. *DND* II 12-15, Long & Sedley translation 54C, modified and completed)

Though Cicero does not formally attribute it to Cleanthes, the first sentence quoted here (from § 12) seems to imply that Cleanthes thought that the notion of the existence of the gods was "innate" (*innatus*) and "so to say engraved in the mind" (*in animo quasi insculptum*). Now, these are the exact terms Cicero has already used in book 1 about Epicurus: "it must necessarily be understood that there are gods, given that we have implanted, or rather innate (*insitas eorum uel potius innatas*), knowledge of them" (§ 44), "nature has also engraved (*natura insculpsit*) in our minds the view of them as everlasting and blessed" (§ 45). Thus, here, either Cicero is just pasting and copying himself, or there was really something in Cleanthes that was borrowed from Epicurus. Both are possible and cannot be decided with certainty. Yet Cleanthes here records four causes that led humankind to the formation of the notions of the gods: (1) divination, (2) the benefits we get from the benevolence of the gods, (3) frightening phenomena, and (4) the order and the regularity of the heavenly motions. As we have seen, the fourth origin of the notion of the gods is similar to one of the two origins that, according to Sextus Emp. *AM* IX 45, Epicurus ascribed to the notion of the existence of the gods, namely, the observation of the world (τὰ κατὰ τὸν κόσμον θεωρούμενα). In chapter I 6 of the *Placita* – titled "from where did human beings obtain a notion of the gods" (πόθεν ἔννοιαν ἔσχον θεῶν ἄνθρωποι), and which is actually a piece of Stoic doxography[70] – one can find a "teaching" (διδαχή) on the gods in seven species that includes the same origin. According to the author of the *Placita*, the first source of the "notion of god" (θεοῦ ἔννοια) is based on the "phenomena and heavenly occurrences" (ἐκ τῶν φαινομένων καὶ μετεώρων): human beings observed the harmony of the heavens, as well as the variety of the seasons and the living beings, and from this they formed a notion of

---

[70] It is sometimes attributed to Posidonius, since the initial definition of the divinity is attributed to him in Stobaeus, *Eclog.* I 11.5c, 133.18-23. On this chapter, see Mansfeld-Runia 2020, vol. 1: 337-369.

divinity.[71] This derivation obviously is equivalent to Epicurus' second origin of the notion of the gods in Sextus Emp. *AM* IX 45 and to the fourth origin of the notion of the gods in Cleanthes.

It is unclear whether the first reason alleged, that of the existence of divination, inducing the idea that the gods are proven to exist since they predict our future, was already mentioned by Zeno,[72] but it is clearly anti-Epicurean. The third source, that of the terrors, does not seem to have been recorded elsewhere as a cause of the belief in the gods for the Stoics, but the second source, though more difficult to identify, seems also to be present in *Placita* I 6. This second source, "the magnitude of the benefits" we get from the land, and the "vast abundance of other advantages" could correspond to the third category in the *Placita*, the "gods who assist", since they are Hera, Zeus, Hermes, and Demeter.[73] It is also possible to identify them in the last class of gods, namely, those human benefactors who have been deified.[74] Such deified benefactors of the human kind were accepted as a "non-implausible" source of faith by the Stoic Persaeus, who borrowed it from Prodicus[75] and Velleius in book 1 of the *De natura deorum* also attributes it polemically to Persaeus, as an erroneous deification of beneficent men.[76] Persaeus in Cicero as well as the *Placita* list among those deified benefactors of the human kind the Dioscuri and Dionysus, while Persaeus adds to the list Demeter, who is precisely listed as one of the deities who give assistance to human beings in the *Placita* I 6, obviously because of the benefits human beings get from agriculture. All this seems to indicate that Cleanthes' second origin for the conception of the gods – the one that derives from the "benefices" and the "advantages" that induce them to deify their benefactors, either nature or human beings – was widely accepted among the Stoics as one of the origins of our notion of the gods. It also suggests that the Stoics were engaged in a polemics with the Epicureans on that issue.

Despite the similarity of approaches that one may observe in Cicero's testimony regarding the fact that, according to him, both Epicurus and Cleanthes maintained that the notion of the gods was "innate" (*innatus*) and "engraved" (*insculptus*), there are remarkable differences, no more explicitly noted by Cicero than this very similarity. It is only in the case of Epicurus that Cicero describes this "notion of the gods" as a preconception. In the case of Cleanthes, it is described as a *notio*, and though it is not formally excluded that *notio* here may translate *prolepsis*, it is more plausible that, if it was the case, Cicero would have marked it by using *anticipatio* as he does in I 43-45, had he meant πρόληψις instead of ἔννοια. This hypothesis

---

[71] [Plutarch], *Plac.* I 6, 880 A-B.
[72] All that we know is that Zeno acknowledged the existence of divination as an expertise (Diog. Laert. VII 149).
[73] [Plutarch], *Plac.* I 6, 880 B.
[74] [Plutarch], *Plac.* I 6, 880 C-D.
[75] Philodemus, *PHerc.* 1428, col. 348-349 in Vassallo 2018: 162-164.
[76] Cic. *DND* I 38.

seems to be confirmed by the fact that in *Placita* I 6, this ἔννοια is described as a teaching (διδαχή), so that it cannot be a *natural* preconception. In addition, only one way of forming this notion is common to Epicurus and Cleanthes: that from the observation of the world's phenomena. Dreams and the extension of the felicity and lifespan of happy human beings are excluded from the modes of concept-formation acknowledged by Cleanthes, as well as the argument of the universality of the notion and the *consensus omnium*, while the recognition that human beings have deified the benefactors of the human race seems to have been criticized by the Epicureans. Therefore it seems quite plausible that Cleanthes was well aware of Epicurus' theory of the preconception of the gods, but that he consciously did not endorse it at face value but modified it and included it as a theory of the origins of the ἔννοια of the gods, which was subsequently developed by later Stoics.

3.2. The third generation: Chrysippus

Evidence of the reintroduction of the *prolepsis* in Stoicism points to Cleanthes' successor at the head of the Stoa, Chrysippus. According to Diog. Laert. VII 54, he had two alternative views about the criterion:

> Κριτήριον δὲ τῆς ἀληθείας φασὶ τυγχάνειν τὴν καταληπτικὴν φαντασίαν, τουτέστι τὴν ἀπὸ ὑπάρχοντος, καθά φησι Χρύσιππος ἐν τῇ β' τῶν Φυσικῶν [...]· ὁ δὲ Χρύσιππος διαφερόμενος πρὸς αὐτὸν ἐν τῷ πρώτῳ Περὶ λόγου κριτήριά φησιν εἶναι αἴσθησιν καὶ πρόληψιν· ἔστι δ' ἡ πρόληψις ἔννοια φυσικὴ τῶν καθόλου. (Diog. Laert. VII 54)

> The criterion of truth they declare to be the cognitive impression, that is that which comes from what is – according to Chrysippus in the second book of his *Physics* [...] while Chrysippus in the first book of his *On Reason* contradicts himself and declares that sense-perception and preconception are the criteria, preconception being a natural notion of universals.

This move is surprising: the first stance follows Zeno, the second reproduces Epicurus. There is no hint that Chrysippus criticized the cognitive impression nor gave it up, but he seems to have completed Zeno's view with Epicurus. To define sense-perception as a criterion may have been not very different in Stoic terms from defining cognition as a criterion since, according to the Stoics, "sense-perception"(αἴσθησις) is both the *pneuma* going from the ruling part of the soul to the senses and a certain kind of cognition[77] consisting in an assent to cognitive sense-perception.[78] Hence, to say that sense-perception was a criterion, though it literally reproduces Epicurus' criterion, may have had the same meaning as saying that a cognition coming from a cognitive sense-perception is a criterion. The brief definition of preconception attributed to Chrysippus by Diog. Laert. VII 54,

---

[77] Diog. Laert. VII 52; [Plutarch], *Plac.* IV 8, 899D.
[78] Cic. *Acad.* I 41; Stobaeus, *Eclog.* I 49, 249.25-26.

"preconception is a natural notion of universals", may be explained by the more comprehensive account of the Stoic doctrine of ἔννοια and πρόληψις given in the *Placita*. The following chapter (IV 12) will be an account of Chrysippus, so there is all likelihood that chapter 11 also represents Chrysippus' views:

> Οἱ Στωικοί φασιν· ὅταν γεννηθῇ ὁ ἄνθρωπος, ἔχει τὸ ἡγεμονικὸν μέρος τῆς ψυχῆς ὥσπερ χαρτίον εὔεργὸν εἰς ἀπογραφήν. Εἰς τοῦτο μίαν ἑκάστην τῶν ἐννοιῶν ἐναπογράφεται. Πρῶτος δὲ [ὁ] τῆς ἀναγραφῆς τρόπος ὁ διὰ τῶν αἰσθήσεων· αἰσθανόμενοι γάρ τινος οἷον λευκοῦ, ἀπελθόντος αὐτοῦ μνήμην ἔχουσιν· ὅταν δ' ὁμοειδεῖς πολλαὶ μνῆμαι γένωνται, τότε φαμὲν ἔχειν ἐμπειρίαν· ἐμπειρία γάρ ἐστι τὸ τῶν ὁμοειδῶν φαντασιῶν πλῆθος. Τῶν δ' ἐννοιῶν αἱ μὲν φυσικῶς γίνονται κατὰ τοὺς εἰρημένους τρόπους καὶ ἀνεπιτεχνήτως, αἱ δ' ἤδη δι' ἡμετέρας διδασκαλίας (C) καὶ ἐπιμελείας· αὗται μὲν οὖν ἔννοιαι καλοῦνται μόνον, ἐκεῖναι δὲ καὶ προλήψεις. Ὁ δὲ λόγος, καθ' ὃν προσαγορευόμεθα λογικοί, ἐκ τῶν προλήψεων συμπληροῦσθαι λέγεται κατὰ τὴν πρώτην ἑβδομάδα. ([Plutarch], *Placita*, IV 11, 900 BC)

When a human being is born, the Stoics say, it has the commanding-part of his soul like a small piece of papyrus ready for writing upon. On this it inscribes each one of its notions. The first method of inscription is through the senses. For by perceiving something, e.g. white, they have a memory of it when it has departed. And when many memories of a similar kind have occurred, we then have experience. For the plurality of similar impressions is experience. Some conceptions arise naturally in the aforesaid way and undesignedly, others through our own instruction and attention. The latter are called "notions" only, the former are called "preconceptions" as well. Reason, for which we are called rational, is said to be completed from our preconceptions during our first seven years. (Long & Sedley, translation slightly modified, 39E)

This passage allows us to understand in which sense the preconception is a natural notion (ἔννοια φυσική): it is natural insofar as it occurs "naturally" (φυσικῶς) without being taught (without a teaching, a διδασκαλία) and even without any attention (ἐπιμελεία) from our part. It turns out to be an exact equivalent of what Cic. *DND* I 43 says about the Epicurean preconception, namely, that it is imprinted by nature without any teaching (*sine doctrina*). Cicero's *doctrina* would perfectly translate διδασκαλία. In addition, the process of inscription of the *prolepsis*, through sense-perception and memory, is similar to the process attributed to Epicurus in Diog. Laert. X 33, if not roughly to the process of acquiring universals in Aristotle's *Posterior Analytics* II 19 as well. Finally, such expressions as "it inscribes (ἐναπογράφεται) each one of its notions" recalls Cicero's description of nature "impressing" (*impressisset*) the notions or "engraving" (*insculpsit*) them in our minds. On the other hand, the definition attributed to Chrysippus in Diog. Laert. VII 54, "a natural notion of universals", is reminiscent of the definition he attributes to Epicurus in X 33 of a "universal stored thought" (καθολικὴ νόησις ἐναποκειμένη). The terms νόησις and ἐναποκειμένη are not found in the description of the preconception in the *Placita* nor in Diog. Laert. VII 54, but they may be found in a definition of the *ennoia* attributed to the Stoics by Plutarch:

τὰς ἐννοίας <ἐν>αποκειμένας τινὰς ὁριζόμενοι νοήσεις, μνήμας δὲ μονίμους καὶ σχετικὰς τυπώσεις. (Plutarch, *Not. Comm.* 47, 1085 A-B)

[The Stoics] define notions as some stored thoughts, and memories as abiding and stable impressions.

With the omission of "universal", this definition of the *ennoia* reproduces the terms of the Epicurean definition of the *prolepsis*. Therefore, if one adds that it is a universal, then one has the Epicurean definition of the *prolepsis*. In other words, Epicurean and Stoic accounts of the *ennoia* as a "stored thought" and of *prolepsis* as a "universal stored thought" seem literally equivalent.

To sum up, the similarities between Epicurus and Chrysippus are the following:
- A *prolepsis* is a stored (ἐναποκειμένη) notion.
- It comes from the sense-perception that "comes first".[79]
- Memory, then, is formed from similar impressions from sense-perceptions, and a *prolepsis* is formed from this.
- A *prolepsis* is a universal thought (a καθολικὴ νόησις according to Epicurus, a ἔννοια φυσικὴ τῶν καθόλου in the words of Chrysippus).
- It is "engraved" in our minds by nature, or it is natural (φυσική), and it is in some sense "innate" (*insita uel potius innata* according to Cicero in Epicurus, while the expression ἔμφυτος πρόληψις occurs in Stoic sources).[80]
- It does not come from teaching (*doctrina* or *didaskalia*).
- When one has an actual sense-perception, one relates it to preconceptions. The example given by Diog. Laert. X 33 – "Is what is standing over there a horse or a cow?" – is echoed in Stoicism when Diog. Laert. VII 42 says that "things are grasped through notions" (διὰ τῶν ἐννοιῶν τὰ πράγματα λαμβάνεται). Probably it may be illustrated by the example given by Cic. *Acad.* II 21: "this is a horse, this is a dog": it seems to illustrate the kind of thing we grasp with the mind, not with senses. As mentioned above, this usage of preception may have its source in Plato's book simile in the *Philebus*.
- In a *prolepsis*, we have some sense of what the object is. Parallel examples are given by Diog. Laert. X 33 concerning Epicurus ("such and such a kind of thing is a human being") and by Cic. *Acad.* II 21 concerning the Stoics: ""if this is a human being, this is rational animal": the notions of things

---

[79] Προηγουμένων τῶν αἰσθήσεων, according to Diog. Laert. X 33 to compare with Diog. Laert. VII 49 (προηγεῖται ἡ φαντασία).
[80] In Plutarch, *Stoic. Repug.*, 17, 1041 E while ἔμφυτος ἔννοια appears in Epictetus, *Diss.* II 11.5 and in Plutarch, fr. 215f.

(*notitiae rerum*) are engraved in us (*nobis imprimuntur*) from this kind of impression."

Like the Epicureans, Chrysippus seems to have admitted that these preconceptions are common to all humans and for that reason they constitute "excellent criteria of truth". This is what Alexander says about our 'common notions' of mixture:

> He tries to support the existence of these different mixtures through the common conceptions (διὰ τῶν κοινῶν ἐννοιῶν), and says that we take these from nature as excellent criteria of truth (μάλιστα δὲ κριτήρια τῆς ἀληθείας φησὶν ἡμᾶς παρὰ τῆς φύσεως λαβόντας): we certainly have one impression (ἄλλην γοῦν φαντασίαν) from the bodies composed by joining, and a different one for those that are fused and destroyed together, and another for those that are blended and mutually coextended through and through so that they each preserve their own nature; we would not have these different impressions (ἣν διαφορὰν φαντασιῶν οὐκ ἂν εἴχομεν) if all things, however they were mixed, lay side by side one another by joining. (Alexander of Aphrodisias, *De mixtione* 3, p. 217, 2-9 Bruns, Long & Sedley translation, 48C).

What Alexander illustrates here is that our common conceptions[81] are based on our sense-perceptions, and we form naturally discriminating notions of the various kinds of mixture because we have different impressions of them: we have those different impressions because the objects that imprint our minds are different, and these differentiated impressions in turn produce differentiated conceptions that are common to all humans.

Some aspects of the preconceptions are not recorded for both schools. For one thing, there is no hint that *prolepsis* plays a role in language in Chrysippus or that a *prolepsis* underlies each name, as it is the case in Epicurus when he says, according to Diog. Laert. X 33, that "as soon as 'human being' is uttered, immediately its delineation also comes to mind by means of preconception". On the other hand, Chrysippus defined reason as an "aggregate (ἄθροισμα) of notions and preconceptions",[82] and there is no hint that Epicurus said something in any way similar. This definition is echoed in the *Placita* passage quoted above when the author says that reason is completed at seven years old from notions. Since "aggregate" (ἄθροισμα) was a technical term of atomism, the use of the term "aggregate" (ἄθροισμα) by Chrysippus in that context may have been discretely polemical or even slightly ironical. In any case, Chrysippus presumably meant something literal here: reason is physically constituted in the soul by an accretion of stored notions.

---

[81] For a defence of the identity of 'common conceptions' and preconceptions, see Dyson 2009.
[82] Galen, *PHP* V 3, p. 304, 34-35 De Lacy: ἐννοιῶν τέ τινων καὶ προλήψεων ἄθροισμα.

4. A COMMON CHALLENGE TO INNATISM?

Preconceptions played similar roles in the epistemology of both schools. For both schools, the *prolepsis* is a criterion. For Epicurus, preconception is an additional criterion to sense-perception; for Chrysippus, it is an additional criterion to cognitive sense-perception. Thus, it does not work exactly in the same way in both schools. All sense-perceptions are true according to Epicurus, and therefore they are the criteria by which we know that something is the case. From these, we form preconceptions, whose causal history – since they are constituted from those true sense-perceptions – warrants their reliability. Zeno disagreed with Epicurus that all sense-perceptions were true, and he separated the true and reliable ones, namely, the 'cognitive' ones from the non-cognitive. He seemed to have admitted similarly to Epicurus that from true sense-perceptions some conceptions were formed, and this view was endorsed later by Cleanthes. Yet it seems to have been only Chrysippus who reintroduced the preconceptions as notions naturally formed from reliable impressions as a criterion, parallel to cognitive impressions.

In both schools, preconception is also a preliminary tool for research, discussion and intelligence, as explicitly said for Epicurus by Diog. Laert. X 33 and Cic. *DND* I 43.[83] Similar views are attributed to the Stoics by Cicero in *Acad.* II 21 and *Acad.* I 42, which was seen as a parallel answer to what was coined as the *Meno* problem:

> That the problem advanced in the *Meno*, namely whether search and discovery are possible (εἰ οἷόν τε ζητεῖν καὶ εὑρίσκειν), leads to a real impasse. For we do not, on the one hand, try to find out things we know –a futile proceeding– nor, on the other, things we do not know, since even if we come across them we do not recognize them: they might be anything. The Peripatetics introduced the conception of "potential intuition" but the origin of our difficulty was actual knowing and not knowing. Even if we grant the existence of a potential intuition, the difficulty remains unchanged. How does this intuition operate? It must be either on what it knows or on what it does not know. The Stoics make the "natural conceptions" responsible (οἱ δὲ ἀπὸ τῆς Στοᾶς τὰς φυσικὰς ἐννοίας αἰτιῶνται). If these are potential, we shall use the same argument as against the Peripatetics; and if they are actual, why do we search for what we know? And if we use them as a starting-point for a search for other things that we do not know, how do we search for what we do not know? The Epicureans introduce "preconceptions"(οἱ δὲ Ἐπικούρειοι τὰς προλήψεις); if they mean these to be "articulated" (διηρθρωμένας), search is unnecessary; if "unarticulated"(ἀδιαρθρώτους), how do we extend our search beyond our preconceptions, to look for something of which we do not possess a preconception? (Plutarch, fr. 215f Sandbach = *Extracts from the Chaeronean*)

---

[83] See also Sextus Emp. *AM* I 57 and XI 21: "according to the wise Epicurus, it is not possible to inquire (ζητεῖν) nor to come to an impasse (ἀπορεῖν) without a preconception".

So Epicureans and Stoics seem to have resorted to "natural conceptions" or "preconceptions" as a solution to the *Meno* problem,[84] alternative to the Platonic doctrine of the reminiscence, and even to the actualization of potential knowledge in the Peripatetic school. Zeno's criticism of Plato's theory of ideas was famous,[85] and he could hardly have adopted one of its corollaries: recollection. It is striking that both Epicurus and the Stoics seem to have borrowed something from some empiricist passages of Plato: the wax analogy in the *Theaetetus* in the case of the Stoics and the book simile in the *Philebus* in the case of the Epicureans. In the *Theatetus*, however, Plato explicitly argues that the wax simile is not a sufficient explanation, since these empiricist views cannot explain intellectual errors, especially in the case of mathematics. Thus, the Hellenistic philosophers needed to account for the origins of our knowledge in cases where empirical concept-formation was not a sufficient explanation. According to Plutarch, Chrysippus as well as Epicurus also needed to explain what we start from, when we want to pursue an enquiry: without a preconception of something, we cannot search for it since we would not even know what we are looking for.

At first sight, this reasoning seems to contradict the criterial value of the preconception: if a preconception is a start for an investigation, then it seems to mean that we do not know yet what the thing is, and then it cannot be used as a criterion. However, what underlies Plutarch's argument seems to suggest how it is possible. For Plutarch says that when the Epicureans introduce the preconception, they do not say whether they mean "articulated" (διηρθρωμένας) or "unarticulated" (ἀδιαρθρώτους) preconceptions. This argument suggests that this is a distinction the Epicureans do not make,[86] but that, if a preconception is articulated, then we do not need any further investigation; whereas if a preconception is not articulated, then we do not completely possess a notion of the thing, and we do not know what to search for. This distinction suggests two kinds or two levels of preconceptions. Actually, it seems to have been practised by the Stoics more than by the Epicureans. An "articulation of ethical notions" is mentioned as a section of the catalogue of Chrysippus' works by Diog. Laert. VII 199, and from Epictetus (II 17.7-22) we may guess that it was a common practice in Stoic epistemology to 'articulate' our preconceptions, namely to develop them from a quite general stage to a more precise content. The titles of the section of the catalogue of Chrysippus' work suggests that 'articulating' notions consists in giving definitions of ethical notions, along

---

[84] See Alesse 1989 for a detailed analysis of the treatment of the *Meno* problem by the Epicureans and the Stoics.

[85] Stobaeus, *Eclog.* I 12.3, t. I, p. 136, 21-137, 6 Wachsmuth.

[86] I retract here what I wrote in Gourinat 2018: 142, following Alesse 1989: 643. I do not believe any more that what Plutarch says here implies that the "articulation of the preconceptions" is of Epicurean origin, but rather that such articulation was missing in Epicurus and his followers.

with practising divisions and distinctions. Plutarch confirms that this practice was largely developed by Chrysippus who, according to him,

> had entirely eliminated the confusion about preconceptions and notions both by articulating each one of them and by assigning each of them to its proper place. (Plutarch, *Comm. Not.* 1, 1059B-C)

Plutarch here suggests that Chrysippus largely developed the process of internal articulation of preconceptions and notions and connected this process to a structuration of notions by *diairesis*.[87] Hence, it must have been similar to what Plato called a division "according to natural articulations".[88] It seems likely that this process of articulation of the preconceptions was more or less directly in debt to Plato, something which Epicurus had not introduced in the context of preconceptions. One can see how an articulated or an unarticulated notion makes a difference. When one has an unarticulated preconception, then it may be a start for enquiry, since a preconception just gives an outline, a general concept, and is not yet fully articulated. Epictetus suggests that we may have a correct preconception, but if we have not sufficiently articulated it, then we may erroneously apply it to particular cases.[89] In other words, a preconception is a criterion of truth, but it may be erroneously applied to particular cases if it is not correctly articulated. That a preconception may be incorrectly developed and filled in by false suppositions is something that was already suggested by Epicurus:

> Πρῶτον μὲν τὸν θεὸν ζῷον ἄφθαρτον καὶ μακάριον νομίζων, ὡς ἡ κοινὴ τοῦ θεοῦ νόησις ὑπεγράφη, μηθὲν μήτε τῆς ἀφθαρσίας ἀλλότριον μήτε τῆς μακαριότητος ἀνοίκειον αὐτῷ πρόσαπτε· πᾶν δὲ τὸ φυλάττειν αὐτοῦ δυνάμενον τὴν μετὰ ἀφθαρσίας μακαριότητα περὶ αὐτὸν δόξαζε. θεοὶ μὲν γὰρ εἰσίν· ἐναργὴς γὰρ αὐτῶν ἐστιν ἡ γνῶσις· οἵους δ᾽ αὐτοὺς <οἱ> πολλοὶ νομίζουσιν, οὐκ εἰσίν· τῶν πολλῶν θεοὺς ἀναιρῶν, ἀλλ᾽ ὁ τὰς τῶν πολλῶν δόξας θεοῖς προσάπτων. (124) οὐ γὰρ προλήψεις εἰσὶν ἀλλ᾽ ὑπολήψεις ψευδεῖς αἱ τῶν πολλῶν ὑπὲρ θεῶν ἀποφάσεις. (Epicur. *Men.* 123-124)

> First, think of god as an imperishable and blessed living being, as the common thought of god is in outline, and attach to him nothing alien to imperishability or inappropriate to blessedness, but believe about him anything that can preserve his combination of blessedness and imperishability. For there are gods: the knowledge of them is evident. But they are not what the multitude believes them to be. For they do not preserve them by believing they are what they think they are. The impious man is not he who denies the gods of the many, but he who attaches to the gods the

---

[87] On such a process, see Gourinat 2021a. I follow Babut's suggestion here in Babut-Casevitz 2002: 126-127 n. 20 that what is at stake here is not the distinction and articulation between notions and preconceptions, "since Plutarch does not distinguish between them" but the very process of articulating notions and conceptions.
[88] Plato, *Phaedr.* 265e. For a suggestion along these lines, see Gourinat 2021a: 48-50.
[89] For the articulation in Epictetus, see Collette-Dučić 2020.

beliefs of the many about them. For the assertions of the many about the gods are not preconceptions but false suppositions.

Epicurus, in § 123, describes the "common thought of god" (ἡ κοινὴ τοῦ θεοῦ νόησις) as "outlined" (ὑπεγράφη), and in § 124 he obviously identifies this with a "preconception". This is in accordance with his definition of a "preconception" as "universal thought" (καθολικὴ νόησις) and as "sketch" (τύπος) in Diog. Laert. X 33. He contrasts this "preconception" with the "false suppositions" (ὑπολήψεις ψευδεῖς) of the multitude about the gods. These false suppositions are later additions to the original preconceptions of the gods; they are presumably the anthropomorphic tales that induce people to fear and superstition.[90] In addition, these false suppositions may be formed as the result of teaching and religious indoctrination (*doctrina*), hence they are not "natural notions". Still, by Epicurus own standards, where does the preconception of the gods end, and when do the false presuppositions start? According to what Epicurus says here, the "true thought" about the gods is that they are imperishable and blessed. Yet these traits are precisely the ones Cicero attaches to the preconception of the gods in the *De natura deorum*. However, from Sextus we learn that such notions about the gods were derived by "transition from humans", by enlarging the happiness of human beings to the extreme and their lifespan to eternity. Are these preconceptions or false presuppositions? Similarly, how could Epicurus consistently believe that a "preconception" of the gods derived from dreams and from the observation of the universe – from which one usually derives the supposition that it is the product of a benevolent god – be something else than a "false supposition" on Epicurus' own account?

The preconception of the gods appears as a true challenge to Epicurus' views on preconceptions as a criterion for the simple reason that such preconceptions were not formed in the same straightforward way as the preconceptions of a human being, a horse, or a cow, namely, by repeated sense-perceptions, memory, and imprint in the mind of a certain sketch. It seems highly plausible that the Epicureans had answers to these quibbles, but it is also highly plausible that the Stoics were not satisfied by these answers. According to them, even if we have notions of the gods, we do not apprehend the gods by a *prolepsis*, but by a demonstration.

Ἡ κατάληψις γίνεται κατ' αὐτοὺς αἰσθήσει μὲν λευκῶν καὶ μελάνων καὶ τραχέων καὶ λείων, λόγῳ δὲ τῶν δι' ἀποδείξεως συναγομένων, ὥσπερ τὸ θεοὺς εἶναι, καὶ προνοεῖν τούτους (Diog. Laert. VII 52)

According to them, cognition of white and black things, of rough and smooth things, occurs through sense-perception, while the cognition of the conclusions of a demonstration, for instance that the gods exist and that they are provident, occurs through reason.

---

[90] See Lucret. I 50-145, III 978-1023.

In *Placita*, IV 11, 900 B (quoted above), whiteness is a typical example of the kind of thing we have a sense-perception of and from which a preconception is imprinted in our minds. We have cognitive perceptions of black and white, and from this perception, we form a preconception of black and white. The existence and providence of the gods is also something of which we may have a cognition, but this cognition cannot come from a sense impression and must be concluded from an argument. What immediately follows in Diogenes Laertius is a description of the various modes of concept formation. Thus, in § 52-53, Diogenes Laertius successively reviews the two criteria, cognition and preconception, or at least what preconception is a species of, namely, concepts. This list obviously integrates and expands the fourfold scheme of concept-formation first introduced by Epicurus, according to Diog. Laert. X 32: encounter, analogy, similarity, and composition.[91] Yet the gods do not appear in the examples he gives:

> Among the products of our thought (τῶν γὰρ νοουμένων), some are thought by direct encounter (τὰ μὲν κατὰ περίπτωσιν ἐνοήθη), some by resemblance (καθ' ὁμοιότητα), some by analogy (κατ' ἀναλογίαν), <some by transposition>, some by composition (κατὰ σύνθεσιν), and some by contrariety. (53) By direct encounter we think sensible things; by resemblance things similar to something before us, as Socrates from his portrait; while by analogy, either by way of enlargement, we conceive Tityos or the Cyclops, or by way of diminution, the Pygmy. And thus, too, the centre of the earth was originally conceived by analogy with smaller spheres. Eyes on the chest are thought by transposition, while the centaur is thought by composition, and death by contrariety. Furthermore, some things are conceived by a transition (κατὰ μετάβασίν) like space and sayables. Something just and good is thought naturally (φυσικῶς δὲ νοεῖται δίκαιόν τι καὶ ἀγαθόν). A man without hands is thought by privation. (Diog. Laert. VII 52-53)

Thus the Epicurean "analogy by enlargement" is preserved by the Stoics – even including the standard example of the Cyclops – but it is not applied to the notion of the gods. By contrast, we know from Cicero and Seneca[92] that the Stoics retained analogy as the mode of formation of the notion of the good:

> (33) Since the notions of things arise in souls (*cumque rerum notiones in animis fiant*), if something is known (*cognitum*) either by direct encounter (*usu*), or by composition (*coniunctione*), or by resemblance (*similitudine*), or by comparison of relation (*collatione rationis*), then it is by the fourth operation, which I have last mentioned, that we arrive at the notion of the good (*ad notionem boni pervenit*). For when the soul rises by comparison of relation from those things which are in

---

[91] Note here that even if the account of concept formation in Epicurus and the Stoics has some similarities with Aristotle's views in the *APo* and with Plato's views in the *Philebus*, the fact that the Stoics took over and expanded the Epicurean fourfold classification shows clearly that the Stoics here depend on Epicurus, and not only on Plato and Aristotle.
[92] Seneca, *Ep.* 120, 4-5.

accordance with nature, it arrives at the notion of the good (*cum enim ab iis rebus, quae sunt secundum naturam, ascendit animus collatione rationis, tum ad notionem boni pervenit*). (34) However, this good itself it is not by addition, nor by increase, nor by comparison with everything else (*non accessione neque crescendo aut cum ceteris comparando*), but it is by its own force (*propria vi sua*) that we feel it and call it "good" For just as honey, though sweeter than all the rest, is felt to be sweet by its own kind of flavour and not by comparison with other things, so this good we are talking about must be esteemed far superior to all the rest, but this value is worth by its own kind, and not by a magnitude. For since the value which we call *axia* is counted neither among goods nor among evils, we can add to it whatever we like, it will remain in its own kind. Hence different is the value of virtue, that gets its value from its own kind, not by increase (*quae genere, non crescendo valet*). (Cic. *De Finibus* III 33-34).

Here again, we find the Epicurean distinction between the four kinds of concept formation, without the extra modes we find in Diogenes Laertius. Still, it is striking that Cicero rejects the idea that it is by "increasing" our notion of what is in accordance with nature that we conceive the good. He thus rejects one of the two standard forms of the formation of a notion by analogy, the one that proceeds by enlargement, as in the case of the formation of the notion of a Cyclops by increasing the size of the ordinary man. The reason for rejecting that the good is an enlargement of what is in accordance with nature is obvious: one must not think that the true good (i.e., virtue) is of the same kind as that which is in accordance with nature, and this is what Cicero explicitly says, namely, that virtue has its proper value. Cicero thus seems to be aiming at a non-quantitative analogy: good is not a superior quantity of the preferables, but it is analogous to them. Seneca goes in the same direction as Cicero, and he explains even more clearly than Cicero that the good is known through a kind of qualitative analogy, not a quantitative one:

> Now I return to the question you wanted to be discussed, how the first conception (*prima notitia*) of the good and the honest reaches us. Nature could not teach us this (*hoc nos natura docere non potuit*), it has given us seeds of knowledge (*semina scientiae*), not knowledge. Some claim that it fell into our conception (*nos in notitiam incidisse*), but this is unbelievable that some appearance of virtue could have met us by accident (*casu occucurrisse*). It seems to us that it is the observation and the mutual comparison of repeated actions which has induced this conception and they judge that the honest and the good are understood through analogy (*per analogiam intellectum*). [...] (5) I must say what is "analogy" We know bodily health. From this we know that there also exists one of the mind. We know bodily strength. From this we know that there also exists one of the mind. (Seneca, *Ep.* 120, 4-5 = LS 60E)

The first sentence of the passage clearly recalls the opposition between a notion conceived by "encounter" (περίπτωσις), which Seneca translates more faithfully by *incidisse* and *casu occucurisse* than Cicero by *usus*, while *notitia* replaces the term *notio* used by Cicero. These two points suffice to establish that Seneca does not only depend on Cicero but that he relies on Greek sources. Like Cicero, Seneca finds it necessary to explain in what sense there is an analogy. Contrary to Cicero, he does not mention the four kinds of notion formations. Yet he seems to have implicitly in mind the usual conception of analogy, since he feels the need to explain what this analogy consists of. It is precisely he who, better than Cicero, explains why there is an analogy. According to him, the health and strength of the soul are analogous to the health and strength of the body. In other words, if we put together the explanations of Cicero and Seneca, we understand that there is an analogous identity between what has value for the body – in Stoic terms the "preferables" like health, strength, and all that contributes to the preservation of the body – and that which has value for the soul, that is, good and virtue: good is to the soul what health is to the body. However, though there is an analogy between bodily health and psychic health, there is no common measure between them, and the analogy is not quantifiable. There is no common measure between the preferable and the good, since it has an unreachable or unsurpassed value (ἀνυπέρβλητος).[93] Diog. Laert. VII 53 maintains allusively that the good "is thought naturally (φυσικῶς)". This qualification obviously alludes to the Stoic distinction between technical notions and "natural" notions (i.e., preconceptions). The Stoic process of "appropriation" (οἰκείωσις) described by Cicero at the beginning of book III of the *De finibus* – long before he discusses the formation of the notion of the good – shows clearly that this notion of good does not appear at birth, but that "appropriation" paves the way. Appropriation is an impulse to search for things in conformity with nature. The impulse develops over the years through a slow transition from animal impulses to a rational concept of the good (§ 19-21). When human beings grasp the harmony and the order of their actions in accordance with nature, then they get a concept of goodness and value it more than the preferables (§ 21). It is a long process. Such views are echoed in Seneca, when he says that "nature could not teach us" the notion of the good, but has given us "seeds of knowledge, not knowledge".[94] Thus the notion of the good is not 'inborn' in the sense that we already have it at birth, but in the sense that we have innate dispositions for knowledge and virtue. This means that our 'innate' or 'inborn' notions or preconceptions[95] are not notions we have at birth but notions we naturally form.[96]

---

[93] Stobaeus *Eclog.* II 7, p. 100.18
[94] Compare with ἀφορμὰς ἐκ φύσεως in Stobaeus, *Eclog.* II 7, p. 65.8. On the role of these innate tendencies, see Scott 1988: 142-146, and more generally on the link between appropriation and preconception of the good, see Jackson-McCabe 2004: 334-336 and Scott 1988: 141-142
[95] For ἔμφυτος πρόληψις, see Plutarch, *Stoic. Repugn.* 17, 1041E.
[96] The problem of the meaning of ἔμφυτος and *innatus* is similar concerning Epicureans and concerning the Stoics. Sedley 2011: 31 confronts Epicurus' views on the "implanted, or rather innate, knowledge" that are our preconceptions of the gods in Cic. *DND* I 44 to a similar passage in *de Finibus* IV 4 where all the old disciples of Plato, Speusippus, Aristotle and their pupils but also Zeno held that

The Stoics' resistance to the use of the analogy by enlargement in conceiving the good seems to indicate that they had changed the kind of confidence they wanted to put into the preconceptions.

If we arrive at the notion of the blessedness of the gods by enlarging the notion of human happiness and at the notion of their eternity by expanding the time span of human life without any limit – although this process is natural in the sense that we naturally do so (we naturally aspire to an everlasting life, for instance), it is not 'natural' in the sense that we do not perceive such blessedness or such eternal life in the same way as we perceive a human being, a horse, or a dog. Now, precisely, what is clear with the way our notions of the gods are constituted by enlargement is that they cannot warrant the reliability of such a notion of the gods as entities existing outside our minds – quite the contrary, it rather indicates that such a notion is a creation of the human mind. This process seems to support what Sedley 2011: 29 calls the "idealist" interpretation of Epicurus' theology, that is, that Epicurean gods are "our own graphic idealization of the life to which we aspire". It may not have been the case,[97] but it seems plausible that the Stoics interpreted such Epicurean genealogies of the concept of god as supporting the view that Epicurus did not believe in the existence of the gods (as the Stoics conceived them), but endorsed the view that they are figments of the human mind.[98] The consequence may have well been that they stepped aside from Epicurus' views on the *prolepsis* of the gods and refused to endorse analogy by enlargement as an acceptable process of formation of our preconceptions.

In ethics, the Stoics backed up the *prolepsis* by "natural seeds of virtues" – in other words, natural impulses towards harmony and goodness. It means that *they did not insist so much on inborn concepts, as they did on natural impulses and tendencies*. And even if they admitted that the notion of the good could be conceived through an analogy with the health and strength of the body, they insisted that it could not be a quantitative analogy: the Stoics presumably deemed that expanding a quantity – as the Epicureans did with the blessedness and the lifespan of human beings – was not a correct way to form a concept, since such a process was rather artificial. A preconception could only be trusted if it derived from the encounter (περίπτωσις) of something that exists (ἀπὸ ὑπάρχοντος), thus from a cognitive impression (καταληπτικὴ φαντασία). Furthermore, to be correctly applied, it needed to be correctly articulated. Hence it seems that when Chrysippus borrowed from

---

we have "a certain implanted, or rather innate, desire for knowledge (*insitam vel potius innatam cupiditatem scientiae*) and have been born for human society and for the fellowship and communality of mankind". On the problem of 'innateness' in Epictetus, see now Flamigni 2020. For more detailed views on analogy in Stoicism in relation with the Epicurean doctrine of concept-formation, see Gourinat 2021b.

[97] Other views may be advocated, in line with the way Tsouna 2016: 174-185 interprets *N. D.* I 43-45 or in line with Konstan 2011. What I mean here is that it was probably not the way the Stoics interpreted Epicurus' views and that their views were an important part of their position regarding the *prolepsis*.

[98] On the Stoic charge of atheism against Epicurus, see Cic. *DND* I 123.

Epicurus preconception as a criterion of truth, he did not do it without cautiously modifying it and harmonizing it with the Zenonian criterion, the famous *katalepsis*. And this, all things considered, should not come as a surprise.

REFERENCES

Alesse, F., 1989, "La dottrina delle προλήψεις nello stoicismo antico", *Rivista di Storia della Filosofia* 44: 629-645.

Angeli, A., 1993, "Frammenti di lettere di Epicuro nei papiri d'Ercolano", *Cronache Ercolanesi* 23: 11-27.

Babut, D., – Casevitz, M., 2004, Plutarque, *Œuvres morales*, XV, 1, texte établi par M. Casevitz, traduit et commenté par D. Babut, Paris: Les Belles Lettres.

Barnes, J., 1993, Aristotle, *Posterior Analytics*, translated with a commentary by J. Barnes, 2nd ed., Oxford: Clarendon Press.

Dyson, H., 2009, *Prolepsis and Ennoia in the Early Stoa*, Berlin: De Gruyter.

Flamigni, G., 2020, "Sull' innatismo di Epitteto. Una nuova interpretazione di Diss. II 11.1.6", *Méthexis* 32: 218-239.

Goldschmidt, V., 1978/2006, "Remarques sur l'origine épicurienne de la 'prénotion'", in J. Brunschwig (ed.), *Les Stoïciens et leur logique*, Paris: Vrin, 1978: 155-169 (2nd ed. 2006: 41-60).

Collette-Dučić, B., 2020, "Division et articulation chez Épictète et Marc Aurèle", in S. Delcomminette – R. Van Daële (eds.), *La méthode de division de Platon à Érigène*, Paris: Vrin: 85-104.

Goulet, R., 2000, "Épicure de Samos" E 36, in R. Goulet (ed.), *Dictionnaire des philosophes antiques*, t. III, Paris: CNRS-Éditions: 154-181.

Gourinat, J.-B., 2000, *La dialectique des stoïciens*, Paris: Vrin.

Gourinat, J.-B., 2005, "L'origine des pensées: un bien commun des épicuriens et des stoïciens", in E. Végléris (éd.), *Cosmos et psychè. Mélanges offerts à Jean Frère*, Hildesheim-Zürich-New York: Olms: 271-291.

Gourinat, J.-B., 2012, "Les polémiques sur la perception entre stoïciens et académiciens", *Philosophie antique* 12: 43-88.

Gourinat, J.-B., 2018a, "Zénon de Citium" Z 20, in R. Goulet (ed.), *Dictionnaire des philosophes antiques*, t. VII, Paris: CNRS-Éditions: 364-396.

Gourinat, J.-B., 2018b, "L'épistémologie stoïcienne", *Lexicon Philosophicum*, special issue 2018: 123-144.

Gourinat, J.-B., 2021a, "La division dans l'ancien stoïcisme et ses applications éthiques", in S. Delcomminette – R. Van Daële (éds.), *La méthode de division de Platon à Érigène*, Paris: Vrin: 59-83.

Gourinat, J.-B., 2021b, "Les notions conçues par analogie dans le stoïcisme et leur enjeu épistémologique et éthique", *Analogia* 1: 201-226.

Hadot, I., 2014, "Getting to goodness ou par quels moyens les stoïciens pensent-ils pouvoir devenir vertueux", in *Sénèque. Direction spirituelle et pratique de la philosophie*, Paris: Vrin: 373-414.

Ioppolo, A. M., 1980, *Aristone di Chio e lo Stoicismo antico*, Naples: Bibliopolis.

Jackson-McCabe, M., 2004, "The Stoic theory of implanted preconceptions", *Phronesis* 49: 323-347.

Kechagia, E., 2010, "Rethinking a professional rivalry: Early Epicureans against the Stoa", *The Classical Quarterly* 60: 123-155.

Konstan, D., 2011, "Epicurus on the gods", in J. Fish – K.R. Sanders (eds.), *Epicurus and the Epicurean Tradition*, Cambridge: Cambridge University Press: 53-71.

Long, A. A. & Sedley, D. N., 1987, *The Hellenistic Philosophers*, Cambridge: Cambridge University Press.

Long, A. A., 2006, "Zeno's epistemology and Plato's *Theaetetus*", in *From Epicurus to Epictetus*, Oxford: Oxford University Press: 223-235 [reprinted from *The Philosophy of Zeno*, T. Scaltsas – A.S. Mason (eds.), Larnaca: The Municipality of Larnaca and the Pierides Foundation, 2002: 113-131].

Mansfeld, J., Runia, D., 2020, *Aëtiana V. An edition and Reconstruction Text of the* Placita *with a Commentary and Collection of Related Texts*, Leiden: Brill.

Morel, P.-M., 2008, "Method and evidence: on Epicurean preconception", *Proceedings of the Boston Area Colloquium in Ancient Philosophy* 23, Leiden: Brill: 25-48.

Robitzsch, J. M., 2022, "Epicurean feelings (*pathe*) as criteria", *Archiv für Geschichte der Philosophie* 79: 1-22.

Sedley, D., 2005, "La définition de la *phantasia kataléptikê* par Zénon", in J.-B. Gourinat – G. Romeyer Dherbey (eds.), *Les stoïciens*, Paris: Vrin: 75-92.

Sedley, D., 2011, "Epicurus' theological innatism", in J. Fish – K.R. Sanders (eds.), *Epicurus and the Epicurean Tradition*, Cambridge: Cambridge University Press: 29-52.

Scott, D., 1988, "Innatism and the Stoa", *Proceedings of the Cambridge Philological Society* 30: 123-153.

Striker, G., 1996, Κριτήριον τῆς ἀληθείας (chap. 2), in *Essays on Hellenistic Epistemology and Ethics*, Cambridge: Cambridge University Press: 22-76.

Togni, P., 2013, "Plato's soul-book simile and Zeno's epistemology", *Methexis* 26: 163-185.

Tsouna, V., 2016, "Epicurean preconceptions", *Phronesis* 61: 160-221.

Vassallo, C., 2018, "Persaeus on Prodicus on the Gods' Existence and Nature", *Philosophie Antique* 18: 153-168.

Verde, F., 2016a, "Epicuro nella testimonianze di Cicerone", in *Testo e forme del testo. Ricerche di filologia filosofica*, a cura di M. Tulli, Pisa-Rome: Fabrizio Serra editore: 335-368.

Verde, F., 2016b, "Aristotle and the Garden", in A. Falcone (ed.), *Brill's Companion to the Reception of Aristotle in Antiquity*, Leiden: Brill: 35-55.

Verde, F., 2018, "Ancora sullo statuto veritativo della sensazione in Epicuro", *Lexicon Philosophicum*, special issue: 79-104.

SCIENCE, ETHICS, AND ἀνάγκη IN EPICUREAN THOUGHT

Phillip Mitsis

Shortly after the Second Word War, Carlo Diano – one of the greatest Epicurean scholars of the twentieth century[1] – produced a notable work of philosophy that examined the relation between forms and 'events' in Greek thought beginning with Homer.[2] It was not an exercise in pure scholarship, however, but in some sense an attempt to diagnose what he took to be a European intellectual and cultural crisis. Early reactions to his larger claims tended to be somewhat muted,[3] but for our present purposes it will be helpful to focus on a more limited aspect of his argument since it can serve as an introduction to the problem addressed in this paper. While examining Stoic treatments of the Aristotelian syllogism, Diano emphasized that they were nominalists who took forms or universals to be unreal, thus removing any stable elements from what they deemed to be an ever-changing universe. General terms, concepts, etc. – i.e., "forms" – were, for them, mere specifications of events or processes, since the providential material *logos* holding the events of the world together was itself, on their view, inherently in motion. Accordingly, this immanent Stoic deity or *logos*, was "not a mind that sees" but "a reason that continually keeps moving". By way of contrast, Aristotle and Epicurus – both of whom Diano thinks are of one mind on this score – defend a more static and stable structure for the world; they construct reality in terms of form or substance, and they consequently recognize eternal unchanging laws of nature. So, for instance, Diano contrasts Epicurus with his atomistic predecessors in the following way regarding the notion of chance in atomism:

> Epicurus does not want to play. If the game has risks, then he will not play. . . Not everything can happen by chance: There has to be necessity too and somewhere in between a place for freedom as well. Chance gives us the possibility of moving where and how we want. Necessity insures that the earth does not give way beneath our feet; it allows us to walk in any direction. Thus, Epicurus amends Democritus and adopts Aristotle's theory of substance. He founds the stability of species on aeterna foedera naturai [the eternal covenant of nature] and declares that forms are eternal. (trans. Campbell)[4]

---

[1] Giannantoni 1986. I would like to thank the participants of the Venice Symposium and, for subsequent discussion, Elizabeth Asmis, David Konstan, Pietro Pucci, and Enrico Piergiacomi. The paper has benefited as well from criticisms by an anonymous referee.
[2] Diano 1952.
[3] Chantraine 1954: 257. For an excellent account see Verde 2016.
[4] Campbell and Lezra 2020: 55.

Diano begins with the claim that Epicurus carves up the world between necessity and chance, with a place in between for freedom, presumably human freedom. After that, things become rather less transparent, especially if we take the argument to be moving between atomic and macroscopic perspectives. Insofar as Diano, as Enrico Piergiacomi points out, seems at times to be leaning on the etymology of *eventum*, which in this context derives from *ex-venio*, "to come out of", the potential linkages among *eventa* and their sources are complex.[5] So, for instance, on the one hand, the *eventum* of human freedom seems to depend on chance, which gives us possibilities for moving where and how we wish; yet it also "comes out of" necessity, which Diano suggests maintains the structure of the world and, in particular, gives the necessary support for, say, our walking in any direction. Yet, by the same token, one inevitably thinks in this context of Lucretius' discussion of *libera voluntas* in *DRN* II where an indeterminate swerve of atoms makes it possible for us to walk in the direction that we choose, though only because it breaks the bonds of necessity and thereby frees us from them. Thus, at least at first glance, there seems to be an initial tension in necessity's roles in our free actions. Diano then has recourse to a notion of *aeterna foedera naturai* which seem to be linked to necessity and, in any case, guarantee the stability of species and the world in the manner of Aristotle. This further move, however, is also somewhat elliptical and puzzling, since whatever one thinks of the relation of Aristotle and Epicurus, the latter's denial of teleology and the eternal stability of species would seem, at least at first glance, to put the two thinkers in different conceptual worlds.

Although these claims are not fully delineated by Diano, no doubt given the larger aims of his argument, they nonetheless bring together key elements for puzzling out how necessity, chance, and the *eventum* of human freedom coexist and operate in Epicurus' thought. They also signal some tensions that I think have been insufficiently explored in the scholarship.[6] How can our freedom, for instance, both be derived from or, at least, be supported by necessity and necessary laws, while at the same time able to function only when these same bonds of necessity are broken? More generally, what exactly is the status of ἀνάγκη, if in one sense it is taken to provide the backbone of support for the Epicurean world and its operative structures, while at the same time it must be abrogated in order to make way for human freedom?

Probably the locus classicus for this particular problem and Diano's rather mysterious trinity of necessity, chance, and human *par'hemas* action – as well as their various relations – is in section 133 of the *Letter to Menoeceus*. Although in the letter Epicurus tends to keep his focus squarely on ethical questions without bringing in

---

[5] Piergiacomi 2019: 198-202.
[6] An important exception is Morel 2000; 2021, whose views I discuss below, cf. nn.36, 40.

much in the way of supporting argument from other areas of his philosophy,[7] we can still perhaps catch a first glimpse, even if through a glass darkly, of some of the wider questions raised by ἀνάγκη in the worlds of both ethics and science. Unfortunately, the text itself is deeply problematic, and I begin with three reconstructions based on Von der Mühll's supplement that, although separated by over a hundred years, give what I take to be the common consensus of how this passage has been generally understood in describing the workings of ἀνάγκη in the ethical world, and by extension, the world at large.

The first is by Usener, followed by Long and Sedley, and finally Jan Erik Hessler:

τὴν δὲ ὑπό τινων δεσπότιν εἰσαγομένην πάντων διαγελῶντος <εἱμαρμένην καὶ μᾶλλον ἃ μὲν κατ' ἀνάγκην γίνεσθαι λέγοντος>, ἃ δὲ ἀπὸ τύχης, ἃ δὲ παρ' ἡμᾶς διὰ τὸ τὴν μὲν ἀνάγκην ἀνυπεύθυνον εἶναι, τὴν δὲ τύχην ἄστατον ὁρᾶν, τὸ δὲ παρ' ἡμᾶς ἀδέσποτον ᾧ καὶ τὸ μεμπτὸν καὶ τὸ ἐναντίον παρακολουθεῖν πέφυκεν.[8]

τὴν δὲ ὑπό τινων δεσπότιν εἰσαγομένην πάντων ἂν γελῶντος <εἱμαρμένην, ἀλλ' ἃ μὲν κατ' ἀνάγκην ὄντα συνορῶντος>, ἃ δὲ ἀπὸ τύχης, ἃ δὲ παρ' ἡμᾶς διὰ τὸ τὴν μὲν ἀνάγκην ἀνυπεύθυνον εἶναι, τὴν δὲ τύχην ἄστατον ὁρᾶν, τὸ δὲ παρ' ἡμᾶς ἀδέσποτον ᾧ καὶ τὸ μεμπτὸν καὶ τὸ ἐναντίον παρακολουθεῖν πέφυκεν.[9]

τὴν δὲ ὑπό τινων δεσπότιν εἰσαγομένην πάντων <εἱμαρμένην οὐκ εἶναι νομίζοντος, ἀλλὰ γίνεσθαι κατ' ἀνάγκην ἃ μὲν πάντων> ἀγγέλλοντος, ἃ δὲ ἀπὸ τύχης, ἃ δὲ παρ' ἡμᾶς, διὰ τὸ τὴν μὲν ἀνάγκην ἀνυπεύθυνον εἶναι, τὴν δὲ τύχην ἄστατον ὁρᾶν, τὸ δὲ παρ' ἡμᾶς ἀδέσποτον ᾧ καὶ τὸ μεμπτὸν καὶ τὸ ἐναντίον παρακολουθεῖν πέφυκεν.[10]

The emendations introduced in the first two reconstructions, διαγελῶντος or ἂν γελῶντος,[11] strike me as unlikely. In merely scorning, laughing or smiling at, mocking, or deriding the "mistress of all things", the possibility is left open that she actually exists.[12] A swashbuckling buccaneer may proclaim that he laughs in the face of death as he is about to fearlessly go meet it, but in so doing he merely affirms its existence. Moreover, the tone of sobriety, judging, understanding, and the like characterizing the preceding list of important Epicurean capacities from the be-

---

[7] We do get a passing reference to *prolepseis* and *hupolepseis* (*Men.* 124) in his compressed discussion of theology and also ἡ κοινὴ τοῦ θεοῦ νόησις (*Men.* 123), but otherwise there is minimal technical epistemological vocabulary and no reference to atomism where one might expect it, for instance, in his discussion of death (*Men.* 124-7). Famously, there is no direct mention of the swerve.
[8] Usener 1887.
[9] Long and Sedley 1987.
[10] Hessler 2014 *ad loc.*
[11] Long and Sedley's introduction of ἂν (Long-Sedley 1987 vol.2 *ad loc.*) adds an unwarranted aspect of potentiality, which occurs nowhere else in the long list of right beliefs held by the one of whom there is no one better; nor does Epicurus use ἂν anywhere else in the letter.
[12] The addition of εἱμαρμένην, I imagine, is supposed to further specify the nature of the δεσπότις, but it leads not only to a direct conceptual conflict with the κατ' ἀνάγκην that follows, but also to a straightforward verbal one. Cf. 134 with ensuing discussion below.

ginning of [133] and continuing on (see below) – does not fit well with the notion of scorn or mocking, which elsewhere in the letter is reserved for those who are foolish (cf. *Men.* 127).

Hessler's "believing that it does not exist" is closer to the mark but less economical than something like, say, ἀναλύοντος, which is easier paleographically. In any case, it should be noticed that the "laughing" versions – by perhaps implicitly suggesting the existence of what is laughed at (i.e., "destiny") – subtly prepare the way for the introduction into the text of what at least at first glance might otherwise seem to be a rather stunning non-sequitur, that is, the claim that there actually are things that are by necessity: ἃ μὲν κατ' ἀνάγκην. After just being told that the Epicurean has no truck with the δεσπότις of τινων – here the indefinite being used in Epicurus' typically dismissive way for opponents – we are then rather abruptly supplied in the reconstructions with various versions of the surprising claim that some things are indeed necessitated or occur by necessity after all. What makes this contention even more difficult to follow as an argument is that in the space of a few short lines [134] we are reminded that we should reject being enslaved to τῇ τῶν φυσικῶν εἱμαρμένῃ – the "destiny" or "fate" of natural philosophers (i.e., the τινων above) – because it possesses implacable necessity (ἡ δὲ ἀπαραίτητον ἔχει τὴν ἀνάγκην). So one might reasonably wonder why after the strong initial denial of something that possesses ἀνάγκη, the text would immediately assert that some things are indeed by ἀνάγκη, especially by means of a contrast made by ἀλλά, where one might expect instead "not by the mistress (which possesses necessity), but by something else which is different." And, in fact, this distinction is precisely what is supported by the manuscripts, ἃ δὲ ἀπὸ τύχης and ἃ δὲ παρ' ἡμᾶς, both of which provide a suitable contrast with the ἡ δεσπότις introduced by, as we are to immediately find out, the natural philosophers.

This is not to say that the text as it stands without supplementation is not lacunose, but the question that arises is whether ἀνάγκη here is merely εἰσαγομένη ὑπό τινων, in this case by the editors, given the harshness, even illogicality, of introducing it in the immediate context of the denial of fate, as well as given the rest of the subsequent argument of this section of the letter. To better assess this change, we can turn to Dorandi's text which is admirably reticent about introducing so much textual conjecture and doctrine without support. My translation then follows.

{133} ἐπεὶ τίνα νομίζεις εἶναι κρείττονα τοῦ καὶ περὶ θεῶν ὅσια δοξάζοντος καὶ περὶ θανάτου διὰ παντὸς ἀφόβως ἔχοντος καὶ τὸ τῆς φύσεως ἐπιλελογισμένου τέλος, καὶ τὸ μὲν τῶν ἀγαθῶν πέρας ὡς ἔστιν εὐσυμπλήρωτόν τε καὶ εὐπόριστον διαλαμβάνοντος, τὸ δὲ τῶν κακῶν ὡς ἢ χρόνους ἢ πόνους ἔχει βραχεῖς· **τὴν δὲ ὑπό τινων δεσπότιν εἰσαγομένην πάντων †ἀγγέλλοντος†**[13]**, ἃ δὲ ἀπὸ τύχης, ἃ δὲ παρ' ἡμᾶς διὰ τὸ τὴν μὲν**

---

[13] ἀναλύοντος is my conjecture. Here is not the place to try to give an account of its possible ratio corruptelae, since more important for its justification from the point of view of its appearance

ἀνάγκην ἀνυπεύθυνον εἶναι, τὴν δὲ τύχην ἄστατον ὁρᾶν, τὸ δὲ παρ' ἡμᾶς ἀδέσποτον, ᾧ καὶ τὸ μεμπτὸν καὶ τὸ ἐναντίον παρακολουθεῖν πέφυκεν(;) [134] (ἐπεὶ κρεῖττον ἦν τῷ περὶ θεῶν μύθῳ κατακολουθεῖν ἢ τῇ τῶν φυσικῶν εἱμαρμένῃ δουλεύειν· ὁ μὲν γὰρ ἐλπίδα παραιτήσεως ὑπογράφει θεῶν διὰ τιμῆς, ἡ δὲ ἀπαραίτητον ἔχει τὴν ἀνάγκην)· τὴν δὲ τύχην οὔτε θεόν, ὡς οἱ πολλοὶ νομίζουσιν, ὑπολαμβάνων (οὐθὲν γὰρ ἀτάκτως θεῷ πράττεται) οὔτε ἀβέβαιον αἰτίαν, (<οὐκ> οἴεται μὲν γὰρ ἀγαθὸν ἢ κακὸν ἐκ ταύτης πρὸς τὸ μακαρίως ζῆν ἀνθρώποις δίδοσθαι, ἀρχὰς μέντοι μεγάλων ἀγαθῶν ἢ κακῶν ὑπὸ ταύτης χορηγεῖσθαι), [135] κρεῖττον εἶναι νομίζει εὐλογίστως ἀτυχεῖν ἢ ἀλογίστως εὐτυχεῖν· βέλτιον γὰρ ἐν ταῖς πράξεσι τὸ καλῶς κριθὲν <μὴ ὀρθωθῆναι ἢ τὸ μὴ καλῶς κριθὲν> ὀρθωθῆναι.

{133}. Since whom do you recognize as being better than one who judges piously concerning the gods as well and who is disposed ever fearlessly concerning death and who has assessed nature's goal, and who holds that the limit of goods is easy to fulfill and easy to come by, while that of evils possesses either fleeting pains or periods of time; and **<who does away with[14]> the mistress of all things adduced by certain ones, but some things are by chance, and others are in our power because of necessity being without responsibility, and (because of) seeing chance to be unstable, and (because of) that which is up to us being without a master, from which both the blameworthy and the opposite naturally follow(?)** [134] For it would be better to acquiesce to the fictions about the gods than to be enslaved to the 'destiny' of the natural philosophers; for the one underwrites hope of placating the gods through recompense, the other possesses implacable necessity; and understanding that chance is neither a god, as the many believe (for nothing in a disorderly fashion is accomplished by divinity) nor that is it a fickle cause, since he does <not> think that either good or evil is given from it to human beings for living a blessed life, but that the beginnings of great goods and evils are supplied by it, {135} and it is better to recognize that one has been unfortunate acting reasonably than fortunate unreasonably. For it is better in one's actions that a good judgment <not succeed than a bad judgment> succeed because of it (i.e., luck).[15]

I suspect the main reason for the initial supplementation of ἀνάγκη – apart from the kind of general outlook represented by Diano – is to create some sort of proleptic symmetry between ἀνάγκη, τύχη, and παρ' ἡμᾶς in parallel with what follows: διὰ τὸ τὴν μὲν ἀνάγκην ἀνυπεύθυνον εἶναι, τὴν δὲ τύχην ἄστατον ὁρᾶν, τὸ δὲ παρ' ἡμᾶς ἀδέσποτον.... If one compares *Men.* 135, for instance, there is an immediate repe-

---

here is its content and philosophical purport. ἀναλύοντος is used elsewhere in the appropriate sense by Epicurus and also has the sense of untying the bonds of fate or setting one free, a common enough metaphor. Dorandi 2013 as editor of Diogenes Laertius prints †ἀγγέλλοντος† thinking this was the text of the archetype of the extant MSS., maybe even the original model for Diogenes. If so, it would have been very difficult for Diogenes to correct it himself and he would have left it as it is. Yet *per litteras*, Dorandi tells me he finds ἀναλύοντος more plausible than its competitors for what Epicurus himself might have written.

[14] Reading ἀναλύοντος.
[15] Translation Mitsis (forthcoming).

tition of a symmetry that is supplied, <οὐδὲ φρονίμως καὶ καλῶς καὶ δικαίως>, but there at least with some Ciceronian justification, and in any case, it is a supplement that is perfectly coherent conceptually. The problem here, though, is that what is being supplemented produces a false symmetry that only engenders further problems, since the διά clause has a different purport. The thought behind introducing the parallel would seem to be that the διά clause is repeating further specifications of the initial, supplemented trinity. Thus, some things are necessitated (ἃ μὲν κατ' ἀνάγκην) *because* necessity is ἀνυπεύθυνον (διὰ τὸ τὴν μὲν ἀνάγκην ἀνυπεύθυνον εἶναι). Yet ἀνυπεύθυνον hardly explains why some things are necessitated, and, indeed, its use here seems to be making the opposite point – that necessity is not accountable to or responsible for anything connected to what is παρ' ἡμᾶς.[16] The scope of necessity in the διά clause seems to be one strictly limited to human agency where necessity plays no role. In contrast, an initial supplement of ἀνάγκη seems to treat necessity generally as one of the three governing forces of things that happen. One might indeed generally wonder whether necessity is accountable or responsible for any features of the world, perhaps like insuring that the ground does not give way under our feet. Even so, it is hard to see what the point would be of such a universal proclamation in the midst of these particular ethical attainments – essentially a summary recapitulation of the teachings of the letter (and the *tetrapharmakon*) – or why the Epicurean would reject the notion of a δεσπότις (especially if it is further glossed as εἱμαρμένη), but then immediately embrace the notion that some things are by necessity – especially when we find that the εἱμαρμένη of the natural philosophers brings necessity in its train and is consequently to be rejected. If necessity is something which is not accountable to us, Epicurus claims, then it would be better to acquiesce to the fictions of the gods, since we might hope to placate them. The text, however, reads ἃ δὲ παρ' ἡμᾶς διὰ τὸ τὴν μὲν ἀνάγκην ἀνυπεύθυνον εἶναι, that is, some things are up to us precisely because necessity is not accountable for anything, not because there is no recourse in the face of its mandates. If, conversely, necessity

---

[16] Long and Sedley, for instance, take ἀνυπεύθυνον to mean "accountable to no one". While it is true that it can mean both "not accountable to" and "not accountable for", the former hardly gives an explanation of why some things are in our power – just the opposite, since if something is not accountable to x it can do what it pleases with it. Hessler prints a comma before *dia*, which makes the point that everything after it is not subordinated to παρ' ἡμᾶς, but refers back to the earlier reconstructed clause. Again, though, this reasoning is circular and still does not account for the question of why things are παρ' ἡμᾶς. They are παρ' ἡμᾶς because they are ἀδέσποτον, and while τύχη exists and has other effects throughout the subsequent passage, ἀνάγκη nowhere is granted any power or existence and is only mentioned negatively in connection with the εἱμαρμένη τῶν φυσικῶν as something whose existence is to be rejected. Even if we accept the rendering "accountable to no one", it does not mean that necessity exists, since the phrase can function purely as a descriptive claim that explains why it should be rejected, i.e., the "necessity" described by some is accountable to no one, hence we must reject it in the ethical realm. Indeed, given human free action, a claim that necessity is accountable to no one tilts more strongly in the direction of necessity's non-existence in the contexts of ethics, which in turn fails to license any inferences about its existence at the physical level and, indeed, tends to undercut it.

existed and were accountable to no one, then things would hardly be up to us. We should therefore take the scope of the διὰ to be explaining why things are παρ' ἡμᾶς, rather than offering a repetition of a questionable threefold symmetry that, in any case, has been introduced into the text.

Accordingly, introducing ἃ μὲν κατ' ἀνάγκην, ἀλλὰ γίνεσθαι κατ' ἀνάγκην, and so forth, creates a false symmetry with what follows, given that necessity is not granted control over anything in the διὰ clause. Even if we grant Long and Sedley's claim that necessity is merely "unaccountable to no one", it does not show that necessity is actually accountable for some things (ἃ μὲν κατ' ἀνάγκην). Nor does it explain why some actions are παρ' ἡμᾶς, which are explicable only if they are not in the grip of a necessity that is not unaccountable to no one. Moreover, in the larger argumentative context, if necessity were accountable for some things, it would cast doubt both forward and backward about the rejection of the claims of natural philosophers who believe themselves to be enslaved by fate, which possesses ἀνάγκη.

As the passage continues, after dismissing fate and necessity, Epicurus denies the divinity of chance and also its ability to provide either goods or evils for the blessed life. Τύχη does, however, offer the ἀρχὰς for great goods and evils. What is most important, however, is to conduct one's life εὐλογίστως, even if one is unlucky and fails. This position is of a piece with Epicurus' emphasis on *phronesis* and rationality throughout his ethical writings, neither of which is possible, however, unless the bonds of necessity are broken. In effect we leave the passage, and the letter generally, with a dyad of chance and free, rational human action. This is not to say that the ethical world generally has no structuring elements beyond chance and human freedom. Indeed, as I will argue, we get glimpses of how that external structure works through Epicurus' use of terms such as πέρας (cf. *Men*. 133). In any case, one is not constrained at this point to conclude that structures supporting our actions in the world are governed by causal laws that are necessary and hence, eternal.

To be sure, even if we rid ἀνάγκη as a structural feature of the ethical world from Epicurus' most important surviving ethical text, a question still arises about the role of necessity beyond the domain of ethics and whether Epicurus believes that anything in the world at large is κατ' ἀνάγκην. On this front, many scholars have followed Diano's claim that ἀνάγκη binds and structures the rest of the non-animate universe through *aeterna foedera naturai*. Yet, for those attempting to find a place for necessity in other areas of Epicurus' system, it seems to me that there arise two significant hurdles, both of which are systematic, pervasive, and ultimately dependent on the doctrine of the swerve.

The first is connected to Epicurus' views about logical necessity. In a recent paper, Alexander Bown has argued that Epicurus distinguishes between semantic and syntactic elements in his arguments about bi-valence (if we want to translate the ancient evidence into terms of Classical propositional logic). He then attempts to construct a "supervaluationist" grounding for Epicurus' account that... "allows the Epicureans to reject the principle of bivalence and the semantic law of the excluded middle in order to avoid being forced to accept fatalism by the argument from truth to necessity, but nonetheless to mitigate the damage this rejection causes by retaining the syntactic law of the excluded middle".[17] Bown's claim is rooted in Ciceronian evidence that gives a crucial role to the swerve in the formulation of Epicurus' arguments. By way of contrast, Anthony Long, in an influential paper, attempts to show that domains outside of free human action are immune from the swerve's effects generally. Accordingly, he fleshes out Diano's linking of necessity with *aeterna foedera naturai* and affirms what we might describe as necessity's grip on what is by far the greatest part of the universe, logical and otherwise. Long writes:

> If the general line of argument in this paper is sound, Epicurus confined the verifiable evidence of the swerve in nature to 'free' animal behaviour. It is worth noting that his denial of necessity to propositions of the form 'Either Hermarchus will be alive tomorrow or he will not' is illustrated by an example referring to man. Epicurus was most anxious to free human actions from necessity. But in other respects he developed a model of the world which conforms to natural law. The *foedera naturae* are probably identical to the *foedera fati* except in the case of *libera voluntas*.[18]

If Long is suggesting that Epicurus' arguments against logical determinism extend only so far as free animal behaviour – especially free human actions, where the effects of the swerve are verifiable – then it seems to be that the claim verges on a kind of category mistake, since the question is one of *logical* necessity, and it is hard to see how voluntary animal behaviour is a particularly relevant constituent term in questions about logical necessity. Yet even if for the sake of argument we entertain this claim, the example itself hardly suggests that Hermarchus' death is an example of *libera voluntas*, much less of an action that is παρ' ἡμᾶς.[19] Hermarchus easily might die unawares in his sleep, for instance. And, of course, horses also exercise *voluntas*, at least in Lucretius, so as Long notices, the swerve's effects at the physical level cannot be confined in any case strictly to human παρ' ἡμᾶς actions, since they extend to the voluntary movements of other animate creatures as well.

More important, Cicero is concerned in his account in *Fato* 37 with the nature of definite future contingent claims such as, say, "Either Hermarchus will die in Lysias' house or he will not", in which case the question of Hermarchus' freedom of action or responsibility is similarly not the relevant focus. Certainly Hermarchus may have freely chosen to go to Lysias' house, or he may have hoped to die peacefully in his

---

[17] Bown 2016.
[18] Long 1977: 86.
[19] I take the distinction here to be between actions that are the result of *libera voluntas*, which both animals and children are capable of, and of rational adult actions, which are παρ' ἡμᾶς and hence those for which individuals can be held responsible.

sleep in Lysias' house, but whether he dies in Lysias' house or not can doubtlessly be independent of any of his particular παρ' ἡμᾶς choices. The focus of Epicurus' argument is on whether necessity attaches to either of the contingent disjunctive outcomes, and this necessity is what he is denies. This is not to deny that our conclusions about the relations of truth, possibility, and necessity here might affect questions of human free will, of course, but from a logical perspective, Epicurus would certainly not view differently the proposition "Either the stone gets wet tomorrow or it does not" just because the disjuncts do not contain a human constituent term. Accordingly, Epicurus is making a completely general logical claim that applies to human and non-human behaviour alike, and in either case, Epicurus is keen to reject the bivalence of future contingents across the board.

By the same token, Long's argument elides the fact that the evidence of Cicero's *De fato* makes the role of the swerve crucial in blocking the causal chains necessary for particular contingent future events to happen *simpliciter*, and not just in connection with free human choice. To be sure, Epicurus' overall argument still presents some well-known problems of its own. For instance, one common complaint against supervaluationist semantics is that it allows for a disjunction to be true even though none of its disjuncts is in fact true. This reasoning is exactly what Cicero in *Fato* 37 finds so shameless on the part of the Epicureans.[20] Bown, however, finds Epicurus' account sufficiently plausible to offer an imaginative reconstruction of his theory based on branching temporal/causal chains that change paths because of indeterminate causal breaks, somewhat in the manner of recent quantum logicians. Whether or not this moves too far from the ancient texts themselves,[21] we only need recognize for our more limited purposes that any attempt to constrict the domains of Epicurus' denial of logical necessity to human action is arbitrary; and however we understand Epicurean views about the relation of logical necessity to metaphysical, physical, or nomological necessity, Epicurus' arguments in this sphere involve a blanket denial of necessity throughout the entire domain of possible constituents.

We can now turn to the second of the major hurdles for partisans of necessity, that of physical necessity, which the Epicureans see as being clearly connected to logical necessity insofar as for something to be true in advance, it must be necessitated by pre-determined causes. Long again argues that the effect of indeterminate swerves at the physical level is sufficiently circumscribed to allow natural laws governing the physical world to be necessary. Certainly at the atomic level of explanation, it seems to me that this claim is unsupportable. There certainly would appear to be reasonably good evidence that at the general level physical laws are not sufficient to determine the path of every atom, and if we follow David Konstan's more precise explanation, this insufficiency is because of the indeterminacy of the rebound after

---

[20] Cicero, *Fato* 37: *aut, cum id pudet, illud tamen dicunt quod est impudentius, veras esse ex contrariis diiunctiones, sed quae in his enuntiata essent, eorum neutrum esse verum.* (Cf. Graff Fara 2010).
[21] Cf. Verde 2013 for a careful delineation of the question.

atomic collisions.[22] As Konstan argues, atomic collisions fall under certain larger statistical criteria, but they are neither necessitated nor do they obey discrete causal laws. Hence there is no necessity at the atomic level. Accordingly, any claims about the existence of necessary natural laws typically must be restricted to macroscopic properties, but exactly how we could move from indeterminism at the micro level to necessity at the macro level is hardly transparent on any of the going theories relating the two realms (i.e., reductionism, identity theory, or emergence). Perhaps Sedley's supervenient dualism (which he describes as a species of "emergence") might allow for the two realms to be sufficiently modally distinct in this respect, but it would still require that linkages of causal necessity somehow supervene on some, but not on other higher order atomic compositions (the human soul, for instance). The argument here typically is that swerves do not have observable effects on less sensitive atomic configurations, which in Long's view turns out to be the vast majority of entities in the world, indeed everything except animal souls. Such an argument, though, does not fully address the question of macroscopic necessity and how it "comes out of" atomic indeterminism. Claims about observable regularities are not equivalent to claims about *necessity*. Thus, even if one atom in one non-animate entity were to swerve – which can occur at any time or any place – we could not say that it and the future atomic movements of its constituents, however seemingly regular, are determined and necessary *stricto sensu*, regardless of any apparent macroscopic behaviour. Luckily, determining exactly how microscopic indeterminacy could ever get cashed out into macroscopic necessity and how we could understand the modal relations between the two realms is something we do not need to pursue further, since it is hardly clear in the first place that Epicurus believes that macro entities are subject to laws of nature that are necessary.

To begin with, it is perhaps worth noticing how both Diano and Long in their arguments immediately slip into Latin for the notion of necessary natural laws. Diano has recourse to a notion of *aeterna foedera naturai*, a phrase that on the surface might look Lucretian but actually never occurs in Lucretius. Long for his part equates *foedera naturai* with *foedera fati* – again, as we shall see, a highly arguable move. To be sure, in discussions of Epicureanism, scholars often have had recourse to such terms as "Naturgesetz", "legge naturale", "loi naturelle", and the like. Yet in turning to Epicurus himself, we find that instead of embracing a notion of *nomos phuseos*, as did the Stoics, he maintains the earlier Greek contrast between *nomos* and *phusis*. There are very few occurrences of the term "*nomos*" at all in Epicurus' writings, and those instances are presented in the following deflationary manner:

ἐὰν δὲ **νόμον** θῆταί τις, μὴ ἀποβαίνῃ δὲ κατὰ τὸ συμφέρον τῆς πρὸς ἀλλήλους κοινωνίας, οὐκέτι τοῦτο τὴν τοῦ δικαίου **φύσιν** ἔχει. (*KD* 36)

---

[22] Konstan 1979: 414 ff.

Yet if someone lay down a law, but it does not result for one another in the advantage of association, it no longer possesses the nature of justice.

A report from Plutarch (*adv. Col.* 1127d) drives the point home:

γράφων πρὸς Ἰδομενέα διακελεύεται μὴ **νόμοις** καὶ δόξαις δουλεύοντα ζῆν, ...

Writing to Idomeneus, he bids him not to live enslaved to laws or opinions, ...

The Stoics likely invented and regularized the use of *nomos phuseos* in the sense of "natural law", which originally sounded rather oxymoronic, and they did so by embracing the notion of Zeus – and hence nature itself – as the source or giver of law.[23] Epicurus' non-teleological atomism would hardly be hospitable to such a view of laws, of course, but even so, it is a matter of some controversy whether the notion of *nomos* as a scientific causal law is even applicable in the case of the Stoics. R.G. Collingwood,[24] for instance, argued that the notion of a scientific causal law is a post-Renaissance achievement that only became possible when laws were freed up from the power of such divine lawgivers. While it is true that Epicurean views were important for these later developments in the early modern period, it was an Epicurean atomism shorn of the doctrine of the swerve – itself widely dismissed as unintelligible even by his most ardent supporters because it abolished causality. Epicurus' own indeterministic atomism would have doubtlessly been inimical to such a concept of the (necessary) laws of nature.

To be sure, even if Epicurus himself does not have a particular word or phrase for a necessary causal law, it might be argued that he still has or needs such a concept to be operative in his account of the world. Even if one grants that a vast number of ordinary natural regularities are exempt from the strict bonds of ἀνάγκη, one might still argue that Epicurus must believe that many might still be necessary. To return to the question of Hermarchus' death, for instance, even if his future death is not subject to logical determinism, one might claim that it is still necessary that Hermarchus die, given that he is a mortal human being. Again, though, one must be careful in one's use of 'necessity' here. Gods do not die, for instance, and the reason is that the chance collocation of atoms that created the worlds in which the gods live gave rise to beings who do not die. Humans were created by other chance collocations of atoms bound by certain *foedera*, but these are not necessitating laws; they are chance collocations. Hence, our mortality is not a necessary feature of the world. To be sure, human mortality is structured by the current temporary *foedera* governing our world, but these *foedera* are not necessary either physically or metaphysically. Nor are they, as claimed by Long and Diano, eternal. So, yes,

---

[23] Striker 1996.
[24] Collingwood 1940.

Hermarchus is going to die. It is not *necessary*, however, that he or any other human being die. It is a contingent feature of this temporary world.

By the same token, one might object that it seems unavoidable in the Epicurean system that several brute metaphysical and physical facts are to be characterized as being necessary.[25] Isn't it necessary that atoms be uncuttable or that atoms move in a void? In the first place, it is not clear how an Epicurean is supposed to answer such a question. Was there some series of necessary causal events that made atoms uncuttable? It seems unlikely. Is it by mere chance that the world is so structured that atoms are uncuttable? Perhaps. Are there metaphysical and physical features of the cosmos that prevent atoms from being cut? Are then atoms necessarily uncuttable, or is this quality a purely contingent feature of the world? Interestingly, Epicurus himself does not seem to address such worries in these terms, and he fails to describe such basic features of the world in ways that suggest they are necessary, which is perhaps one reason scholars typically turn to Lucretius and his use of *foedera* to support their notions of necessary causal laws. Such a strategy raises difficult questions in turn about the prospect of Lucretian linguistic and conceptual innovations, but I think when all the dust clears, none are sufficient to suggest that he explicitly embraces a conception of necessary laws. To see this point, it might be helpful to begin with Lucretius' detailed declaration at *DRN* V 55, since it has often been taken to be a particularly salient example of the claim that each created thing is of necessity bound by inviolable laws:

> Cuius ego ingressus vestigia dum rationes persequor ac doceo dictis,
>   quo quaeque creata
> foedere sint, in eo quam sit durare necessum
> nec validas valeant aevi rescindere leges,
> quo genere in primis animi natura reperta est
> nativo primum consistere corpore creta,
> nec posse incolumem magnum durare per aevum,
> ...quod super est, nunc huc rationis detulit ordo,
> ut mihi mortali consistere corpore mundum
> nativomque simul ratio reddunda sit esse;
> ...
> praeterea solis cursus lunaeque meatus.   76
> expediam qua vi flectat natura gubernans,
> ne forte haec inter caelum terramque reamur
> libera sponte sua cursus lustrare perennis,
> morigera ad fruges augendas atque animantis,
> neve aliqua divom volvi ratione putemus.
> ... ignari quid queat esse,
> quid nequeat, finita potestas denique cuique
> quanam sit ratione atque alte terminus haerens.

---

[25] Morel 2000: 45-52.

> His steps I trace, his doctrines I follow, teaching in my poem
> how all things are bound to abide in that law (*foedere*) by which they were
> made, and how they are impotent to annul the strong statutes (*leges*)
> of time; and herein first of all the nature of the mind has been
> found first to consist of a body that had birth, and unable to endure
> intact through a long time ...
> Now for what remains the order of my design has brought me
> to this point, that I must show how the frame of which the world
> consists is subject to death and has also had birth; ...
> Besides, I will explain by what force pilot nature steers 76
> the courses of the sun and the goings of the moon;
> lest by any chance we think that these
> between heaven and earth traverse their yearly courses free, of
> their own will, and obliging for the increase of crops and of animals,
> or deem them to revolve by some plan of the gods....
> not knowing what can be and what cannot, in a word
> how each thing has limited power and a deep-set boundary mark.
> (trans. Rouse, revised M.F. West)

I will take up questions about "*foedera*", "*leges*", and the meaning of "*necessum*" in the poem in turn. Certainly one of the things that Lucretian scholarship since the time of Diano and Long has made clear is how richly embedded Lucretius' use of *foedus* is in Roman cultural preoccupations.[26] Diano assumes, while Long explicitly argues for the claim that "Lucretius is playing on the meaning of *foedus* as both something concrete – a bond or union of atoms with congruent shapes – and the more abstract notion of law."[27] The question arises, though, does what Long describes as a "more abstract notion of law" ever rise to the level of universal necessary causal laws? Or, as he claims, does Lucretius deem them to be the equivalent of *foedera fati*?[28] It is certainly the case that for Lucretius, *foedus* has Roman ritual,[29] juridical,[30] and political nuances,[31] along with larger cosmological ones.[32] Yet the very point of these various uses in Lucretius typically is to show the fragility and contingency of such pacts and alliances – as we find out, for instance, shortly in this same passage with

---

[26] Gladhill 2008: 133-200 gives an excellent overview of this scholarship.
[27] Long 1977: 88.
[28] Lucretius famously describes how the swerve breaks (*rumpere*) the *fati foedera* (II 254), which may suggest that there are *fati foedera* in force until the swerve breaks them; but the swerve is an eternal feature of the universe, hence the power of fate has always been brokeback. It is not that necessity is in force and then somehow interrupted on occasion. At V 306-10, Lucretius argues that stones cannot carry forward the *finis fati* or strive against *naturae foedera*, linking the two notions. Still, the point of this argument is that there are limits to the physical integrity of material objects, even the stones in the temples of the gods, not that such physical limits are a matter of metaphysical necessity.
[29] Gladhill 2016.
[30] Schiesaro 2007.
[31] Fowler 1989.
[32] Asmis 2008.

respect to the material compound of the mind at *DRN* V 61: "nec posse incolumem magnum durare per aevum". Lucretius takes seriously the analogy between the way that atomic compounds come together and the various kinds of treaties, pacts, agreements, and so forth, that are made at the human level. Yet just as atomic compounds are subject to contingency and dissolution, so are human pacts, agreements, laws, and so on. Nature's pacts in Lucretius are not like the Stoic mandates of a divine eternal intellect, and they are not *foedera naturai* that are *aeterna* in Diano's sense. As Fowler and others have pointed out, they are deeply coloured by the contingency and vulnerability of human pacts. Lucretius, that is, extends an anthropomorphic notion and the linguistic nuances of human compacts to the natural world. By way of contrast, Epicurus uses *synthēkai* for human compacts but does not read such human agreements in an unmediated linguistic fashion onto the natural physical world. Perhaps one reason for this perspective is signaled by Lucretius at *DRN* V 419-21:

> nam certe neque consilio primordia rerum
> ordine se suo quaeque sagaci mente locarunt
> nec quos quaeque darent motus pepigere profecto;

> For certainly it was no design of the first beginnings
> that led them to place themselves each in its own order
> with keen intelligence, nor assuredly did they make
> any bargain what motions each should produce;

Be that as it may, the root analogy that is of overriding importance for Lucretius, and which ties the realms of humanity and cosmos together, remains the idea that *foedera* are contingent agreements that set out conditions within certain limits, typically involving boundaries. These limits result, at best, in a temporary stability in a world characterized by change and strife. They themselves, moreover, are subject to individual variation. As Philip De Lacy[33] argued in a seminal paper, Lucretius perhaps goes beyond Epicurus in specifying where these limits are,[34] but the dual emphasis on limits in Epicurus' ethical works and in his natural philosophy is helpfully captured by Lucretius. So, for instance, at *DRN* I 75-77, he describes the great prize that Epicurus as victor brought to humankind from his triumphant exploration of the universe:

> Unde refert nobis victor quid possit oriri,
> quid nequeat, finita potestas denique cuique
> quanam sit ratione atque alte terminus haerens

---

[33] De Lacy 1969.
[34] See Morel's discussion in this volume on *akribeia*. He raises the question of whether precision about limits is an objective ontological property of things or whether it consists in a safe disposition of the mind, i.e., a species of epistemic virtue. He defends the latter, which is in keeping with the claim that Epicurus himself does not think there can be limits in accordance with necessary causal laws.

This generalization, which he repeats at I 594-596, served as the conclusion to his syllabus above at V 88-90, and it is repeated again at VI 64-66. As De Lacy shows, the notion of limits is reinforced by the poem's frequent use of such terms as *finis*, *certus*, and the like, and represents for Lucretius a crucial principle structuring the Epicurean account. It is applicable not only to the *foedera naturae* (I 586) that insure to natural processes a certain regularity, but also to death, *the terminus malorum* (III 1020; cf. *terminus vitae*, II 1087), and into the ethical realm as well, as in the *finis cuppedinis atque timoris* (VI 25) and *quae sit habendi finis et omnino quoad crescit vera voluptas* (V 1432-33).

The central importance of limits is underlined in the *Letter to Menoeceus*, while πέρας and ὅρος are key terms in Epicurus' account of the natural limits of pleasure – as spelled out in greater detail, for instance, at *KD* 20 – along with the limits of life itself and of what counts as a complete life and of living blessedly, τοῦ μακαρίως ζῆν.

Ἡ μὲν σὰρξ ἀπέλαβε τὰ πέρατα τῆς ἡδονῆς ἄπειρα, καὶ ἄπειρος αὐτὴν χρόνος παρεσκεύασεν. ἡ δὲ διάνοια τοῦ τῆς σαρκὸς τέλους καὶ πέρατος λαβοῦσα τὸν ἐπιλογισμὸν καὶ τοὺς ὑπὲρ τοῦ αἰῶνος φόβους ἐκλύσασα τὸν παντελῆ βίον παρεσκεύασεν, καὶ οὐθὲν ἔτι τοῦ ἀπείρου χρόνου προσεδεήθη, ἀλλ' οὔτ' ἔφυγε τὴν ἡδονήν, οὔθ' ἡνίκα τὴν ἐξαγωγὴν ἐκ τοῦ ζῆν τὰ πράγματα παρεσκεύαζεν, ὡς ἐλλείπουσά τι τοῦ ἀρίστου βίου κατέστρεψεν.

The flesh viewed the limits of pleasure to be unlimited, and unlimited time produced it (pleasure). But the mind, grasping the proper assessment of the goal and limit of the flesh and dissolving fears about eternity, produces the complete [i.e., fulfilled, perfect] life and no longer is in need of unlimited time, yet the mind did not flee from pleasure, nor when events caused it to exit from life, was it destroyed having missed anything of the best life.

Within these limits, however, are variations: kinetic pleasures are varied within the proper limits of katastematic pleasure; there are limits to the variety of atoms and of their size, and that of their minimal parts; only a limited number of atomic combinations is possible, and of only certain variations; a finite space can be occupied by a limited number and variety of atoms, and every cosmos is of a finite magnitude; there are limits to the possible various shapes of the cosmos, and so on and so forth. Our understanding of the nature of the principles behind these individual and potentially spontaneous variations is inflected no doubt by various conceptions of the Epicurean notions of ποικιλός and παραλλαγή.[35] Since space does not permit, however, I want to turn directly and somewhat schematically to the general question of whether these fixed boundaries within which all these variations occur can be identified with natural laws, much less necessary natural laws.

As we have seen, Epicurus does not think of nature in terms of laws *per se*, but in Lucretius, the word *lex* occurs three times: once describing the *lege leti* (III 687);

---

[35] De Lacy 1969: 107 ff.

again at V 58 above describing the strong laws of time (*validas leges aevi*); and in the following passage at II 707-723, where he concludes that all things in nature are held apart by their limits, which he identifies as laws (719):

> quorum nil fieri manifestum est, omnia quando
> seminibus certis certa genetrice creata
> conservare genus crescentia posse videmus.
> scilicet id certa fieri ratione necessust.   710
> nam sua cuique cibis ex omnibus intus in artus
> corpora discedunt conexaque convenientis
> efficiunt motus; at contra aliena videmus
> reicere in terras naturam, multaque caecis
> corporibus fugiunt e corpore percita plagis,   715
> quae neque conecti quoquam potuere neque intus
> vitalis motus consentire atque imitari.
> sed ne forte putes animalia sola teneri
> legibus his, quaedam ratio res terminat omnis.
> nam vel uti tota natura dissimiles sunt   720
> inter se genitae res quaeque, ita quamque necessest
> dissimili constare figura principiorum;

> But that none of these things happen is manifest, since
> we see that all things bred from fixed seeds by a fixed mother
> are able to conserve their kind as they grow.
> Assuredly this must come about in a fixed way.
> For in each thing, its own proper bodies are spread abroad
> through the frame within from all its foods, and being combined
> produce the appropriate motions; but contrariwise we see alien elements
> to be thrown back by nature upon the earth, and many, beaten by blows,
> escape from the body with their invisible bodies,
> which were not able to combine with any part nor within the body
> to feel the life-giving motions with it and imitate them.
> But do not think that animals only are are held by these laws,
> for the same principle holds all things apart by their limits.
> For just as all things made are in their whole nature different one from another,
> so each must consist of first-beginnings differently shaped;
> (trans. Rouse, revised M.F. West)

In these passages where Lucretius talks about laws, he also uses the phrase "necessum est" which has led some scholars to import the notion of necessity into the discussion and hence, necessary laws. Something parallel happens on the Greek side with uses of ἀνάγκη. As is well known from Aristotle's logic, for instance, ἀνάγκη can easily slip between the meaning of metaphysical necessity and its uses as a simple linguistic operator meaning something like "it is indispensable that" or "one must" do *x*, and so forth. A clear instance of this latter use, for instance, is at *Hrdt.* 38:

ἀνάγκη γὰρ τὸ πρῶτον ἐννόημα καθ' ἕκαστον φθόγγον βλέπεσθαι καὶ μηθὲν ἀποδείξεως προσδεῖσθαι...

One must look thus to the first meaning of each sound and not require demonstration...

So, too, in Epicurus' account in the *Letter to Menoeceus* some desires are ἀναγκαῖαι. These are typically treated as being "necessary" desires, but they are certainly not necessary in the sense of being metaphysically determined desires. Such desires are, as it were, indispensable for a blessed life, but they are not metaphysically necessary in the required sense since they are features of human beings whose present configurations are temporary and contingent.[36] There are all sorts of contexts in Epicurean texts where ἀνάγκη or *necesse* are merely serving as such linguistic operators and not signaling instances of metaphysical necessity.[37] I would argue that even in these particular instances in Lucretius, where such uses of *necesse* are linked with "laws", we are to understand this against the background of Lucretius' wider views about the contingency and limits of atomic compounds and their higher order creations.[38] In any case, if he ascribes more to these notions, he would appear to be innovating or indulging in the kind of poetic license or imprecision that allows him to speak of *"natura gubernans"* (V 77).

---

[36] Morel 2021: 141 argues that while Epicurus rejects necessitarianism, he retains a weakened though positive notion of necessity that corresponds to causal efficacy. No doubt, such physical ἀναγκαῖαι desires are efficacious in achieving the blessed life, but are they "causally efficacious", and do they fall under general causal laws? They clearly are efficacious in helping to achieve *eudaimonia*, the well-being of the body, and living itself. However, it is unclear to me the advantage of viewing these as embodying a positive notion of causal necessity. Their proper fulfilment may be crucial for *ataraxia*, and my ἀναγκαῖαι desires for food may induce me to preserve my life. Yet they do so in ways that are up to me, including, for instance, eating too much or too little. Thus, even their causal efficacy is ultimately up for grabs, and any notion of even weakened necessity (however construed) seems little more than a *façon de parler*.

[37] In some of the more difficult passages of the *Peri Phuseos*, Epicurus uses the expression κατ' ἀνάγκην in ways that can be taken as suggesting metaphysical necessity, though it often is probably just functioning as an operator. So, for instance, Fr. 17: ὥστε παρ ἡμᾶς π[οθ] ἁπλῶς τὸ ἀπογεγεννημένον ἤδη γίγνεσθαι τοῖα ἢ τοῖα καὶ τὰ ἐκ τοῦ περιέχοντος κ[α]τ ἀνάγκη ν διὰ τοὺς πό[ρο]υς εἰσρέοντα παρ ἡμᾶς π[ο]τε γείγεσθαι καὶ παρὰ τὰς ἡμετέρας [ἐ]ξ ἡμῶν αὐτῶν δόξ[ας] (Masi). Here the claim is not that τὸ ἀπογεγεννημένον becomes autonomous in the face of things from the outside externally determined by necessity, but in the face of things which flow in from the outside κατ' ἀνάγκην – i.e., they just flow in for our development, perception, etc. – 'of necessity' in the sense of 'unavoidably as a matter of course', like the air we breathe.

[38] Keeping in mind De Lacy's worry that Lucretius is too optimistic about specifying limits at an ontological level. Here it is worth remembering perhaps, *De Signis* cols. 1 and 2 where Philodemus vitiates attempts to set the limits to what can happen too precisely, given that possible variations can never be determined empirically.

In conclusion, I want to take up the assumption that somehow necessity is still required as a kind of backdrop in the Epicurean world and the idea that there is a settled necessary condition of the world that is momentarily interrupted piecemeal by the swerve. If we take the famous self-refutation argument (*SV* 40),[39] we can see how problematic such an assumption is:

> Ὁ λέγων πάντα κατ' ἀνάγκην γίνεσθαι οὐδὲν ἐγκαλεῖν ἔχει τῷ λέγοντι μὴ πάντα κατ' ἀνάγκην γίνεσθαι· αὐτὸ γὰρ τοῦτό φησι κατ' ἀνάγκην γίνεσθαι.

> The one saying all things happen in accord with necessity has no charge to bring against the one saying not all things happen in accord with necessity. For this very thing he is saying is in accord with necessity.

It might be objected that although Epicurus is refuting the claim that all things happen by necessity, his argument still leaves open the possibility that some things still happen by necessity,[40] or even almost all of them. Epicurus is not suggesting, though, that someone can escape self-refutation by saying that only some things happen by necessity – the problematic supplemented claim that we saw at the beginning of the *Letter to Menoeceus*. In the first instance, of course, there is the epistemological problem of never knowing if or when some aspect of the world of necessity is impinging on the one claiming that some things happen by necessity and others do not. Epicurus' defense of the freedom of reason to think and choose depends precisely on the claim that we are always free of such necessity, not that we are necessitated in some cases and then sometimes liberated by a swerve. Nor is it only in those latter instances that we can criticize someone who claims that some things are by necessity – which in turn again would depend on that person not being in the grips of necessity at that particular moment. So I strongly doubt that we can plausibly assume that Epicurus relies on an occurrent backdrop of necessity to highlight the conditions of our freedom. In other words, the *eventum* of free human action is supported not by necessity in some unchartered way, but depends on its elimination. And as I have argued, a supporting backdrop of necessity in the

---

[39] Some scholars – strangely, in my view – take *SV* 9 to be another version of the self-refutation argument. Κακὸν ἀνάγκη, ἀλλ' οὐδεμία ἀνάγκη ζῆν μετὰ ἀνάγκης: I take this claim to be just a bit of homey advice that one does not need to live in need (or poverty), i.e., more a matter of clever wordplay than of logical paradox.

[40] Morel defends the view that Epicurus' self-refutation arguments do not preclude the claim that some events occur by necessity. His key text is *On Nature* 34.29 (Arrighetti): "he will not be modifying any actions in the way in which in some cases the man who regularly sees what sort of actions are necessitated regularly dissuades those who desire to do something in the face of compulsion" (trans. Long and Sedley). Morel takes this as being a description of the Epicurean view, rather than an attribute of the opponents who are merely changing names by ascribing responsibility to actions that have been compelled by necessity, even if at times trying to dissuade others from actions they believe to be compelled. I take this, however, to be yet another characterization of the incoherence of compatibilists, not an affirmation of dichotomous necessity. And in any case, this hardly serves as an example of a general sort of positive, though weakened, necessity that remains casually efficacious (cf. n. 36).

world is not likely, given Epicurus' larger commitments in his logical and physical theory. Our freedom is carried on against a background of chance, which gives us starting points for opportunities, and in a world that is structured by limits that themselves are ontologically variable and which offer us a further world of variation among those changing limits. Necessity need not enter the picture, since for the Epicureans such a world of limits on its own offers sufficient support and regularity for the pursuit of knowledge and happiness. If Epicurus therefore parts company with Aristotle, it does not mean conversely that he takes aboard the ever-changing instability of the Stoic outlook. Rather, as we might expect, Epicurus offers a healthier alternative in keeping both with the sobriety and lack of hubris that characterizes his physical theory and with the attractive and welcoming flexibility of his ethics – both of which depend on sensible and balanced limits that avoid the twin defects of inflexible rigidity and turbulent change that are espoused by the competition.

REFERENCES

Asmis, E., 2008, "Lucretius' New World Order: Making a Pact with Nature", *The Classical Quarterly* 58.1: 141-157
Bown, A., 2016, "Epicurus on Bi-valence and the Excluded Middle", *Archiv für Geschichte der Philosophie* 98.3: 239-271.
Campbell, T. C., – Lezra, J. (eds.), 2020, *Form and Event: Principles for an Interpretation of the Greek World* (Carlo Diano), New York: Fordham University Press.
Chantraine, P., 1954, "C. Diano, *Forma ed Evento*", *Revue de Philologie, de Littérature et d'Histoire Anciennes* 28: 257.
Collingwood, R. G., 1940, *An Essay on Metaphysics*, Oxford: Oxford University Press.
De Lacy, P., 1969, "Limit and Variation in the Epicurean Philosophy", *Phoenix* 23.1: 104-113.
Diano, C., 1952, *Forma ed evento. Principii per un'interpretazione del mondo greco. Giornale Critico Della Filosofia Italiana* 6:1-111.
Dorandi, T. (tr.), 2013, *Diogenes Laertius: Lives of Eminent Philosophers*, Cambridge: Cambridge University Press.
Fowler, D. P., 1989, "Lucretius and Politics", in *Philosophia Togata. Essays on Philosophy and Roman Society*, M. Griffin – J. Barnes (eds.), Oxford: Oxford University Press: 120-507.
Giannantoni, G., 1986, "Gli studi epicurei di Carlo Diano", in Aa. Vv., *Il segno della forma, Atti del convegno di studio su Carlo Diano (1902-1974)*, Padua, Antenore, 1984, 1986: 167-180.
Gladhill, C. W., 2008, "*Foedera*: A Study in Roman Poetics and Society", Stanford [diss.].
Gladhill, C. W., 2016, *Rethinking Roman Alliance: A Study in Poetics and Society*, Cambridge: Cambridge University Press.
Graff Fara D., 2010, "Scope Confusions and Unsatisfiable Disjuncts: Two Problems for Supervaluationism", in R. Dietz – S. Moruzzi (eds.), *Cuts and Clouds: Vagueness, Its Nature and Its Logic*, Oxford: Oxford University Press: 373-382.
Konstan, D., 1979, "Problems in Epicurean Physics", *Isis* 70.3: 394-418.

Long, A. A., 1977, "Chance and Necessity in Epicureanism", *Phronesis* 22: 63-88.

Long, A. A., – Sedley, D., 1987, *The Hellenistic Philosophers*, Cambridge: Cambridge University Press.

Mitsis, P., forthcoming, *How to be a Hedonist: An Ancient Guide to the Epicurean Life*, Princeton: Princeton University Press.

Morel, P.-M., 2000, *Atome et nécessité. Démocrite, Épicure, Lucrèce*, Paris: PUF.

Morel, P.-M., 2021, *Le plaisir et la nécessité. Philosophie naturelle et anthropologie chez Démocrite et Épicure*, Paris: Vrin.

Piergiacomi, E., 2019, "La libertà: un evento?" in P. Mitsis, *La teoria etica di Epicuro. I piaceri dell'invulnerabilità* (Studia Philologica, 22), Rome: L'Erma di Bretschneider: 198-202.

Schiesaro, A., 2007, "Lucretius and Roman Politics and History", in *The Cambridge Companion to Lucretius*, S. Gillespie – P. Hardie (eds.), Cambridge: Cambridge University Press: 41-58.

Striker, G., 1996, "Origins of the concept of natural law", in *Essays on Hellenistic Epistemology and Ethics*, Cambridge: Cambridge University Press: 209-220.

Usener, H., 1887, *Epicurea*, Leipzig: Teubner.

Verde, F., 2013, "Cause epicuree", *Antiquorum philosophia*, Pisa: Fabrizio Serra: 127-144.

Verde, F., 2016, "Carlo Diano interprete del mondo greco", *Archivio di Storia della Cultura* 29: 265-280.

Part II

Ethics and its scientific background

MEDICINA ANCILLA PHILOSOPHIAE: THE EPICUREAN REMEDY FOR THE FEAR OF A CHILDLESS LIFE

Wim Nijs

1. INTRODUCTION

If ever there was a sickness that the Epicureans dearly desired to root out once and for all, it must certainly be irrational fear and the plethora of false notions that underlies it.[1] This sort of fear is, after all, responsible for spoiling countless people's chances of achieving the Epicurean ideal of a tranquil and happy life. First and foremost among these harmful fears are, no doubt, the fear of death and the fear of divine punishment. These two topics are dealt with at great length in extant Epicurean texts and feature prominently in the Garden's famous fourfold remedy.[2] Yet that does not mean that there were not countless other, often somewhat less obvious issues that filled unenlightened people with dread and anxiety. In a society where children were considered a family's pride and joy and where the survival of one's name and remembrance was believed to depend largely upon one's ability to produce heirs, the fear of remaining childless haunted many a couple's troubled dreams. Although the fear of childlessness occupies a less prominent position in extant Epicurean writings than the more universal fears of death and the gods, it is in many ways tangential to either of these, as we will see in what follows. Many people in antiquity tended to view childlessness as a terrible curse. The childless were, after all, destined to spend their old age and dying hours without the warmth and support of their caring sons and daughters. People were, moreover, terrified by the idea that the further growth of their family tree would be cut short and that the until then unbroken continuation of their family name would at last grind to an ignominious end.[3] Many blamed the gods or an envious fate for this sort of misfortune and foolishly gave themselves over to irrational bouts of religious zeal in a fruitless attempt to appease supernatural entities.[4] It should be no surprise, then, that the Epicureans, who presented themselves as veritable doctors of the soul, did not completely neglect this nasty source of anxiety and fear.

---

[1] Diogenes of Oinoanda famously wrote that the whole world is suffering from a common disease in this respect (fr. 3.4.3-13). For the Epicurean view on irrational fears and false notions like sicknesses and philosophy as medicine, see, for example, Gigante 1975; Duvernoy 1984; Nussbaum 1994: 102-139; Konstan et al. 1998: 20-23; Giovacchini 2007.

[2] Phld. *PHerc*. 1005.5.9-14: "God is not to be feared; death is no cause for worry; the good is easy to achieve; the bad is easy to endure". Cf. *KD* I-II; *SV* 1-2. Philodemus devoted entire treatises to the fear of death and dying (*De Morte*), the gods (*De dis*), and our piety towards them and (*De pietate*).

[3] Cf. Tutrone 2016: 775.

[4] For the ancient belief in a causal relationship between (in)fertility, divine agency, and religious practice, see, e.g., Brown 1987: 336-337; Flemming 2013: 580-588; Tutrone 2016.

In spite of ancient superstitions, infertility is, of course, a medical issue first. As such, the study of its causes and possible remedies belongs to the domain of medical science.

Extant textual evidence on meteorological phenomena shows that the Epicureans were willing to engage with natural science in order to demonstrate to people that these phenomena are natural occurrences rather than supernatural manifestations of divine wrath. To this end they developed their emblematic method of multiple explanations.[5] Although we cannot and should not always pinpoint the exact cause for a given natural phenomenon, so the Epicureans tell us, we can at all times rest assured that a rational explanation is in order and that the supernatural has absolutely nothing to do with it. A typically Epicurean brand of natural science and the key principles of the School's ethical doctrine are combined into a therapy for ungrounded fears that may help people achieve the Epicurean ideal of an unperturbed life.[6]

The problem of childlessness as a result of infertility, then, provides us with an interesting opportunity to investigate whether the Epicureans made similar inroads into the domain of medical science in general and gynecology/embryology in particular as part of their ethical project of freeing people from their fear of a life without children.[7] We will try to determine whether and how medical insights were combined with ethical precepts in service of Epicureanism's overarching objectives.

In what follows, we will discuss the arguments that the Epicureans used to help people get rid of their fear of childlessness. Ultimately, we will try to reconstruct and assess the different components of what may very well have been an all-in-one Epicurean therapy for the fear of a childless life.

2. EPICUREAN THERAPY FOR THE FEAR OF CHILDLESSNESS

2.1. Epicurus on having children

Undetected though they chose to live, the Garden's denizens were very much aware of the problems and exigencies of everyday life. It should not come as a surprise that Epicurus himself already gave some thought to the issues of marriage and

---

[5] Cf. Epic. *Pyth.* 86-88. The Epicurean method of multiple explanation has received a lot of scholarly attention in recent times. Some excellent studies can be found in Bénatouïl 2003; Taub 2009; Hankinson 2013; Masi 2014; Bakker 2016; Corsi 2017; Leone 2017; Verde 2018, 2020, and 2022: 53-99; Tsouna 2023.

[6] Cf. Epic. *Pyth.* 85-86: "In the first place, remember that, like everything else, knowledge of celestial phenomena, whether taken along with other things or in isolation, has no other end in view than peace of mind and firm conviction" (transl. Hicks 1931).

[7] Of course, involuntary childlessness is not necessarily caused by infertility. It can also be the result of a person's inability (or unwillingness) to find a suitable partner of the opposite sex. However, as far as I can tell, ancient Epicurean texts do not seem to have any explicit attention for this sort of scenario. Perhaps this sort of thing was much less of a problem in antiquity, when arranged marriages were still common practice, than it is nowadays.

children. Judging that a wife and children are likely to be a needless burden for the Epicurean's ataractic life – if not a downright distraction from philosophical pursuits – his advice was simply not to marry, nor to sire children.[8] However, so he concedes in typically qualifying fashion,[9] even the Epicurean sage may under certain circumstances diverge from this general precept.[10] It would seem, then, that childlessness is not entirely mandatory, but that it is, at any rate, the most ideal situation. We may well presume that, as far as Epicurus is concerned, people struggling to conceive should not at all be unhappy about their predicament. In sum, the Epicurean answer to people with infertility issues could easily have been a very short one. Yet it remains to be seen whether these troubled people would find such a curt dismissal of their worries satisfactory, let alone that it would be able to free them from all their fears. The Epicureans seem to have been well aware of this and, as a result, their extant writings allow us to reconstruct a more nuanced Epicurean therapy for the fear of childlessness.

This Epicurean treatment seems to consist in a two-pronged approach: a first part deals with people's fear of the causes of their infertility, while a second part is concerned with the fear of the impact that childlessness might have on the rest of their lives.

2.2. Fear not infertility's causes: Epicurean lessons in medicine

As mentioned above, many people in antiquity adhered to the traditional belief that infertility is caused by supernatural forces. Such a superstitious view attributes a failure to conceive entirely to the agency of disgruntled or envious gods, thus placing the fate of couples with fertility issues squarely in the hands of intractable higher powers. As a result, many childless people lived in a state of fear and despair and devoted enormous amounts of time, energy, and resources to sacrifices and prayer.[11] Seeing that the removal of such superstitious fears was very much part of the Epicurean ethical project, it should be no surprise that the Epicureans tried to counter the misguided belief that the blissful gods might somehow be the cause of infertility. As is the case with their explanations of meteorological phenomena, the ancient Epicureans tried to offer a rational alternative for the widely held superstitious beliefs that caused people to quiver in fear of divine punishment. To this end, they seem to have taken an interest in matters of gynecology and embryology.[12]

---

[8] Diog. Laert. X 119.
[9] See Roskam 2007a: 148 and *passim* on Epicureanism as a qualifying philosophy.
[10] For important discussion of the problematic textual basis for this qualification, see Chilton 1960; Gigante 1962: 380-381; and especially Brennan 1996: 348-352.
[11] Cf. Tutrone 2016: 779-780.
[12] For the (scant) evidence on Epicurus' interest in this topic, see fr. 329-333 Us. We also know that Epicurus' *Symposium* included a passage about the physical dangers involved in after-dinner sex (Plut. *Quaest. conv.* 653E-654A = fr. 61 Us.): cf. Nijs 2022a: 73-77. Philodemus' teacher Zeno of Sidon is also reported to have dealt with matters of procreation (Sor. *Gyn.* 3.3); cf. Angeli – Colaizzo 1979: 85.

This theme is perfectly illustrated by Lucretius' Book 4 of *De rerum natura* and the Epicurean treatise preserved in *PHerc.* 908/1390, which has been tentatively yet, in my view, convincingly attributed to Demetrius Lacon.[13]

Lucretius' text is, of course, far better preserved than the papyrus and, as a result, his argumentative aims can be more easily discerned than those of Demetrius. In Book 4 he launches into an all-out polemical attack against the conventional views on love, marriage, sex, and procreation.[14] His aim is to demystify these aspects of human life and to expose our sentimental approach to them for what it is: a collection of self-imposed illusions and superstitions that mask the straightforward natural principles that really underlie our behaviour. The misguided tendency to sugarcoat and romanticize sex and procreation as some sort of sacred spiritual experience is by no means harmless. In fact, it relegates this particular form of natural behaviour to the dangerous realm of superstitious fears and emotional obsessions where the practices of ritual sacrifice and fearful prayer reign supreme. In Book 4, Lucretius first addresses and ridicules the traditional beliefs about love and sexual desire (4.1037-1191), after which he turns to the matter of procreation and, indeed, infertility and people's fear thereof:[15]

> Nec divina satum genitalem numina cuiquam // absterrent, pater a gnatis ne dulcibus umquam // appelletur et ut sterili Venere exigat aevom; // quod plerumque putant, et multo sanguine maesti // conspergunt aras adolentque altaria donis, // ut gravidas reddant uxores semine largo. // nequiquam divom numen sortisque fatigant;

> It is not the divine powers that deprive any man of procreative capacity so that he is prevented from ever being called father by sweet children and is condemned to live a life cursed with sterility. This is indeed a widespread belief, which induces men mournfully to saturate the sacrificial slabs with streams of blood and set the altars ablaze with offerings, in the hope of making their wives pregnant with a full flow of semen. They importune the gods and their oracles in vain.

Many people wrongly believe that the gods have deprived them of their capacity to beget children, so Lucretius affirms. As a result, they spend their days bewailing their fate and waste their time and energy on sacrifices and the senseless mutterings of oracles and soothsayers.[16] Ironically, they do not only make a mistake in vainly

---

[13] Giorgianni – Ranocchia (and Corti) 2019: 45-50 and Ranocchia 2022. Before this new edition and commentary, the authorship of the text had been debated by various scholars (e.g., Cavallo 1983: 30, 56, 58; Brown 1987: 103 n. 7; Puglia 1992: 180-181) and was sometimes attributed to Epicurus' *De natura* (cf. Comparetti 1972: 78; Usener 1887: 129 and 1977; see also Piergiacomi 2023: 147).

[14] Brown 1987: 60-91; Tutrone 2016.

[15] Lucr. 4.1233-1239. Text by Rouse – Smith 1992 and translation by Smith 2001.

[16] The negative Epicurean view on oracular practice is well attested. See, e.g., Diog. Oen. fr. 23-24. See also Gordon 1996: 105-116; Clay 1989: 333; Warren 2000: 148; Bendlin 2011: 181-185; Nijs 2020. Also of interest is Plutarch's characterization of his critical Epicurean friend Boethus in *De Pythiae oraculis*. Here the latter formulates a whole series of cogent and thoroughly Epicurean criticisms against the

putting their trust in higher powers, but also tend to ask the gods for the wrong thing, begging them to grant them a more abundant flow of semen, which they believe will allow them to successfully impregnate their wives. Yet even if the gods were able and willing to grant that wish, there would still not be any guarantee that it would do these people much good, so Lucretius suggests in the verses that follow.[17] A correct medical appraisal of the issue of infertility demonstrates that a failure to conceive can be caused by a number of things. There may indeed be cases in which a shortage of semen is the problem, but it would be wrong to think that every patient may be helped in that way. There are, in fact, people who fail to conceive precisely because the flow of their semen is too abundant, so Demetrius Lacon tells us.[18] The list of issues of which the Epicureans believed that they might lead to infertility may have been quite lengthy. PHerc. 908/1390 mentions some causes which are absent from Lucretius' account and, seeing that only a small number of columns and fragments of the papyrus have been preserved, we may well assume that the complete list was far more elaborate. If we combine Lucretius' account and the extant passages from the papyrus, we see that, according to the Epicureans, infertility can be caused by the following things: (1) a shortage or abundance of semen;[19] (2) an ejaculatory duct and/or uterus that does not properly align;[20] (3) sexual positions that do not guarantee a sufficient alignment of the reproductive organs;[21] (4) incompatibility between man and woman, which may be caused by: (a) a lack of proportionality between the size of the membrum virile and the uterus,[22] (b) incompatibility of the male and female semen;[23] (5) excessive thickness or thinness of the semen causing it either to fall short of the mark or to be dispersed too easily (an unsuitable diet might play a role here);[24] (6) a uterus that offers an unfavourable environment for procreation on account of it being either too hot or too cold.[25] In sum, childlessness may be caused by many things, but divine punishment is definitely not one of them.[26] The fact that so many explanations are possible means also that there is no universal remedy for all cases of infertility. Therefore, one must certainly not make the mistake to conclude that medical science should be

---

credibility of the Delphic oracle and against oracular practice at large: cf. Ferrari 2000: 149-163 on this. An excellent in-depth discussion of Boethus' Epicureanism can be found in Verde 2015.

[17] Lucr. 4.1240-1277.
[18] PHerc. 908/1390.5.2-5.
[19] PHerc. 908/1390.4.
[20] PHerc. 908/1390.5-7.
[21] Lucr. 4.1263-1277.
[22] PHerc. 908/1390.6.
[23] Lucr. 4.1257-1259. Like Pythagoras and Democritus, the Epicureans also held that both men and women produced semen (Aet. 5.5.1 = fr. 330 Us.; Censorinus, *DN* 5.4 = fr. 331 Us.). For discussions on Lucretius' view on male and female semen, see Brown 1987: 321-360 and Pope 2019.
[24] Lucr. 4.1240-1247; 1260.
[25] PHerc. 908/1390.9.
[26] The Epicureans held, after all, that the gods never interfere in our affairs. They should be thought of as perfect beings, entirely unburdened by petty emotions like spite or jealousy (*KD* I).

abandoned in favour of religious practice should one or more medical therapies fail to solve the problem.

Our aim here is, of course, to study the Epicurean therapy of the fear of childlessness and infertility, not to discuss the aforementioned scientific explanations in detail, nor again to go looking for parallels in non-Epicurean medical texts.[27] It suffices to note that at least some Epicureans seem to have gone to considerable lengths in order to come up with an extensive set of possible explanations for the distressing issue of infertility. This indeed reminds us of their engagement with meteorology and natural sciences. When it comes to medical ailments, however, the Epicureans' methodological choice for multiple explanations is, of course, far less novel or controversial than it is in the domain of natural sciences.[28] Medical diagnosis and treatment are, after all, conjectural practices, as the Epicureans well knew and acknowledged.[29] Although natural philosophers liked to deal in absolutes, much to the disapproval of Epicurus and his followers,[30] medical doctors know very well that their craft inevitably involves a considerable amount of conjecture. In spite of the fact that the human body is much closer to us than the celestial bodies, its inner workings and defects are not always that much easier to discern. This is, no doubt, especially true for ancient doctors who did not have the means to inspect their patient's inner organs without performing a dangerous, if not downright unfeasible operation on them. Hence, it is not at all unusual for medical texts to propose a multitude of possible explanations for a given problem. Of course, in order to cure his patient, a doctor will eventually have to select the most likely explanation upon which he may then base the ensuing treatment. Epicurean philosophers, on the other hand, may not have felt any real need to choose between the multiple explanations which they listed in their writings on fertility issues.[31]

As with his multiple explanations for natural phenomena, the Epicurean philosopher's goal is above all to convince people that they need not fear some sort of supernatural interference in our world. Lucretius offers his list of possible causes of infertility in the context of his polemical attack against the superstitions that permeated Graeco-Roman culture. Demetrius Lacon also seems to add that people are often pained by their infertility, because they wrongly think that it does not occur

---

[27] Such discussions can, for example, be found in Brown 1987: 336-340 for Lucretius and in the commentary by Giorgianni – Ranocchia (and Corti) 2019 for Demetrius Lacon. See also Nijs 2022b for some additional parallels with either text.

[28] Cf. Giorgianni – Ranocchia (and Corti) 2019: 85; 97-98.

[29] Phld. *Rhet.* 2.2 (= Longo Auricchio 47); 2.26 (= Longo Auricchio 99).

[30] Epic. *Pyth.* 87.

[31] We shall return to this point at the end of this paper. In their capacities as doctors of the soul, however, the Epicureans faced more or less the same challenges as their medical colleagues. The Epicureans acknowledged that their moral therapy is no less conjectural than traditional medicine and that their diagnosis of a patient's sicknesses of the soul is often based on inferences drawn from visible signs (Phld. *Lib. dic.* fr. 57.1-11): cf. Gigante 1975: 55; 57 and 1983: 62-67.

through natural causes.[32] Both Epicureans, then, are certainly doing their part as true doctors of the soul, by curing patients of their irrational fears and superstitions. Their texts, then, may rightly be considered potent medicines for the fear of what people erroneously think is causing their childlessness.

2.3. Fear not infertility's consequences: Ethical arguments from Herculaneum

If we accept that our problems are not caused by the gods, we may grow to understand that infertility and childlessness are merely natural occurrences, rather than instances of divine punishment. Yet even if we now know and accept that the causes of our predicament are not at all frightening, we may still be worried about the *consequences* that this medical problem will have for the rest of our life.

We may, for instance, be deeply concerned about the fact that we will be missing out on the joy that children provide their parents. The prospect of not being able to start a family may make us fear that our overall life quality will in some way be diminished by this.

On the short term, we will not enjoy the affection or company of our children, nor will they in a more distant future be there to save us from a lonely and unassisted old age. Especially the fear of childlessness in connection to our old age and death is discussed at some length in extant Epicurean texts. In what follows, we will take a look at the Epicurean answer to a series of worries that appear to have plagued the childless person in antiquity.

2.3.1. Loneliness and a diminished life quality

First of all, the prospect of being forced to spend our entire life destitute of children may cause a person to imagine a bleak future in which he or she will languish in a state of helpless solitude. Parents may, after all, expect that their children will be there for them in their old age. They are comforted by the pleasant thought that their offspring will stay by their side to provide them with pleasant company and to care for them during their final years. Childless people, on the other hand, have no such consolation and may come to spend their days dreading a future when they will be left to their own devices to cope with the discomforts of their aging bodies.[33] Indeed, they may grow desperate at the thought of living their final moments in a

---

[32] *PHerc.* 908/1390.10.4-8: αἴτια τ[. .] . [. . .] ἡμῶν πλέον ἐπ[ὶ τού]των ἐχόντων λύπην, πλὴν ὅτι πέφυκεν, καὶ ὡς τὰ πράγματ[α . . . (.)]ου.: "cause (...) (of) us who are rather pained because of that, except that it happens naturally and like the matters...". It should, however, be noted that many of the preserved letters are barely readable and that we should therefore be careful not to lean too heavily upon this passage.

[33] Incidentally, Diogenes of Oinoanda seems to have had arguments ready to assuage the fear of the various physical ailments that may be brought on by old age (e.g., fr.144-145 + NF 133: on poor eyesight; fr. 146 + NF 177 + NF 134: on slowness of movement; NF 211 + fr. 151: on the loss of teeth). For Diogenes' treatise on old age, see Hammerstaedt 2015 and the comments *ad loc.* in Smith 1993.

state of complete loneliness when there will be no one left to care if they live or die, let alone that they will be remembered once they are gone.

And yet, the idealized image of a parent's old age entails an important condition. The idea that children will take care of their elderly parents hinges upon the prerequisite that these children do, in fact, feel genuine love for their parents and that they are, moreover, inclined to act upon that love. There is, however, no absolute guarantee that this will indeed be the case.[34] Lactantius reports that Epicurus once claimed that *habenti malos liberos orbitas praedicatur* ("to him who has bad children, childlessness is recommended").[35] It is all well and good to have morally outstanding, dutiful children, but one might as easily end up with a far less desirable progeny.[36] Despite one's best efforts to raise one's children to be thoroughly virtuous people, there is always the chance that they will somehow go astray, be it under the influence of bad friends or simply on account of their own rebellious temperament.[37] If any of the Epicureans ever doubted that even the best families can spawn some unexpectedly hateful people, they surely ceased to harbour any such illusions having witnessed the many spiteful actions of Metrodorus' own brother, Timocrates.[38]

Epicurus famously made the highly provocative claim that a parent's affection for his or her children is not natural, in the sense that it does not arise by necessity.[39] Parents do not always love their children spontaneously, nor does this bond automatically come into existence, so the Epicureans argue. Unlike hunger or pain, which arise of their own accord whether we want it or not,[40] the emotional connection between ourselves and our offspring is reliant upon our willingness to give that bond the opportunity to grow. If even our love for our children should not be taken for granted, it certainly remains to be seen to what extent the reverse feeling of affection may be counted upon. There are, after all, countless examples of children who have treated their own parents in the most appalling of ways.[41] All things considered, then, the pleasant dream of spending one's old age surrounded

---

[34] Cf. Phld. *Morte* 24.8-10.

[35] Lact. *Div. inst.* 3.17.5 = fr. 526 Us.

[36] Cf. e.g. *Alcib. II* 142b4-7; Juv. 10.350-353.

[37] Although Philodemus does not explicitly address the matter of teaching one's own children, he definitely acknowledges that some students may react very poorly to their Epicurean teacher's moral lessons (e.g., *Ira* 19.12-20.3; *Lib. dic.* fr. 67.9-12; fr. 70.7-15; fr. 7; 22a-24b). It is probably no coincidence that Epicurus' will stipulates that the surviving members of the Garden should take care of the children of Metrodorus and Polyaenus, on the condition that they continue to behave themselves in a way that befits the principles of the School (Diog. Laert. X 19; 21). If they ever go astray, the Epicureans are completely free to cut them off entirely. See Roskam 2020: 133-136 on this point.

[38] See Roskam 2007b: 43-49 on this point.

[39] Demetr. Lac. *PHerc.* 1012.66-68; Plut. *Am. prol.* 495A; *Adv. Col.* 1123A; Cic. *Ad Att.* 7.2.4; Cf. Alesse 2011. See also Roskam 2011 for Plutarch's polemical discussion of Epicurus' position.

[40] Cf. Demetr. Lac. *PHerc.* 1012.67.1-5.

[41] In Graeco-Roman mythology alone, the examples of Medea and Ariadne immediately spring to mind, who both betrayed their father and family. Even more shocking is the story of Pelias' daughters, who literally murdered their own father, albeit with good, yet terribly misguided intentions.

by dutiful and caring children might eventually turn out to be as unrealistic for the parent as it is for the childless person.

That possibility does not, however, mean that it would not be very unfortunate and even downright painful to end up in a state of utter loneliness.[42] In fact, Philodemus is willing to concede as much in *De morte*:[43]

τό γε μὴν ἐπὶ τῶι πρὸς μηδενὸς ὅλως μνημονευθή[σε]σθαι δηγμὸν ἀναδέχε[σ]θαι φυσικὸ[ν] ἔοικεν εἶν[αι·ᵛ] ζω{ι}ῆς γὰρ ἐνίοτ' ἀφίλο[υ] καὶ μηδὲν [ἀγα]θὸν ἐσχηκυίας ἐπιγέ[νη]μ' ἐστί[ν·ᵛ]

On the other hand, to experience suffering at the prospect of not being remembered by anyone at all seems to be natural: for it is sometimes the consequence of a life (that is) friendless and has nothing good.

Even though death itself is nothing to us,[44] Philodemus admits that it is only natural for the lonely person who is unlikely to be remembered after his death to be pained by this.[45] This condition is indeed the kind of future that the desperate childless person is likely to fear. Yet, as we have seen above, children are by no means the surest way to avert this dismal fate. The problem with the life of the painfully forsaken person of whom Philodemus speaks is not so much that it is childless, but above all that it is friendless. Friends are, after all, a crucial component of the Epicurean ideal of a happy life. A person who does not have any should indeed expect nothing good from the future.[46] The person who spends his life with neither family nor friends is not pitiable because he does not have the former, but very much so because he lacks the latter. As far as the Epicureans are concerned, friends are, in fact, superior to children in every single respect, as we will see in what follows.

First of all, the privilege to have children is not open to everyone. Although some couples may be blessed (or cursed?) with an unusually high fertility rate, many others struggle to fulfil their desire for children, growing increasingly frustrated and unhappy in the process. The ability to successfully beget children hinges upon natural factors, which lie outside our own control. It can be difficult to pinpoint the precise cause of a specific infertility problem, as it may be due to a variety

---

[42] For the Epicurean views on social isolation and its connection to vice, see Nijs 2024: 18-29.
[43] Phld. *Morte* 35.34-39 Henry (= 114.34-39 Delattre) – text by Delattre 2022 and translation by Henry 2009. A more detailed discussion of this passage can be found in Nijs 2024: 38-40.
[44] KD II; SV 2.
[45] They experience, as it were, a natural "bite" (δηγμός). See Tsouna 2007: 44-51 and Nijs 2024: 165-174 on the topic of "bites" in Philodemus.
[46] The Epicureans' enthusiastic praise of friendship is well attested (see, e.g., KD XXVII-XXVIII; SV 52), but its precise role within Epicurean ethics is not entirely unproblematic. Here is not the place to provide an exhaustive overview of scholarship on this topic, but some important discussions can, at any rate, be found in Rist 1980; Mitsis 1988: 98-128; O'Connor 1989; O'Keefe 2001; Brown 2002; Evans 2004; Armstrong 2011; Frede 2016; and not in the least Mitsis 2020, offering an excellent critical appraisal of past scholarship.

of factors. There is, moreover, no guarantee that the problem can be remedied at all. In fact, even if there is a remedy, it may sometimes come at too high a cost. It may, for example, be necessary to change partners in order to maximize sexual compatibility, as we read in Lucretius' Book 4.[47] Although orthodox Epicureans are, by principle, not particularly attached to the institution of marriage, it is not at all unthinkable that a couple sharing the unfulfilled wish to start a family together will not necessarily be happy with the advice to separate in order to seek out a more sexually compatible new partner.

The ability to acquire friends, on the other hand, is not dependent on factors beyond our own power. We only need to be kind and welcoming towards the people we meet and show a willingness to improve any shortcomings in our own mental disposition, so as to become even better suited for friendships with good people. If we are open to it, we can, in fact, befriend as many people as we like. Philodemus states that the Epicurean sage is always looking for new friends, regardless of his life stage.[48] Thus he continuously enriches his existence and fortifies himself against whatever turns of fortune the unforeseeable future might yet have in store for him. Whilst one may sometimes find it impossible to produce even a single child, friends can be acquired in any quantity we like.[49]

Finally, and perhaps most importantly, our affection for our friends is both natural and necessary. If we do not love our friend, it would simply be incorrect to call him a friend in the first place. We can have children whom we do not love, but who will still be our children nonetheless. *Mutatis mutandis*, our children may not love us either, in spite of our biological relationship. Yet we cannot have friends without loving them. Perhaps even more important from an egocentric Epicurean perspective is that it is impossible for anyone to be our friend if they do not love us back as well.[50] In the same way that we are inclined towards virtuous behaviour, precisely because it helps us in our pursuit of a happy life,[51] we will also feel genuine affection for our friends, who are, after all, an important factor for our happiness.

---

[47] Lucr. 4.1248-1256.

[48] Phld. *Elect. et fugae* 22.9-12: "And since he does not cut short the long extent of his life, he always begins new activities and friendly attachments" (transl. Indelli – Tsouna-McKirahan 1995).

[49] Epicurus famously opened the doors of the Garden to a heterogenous multitude of friends. It should be added that he also drew a fair amount of criticism for this, especially from Cicero, who held that it is better to cultivate a small number of friends. In his opinion – which echoes Aristotle (*EN* 1171a7-13) – the quality of friendship will be diluted when it is spread among too many people (Cic. *Amic.* 45); cf. Glad 1995: 165-175; Nijs 2022c: 164. Plutarch argues more or less to the same effect in his treatise *De amicorum multitudine*. For a detailed discussion of Plutarch's arguments, I refer to Van der Stockt 2011.

[50] It is, in fact, said that the Epicurean sage will love his friend as much as he loves himself (Cic. *Fin.* 1.67). Of course, there may also be people who feign affection for the person whose friend they pretend to be. These are, however, no friends at all and the wise Epicurean will take great care to distinguish flatterers from friends, as appears from Philodemus' elaborate engagement with the issue in his work *De adulatione*.

[51] Cf. Demetr. Lac. *PHerc.* 1012.67.5-7.

Mutual affection, then, is a natural and necessary characteristic of the bond between friends, but it will not necessarily be found in every relationship between a parent and his or her offspring.

In sum, the childless person has little or no reason to bewail his fate. If indeed he ends up in a wretched state of loneliness, he has only himself to blame. The time and energy that he wasted on his fruitless desire to start a family might have been spent far more usefully on the acquisition of friends. Friends are, after all, not merely a perfectly acceptable alternative for offspring, but are, in fact, simply the better choice in every single way. They provide us with all the good things one might hope to receive from one's children, but, contrary to the latter, they are easy to acquire and provide us with absolute guarantees for a happy and secure future.

2.3.2. Inheritance

Another worry that may be on the childless person's mind concerns the matter of inheritance. With no natural heirs at one's disposal, one may be disturbed by the thought that undeserving strangers will one day reap the fruits of one's labour. This second worry is not overlooked by Philodemus, either:[52]

> εἰ μή, νή [Δία], κατὰ τοῦτο λυπηρόν ἐστιν ἄπαι[δ]ος [κ]αταστροφή, διότι τοῖς κληρονόμο[ις] ἔστα[ι] τὰ πονηθέντα, καθαπερεὶ οὐχὶ πολλάκις ἅπασιν καταλείπειν ἡδεί[ο]νος [ὄ]ντος ἤ τισιν τέκνοις.ᵛ χωρὶς [τοῦ] μηδὲ φαύλους εἶναι μηδ' ἀναξ[ί]ους ἐνίοτε τοὺς κληρονομήσαντ[ας]· ἐὰν δ' ὦσιν πονηροί, προφυλάξασθ[αι] δυνατόν [ἐστιν κα]ὶ σπουδαίοις καὶ φίλοις ἀπολεί[ψειν· εἰ δ]έ τις οὐκ ἔχει, διὰ [το]ῦτ' ἔστιν ο[ἰ]κτρός, οὐχ ὅτι χη[ρ]ωστα[ὶ] γ' οἱ κάκ[ιστο]ι δύναντ]αι ε[ἶναι·]

> Unless indeed the death of a childless man is painful in this respect, because the fruits of his labors will go to his inheritors: as through it were not frequently more pleasant to leave things to anyone than to certain children! Besides, sometimes those who will inherit are not even bad, nor unworthy: and if they should be wicked, [it is] possible to take precautions [and] to bequeath to good men and to friends; and if someone does not have (any), he is pitiable for that reason, not because distant relatives can be the worst.

Once again friends are presented as the ultimate solution for the childless person's worries and insecurities. As we saw earlier, one cannot always choose what sort of people one's children will turn out to become, nor can it be ruled out that children will sometimes grow up to become bad people who might even bear their own parents ill will. For that reason, it is not always true that our children are more deserving of our goods than people to whom we are not related by blood.[53] Philode-

---

[52] Phld. *Morte* 24.5-17 Henry (= 103.5-17 Delattre). Text by Delattre 2022 and translation by Henry 2009 (modified).

[53] Moreover, even people who have children cannot be entirely sure that their heirs will not die prematurely. If such a thing were to happen, their possessions might still fall into the hands of unde-

mus' advice to the childless person is simply to write a will and to bequeath his or her belongings to friends.[54] It would seem, then, that good people are never really forced to leave their things to distant relatives whom they dislike. Of course, this situation does not apply to the deplorable loners who are just too misanthropic or too lazy to step outside and build some meaningful interhuman relationships. Such people have only themselves to blame for their predicament, and, truly wretched as their entire existence is, the matter of their inheritance is but the very least of their troubles.

The proper course of action, then, is to treat one's friends as one would treat one's lawful children. The wise Epicurean arranges his finances and property in such a way that he can always put something aside for his friends and makes sure that they will be taken care of after his own death:[55]

> φίλων μὲν τοίνυν ὑπαρχό[ν]των φειστέον μᾶλλον, ἵν' ἔχωσιν καὶ τελευτήσαντος ἐ[φ]ό[διον], καὶ οἷα τ[έ]κνα θετέον ...

> Thus, if one has friends, one should save more in order that they may have [means of maintaining themselves] even after one's death, and one should regard them as one's children.

In other words, childlessness is no reason to neglect one's finances and legacy. One should not make the mistake to think that narrowly avoiding bankruptcy until one's own death is acceptable if there are no direct heirs to whom one might bequeath one's possessions. Surely, such behaviour might be normal for the friendless person, whose life does not amount to much good anyway. Yet, childlessness does not at all preclude a happy life filled with friendship and pleasant companionship. A good person who has no children will still administer his affairs as diligently as an actual *pater familias* would – perhaps even more so, motivated as he is by the warm bond of genuine affection that exists between himself and his many likeminded friends.[56]

---

serving people (Phld. *Morte* 24.31-25.2), cf. Tsouna 2007: 284-285. Of course, from an Epicurean point of view, one should hardly worry about such events which may or may not occur after one's own death. It is fitting that we make arrangements for the benefit of the people we care about, but to be worried about anything that might happen to our legacy beyond that point is, of course, absurd and, as such, a needless source of disturbance for our mental equilibrium.

[54] See also Tsouna 2007: 283-285 on this point. Epicurus himself set the example for all future generations of Epicureans when he wrote the famous will that has been preserved in D.L. 10.16-22. For the Epicurean tradition of will-writing, see the discussions in Leiwo – Remes 1999; Warren 2001a; 2006: 162-199; Suits 2020: 185-188.

[55] Phld. *Oec.* 27.5-9. Text and translation by Tsouna 2013.

[56] Cf. Phld. *Elect. et fugae* 21.1-10, where we read that the sage will actually be prepared to work harder than usual if it is for the sake of his friends.

2.3.3. Living on through one's children

Some people may also be troubled by the idea that their bloodline will die out because of their failure to produce offspring. Especially members of aristocratic families who traditionally take great pride in their ancestry might be unpleasantly affected by the prospect that they will be responsible for the discontinuation of their long and illustrious bloodline. Many people in antiquity believed that having children amounted to acquiring some sort of immortality and that one might thus 'live on' through one's offspring.[57] As a result, the fear that childlessness might jeopardize this sense of 'immortality' falls firmly within the remit of the Epicurean therapy for the fear of death and is discussed by Philodemus in his treatise *De morte*. Philodemus' answer to this kind of concerns reads as follows:[58]

μάταιον δ ἐστὶ καὶ τ[ὸ] λυπεῖσθαι τελευτῶνας ἐπὶ τῷ[ι] τέκνα μὴ καταλείπειν δι' ἃ λέγου[σι]·ᵛ χ[ά]ριν γὰρ τοῦ διατηρεῖσθαι τοῦ[νο]μα, καθεύδειν ἔξεστιν ἐπ' ἀμφ[ότερα], μυρίων, μᾶλλον δ ἀπείρων τ[οῖς αὐ]τοῖς ὀ[νό]μασιν πρ[ο]σαγο[ρε]υθη[σο]μ[έν]ων […]

It is also foolish (for men) when dying to be distressed at not leaving behind children for the reasons they mention. For as to the maintenance of their names, it is possible to sleep on both (ears), as countless, or rather infinitely many (men) will be called by the same names …

Obviously, a proper Epicurean like Philodemus could not care less about idle pursuits such as the continuation of an aristocratic name, let alone the vain desire to amplify its future glory or influence. The Epicureans preferred to lead their lives unnoticed and were not at all interested in the role that having an illustrious name might play within the intricate game of politics. As a result, Philodemus can easily ignore that in the act of passing on one's name to one's children, it is not really the name as such that counts, but rather the affiliation to an important socio-political faction. Indeed, after Metrodorus' death, countless other Metrodoruses have walked the earth, none of whom were related to the famous Epicurean. So, as far as Philodemus is concerned, the name Metrodorus was perfectly able to survive the death of one of its most renowned bearers. Philodemus can make this claim with confidence because the Epicureans held that there is an infinite number of worlds and an infinity of time, which means that even less common names than the aforementioned Metrodorus will at some point resurface.[59] It remains, however, to be seen whether, for example, a member of the noble *gens Claudia* would find it satisfying to hear that his bloodline will be broken off, but that his name will

---

[57] Cf. Tutrone 2016: 775; Dixon 1992: 115.
[58] Phdl. *Morte* 22.9-16 Henry (= 101.9-16 Delattre) – text by Delattre 2022 and translation by Henry 2009.
[59] For this so-called principle of plenitude in Epicureanism, see fr. 266 Us.; Lucr. 1.232; 5.422-431; cf. Sedley 1998: 175 n. 29; Bakker 2016: 21-32 and *passim*.

endure thanks to some completely unrelated peasants who will also happen to bear the name Clodius somewhere in the distant future. Although the Epicureans have no reason to acknowledge the socio-political aspect of a given family name as a relevant factor, the objection that bearing the same name is not the same as being related would appear to have at least some validity to it. It should be noted that, even though the extant text does not pursue this line of reasoning, Epicurean doctrine would have allowed Philodemus to counter this objection as well. Had he wished to do so, he could have gone so far as to make the even stronger claim that there will not only be people who bear our name, but that people who are in all respects atomically identical to ourselves will walk the earth after our death. The Epicurean view on the combination and recombination of atoms and the plurality of worlds does, after all, leave room for the concept of *palingenesis*.[60] When we die, our atoms do not simply vanish. Instead, they are dispersed and float around until they meet with other atoms so as to form new composite bodies. It may, obviously, take countless centuries for every single atom of a given body to come back together in an identical combination, but – in light of the infinity of time and the indestructability of atoms – it is a logical necessity that every combination of atoms will occur an infinite number of times. In sum, even if we are unable to pass our genetic makeup on to our children, our DNA, so to speak, will not be irretrievably lost, but will simply recombine again with the passing of time. Based on the principles of Epicurean cosmology, then, neither our name, nor our exact bodily composition will ever be truly lost, regardless of whether or not we are able to produce children. Yet neither the strangers who will bear our name nor those who will actually be identical to us will have anything to do with ourselves. The dead no longer exist and true *repetentia nostri* cannot occur, as there is no meaningful continuity between ourselves and our future or past incarnations. In the end, none of these things will have any bearing whatsoever upon our own life, nor should we allow it to influence our happiness or peace of mind.

Moreover, so Philodemus seems to add in the damaged lines that follow, there is no need to worry about the fact that we are letting down countless generations of ancestors who all made an effort to pass on their name. These ancestors are, after all, long dead and are as such in no position to care about whatever happens to their legacy.[61]

---

[60] Lucr. 3.847-861: "Furthermore, if in course of time all our component atoms should be reassembled after our death and restored again to their present positions, so that the light of life was given to us a second time, even that eventuality would not affect us in the least, once there had been a break in the chain of consciousness. (...) When you survey the whole sweep of measureless time past and consider the multifariousness of the movements of matter, you can easily convince yourself that the same seeds that compose us now have often been arranged in the same order that they occupy now." (transl. Smith 2001). For insightful, in-depth discussions of Epicurean *palingenesis* and its repercussions for our sense of identity, see Warren 2001b and Lentricchia 2020.

[61] Phld. *Morte* 23.33-36 Henry (= 102.33-36 Delattre).

In sum, a misguided desire to 'live on' by passing on one's name is certainly not a valid reason to desire children. If one really is determined to be remembered for centuries to come, which is in itself an utterly useless desire, one should simply bear in mind that this can also be accomplished without legitimate children or the direct continuation of one's name.

Epicurus himself advised against marriage and family life and, as far as we know, he never fathered any (legitimate) children.[62] Yet more than two thousand years after his death, his name has still not been forgotten, even though he never passed it on to a son or a daughter. For this enduring remembrance he has his many friends and later followers to thank,[63] although, of course, he is no longer able to be thankful and would have cared very little about *post mortem* fame to begin with. As Philodemus points out, the members of the Garden have done much more to keep the memory of its Founding Fathers alive than most children ever did for their biological parents. Mythical figures such as Danaus, Aegyptus, and Heracles may have sired scores of children, but, in the end, none of these added much to whatever fame their fathers had already acquired for themselves during their lives:[64]

εἰ δὲ τοῖς [ἀ]ποτελέσμ[α]σιν χρὴ τεκμα[ίρ]εσθαι, τ[ί]ς ἔτυχεν [κη]δεμόνων οἵων Πολύαινος καὶ Μη[τρό]δωρος καὶ Λεοντε[ὺ]ς καὶ Ἐπίκουρ[ος αὐ]τός, ἀπὸ τῆς τελευτῆς ἄχρι καὶ νῦ[ν, κ]αὶ κατὰ λόγον ἅπαντ[ε]ς οἱ κατὰ τὴν αἵρε[σι]ν ἡμῶν προκόψαντε[ς];ᵛ ὁρῶμεν δὲ κ[α]ὶ τῶν ἰδιωτῶν πολλοὺς τυγχάν[ο]ντας ἁπαξαπάσης τ[ι]μῆς ἐννόμο[υ κ]αὶ φυσικῆς ὑπὸ φίλων ἀξιολόγως ε[ὐ]νοησάντων, πολὺ μᾶλλον ἢ τοὺς [ἀ]π[ὸ] Δαναοῦ καὶ τἀδελφοῦ καὶ τοῦ κα[ὶ πλε]ί[ους α]ὐ[τῶν ἥρω]ος Ἡρακλ[έ]ους κατ[α]λιπόν[τος, ὥσ]τ' ο[ὐ] περίεστ[ὶ] γε κερδαίνειν […]

But if one must judge by the results, who gained protectors such as Polyaenus and Metrodorus and Leonteus and Epicurus himself (gained) from (the moment of) death right up to now, and similarly all those who progressed in our school? And even among laymen we see many obtaining lawful and natural honor to the full extent from friends who displayed noteworthy goodwill, much more than those men (obtain such honor) who left behind the children of Danaus and of his brother and of him who [fathered an even greater number], Heracles, so that there is left over (?) to profit (...)

---

[62] The polemical doxographic tradition reports that, although Epicurus may not have had any lawful children, he conceived at least one child with an unnamed prostitute from Cyzicus (Plut. *Non posse* 1098B). Although Epicurus would hardly have considered it shameful to consort with such a woman, it is far from certain that this sort of slander contains any truth. It certainly fits the doxographic anti-Epicurean tradition which has no shortage of greatly exaggerated polemical accounts meant to attest to Epicurus' alleged licentiousness and gluttony.

[63] In fact, we know of at least one instance in which Epicurus' friends and followers literally kept his name alive: Metrodorus and Leontion named their son Epicurus in honor of their dear friend and mentor who was still alive at that time (Diog. Laert. X 19).

[64] Phld. *Morte* 23.2-15 Henry (= 101.2-15 Delattre) – text by Delattre 2022 and translation by Henry 2009. See also Delattre 2022: 121 on Philodemus' reference to Danaus, Aegyptus, and Heracles.

Of course, this is a mere *obiter dictum*, seeing that these famous Epicureans could not have cared less about whether or not future members of their school might continue to hold them in high esteem. It is, however, a neat illustration of the unreliability of offspring as compared to the steadfast commitment of one's dear friends and students. The true Epicurean will not at all be preoccupied by thoughts about enduring *post mortem* fame and remembrance, nor about the role that descendants might play in this. However, the childless unenlightened person should definitely take Philodemus' *obiter dictum* to heart. Such a person would, after all, do well to keep in mind that his inability to father children will not harm him in any way and that having many friends is always better than having many children. In sum, the way of life of the Epicurean philosopher, who makes friends wherever he goes, will always yield much better results than that of the misguided fool, sometimes even in areas where the former does not even seek to be successful.[65]

3. CONCLUSION: WHAT SHALL THE EPICUREAN THERAPIST TELL HIS CHILDLESS PATIENT?

As we saw above, the Epicureans did not at all neglect childlessness and the fears to which it might give rise. Approaching the matter from different angles, Epicureans like Lucretius, Demetrius, and Philodemus came up with arguments to cover both the fear of supernatural causes and the manifold worries that people may have about a childless life, old age, and death. The childless person's Epicurean medicine, then, is a potent cocktail of scientific insights and ethical arguments. If he undergoes this Epicurean therapy, he will soon come to see that he does not really need children to enjoy a happy life and that a physical incapacity to produce offspring should not be allowed to become a source of distress.

Yet, although it is not necessary to have children, even the sage may sometimes choose to start a family nonetheless. Famous first generation Epicureans like Metrodorus, Polyaenus, Idomeneus, and Leonteus had children,[66] as did Diogenes of Oinoanda, of whom we know that he delivered a thoroughly Epicurean eulogy at his son's funeral.[67] This fact appears to suggest that some, if not all of these full-fledged Epicureans decided to have children on the basis of a careful rational appraisal of their personal circumstances and the benefits and drawbacks of starting a family.[68] What, then, if someone rationally decides that children are the right option for him,

---

[65] Plutarch capitalizes precisely upon the striking discrepancy between Epicurus' lofty claims about the superiority of an anonymous life, on one hand, and his actual famousness on the other (*Lat. viv.* 1128F-1129A).
[66] Diog. Laert. X19; Plut. *Adv. Col.* 1117DE; Sen. *Ep.* 98.9; Diog. Laert. X 26.
[67] Diog. Oen. NF 215-fr.73-NF209.
[68] Such a rational calculus should, after all, be the yardstick of every decision (Epic. *Men.* 130-132).

but finds himself hampered by fertility issues? Perhaps this person will assure his Epicurean teachers that he harbours no false illusions about the natural causes of his ailment and promises that he will not grow frustrated or depressed when his attempts to impregnate his partner fail. In sum, he accepts and understands all relevant causes and consequences of his situation and is prepared to undergo fertility therapy *sine ira et studio*. Would this person then be able to count upon his Epicurean teachers to offer him some helpful medical advice or does their enㅡgagement with the topic of infertility remain strictly limited to the removal of the fear that it might engender?

If we look at the textual evidence, Lucretius' account seems to hint at some possiㅡble solutions for infertility problems. If procreational incompatibility between man and woman is to blame, a change of partners may solve the problem, so he seems to suggest (*et quibus ante domi fecundae saepe nequissent uxores parere, inventast illis quoque compar natura, ut possent gnatis munire senectam*).[69] Moreover, incomㅡpatibility of the male and female semen may perhaps be remedied by a change of diet.[70] Some foods thicken semen (*aliis rebus concrescunt semina membris*), while others make it thin (*aliis extenvantur tabentque vicissim*). Fertility is enhanced by a combination of thin semen from one partner with thick semen from the other.[71] Based on what Lucretius tells us, it seems a reasonable course of action to put one partner on a rigorous diet of food that make semen thicker, while the other should only consume foodstuffs that are known to render semen more watery. Lastly, it would seem that an insufficient alignment of the male and female reproductive organs may be countered with the choice for a more "animal-like" coital position on all fours (*more ferarum quadrupedumque ritu*).[72]

At first glance, these elements from Lucretius' Book 4 seem to go somewhat beyond the removal of superstitious fear. Indeed, they appear to open the door to a glimmer of hope that there might in fact be a cure for one's infertility. Be that as it may, it remains to be seen exactly to what extent Lucretius' suggestions were effectively intended for practical use. His recommendations are, after all, mostly too unspecific to be usable and, as *PHerc.* 908/1390 demonstrates, his list of Epicuㅡrean explanations for infertility is far from exhaustive. More importantly, Lucretius seems to have chosen this handful of 'helpful' suggestions in service of his larger polemical goal. We should bear in mind that much of Book 4 is devoted to the

---

[69] Lucr. 4.1248-1256.
[70] Lucr. 4.1260-1262. Although the surviving sections of *PHerc.* 908/1390 do not seem to contain any such practical advice, we know that Demetrius took a vivid interest in dietary prescriptions, on which topic he seems to have written an entire treatise Περί τινων συζητηθέντων [κ]ατὰ δίαιταν (*PHerc.* 1006; cf. Assante 2008); see also Giorgianni – Ranocchia (and Corti) 2019: 22-23. There is, however, no way to determine whether or not he ever discussed the importance of a healthy diet in the context of procreation and infertility.
[71] Lucr. 4.1257-1259.
[72] Lucr. 4.1264-1267.

complete demystification of the concepts of love, sex, and marriage. The advice to disband a marriage and to seek a more fertile partner contributes to this goal, as it radically demystifies the idealized concepts of marriage and love and exposes the opportunism of people's underlying animalistic desire for sex and procreation. The same can be said of Lucretius' advice to have sex in the way of four-footed animals.[73] In sum, if our Epicurean-minded childless person is in search of concrete solutions for his infertility, *De rerum natura* is probably not the right place to look.

More important here are the ethical repercussions of our childless person's desire for children. His Epicurean teachers will, in all likelihood, tell him that his willingness to undergo fertility therapy is, in fact, already at odds with one of Epicureanism's core principles. Natural goods are, after all, easily acquired and only unnatural ones require a real effort.[74] The *desire* to have children may under certain circumstances be natural,[75] but in itself it is never truly necessary, quite simply because we do not really need children for the achievement of happiness. Yet that does not necessarily mean that *having children* cannot be a natural good in some cases. A true orthodox Epicurean like Metrodorus may never even have had an outspoken desire to become a father. It is, at any rate, highly unlikely that he would have pursued parenthood if it had been difficult to achieve. Instead, he may simply have decided that being a parent would not per se be a bad thing if he ever happened to become one. In other words, his rational calculus may not have revolved around the question whether or not he wanted children. Instead, it might have concerned his sex life in general. The central question may very well have been whether the possibility to have intercourse with Leontion at any given time without the need

---

[73] Cf. Fratantuono 2015: 298-299: "(...) and once again, the sexual life of mortals is reduced to animalistic terms. We are now in a world of the habits and customs of wild beasts, indeed of the 'rite of quadrupeds' (*quadrupedumque ... ritu*); men are reduced to the seeming indignity of rear-entry intercourse." Only Lucretius' remark about the importance of a good diet seems unrelated to this specific polemical goal. Yet, the fact that he neglects to specify which foods will help us renders his dietary advice unusable. Lucretius' remark on the importance of a healthy diet may to some extent foreshadow his criticism of the harmful dietary habits that had become popular among his Roman contemporaries. At 5.1006-1010, he blames them for poisoning themselves with an immoderate consumption of food and drink. Even if a positive change of diet will not automatically remedy one's fertility issues, it will, at any rate, have a positive effect on one's general health and wellbeing. We should also bear in mind that Epicurus taught his students that the emission of seed which has for some reason become clotted does not occur smoothly and may very well cause internal damage to the body (Plut. *Quast. conv.* 653E-654A, where clotted seed as a result of indigestion is discussed). It would seem that the correlation between the consumption of food and clotted semen is not restricted to *De rerum natura*. Lucretius writes that clotted seed *concretius aequo mittitur* (4.1244-1245), while Epicurus states that indigestion causes semen to συμπεφυρμένην ἀποσπᾶσθαι (*Quaest. conv.* 654A). In light of the obvious similarities between both descriptions, it seems likely that both an unhealthy diet and an abundance of food were believed to lead to one and the same situation of seed becoming too clotted, which may in turn impact not only fertility, but also one's general health.

[74] *KD* XV.

[75] As always, desires are to be evaluated case by case: a desire for fresh figs, for example, may be natural if you happen to live in Greece, but probably somewhat less so if you spend your days in a secluded cabin in the middle of the Alaskan wilderness.

to worry about a potential pregnancy would outweigh the risk that children might become a hindrance.[76]

We know that Epicurus' view on sex was somewhat ambivalent: he categorized it as a natural, yet unnecessary desire and acknowledged that it could be a source of pleasure.[77] Yet, he also proclaimed that it entails risks.[78] We may well imagine that the chance of involuntarily impregnating someone may have been one of these risks. In fact, one's peace of mind could even be affected by the fear that a sexual encounter might, despite all precautions, result in unwanted parenthood. If so, then Metrodorus and Leontion may have decided to rid themselves of this fear once and for all: even though a wise Epicurean is not generally supposed to have an explicit desire for children, they may simply have agreed that, at least for them, pregnancy was nothing to be afraid of and that sexual pleasure could henceforth be enjoyed freely and unmarred by any concerns whatsoever. For Epicureans who have children without trying, then, their offspring can, under certain circumstances, indeed be considered a natural good.

For the infertile person, on the other hand, children are unlikely ever to become a natural good. From an Epicurean point of view, people should definitely not subject themselves to a series of fertility therapies, considering that infertility is in fact something that enables them to enjoy sexual intercourse without the need to worry about inconvenient pregnancies. Even if a person were able to try out fertility treatments without becoming frustrated or depressed by the many setbacks, he or she would still be pursuing an unnecessary desire, which is, essentially, a pure waste of time and energy.[79] In sum, if our childless student were to explain his predicament to his Epicurean teachers and ask them for help, it is very unlikely that they would offer him medical advice of any sort.

Granted, the Epicurean sage always takes the utmost care of his own bodily health and is prepared to entrust himself to the care of doctors and to take any medicine they prescribe if it is likely to enhance the quality of his life and to prolong

---

[76] An important factor in this rational calculus may have been the firm and reassuring knowledge that their many Epicurean friends would always be more than willing to step in and help alleviate their tasks as parents.

[77] Cf. Brown 1987: 120: "(...) both [Epicurus and Lucretius] acknowledge the pleasure of sex, if untainted by love, but view it as a secondary factor in the sum of human happiness."

[78] Diog. Laert. X 118; *SVF* 51; Plut. *Quaest. conv.* 653D. For Epicurus' view on the (un)desirability of sexual intercourse, see, e.g., Arkins 1986; Brown 1987: 108-111; Nussbaum 1994: 141-191; Brennan 1996: 346-348; Gordon 2002; Arenson 2016 and Morel 2019.

[79] This person should, moreover, keep well in mind that even a natural and unnecessary desire may eventually turn into an unnatural one if one becomes overly fixated on the desired object and starts to develop false beliefs about its value for one's happiness: cf. Annas 1993: 191-193. From an Epicurean's point of view, a readiness to go through the trouble of undergoing various fertility treatments might already seem alarmingly symptomatic of the development of false opinions about the necessity or value of having children.

its duration.[80] Yet infertility is in itself no life-threatening affliction.[81] So, rather than to hand out medical advice, our Epicurean teachers will, no doubt, try to help their student with some philosophical advice instead and will tell him that he should, in fact, be happy with his infertility. It allows him, after all, to have sex without the need to worry about the risk of becoming a parent. Neither will they neglect to point out all the benefits of not having any children of one's own. There is, moreover, nothing that would keep a childless person from playing with or even caring for other people's children whenever he feels like it. Epicurus himself seems to have been fond of children,[82] even though he did not want to have any of his own, and from his testament we know that the Epicurean community as a whole was instructed to take care of the children of Metrodorus and Polyaenus.[83]

Be that as it may, the Epicurean teachers will above all remind their student of the importance of having good Epicurean friends. An infertile person may have a very hard time fulfilling his unnatural desire for children, but a natural desire for friends can always be fulfilled with the greatest ease.

In sum, the childless reader should not keep thumbing through Lucretius' Book 4 or Demetrius' treatise *ad infinitum* in a fruitless search for a medical cure. Instead, he should simply put both books aside when he is confident that his fear for the cause of his infertility has safely been removed. At that point, this particular Epicurean medicine will have served its purpose and will have nothing left to offer, other than a repeated affirmation of what the reader already knows.[84] There is, in any case, no need to keep looking for an Epicurean therapy for infertility itself, nor, in fact, for fertility therapy in general: why would one even try to cure something that should not even be considered an ailment in the first place?[85]

---

[80] Phld. *Elect. et fugae* 23.3-14: "And when he encounters whatever can lead to an improvement, he spares no effort in the hope of surviving for a while. Indeed, he takes the greatest care of his health. And feeling confidence against illness and death, he endures with strength the therapies that can remove them" (transl. Indelli – Tsouna-McKirahan 1995).

[81] Cf. Senkova 2015: 129.

[82] Cf. *SV* 62; Diog. Laert. X 22 and possibly also the *Letter to Apia* (fr. 176 Us.; cf. Longo Auricchio 1988: 109-111). See also Roskam 2020: 129.

[83] Diog. Laert. X 19.

[84] Of course, the Epicureans strongly believed that it could be useful to revisit texts that one has already studied in the past (cf. Epic. *Men.* 135). The purpose of this is, however, to rehearse and reaffirm earlier lessons, not to find solutions for problems which the text's authors never intended to address.

[85] The Epicureans may not have been the only ones to hold the view that infertility need not always be seen as a serious health issue. Senkova 2015: 129 notes that male infertility was not usually considered to be dangerous for the patient's health, as opposed to female infertility which was effectively believed to be a potential health hazard. It is, in fact, exceedingly rare for ancient medical texts to devote any attention whatsoever to the possibility that the man might be responsible for a couple's failure to conceive. The elaborate Epicurean engagement with male infertility as seen in the writings of Lucretius and Demetrius is, in fact, quite remarkable in that respect. The few instances in the *Corpus Hippocraticum* and other medical texts where male infertility is acknowledged are not at all concerned with suggesting any sort of possible remedy for the problem; cf. Flemming 2013: 571. In fact, it remains to be seen whether the Epicureans even shared the belief that female infertility is always harmful. Male doctors might perhaps have seen it that way, but the prostitutes who had become valued members of

If there is anything at all that the childless person needs to be happy, it is the very thing that we all require: true friends who will unfailingly provide us with pleasure and security well above and beyond whatever any parent might ever hope to derive from his offspring. Fortunately, the Garden could not only boast of fine doctors of the soul and a cabinet well stocked with a potent compound medicine for the fear of childlessness, but was also ready to offer its patients the best possible medical aftercare under the form of an abundance of genuine Epicurean friendship.

REFERENCES

Alesse, F., 2011, "ΤΕΚΝΟΠΟΙΙΑ e amore parentale in Epicuro e nell'epicureismo", *Cronache Ercolanesi* 41: 207-215.
Angeli, A., – Colaizzo, M., 1979, "I frammenti di Zenone Sidonio", *Cronache Ercolanesi* 9: 47-133.
Annas, J., 1993, *The Morality of Happiness*, Oxford: Oxford University Press.
Arenson, K. E., 2016, "Epicurean on Marriage as Sexual Therapy", *Polis* 33: 291-311.
Arkins, B., 1984, "Epicurus and Lucretius on Sex, Love, and Marriage", *Apeiron* 18: 141-143.
Armstrong, D., 2011, "Epicurean Virtues, Epicurean Friendship: Cicero vs the Herculaneum Papyri", in J. Fish – K. R. Sanders (eds.), *Epicurus and the Epicurean Tradition*, Cambridge: Cambridge University Press: 105-128.
Assante, M. G., 2008, "Per un riesame del *PHerc.* 1006 (Demetrio Lacone, *Alcune ricerche comuni sul metodo di vita*)", *Cronache Ercolanesi* 38: 109-160.
Bakker, F. A., 2016, *Epicurean Meteorology: Sources, Methods, Scope and Organization*, Leiden-Boston: Brill.
Bénatouïl, T., 2003, "La méthode épicurienne des explications multiples", *Les Cahiers Philosophiques de Strasbourg* 15: 15-47.
Bendlin, A., 2011, "On the Uses and Disadvantages of Divination. Oracles and their Literary Representations in the Time of the Second Sophistic", in J. A. North – S. R. F. Price (eds.), *The Religious History of the Roman Empire. Pagans, Jews, and Christians*, Oxford: Oxford University Press: 175-250.
Brennan, T., 1996, "Epicurus on Sex, Marriage, and Children", *Classical Philology* 91: 346-352.
Brown, E., 2002, "Epicurus on the Value of Friendship (*Sententia Vaticana* 23)", *Classical Philology* 97: 68-80.
Brown, R. D., 1987, *Lucretius on Love and Sex. A Commentary on De Rerum Natura IV, 1030-1287 with Prolegomena, Text, and Translation*, Leiden-New York-Copenhagen-Cologne: E. J. Brill.
Cavallo, G., 1983, *Libri, scritture, scribi a Ercolano. Introduzione allo studio dei materiali greci*, Napoli: Macchiaroli.

---

the Garden may very well have had a thing or two to say about the benefits of *not* being all too fertile. For studies on the women of the Epicurean Garden, see Gordon 2004 and Di Fabio 2017.

Chilton, C. W., 1960, "Did Epicurus Approve of Marriage? A Study of Diogenes Laertius X, 119", *Phronesis* 5: 71-74.

Clay, D., 1989, "A Lost Epicurean Community", *Greek, Roman, and Byzantine Studies* 30: 313-335.

Comparetti, D., 1972, "Relazione sui papiri ercolanesi", in D. Comparetti – G. De Petra (eds.), *La Villa ercolanese dei Pisoni. I suoi monumenti e la sua biblioteca*, Turin: Loescher: 55-85.

Corsi, F. G., 2017, "Il metodo delle molteplici spiegazioni in Diogene di Enoanda", *Syzetesis* 4: 253-284.

Delattre, D., 2022, *Philodème de Gadara. Sur la mort. Livre IV. Texte établi, traduit et annoté*, Paris: Les Belles Lettres.

Di Fabio, T., 2017, "Donne epicuree. Cortigiane, filosofe o entrambe?", *Bollettino della Società Filosofica Italiana* 221: 19-36.

Dixon, S., 1992, *The Roman Family*, Baltimore-London: Johns Hopkins University Press.

Duvernoy, J.-F., 1984, "Le modèle médical de l'éthique dans l'épicurisme", in *Justifications de l'éthique*, XIXe Congrès de l'Association des Sociétés de philosophie de langue française Bruxelles – Louvain-la-Neuve 6-9 septembre 1982, Brussels: Éditions de l'Université de Bruxelles: 171-177.

Evans, M., 2004, "Can Epicureans Be Friends?", *Ancient Philosophy* 24: 407-424.

Ferrari, F., 2000, "La falsità delle asserzioni relative al futuro: un argomento epicureo contro la mantica in Plut. Pyth. orac. 10", in M. Erler – R. Bees (eds.), *Epikureismus in der späten Republik und der Kaiserzeit. Akten der 2. Tagung der Karl-und-Gertrud-Abel-Stiftung vom 30. September – 3 Oktober 1998 in Würzburg*, Stuttgart: Franz Steiner Verlag: 149-163.

Flemming, R., 2013, "The Invention of Infertility in the Classical Greek World: Medicine, Divinity, and Gender", *Bulletin of the History of Medicine* 87: 565-590.

Fratantuono, L., 2015, *A Reading of Lucretius' De Rerum Natura*, Lanham-Boulder-New York-London: Lexington Books.

Frede, D., 2016, "Epicurus on the Importance of Friendship in the Good Life (*De Finibus* I.65-70; 2.78-85)", in J. Annas – G. Betegh (eds.), *Cicero's De Finibus: Philosophical Approaches*, Cambridge: Cambridge University Press: 96-117.

Gigante, M., 1962, "Note Laerziane", *La Parola del Passato* 17: 371-381.

Gigante, M., 1975, "*Philosophia medicans* in Filodemo", *Cronache Ercolanesi* 5: 53-61.

Gigante, M., 1983, *Ricerche filodemee. Seconda edizione riveduta e accresciuta*, Naples: Macchiaroli.

Giorgianni, F. – Ranocchia, G. (in collaboration with A. Corti), 2019, "Scrittore epicureo anonimo. Opera incerta *PHerc.* 1390/908. Edizione, introduzione e commentario, tavole", *Galenos* 13: 17-110.

Giovacchini, J., 2007, "La méthode épicurienne et son modèle medicale", Paris [diss.].

Glad, C. E., 1995, *Paul and Philodemus. Adaptability in Epicurean and Early Christian Psychagogy*, Leiden-New York-Cologne: E. J. Brill.

Gordon, P., 1996, *Epicurus in Lycia. The Second-Century World of Diogenes of Oenoanda*, Ann Arbor: University of Michigan Press.

Gordon, P., 2002, "Some Unseen Monster. Rereading Lucretius on Sex", in D. Frederick (ed.), *The Roman Gaze. Vision, Power and the Body*, Baltimore-London: Johns Hopkins University Press: 86-109.

Gordon, P., 2004, "Remembering the Garden. The Trouble with Women in the School of Epicurus", in J. T. Fitzgerald – D. Obbink – G. S. Holland (eds.), *Philodemus and the New Testament World*, Leiden-Boston: Brill: 221-244.

Hammerstaedt, J., 2015, "Considerazioni epicuree sul tema della vecchiaia", in D. De Sanctis – E. Spinelli – M. Tulli – F. Verde (eds.), *Questioni epicuree*, Sankt Augustin: Academia Verlag: 199-212.

Hankinson, R. J., 2013, "Lucretius, Epicurus, and the Logic of Multiple Explanations", in D. Lehoux – A. D. Morrison – A. Sharrok (eds.), *Lucretius: Poetry, Philosophy, Science*, Oxford: Oxford University Press: 69-97.

Henry, W. B., 2009, *Philodemus, On Death. Translated with an Introduction and Notes*, Atlanta: Society of Biblical Literature.

Hicks, R. D., 1931, *Diogenes Laertius. Lives of Eminent Philosophers, with and English Translation*, Cambridge, MA-London: Harvard University Press.

Indelli, G., – Tsouna-McKirahan, V., 1995, *[Philodemus]. [On Choices and Avoidances]. Edited with Translation and Commentary*, Naples: Bibliopolis.

Konstan, D., – Clay, D., – Glad, C. E., – Thom, J. C., – Ware, J., 1998, *Philodemus. On Frank Criticism. Introduction, Translation, and Notes*, Atlanta: Society of Biblical Literature.

Leiwo, M., – Remes, P., 1999, "Partnership of Citizens and Metics: the Will of Epicurus", *Classical Quarterly* 49: 161-166.

Lentricchia, M., 2020, "Our Atoms, Ourselves: Lucretius on the Psychology of Personal Identity (*DRN* 3.842-864)", *Elenchos* 41: 297-328.

Leone, G., 2017, "Diogène d'Oenoanda et la polémique sur les meteora", in J. Hammerstaedt – P.-M. Morel – R. Güremen (eds.), *Diogenes of Oinoanda. Epicureanism and Philosophical Debates / Diogène d'Oenoanda. Épicurisme et controversies*, Leuven: Leuven University Press: 89-110.

Longo Auricchio, F., 1988, *Ermarco. Frammenti*, Naples: Bibliopolis.

Masi, F. G., 2014, "The Method of Multiple Explanations. Epicurus and the Notion of Causal Possibility", in C. Natali – C. Viano (eds.), *Aitia II. Avec ou sans Aristote. Le débat sur les causes à l'âge hellénistique et impérial*, Louvain-la-Neuve: Peeters: 37-63.

Mitsis, P., 1988, *Epicurus' Ethical Theory. The Pleasures of Invulnerability*, Ithaca-London: Cornell University Press.

Mitsis, P., 2020, "Friendship", in P. Mitsis (ed.), *The Oxford Handbook of Epicurus and Epicureanism*, Oxford: Oxford University Press: 250-283.

Morel, P.-M., 2019, "Sexe, amour et politique chez Lucrèce", *Philosophie Antique* 19: 57-84.

Nijs, W., 2020, "Failing Epicureans and Cynics Hiding in Plain Sight: Lucian of Samosata's *Alexander* Revisited", *Quaderni Urbinati di Cultura Classica* 125: 153-176.

Nijs, W., 2022a, "Epicurus at Plutarch's Dinner Table: A Tale of After-Dinner Sex and Questionable Polemics (*Quaest. conv.* III, 6)", *Rivista di Filologia e di Istruzione Classica* 150: 70-105.

Nijs, W., 2022b, "Straightening the Uterus with Epicurus. Some Parallels for *PHerc. 908/1390*", *Mnemosyne* 75: 467-482.

Nijs, W., 2022c, "The Use and Misuse of an Epicurean Dictum in Erycius Puteanus' *Somnium*", *Latomus* 81: 160-168.

Nijs, W., 2024, *The Epicurean Sage in the Ethics of Philodemus*, Leiden-Boston: Brill.

Nussbaum, M. C., 1994, *The Therapy of Desire. Theory and Practice in Hellenistic Ethics*, Princeton-Oxford: Princeton University Press.

O'Connor, D. K., 1989, "The Invulnerable Pleasures of Epicurean Friendship", *Greek, Roman, and Byzantine Studies* 30: 165-186.

O'Keefe, T., 2001, "Is Epicurean Friendship Altruistic?", *Apeiron* 34: 269-305.

Piergiacomi, E., 2023, "Medicine and Responsibility. Hippocratic and Democritean Influences on Epicurus' Περὶ φύσεως Book XXV?", in F. Masi – P.-M. Morel – F. Verde (eds.), *Epicureanism and Scientific Debates. Antiquity and Late Reception. Vol. I: Language, Medicine, Meteorology*, Leuven: Leuven University Press: 141-166.

Pope, M., 2019, "Embryology, Female Semina and Male Invincibility in Lucretius *De Rerum Natura*", *Classical Quarterly* 69: 229-245.

Puglia, E., 1992, "Verso una nuova edizione dell'opera adespota sulla procreazione conservata da PHerc. 908/1390", in A. H. S. El-Mosallamy (ed.), *Proceedings of the XIXth International Congress of Papyrology. Cairo 2-9 September 1989 Vol. 1*, Cairo: Ain Shams University Center of Papyrological Studies: 179-188.

Ranocchia, G., 2022, "Intorno all'autore del trattato ercolanese adespota *Sulla procreazione* (*PHerc.* 1390/908). Non Epicuro, ma Demetrio Lacone?", *Analecta Papyrologica* 34: 71-99.

Rist, J. M., 1980, "Epicurus on Friendship", *Classical Philology* 75: 121-129.

Roskam, G., 2007a, *Live Unnoticed (λάθε βιώσας). On the Vicissitudes of an Epicurean Doctrine*, Leiden-Boston: Brill.

Roskam, G., 2007b, *A Commentary on Plutarch's* De latenter vivendo, Leuven: Leuven University Press.

Roskam, G., 2011, "Plutarch Against Epicurus on Affection for Offspring. A Reading of *De amore prolis*", in G. Roskam – L. Van der Stockt (eds.), *Virtues for the People. Aspects of Plutarchan Ethics*, Leuven: Leuven University Press: 175-201.

Roskam, G., 2020, "Epicurus on Marriage", in J. Beneker – G. Tsouvala (eds.), *The Discourse of Marriage in the Greco-Roman World*, Madison: University of Wisconsin Press: 119-141.

Rouse, W. H. D., – Smith, M. F., 1992, *Lucretius, De Rerum Natura, with an English Translation*, Cambridge, MA-London: Harvard University Press.

Sedley, D. N., 1998, *Lucretius and the Transformation of Greek Wisdom*, Cambridge: Cambridge University Press.

Senkova, M., 2015, "Male Infertility in Classical Greece: Some Observations", *Graeco-Latina Brunensia* 20: 121-131.

Smith, M. F., 1993, *Diogenes of Oinoanda. The Epicurean Inscription. Edited with Introduction, Translation, and Notes*, Naples: Bibliopolis.

Smith, M. F., 2001, *Lucretius. On the Nature of Things. Translated, with Introduction and Notes*, Indianapolis-Cambridge: Hackett.

Suits, D. B., 2020, *Epicurus and the Singularity of Death. Defending Radical Epicureanism*, London: Bloomsbury.

Taub, L. C., 2009, "Cosmology and Meteorology", in J. Warren (ed.), *The Cambridge Companion to Epicureanism*, Cambridge: Cambridge University Press: 105-124.
Tsouna, V., 2007, *The Ethics of Philodemus*, Oxford: Oxford University Press.
Tsouna, V., 2013, *Philodemus, On Property Management. Translated with an Introduction and Notes*, Atlanta: Society of Biblical Literature.
Tsouna, V., 2023, "The Method of Multiple Explanations Revisited", in F. Masi – P.-M. Morel – F. Verde (eds.), *Epicureanism and Scientific Debates. Antiquity and Late Reception. Vol. I: Language, Medicine, Meteorology*, Leuven: Leuven University Press: 221-256.
Tutrone, F., 2016, "Physiologizing (In)fertility in the Roman World: Lucretius on Sacrifice, Nature, and Generation", *Medicina nei Secoli* 28: 773-804.
Usener, H., 1887, *Epicurea*, Leipzig: Teubner.
Usener, H., 1977, *Glossarium Epicureum, edendum curaverunt M. Gigante et W. Schmid*, Rome: Edizioni dell'Ateneo & Bizzarri.
Van der Stockt, L., 2011, "*Semper duo, numquam tres?* Plutarch's *Popularphilosophie* on Friendship and Virtue in *On having many friends*", in G. Roskam – L. Van der Stockt (eds.), *Virtues for the People. Aspects of Plutarchan Ethics*, Leuven: Leuven University Press: 19-40.
Verde, F., 2015, "Boethus the Epicurean", *Philosophie Antique* 15: 205-224.
Verde, F., 2018, "L'empirismo di Teofrasto e la meteorologia epicurea", *Rivista di Filosofia Neo-Scolastica* 90: 889-910.
Verde, F., 2020, "Epicurean Meteorology, Lucretius, and the Aetna", in P. R. Hardie – V. Prosperi – D. Zucca (eds.), *Lucretius Poet and Philosopher*, Berlin-Boston: De Gruyter: 83-102.
Verde, F., 2022, "La meteorologia epicurea", in F. Verde (ed.), *Epicuro: Epistola a Pitocle*, Baden-Baden: Academia Verlag: 27-107.
Warren, J., 2000, "Diogenes Epikourios: Keep Taking the Tablets", *Journal of Hellenic Studies* 120: 144-148.
Warren, J., 2001a, "Epicurus' Dying Wishes", *Cambridge Classical Journal* 47: 23-46.
Warren, J., 2001b, "Lucretian *Palingenesis* Recycled", *Classical Quarterly* 51: 499-508.
Warren, J., 2006, *Facing Death. Epicurus and his Critics*, Oxford: Oxford University Press.

PLUTARCH ON EPICURUS ON WINE

Mauro Bonazzi

Quidquid recipitur ad modum recipientis recipitur

1.

The aim of this paper is an analysis of some testimonies of Epicurus' lost dialogue *Symposium* (Συμπόσιον). A complete and exhaustive overview of this text is impeded by the scarce number of fragments, so much so that scholars disagree on its structure and actual content.[1] The title clearly indicates that it belonged to the literary genre of symposiastic literature. From the surviving evidence we also know that it was a dialogue, which further suggests the idea of a comparison (and confrontation) with Plato and Aristotle. Unlike the latter, however, we also know that Epicurus did not pay much attention to the formal aspects of the style, as it is customary of so many of his works, and he was for this reason reproached by ancient critics such as Athenaeus. Athenaeus also informs us that the main interlocutors were philosophers, all sharing the same basic tenets (προφήτας ἀτόμων, 187b; "flatterers who praise each other", 179d; one of these interlocutors is Polyaenus), thereby showing another difference from his predecessors Plato and Aristotle. Despite Athenaeus' dismissive comments about the random choice of the topics, in the surviving fragments the interlocutors appear to raise issues fitting to a symposiastic context, such as sex and wine (and their interrelation). Some scholars also argued that another topic under discussion was rhetoric, but this view is more controversial. In this paper I will explore the fragments dealing with wine because they raise some interesting issues, not only philosophically but also methodologically. Our major source for them is Plutarch of Chaeronea, a Platonist philosopher, who is well known for

---

[1] See fragments 57-65 Usener. For a quick but clear overview, see Erler 1994: 92-93, with further bibliography. On the form and style, the three most interesting (and critical) testimonies come from Athenaeus; see Athen. 5.186e ("We will now talk about the Homeric symposia. In these, namely, the poet distinguishes times, persons, and occasions. This feature Xenophon and Plato rightly copied, for at the beginning of their works they explain the occasion of the symposium, and who are present. But Epicurus specifies no place, no time: he has no introduction whatever. One has to guess, therefore, how it comes about that a man with cup in hand suddenly propounds questions as though they were discoursing before a class"); 5.187b ("Epicurus introduced none but the prophets of atoms, although he had before him these as his models, I mean the variety of the symposia in Homer, and the charm of Plato and Xenophon as well"); 5.187c ("Again, Epicurus in his symposium puts questions about indigestion in order to get omens for it; following that he asks about fevers. What need is there even to speak of the lack of proportion which pervades his style?") – all transl. Gulick.

his hostility to Epicurus. By investigating these testimonies, it will be also possible to assess how Plutarch he uses his sources for his polemics.

2.

Plutarch mentions Epicurus' *Symposium* and the discussion on wine in two different passages, from two different treatises (fragments 58-60 Usener).[2] In both cases, under investigation is his account of the effects of wine on human bodies.

The first reference comes from one of the *Table Talk Questions*:

> "Now for wine! I should like to know what made you suspect that it is cold". I replied: "Do you actually think that this is my own theory?" "Whose else?" Florus said. And I answered: "I remember coming on Aristotle's discussion also of this question, not recently but a long enough time ago. And Epicurus in his *Symposium* has discussed the matter at great length. The sum of what he has to say, I think, is this: he holds that wine is not hot in an absolute sense, but has in it certain atoms productive of heat and others of cold; some of these it throws off when it comes into the body and others it attracts out of the body until it adapts itself to us, whatever our constitution and nature may be. Accordingly, some men become thoroughly hot when drinking, others experience the contrary". "This", said Florus, "carries us via Protagoras straight to Pyrrho; for it is clear that we shall go on about oil, about milk and honey, and other things in like manner and shall avoid saying about each what its nature is by defining them in terms of their mixtures and union with each other (ταῦτ', εἶπεν ὁ Φλῶρος, ἄντικρυς εἰς τὸν Πύρρωνα διὰ τοῦ Πρωταγόρου φέρει ἡμᾶς· δῆλον γὰρ ὅτι καὶ περὶ ἐλαίου καὶ περὶ γαλάκτος μέλιτός τε καὶ ὁμοίως τῶν ἄλλων διεξιόντες ἀποδρασόμεθα τὸ λέγειν περὶ ἑκάστου ὁποῖον τῇ φύσει ἐστίν, μίξεσι ταῖς πρὸς ἄλληλα καὶ κράσεσιν ἕκαστον γίνεσθαι φάσκοντες; Plut. *QC* 651e-652a; transl. Hoffleit).

What is remarkable in this testimony is the final reference to Protagoras and, even more, to Pyrrho. With this mention, it appears that Plutarch was reading Epicurus' text from an epistemological perspective, arguing that empiricism leads to scepticism. This is not just an erudite quotation, as it sometimes happens in symposiastic literature, but part of a polemical argument against the limits of Epicurus' philosophy. It is not by accident, therefore, that the same idea returns also in the *Adversus Colotem*, a virulent anti-Epicurean treatise:

> Consider the discussion that Epicurus in his *Symposium* presents Polyaenus as holding with him about the heat in wine. When Polyaenus asks, 'Do you deny, Epicurus, the great heating effect of wine?', he replies, 'What need is there to generalize that wine is heating?' A little later he says, 'For it appears that it is not

---

[2] In the *Quaestiones conviviales* (653b, 654d) he also quotes and discusses Epicurus' views on sexual intercourse. In this case as well there are references to wine, in a physiological perspective.

a general fact that wine is heating, but a given quantity of wine may be said to be heating for a given person.' Again, after assigning as one cause the crowding and dispersal of atoms, and as another, the mixture and alignment of these with others, when the wine is mingled with the body, he adds in conclusion, 'Therefore one should not generalize that wine is heating, but only say that this amount is heating for this constitution in this condition, or that that amount is chilling for another. For in an aggregate such as wine there are also certain natural substances of such a sort that cold might be formed of them, or such that, when aligned with others, they would produce a real coolness. Hence, deceived by this, some generalize that wine is cooling, others that it is heating.' If then the man who asserts that the majority are deceived in supposing that what heats is heating or what cools is cooling should refuse to recognize 'Everything is no more this than that' as a conclusion from his premises, he is himself deceived. He proceeds to add, 'And often the wine does not even possess the property of heating or cooling as it enters the body. Rather, the bodily mass is so set in motion that the corpuscles shift their position: the heat-producing atoms are at one time concentrated, becoming numerous enough to impart warmth and heat to the body, but at another time are driven out, producing a chill.' (Plut. *Adv. Col.* 1109d-1110d; transl. De Lacy).

As several scholars have shown, the *Adversus Colotem* takes over and develops the same polemical reference we found in the *Quaestiones convivales* as part of a wider argument in favour of the superiority of Platonist philosophy.[3] The assumption, implicitly shared by both the Platonist Plutarch and the Epicureans, is that scepticism is not a viable option. Yet the analysis of Epicurus' text, as confirmed by the specific case of the effects of wine, shows that scepticism is precisely the outcome of his empiricist stance. By implying (and this is a second assumption) that what can be said of Epicurus is valid also for any kind of empiricist and materialistic approach, Plutarch's conclusion will be that knowledge must be grounded not in data provided by senses – which are always inconsistent and unstable – but in reason and intellect. And this is Platonism. In short, the general argument of Plutarch's anti-Epicurean polemic in the *Adversus Colotem* is: either empiricism or Platonism; but not empiricism (because of scepticism), therefore Platonism, which turns out to be the solution.

The essential point is therefore the link between empiricism and scepticism. Plutarch's answer seems to rely on the fact that empiricism presupposes the existence of matter only (atoms, in the specific case of Epicurus); a reality made of colliding atoms, though, does not have any stability, nor does it allow for any kind of stable knowledge, because everything is perpetually changing. Given this materialistic approach, we cannot determine any given thing as it really is, but can only state how it appears to us. Since appearances vary from subject to subject and from time to time also in the same object, the materialistic approach inevitably paves

---

[3] See, for instance, Kechagia 2011; Bonazzi 2012.

the way to scepticism, meant to be a kind of philosophy that makes any discourse about reality untenable and, therefore, life impossible. This conclusion is what Epicureanism ultimately amounts to.

That this view is a legitimate description of scepticism is highly debatable. Yet it remains that this is a standard account of scepticism in non-sceptical circles in the early Imperial centuries. An interesting parallel comes, for instance, from Sextus Empiricus' *Outlines of Pyrrhonism*, where he discusses the same author discussed by Plutarch, that is, Protagoras:

> What he states is this – that matter is in flux, and as it flows additions are made continuously in the place of effluxions, and the senses are transformed and altered according to the times of life and to all the other conditions of the bodies. [...] And men, he says, apprehend different things at different times owing to their differing dispositions [...]. We see, then, that he dogmatizes about the fluidity of matter [...], this being a non evident matter about which we suspend judgment (Sext. Emp. *PH* I 217-218; transl. Bury).

In the background, as it has now been demonstrated by several scholars, we have Plato's *Theaetetus*:[4]

> I mean the theory that there is nothing which in itself is just one thing; nothing which you could rightly call anything or any kind of thing. If you call a thing large, it will reveal itself as small [...] What is really true, is this: the things of which we naturally say that they 'are', are in process of coming to be, as the results of movement and change and blending with one another. We are wrong when we say that they 'are', since nothing ever is, but everything is coming to be (Plat. *Tht.* 152d-e; transl. Levett).

3.

The relevance of the *Theaetetus* has been recently underlined by Francesco Verde in an interesting paper reconstructing the influence of Plato's dialogue on Epicurus' epistemology.[5] More precisely, Verde refers to a section in the dialogue where reference is made to wine and its effects:

> Now, if I drink wine when I am well it appears to me present and sweet – Yes. – Going by what we earlier agreed, that is so because the active and passive factors moving simultaneously, generate both sweetness and perception; on the passive side, the perception makes the tongue percipient, while on the side of wine, sweetness moving about it makes it both to be and appear sweet to the healthy tongue [...]. Then this

---

[4] See the seminal Decleva Caizzi 1988.
[5] Verde 2020: 13-44, *praes.* 21-23.

pair, Socrates, Socrates ill and the draught of wine, generates, presumably, different things again: a perception of bitterness in the region of the tongue, and bitterness coming to be and moving in the regions of the wine. And then wine becomes, not bitterness, but bitter; and I become, not perception, but percipient (Plat. *Tht.* 159b-e; transl. Levett).

This reference, along with the epistemological context, does seem to find a confirmation at the very beginning of the discussion, before the quotation of Epicurus' *Symposium*:

But whatever we think of that, whoever held that nothing is any more of one description than of another is following an Epicurean doctrine, that all impressions reaching us through the senses are true. For if one of two persons says that the wine is dry and the other that it is sweet, and neither errs in his sensation, how is the wine more dry than sweet? (Plut. *Adv. Col.* 1009a-e [= fr. 250 Usener]; transl. Einarson-De Lacy).

Verde's general hypothesis is interesting and can further confirm the importance of the role played by the *Theaetetus* in the Hellenistic and post-Hellenistic debates. In the specific case of Plutarch's quotation, however, a close scrutiny of the text seems to suggest that something else is also at stake, and that we must distinguish between Plutarch's use of Epicurus and Epicurus' own words and stance. That Epicurus is primarily dealing with epistemological issues is indeed Plutarch's inference, as part of the above-mentioned argument against empiricism.[6] The reference to the *Theaetetus*, in other words, comes more from Plutarch's pen than Epicurus'. Epicurus' use of wine in the above-quoted fragment, instead, seems to point in a different direction. Epicurus is indeed dealing with the issue of the wine producing heat, which is not the same as saying it to be or appear hot (or sweet or bitter). An alternative, more reasonable hypothesis is that Epicurus is addressing another important issue, related to his atomist philosophy, yet as an ontological problem more than an epistemological one.

Under investigation, it is the problem of sensory qualities. In this specific case, the (polemical) reference point would be more Democritus than Plato (and the *Theaetetus*). Indeed, the problem of the status of sensory qualities is a major problem for the Epicureans, given their atomist stance and Democritus' influence.[7] Interestingly, Plutarch's quotation comes precisely from the section devoted to a discussion and defense of Democritus. For a better understanding of Plutarch's polemic, we also need to consider the context of the quotation in the *Adversus Colotem*.

---

[6] In this sense, the passage can be used as further evidence of the importance of the *Theaetetus* for early Imperial Platonists; see, for instance, Opsomer 1998: 27-82.
[7] See, for instance, Sedley 1988; Furley 1993.

4.

As is well known, Plutarch's *Adversus Colotem* is a treatise written in response to another treatise by the Epicurean Colotes. Colotes had accused several philosophers of making life impossible with their doctrines. Plutarch's goal is to show that it is indeed Colotes and, therefore, Epicurus who make life impossible with their philosophy. The section where the *Symposium* is quoted is part of a discussion devoted to Democritus, who is the first to be introduced (by both Colotes and Plutarch).[8] More specifically, Colotes had levelled two charges against Democritus:

1. *Oude mallon*-thesis. The *ouden mallon* makes life impossible: "Colotes first charges him with asserting that no object is any more of one description than of another, thus throwing our life into confusion" (1108f-1009a).
2. *Nomoi*-thesis. In the famous fragment on everything being by *nomos* apart void and atoms he made everything worse, if possible, by attacking the senses: The thesis, propounded by Democritus, that "colour is by convention, all compound by convention, <but in reality the void and> the atoms [are]" goes against the senses and he who abides by, and employs, this argument could not even think of himself that he is a human being or living. (1110e-f)

Interestingly, Plutarch's quote seems to match the second charge better than the first. Yet the quotation occurs in relation to the first charge. Be that as it may, this context seems to suggest that what was at stake was not so much Plato and the epistemological problem of sense-perception as it was about the attempt to detach atomistic philosophy from Democritus' reductionism about sensible qualities.[9] If the only properties for atoms are shape, form, and size, what about colour, smell, and the other properties? Democritus' thesis risks leading to paradoxical outcomes, which was Colotes' criticism. By tracing back Epicurus' position, as presented in discussion of wine, to the *oude mallon* formula, Plutarch shows that it is instead (or also)[10] Epicurus' problem.

Indeed, a) if one takes the *ouden mallon* formula too strictly, the outcome would be Parmenidean: since they do not even exist, it makes no sense to consider these properties; and b) if one takes the formula less strictly, the problem would be relativism (and by consequence subjectivism and scepticism – that is, Protagoras and Pyrrho – as in the above text from the *Quaestiones convivales*): these properties depend on the encounter with the perceiving subjects. Yet the perceiving subjects

---

[8] On this section of the *Adversus Colotem*, see Morel 1996: 336-346; Kechagia 2011: 179-212; Castagnoli 2013.

[9] On the reasonable assumption that Democritus is an eliminativist, a problem that we cannot discuss here.

[10] On Plutarch and Democritus, see Hershbell 1982: 81-111, *praes.* 82-95.

differ, therefore the same things bring about different experiences, and nothing can be said about the object itself (there is a severe discontinuity among the properties to which we have access and the real object), and our life is thrown into confusion.

To confirm the claim that Epicurus and his followers are faced with the same limits they level against Democritus, Plutarch quotes the *Symposium*. *Pace* Plutarch, however, what Epicurus is doing in the *Symposium* is precisely to find an alternative solution to this problem, by defending the reality of sensible qualities without dismissing atomism. The quotation indeed shows that Epicurus' goal is to explain how properties or effects are produced from quality-less atoms and do in fact exist. In this sense he is opposing both readings of the *ouden mallon* formula. As opposed to a), secondary properties do indeed exist; as opposed to b), most importantly, they are relative but not subjective. Whatever is sensible – be it a compound body or one of its properties – is real and does exist. Just to give an example,[11] we could observe that peanuts are healthy for some and dangerous for others. This quality does not mean that this property is not real, in relation to the person with the allergy. It is a real property, albeit a relational one, of the peanut. It is not subjective, however. In other words, these qualities emerge as a result of the atoms colliding with the sense organs and are real properties of the bodies.[12] This seems to be Epicurus' point in the discussion about wine's effects: sensible qualities are dispositional qualities that cause certain effects and sensory affections under certain conditions.[13] In this sense Epicurus can react to Democritus' reductionism, without abandoning atomism.

5.

If this reconstruction is correct and it is Epicurus' position, what about Plutarch's criticism? From a philosophical perspective, it is difficult to give a balanced judgment. On the one hand, as far as the problem of sensible qualities is concerned, one may argue that Plutarch's objection has little force. As a matter of fact, Plutarch's criticism that the relativity of perceptual properties undermines the claim that they are real properties (and thus constitute a typical application of the *oude mallon* formula) does not seem to consider with due attention Epicurus' position. As we

---

[11] I borrow this example from O'Keefe 2010: 37-38, repeating O'Keefe 1997.
[12] An interesting parallel comes from Polystratus, who in his *On irrational contempt* (XXIII 26-XXVI 23 Indelli) also "subsumes observer-dependent attributes under the broader heading 'relative', then shows excellent reasons why the relative, albeit different in status from the *per se*, is not in consequence any less real" (Long – Sedley 1987, I: 37). I thank the anonymous reviewer to this text, which clearly confirms the importance of this problem in the Epicurean circles, not only from an ontological perspective but also from an ethical one.
[13] See O'Keefe 2010: 38: "this theory would allow Epicurus to admit the phenomena of sensory variability and retain the basic Democritean account of how sensations arise as a result of the interactions of atoms, while still holding that sensible qualities are real properties of bodies".

have seen, his point lies precisely in the attempt to show that a relative property does not automatically imply that it is also subjective or non-existent. So far so good. Yet how is this so? How does Epicurus really account for the reality of sensible qualities, apart from asserting the evident fact that they exist? And what about the epistemological consequences of his doctrine, in addition to the problem of scepticism? Here Plutarch might have a point, as Eleni Kechagia has argued.[14] For it is well known that the thesis that all senses are true, which Plutarch (correctly) linked to the thesis about the reality of sensible qualities, risks ending up in a sceptical outcome.[15] Still, it could also be countered that it is equally well known that Epicurus' epistemology was much more sophisticated and included more than the simple claim about the senses being true. In order to properly address the problem Plutarch should have addressed Epicurus' position in all its complexity, not focusing on the senses merely. Since he did not do it, what we can learn from his polemics is probably more useful to reconstruct his views and assumptions than Epicurus' views – which is the typical problem of ancient (and modern) polemics: they help to understand more the one who is attacking than the doctrine under attack.

After all, it might be remarked that Plutarch is liable of the same charge he levelled against Colotes, that is, of misusing the fragments he quotes (*Adv. Col.* 1108d-e: Colotes detaches certain sayings shorn of their real meaning and rips from their context mutilated fragments of argument). Indeed, it is a recurrent problem of ancient philosophical polemics, whose goal is more to emphasize one own's views than to account for a given problem.[16] On this point at least, Plutarch and Epicurus are much closer than they would have expected to be. In Epicurus' *Symposium* there were only atomist philosophers; likewise, in Plutarch's treatise against Colotes, Epicureans are explicitly rejected at the very beginning of the discussion. In both cases, it is not an ideal context for a fruitful discussion.

---

[14] Kechagia 2011: 200-201.
[15] For a typically Academic move, see for instance Cic. *Ac.* 2.79.
[16] De Lacy 1964: 77: "ironically, Plutarch in his reply is at times guilty of the same faults he complains of in Colotes: he does not give careful consideration to the Epicurean explanation of their views but rather draws his own inferences from them and on the basis of these inferences undertakes to demolish the school."

REFERENCES

Bonazzi, M., 2012, "Plutarch on the Difference between Academics and Pyrrhonists", *Oxford Studies in Ancient Philosophy* 43: 271-298.

Castagnoli, L., 2013, "Democritus and Epicurus on sensible qualities in Plutarch's *Against Colotem* 3-9", *Aitia* 3 https://doi.org/10.4000/aitia.622.

Decleva Caizzi, F., 1988, "La materia scorrevole. Sulle tracce di un dibattito perduto", in J. Barnes – M. Mignucci (eds.), *Matter and Metaphysics. Fourth Symposium Hellenisticum*, Naples: Bibliopolis: 425-470.

De Lacy, P. H., 1994, "Colotes' First Criticism of Democritus", in J. Mau – E. G. Schmidt (eds.), *Isonomia. Studien zur Gleichheitsvorstellung im griechischen Denken*, Berlin: Akademie-Verlag: 67-77.

Erler, M., 1994, "Epikur", in H. Flashar (ed.), *Die Philosophie der Antike*, Band 4: *die Hellenistische Philosophie*, Basel: Schwabe: 29-202.

Furley, D., 1993, "Democritus and Epicurus on Sensible Qualities", in J. Brunschwig – M.C. Nussbaum (eds.), *Passions and Perceptions. Studies in Hellenistic Philosophy of Mind*, Cambridge-Paris: Cambridge University Press – Maison de l'Homme: 72-94.

Hershbell, J.P., 1982, "Plutarch and Democritus", *Quaderni Urbinati di Cultura Classica* 10: 81-111.

Kechagia, E., 2011, *Plutarch against Colotes. A Lesson in History of Philosophy*, Oxford: Oxford University Press.

Morel, P.-M., 1996, *Démocrite et la recherche des causes*, Paris: Klincksieck.

O'Keefe, T., 1997, "The Ontological Status of Sensible Qualities for Democritus and Epicurus", *Ancient Philosophy* 17: 119-134.

O'Keefe, T., 2010, *Epicureanism*, Durham: Acumen.

Opsomer, J., 1998, *In Search of the Truth. Academic Tendencies in Middle Platonism*, Brussels: KNAWSK.

Sedley, D. N., 1988, "Epicurean Anti-Reductionism", in J. Barnes – M. Mignucci (eds.), *Matter and Metaphysics. Fourth Symposium Hellenisticum*, Naples: Bibliopolis: 295-327.

Verde, F., 2020, "L'epistemologia di Epicuro e il *Teeteto* di Platone", *Historia philosophica. An International Journal* 18: 13-44.

DIOGENES OF OINOANDA AND THE EPICUREAN EPISTOLARY TRADITION

Attila Németh

Diogenes of Oinoanda, although much appreciated by scholars, has rarely been viewed as an innovative thinker.[1] This assessment fits a general trend in modern scholarship, in harmony with Cicero's criticism of the Pythagoreans – "ipse dixit" (*DND* I.10) – and the Epicureans – "ista [praecepta]...quasi dictata redduntur" (*DND* I. 72) – to see the Epicurean tradition as a long line of fundamentalists who may have renewed the literary presentation of the master's ideas, like Lucretius' poem in Latin hexameters, or innovated with respect to the medium, like Diogenes' inscriptions in rock solid; otherwise, however, they were rigidly faithful to the teachings of Epicurus. On this view, the Epicureans did little more than replicate what they had learned from their founder. This position was already questionable in the light of Cicero's testimony on Epicurean ethics in his *De Finibus* I, where at the end of Torquatus' summary of the movement's positive doctrines, the Epicurean protagonist of the dialogue lists three different positions on Epicurean friendship that most likely reflect existing disagreements between Cicero's Epicurean contemporaries – Cicero mentions hearing in person the Epicurean Phaedrus and Zeno of Sidon lecturing (*De Fin.* I.16), and Philodemus and Siro are spoken of as Epicurean authorities and as fine and learned men (*De Fin.* I.119). Philodemus' own distinct brand of scholarship has been corroborated as increasing numbers of Herculaneum papyri come to the fore: these papyri not only bear witness to their author's ingenuity and to Epicurus' own writings, but also to a distinguished Epicurean philologist, Demetrius of Laconia (*P.Herc.* 1012), whose work aptly reflects the diversity of interpretations within the Epicurean tradition by the first century BCE, within a couple of hundred years of the master's death.

In this paper, I wish to argue that Diogenes of Oinoanda was not innocent of all originality. He obviously transformed the way Epicurus' teachings were presented to the public – namely, by having an enormous wall built probably on the southern side of the Oenoandan agora, on which he had Epicurean doctrines inscribed in different sections (the wall had an estimated 260-square-metre surface and carried a text of approximately 25,000 words, of which we have less than a third in over 300 fragments).[2] Moreover, Diogenes stands out in another significant respect, by having many of his own letters inscribed onto the same wall. The significance of these epistles is normally played down: they report important Epicurean doctrines

---

[1] A picture challenged by the first collection of papers on Diogenes: Hammerstaedt, Morel, Güremen 2007; also cf. Gordon 2020.
[2] Cf. Smith 1993 & 1998.

in the same literary genre that Epicurus famously used. On some views, they are mere imitations of the master, and the authorship of the *Letter to Mother* is debated, with some scholars attributing it to Epicurus, some to Diogenes.[3] The question of certain fragments' authorship aside, many of the surviving epistle fragments are undoubtedly from Diogenes' own 'chisel', yet it has been rarely asked what these epistles tell us about Diogenes: not about the historical figure but about the philosopher or, more particularly, about the (literary) methods of the philosopher.

Even upon superficial scrutiny, it becomes obvious that Diogenes' own epistle fragments do not engage exclusively with the principal Epicurean doctrines, but also discuss quite ordinary matters at length: the weather, certain expected or past visits and related events, and personal affairs that on a first look appear rather unphilosophical. Considering the limited space and the expense of having such an enormous inscription cut and erected, it is hard to imagine that this undertaking was all functionless chatter or noise, especially since it even seems to be in direct tension with Diogenes' stated purpose. This is true most of all if we agree with the statement that "no writing is an 'unloaded tool' whose purpose and function is merely to inform, but rather it is a reflection of the culture and the purpose which had produced it."[4] As Diogenes says in the introduction of the inscription (Fr. 2 & Fr. 3), having reached the sunset of his life, he wanted to help those who are constituted well and suffering from the false notions they have about things (περὶ τῶν πραγμάτων ψευδοδοξίᾳ Fr. 3 IV 6-7). Given their large number, and that Diogenes was also a philanthropist and a man considerate towards future generations, he had his inscription erected as a remedy for the public based on a medicine that he had already tested. It is unclear how Diogenes' personal business (as opposed to the Epicurean doctrines) that is also made public in his letters – incidentally documenting an otherwise lost Epicurean community (as discussed well by Diskin Clay)[5] – helps the objectives he so eloquently articulated in the introduction of the inscription (Fr. 2 & Fr. 3). Therefore, the way in which Diogenes used his epistles – and more generally the epistolary genre – to accomplish his goals for the inscription, as well as what that tells us about Diogenes the philosopher, is still to be investigated. I wish to explore this topic in this chapter, first by presenting an overview of the Epicurean tradition of epistles, and then by scrutinizing, on the one hand, how Diogenes' letters fit into this tradition of letter-writing and, on the other, the function of his epistles in relation to the whole inscription.

*
* *

---

[3] Cf. Gordon 1996, though she seems to change heart in her 2013 paper.
[4] Rosenmeyer 2001: 28.
[5] Cf. Clay 1989/1998.

Epicurus was the first Greek philosopher to leave behind some undoubtedly genuine and complete letters as well as many in fragments. Book 10 of Diogenes Laertius' *Lives of the Eminent Philosophers* preserves three complete letters (*Letter to Herodotus*; *Letter to Pythocles*, *Letter to Menoeceus*), all of which meet formal epistolary requirements. Only the authenticity of the second (the *Letter to Pythocles*) is debated, actually by no lesser authority than the ancient Epicurean, Philodemus. For this reason, Hermann Usener proposed that the *Letter to Pythocles* is a patchwork from Epicurus' *Peri Physeōs* (*P.Herc.* 1005; Usener 1881: xxxix; Angeli 1988). Francesco Verde, however, in his latest edition of the letter, argues for its originality.[6] Yet these so-called epistles are essentially treatises or, rather, summaries of Epicurus' physical, meteorological, and ethical doctrines; if we deprived them of their epistolary formulas, it would be harder to recognize them as letters. In fact, Epicurus himself refers to his letter to Herodotus as a small epitome (*Ep. Pyth.* 10.85). The letters to Herodotus and Pythocles have a few vocatives, but as Pamela Gordon has already pointed out, all these function as introductions or signposts for a new topic or for their conclusions, thus being rather generic and paying no very close attention to their addressees. The *Letter to Menoeceus* has the most characteristics of an epistle, being comparatively short and directly exhorting its addressee from time to time.[7]

Besides these three complete epistles, there are 204 fragments from 146 letters collected by Margherita Erbì in her wonderful volume on the fragments and testimonies of Epicurus' epistles.[8] The fragments she has edited and commented on have 91 identifiable addressees. Seventy-seven are written to individuals (5F-77F), five to a few people (78F-82T), and nine to groups of recipients sharing the same condition (83T-91F). These latter include the friends in Lampsacus, the philosophers of Mytilene, friends in Asia and perhaps in Egypt, friends on Samos, and the problematic μεγάλοι and the ἄσχολοι, the ones who have no free time. And even some more fragments are coming to light on papyri or among the inscriptions.

Epicurus had a very simple reason to write various types of letters: before he founded his Garden outside the walls of Athens around 307/6 BCE, he had taught philosophy in Mytilene on Lesbos and afterwards on the western shore of Asia Minor in Lampsacus, and he had to keep in touch with his disciples in all these places, sending them epitomes of his latest doctrines or explanatory letters concerning either his teachings or how to put them into practice. He met such formative students as Hermarchus in Mytilene, and Metrodorus, Polyaenus, Idomeneus, and Pythocles in Lampsacus. Hermarchus, Metrodorus, and Polyaenus became the καθηγέμονες or the leaders of the Garden along with Epicurus, and even though he often visited his remaining circles outside Athens, he primarily kept in touch with them and with the new recruits of the colonies via epistles.

---
6 Cf. Verde 2022.
7 Gordon 2013: 136-7.
8 Erbì 2020.

The fragments of Epicurus' epistles read strikingly differently from his complete letters preserved by Diogenes Laertius. They are not so dense or abstract, even if the philosophical content, if there is any, is in some cases rather similar to Epicurus' principal doctrines or to the *sententiae* found in the Vatican library in the eighteenth century. Brad Inwood even believes that Epicurus' mainly lost correspondence may have been the prototype of Seneca's *Epistulae Morales*.[9] According to Erbì, though, the primary function of Epicurus' correspondence was to help his φίλοι or friends who, not being able to be with their master, needed support to put theory into practice. Therefore, his letters were instructional and exegetic rather than educational or protreptic like Seneca's epistles. I think, nevertheless, that this difference is merely in emphasis, since Seneca's epistles clearly offer practical advice, and Epicurus must also have used his epistles after settling in Athens for spreading his latest doctrines. That they mediated important doctrinal content is not only clear from some fragments (Porph. *ad Marc.* 27, p. 207, 31 Nauck; *ad Marc.* 29, p. 209, pp. 132-3 in: Bailey 1926), but also from the fact that Diogenes Laertius lists a collection of letters (Ἐπιστολαί; Diog. Laert. X 28) among Epicurus' best writings – τὰ βέλτιστά ἐστι τάδε (Diog. Laert. X 27).

To write epistles also seems to have been a desirable activity among the leaders (καθηγέμονες or οἱ ἄνδρες). The title of one of the works attributed to Hermarchus is Ἐπιστολικά or *Collected Correspondence* (Diog. Laert. X 25), and some of its fragments in Philodemus' *Rhetorics* (Fr. 35–36) preserve Hermarchus addressing an otherwise unknown Theopheides. In this fragment, Hermarchus is arguing against the Megarian philosopher Alexinus of Elis for the position that only sophistic rhetoric alone has the status of τέχνη or art.

Also, among the *Vatican Sayings* attributed to Metrodorus (*SV* 10, 30–31, 47, 51), *SV* 51 is identified as a letter fragment that illustrates Metrodorus gently giving directions to Pythocles concerning his overabundant sexual desires.

The activities of later prominent Epicureans in more distant regions – such as Philonides of Laodicea in Syria, or Protarchus of Bargylia (end of second century/ early first century BCE) – indicate that Epicurus' letters were widely diffused in Asia Minor relatively soon after his death. Philonides, a member of a politically influential family, composed epitomes of the epistles written by Epicurus, Metrodorus, and Hermarchus because he found this exercise was "useful for lazy young people", and he also organized these epistles by genre (*P. Herc.* 1044 fr. 14.3-10). This information shows that 150 years after Epicurus, many and indeed all sorts of Epicurean letters were still in circulation, and that these could be arranged and excerpted according to various considerations.

The fragments of Philodemus' works in the Herculaneum papyri (*Memoirs P.Herc.* 1418/310; *On Piety P.Herc.*1077, *P.Herc.*1428, *P.Herc.*1098; *On Wealth P.Herc.*

---

[9] Cf. Inwood 2007 (a): xiv, and 2007 (b): 136-7.

1570) preserve many letter fragments by Epicurus and by other members of the Garden. An anonymous papyrus (*P.Herc.* 176) preserves evidence for epistles from the school in Lampsacus, written by Polyaenus, Leonteus, Idomeneus, and Batis, who was Metrodorus' sister and Idomeneus' wife, her presence illustrating very well the active participation of women in a philosophical community for the first time in antiquity. What is common and striking in this epistolary evidence, and indeed in all these fragments, is that they all originate from Epicurus or from the first generation of his school, and that later generations edit and transmit them in some form without taking up the task or challenge of writing new Epicurean epistles themselves.

There are, however, some exceptions to this rule: the forgeries of Epicurean epistles. Diogenes Laertius records that Diotimus the Stoic (c. 100 BCE) forged fifty "dirty letters" and claimed that they were written by Epicurus (ἐπιστολὰς φέρων πεντήκοντα ἀσελγεῖς ὡς Ἐπικούρου, 10.3). Athenaeus evidently alludes to the same story, while naming the imitator as a certain Theotimus, who was sued by the Epicurean Zeno, convicted for the forgery, and eventually executed. Diogenes Laertius also mentions another misattribution of some obscene letters to Epicurus which others assigned to Chrysippus (Diog. Laert. X 3).[10]

These forgeries of personal epistles evidently functioned as ideal starting points for anti-Epicurean discourse and could be easily mistaken for the originals, since many of the authentic fragments of Epicurus' letters are reports *in imago suae vitae*, that is, in the image of his life, which served as an example and was meant to be imitated. This purpose can be best illustrated by the famous fragment that Diogenes Laertius presents together with Epicurus' extensive will, which is addressed to Idomeneus and probably to his circle in Lampsacus,[11] in which Epicurus balances his sufferings with the memories of their earlier conversations and the pleasure that they still provide:

τὴν μακαρίαν ἄγοντες καὶ ἅμα τελευταίαν ἡμέραν τοῦ βίου ἐγράφομεν ὑμῖν ταυτί. στραγγουρικά τε παρηκολούθηκει καὶ δυσεντερικὰ πάθη ὑπερβολὴν οὐκ ἀπολείποντα τοῦ ἐν ἑαυτοῖς μεγέθους. ἀντιπαρετάττετο δὲ πᾶσι τούτοις τὸ κατὰ ψυχὴν χαῖρον ἐπὶ τῇ τῶν γεγονότων ἡμῖν διαλογισμῶν μνήμῃ. σὺ δ' ἀξίως τῆς ἐκ μειρακίου παραστάσεως πρὸς ἐμὲ καὶ φιλοσοφίαν ἐπιμελοῦ τῶν παίδων Μητροδώρου.

Passing a delightful day, which will also be the last of my life, I write you (ὑμῖν) this note. Dysentery and an inability to urinate have occasioned the worst possible sufferings. But a counterweight to all this is the joy in my heart when I remember our conversations. I beseech you – in light of how admirably, from childhood, you

---

[10] As Gordon 2013 has shown, the New Comic playwrights began parodying Epicurean language in the times of Epicurus himself. Diogenes Laertius' judgment is corroborated by the testimonies of Aelius Theon, a first-century CE teacher of grammar and rhetoric, who lists a few texts circulating as spurious Epicurean letter fragments.
[11] Cf. Erbì 2020: 143-5.

have stood by me and by philosophy – to keep watch over Metrodorus' children. (Diog. Laert. X 22)[12]

I quoted this well-known fragment – which also survives in Latin translation by Cicero, with the variation that in the *De Finibus* it is addressed to Hermarchus (*De Fin.* 2.96)[13] – because it compares rather well with Fr 117 of Diogenes of Oinoanda:

> Διογένης τοῖς συνγενέσι καὶ οἰκείοις καὶ φίλοις τάδε ἐντέλλομαι. νοσῶν οὕτως ὥστε μοι νῦ[ν] τὴν τοῦ ζῆν ἔτι ἢ μηκέτ[ι] ζῆν ὑπάρχειν κρίσιν (καρδιακὸν γάρ με διαφερει πάθος), ἂν μὲν διαγένωμαι, διδόμενον ἔτι μοι τὸ ζῆν ἡδέως λήμψ[ο]μαι· ἂν μὴ διαγένωμαι δ', ὁ Fr. 117 (HK fr. 2)

> I, Diogenes, give these directions to my relatives and family and friends. I am so sick that I am now at the critical stage which will determine whether I continue to live or not; for a cardiac complaint is afflicting me. If I survive, I shall gladly accept the continuation of life granted to me; while if I do not survive, [death will not be unwelcome to me(?)] [...].[14]

Martin Ferguson Smith believes that this passage was not part of a will, although it sounds very similar to Epicurus' deathbed testament. I think Smith is correct to the extent that linguistically speaking the fragment does not have the characteristics of how some more formal wills started in antiquity. Here are some examples:

a) Κατὰ τάδε δίδωμι <u>τὰ ἐμαυτοῦ</u> πάντα Ἀμυνομάχῳ... / I hereby give all my goods to Amynomachus... (Epicurus' will, Diog. Laert. X 16)

b) Ἀρκεσίλαος Θαυμασίᾳ χαίρειν. δέδωκα Διογένει <u>διαθήκας ἐμαυτοῦ</u> κομίσαι πρὸς σέ· / Arcesilaus to Thaumasias, greetings. I have given Diogenes my will to be conveyed to you. (Arcesilaus' will, Diog. Laert. X 4.43-4)

c) τάδε διατίθεμαι περὶ τῶν <u>κατ' ἐμαυτόν</u>, / I make the following dispositions about my property (Lyco's will, Diog. Laert. X 5.69)

This comparison immediately makes it obvious that all these more formal wills have the reflexive pronoun, ἐμαυτοῦ in common. This feature, at least, is certainly missing from the beginning of Diogenes' fragment. Nonetheless, it is also absent from Epicurus' letter to Idomeneus, hence there is no reason why we ought not to read the Diogenes fragment as a deathbed testament, as Diskin Clay has done (albeit without any argument).[15] Already Plato tacitly assumed that wills are made, in general, on a sick bed or in fear of immediate death (*Leg.* 922b-923a). This premise agrees with

---

[12] Transl. from Mensch/Miller 2018. For authenticity, cf. Erbì's commentary on 56 T.
[13] Cf. Laks 1976.
[14] Transl. by Martin F. Smith 1993, with minor modification.
[15] Clay 1973/1998.

the same allusion that Greek orators made, and which we have several examples of.[16] However, there is also a reason, integral to the fragments of Diogenes, why Fr. 117 is different from other fragments: the emphatic position of Diogenes' name in line 1. If we compare it with all those fragments in which we have Diogenes' name inscribed, then we find that it is either in the vocative somewhere in the middle of a text "ὦ Διόγενες" (Fr. 63 IV 10 and Fr. 154 (NF 49) I 2-3) or in the genitive as part of a title:

Fr. 28 (HK fr. 55)
Διογένους τοῦ [Οἰνο]ανδέως [περὶ τῶν] παθῶν καὶ [πράξεων] ἐπιτομ[ή].
Diogenes of Oinoanda's epitome [on] emotions and [actions].

Fr. 137 (HK fr. 1)
Διογένο[υς τοῦ Οἰωοανδέω]ς συγκει̣π̣[όντος τῷ γήρᾳ ἐπιτομή].
[Epitome] of Diogenes [of Oinoanda in support of old age].

Or it is in the starting formula of a letter:

Fr. 62 (HK fr. 56)
[Διογέν]ης Ἀντι[πάτρῳ ε]ὖ χαίρειν.
Diogenes to Antipater, greetings,

Or (among Jürgen Hammerstaedt and Martin Ferguson Smith's most recent findings[17]) it occurs even in the title of a letter:

NF 215 I
[οἱ ῥη]θέντες [λόγ]οι ὑπὸ [Διο]γένους [μετ]ὰ τὴν [ἐκκ]ομιδὴν [τοῦ] παιδὸς [αὐτ]οῦ
[The words spoken] by [Dio]genes [after] the funeral of [his] son

Nowhere else, though, does it stand in such an emphatic position in the surviving fragments. That of course in and of itself is not conclusive, but coupled with the surviving content, it strongly resembles Epicurus' letter to Idomeneus or Hermarchus, which both Cicero and Diogenes Laertius treated as a deathbed testament and as a letter. Hence, we have strong reasons to recognize the Diogenes fragment as a letter fragment and an imitation of Epicurus, in which Diogenes also constructs his image and life in the mirror of his philosophy.

Diogenes' imitation also chimes in well with the culture of the period in which he lived, if we are to date him to the early second century CE.[18] This time is known as the Second Sophistic "because of its creative re-use of fourth century Athenian cultural and literary models, when the first sophists reigned supreme."[19] Many of

---

[16] Cf. Fitzgerald 2003: 654, n.71 in particular.
[17] Hammerstaedt – Smith 2018.
[18] This is Smith's 1993 dating, which Clay 1989 puts later; also cf. Hall 1979.
[19] Rosenmeyer 2006: 29.

the literary and philosophical products of this period were written in an allusive style that according to some even served as an invitation to readers to join in the "affirmation of a common heritage".[20] Diogenes' deathbed testament fragment fits in well, on the one hand, with the Epicurean tradition that promoted the idea of one's assimilation to Epicurus based on practicing his philosophy,[21] and, on the other hand, it also conforms to popular trends in Diogenes' culture. I believe his epistles, to which now I turn, also manifest these connections.

Let us first study one of the most recent Oinoandean finds: the letter fragment concerning Diogenes' speech at his son's funeral.

> NF 215 = YF 284
> (Col. II) Archelaus to Dion, greetings!
> You are eager to know the words spoken by our Diogenes after the funeral of his son. I most gladly addressed myself to this matter, for I want to bestow on you every favour as if I were actually doing it for myself. The business turned out very fortunately for me, in my wish to give you something better than my own version; for, some accurate shorthand-writers having made a record of the address, I made a copy of this (MFS: I made this copy) for myself and [took it] away.[22]

This is the only letter that has its title preserved in "large" letters on a separate stone (Col. I), while the epistle itself (Col. II) is written in "small" letters, the two fragments amounting to 17 lines in total. It is still regarded as an exception within the group of the so-called FLC Letters (i.e., fourteen-line-column letters), aptly named after the number of lines in most of the fragments.

Jürgen Hammerstaedt has already drawn attention to the compositional similarities between this epistle fragment and the *Letter to Antipater*. In both, the apparent authors are replying to a request by someone who is eager to learn about the matter in question – in this fragment, about Diogenes' speech at the funeral of his son; in the *Letter to Antipater*, about Epicurus' teachings on the infinite number of worlds (Fr. 62-67). In both, an enthusiastic reply is provided, coupled with the lucky position that the author of the epistle happens to be in to satisfy the correspondent's curiosity: in NF 215, Archelaus does not have to rely exclusively on his memory, but owns a copy of the record made by some accurate shorthand-writers, while in the *Letter to Antipater*, Diogenes relies on a recent discussion of the matter in question. Both authors, Archelaus and Diogenes, take pleasure in helping their correspondents. These compositional similarities strongly suggest, I believe, that even if Archelaus and Dion were real contemporaries of Diogenes, the actual author of NF 215 is

---

[20] Jones 1986: 159.
[21] Cf. that of Lucretius' in Németh 2017: *Epilogue*.
[22] Transl. from Hammerstaedt – Smith 2018: 61, as well as for the possible different readings of the inscription.

Diogenes himself – a possibility Martin Ferguson Smith has already noted.[23] This impression is further enhanced by the fact that both letters concern biographical matters important in Diogenes' life: in this fragment the funeral speech, and as we shall see, in the *Letter to Antipater* a dialogue with a member of the Epicurean school in Rhodes, Theodoridas of Lindus. If this attribution of authorship is correct, it already displays the much greater freedom in which Diogenes used the epistolary genre compared to his predecessors.

In order to grasp why Diogenes might have played such a literary game – writing about a speech he himself gave in the voice of another person, Archelaus – we need first to understand the philosophical functions Diogenes may have attributed to his letters. On the one hand, the epistolary form provided variation in Diogenes' presentation of the Epicurean doctrines. The way in which Diogenes uses epistolary form not only mediates but enacts Epicurus' teachings. Both the funeral speech fragment and the *Letter to Antipater* display the pleasure Archelaus/Diogenes takes in satisfying the requests of different correspondents, and thus they also reflect indirectly the basic goal of Diogenes' inscription: providing aid and pleasure to the many. This time, though, readers of the inscription are assisted by themselves becoming additional or supplementary beneficiaries of those favours bestowed on individuals in Diogenes' publicly displayed correspondence. By the very nature of the epistolary genre, they are invited to become a part of a lively discussion and not merely witnesses to the correspondence. The consequent intellectual joy they may experience presents an immediate phenomenal effect in the reader which may encourage them to study the whole inscription and derive some or all its consequent benefits. The literary game by which Diogenes assumes a different voice in the Archelaus letter facilitates this intellectual stimulus in his readers: we know all too well that Diogenes is the sponsor of the inscription that, as we have seen, credits him as the author of most of the epitomes, and hence it is difficult not to read Archelaus' epistle as penned by Diogenes.

Yet perhaps a further reason why he was willing to assume a different voice in the letter, pretending as though Archelaus were writing to Dion, was to create some distance from how he constructed himself in his funeral speech in the part of the letter that has not yet been recovered. Diogenes perhaps wished to embed his reflections on his son's death in an epistolary report, with the shorthand-writers warranting "accuracy" and thus lending verisimilitude to a self-portrayal that was, in fact, a construction, not necessarily reflecting his real self.[24]

Furthermore, as his letters show, Diogenes did not simply preserve already made epitomes or arrange some of Epicurus' letters or those by the first generation of the Garden, but even composed some of his own *in imago suae vitae*, that is, in reflec-

---

[23] Hammerstaedt – Smith 2018: 63.
[24] Cf. Morel on the notion of ἀκρίβεια in this volume.

tion of *his own* life. This fact, I believe, demonstrates another philosophical function of the letters in the whole inscription: Diogenes presents his transformation in his epistles in order to display how he practises his Epicureanism or, more generally, how to practise the Epicurean doctrines he mediates in the *Physics* and *Ethics* sections or through the *Maxims*. We may attribute a similar function to his treatise on *Old Age*. This enactment may effortlessly accommodate insignificant chatter of the sort we find in the *Letter to Antipatros*, which can be read simply as a firsthand demonstration of how to practise the art of Epicurean friendship.

These epistolographic variations, therefore, serve to reflect the main goals of the inscription, enhancing its message and even justifying the functioning of the whole: if it was possible to help others, while absent, through letter-writing, it should also be possible to help the readers of the inscription even in the absence of its author, Diogenes. If this is correct, then it also reveals Diogenes' concern with Plato's critique of writing in the *Phaedrus*, as well as, perhaps, with Seneca's struggle in his own epistolary series to overcome Plato's evaluation that writing is not an effective means of communicating knowledge.[25] Viewed from this perspective, Diogenes' epistles appear to have had an even more significant role: they made the whole inscription come to life. This last point perhaps can be best demonstrated by Fr. 63 from the fragments of the *Letter to Antipater*:

Fr. 63
... our own land being hit by snow. So, as I was saying, having had my appetite most keenly whetted by all the advantage of the voyage, I shall try to meet you as soon as winter has ended, sailing first either to Athens or to Chalcis and Boeotia.

But since this is uncertain, both on account of the changeability and inconstancy of our fortunes and on account of my old age besides, I am sending you, in accordance with your request, the arguments concerning an infinite number of worlds. And you have enjoyed good fortune in the matter; for, before your letter arrived, Theodoridas of Lindus, a member of our school not unknown to you who is still novice to philosophy, was dealing with the same doctrine. And this doctrine came to be better articulated as a result of being turned over between the two of us face to face; for our agreements and disagreements with one another, and also our questionings, rendered the inquiry into the object of our search more precise.

I am therefore sending you that dialogue, Antipater, so that you may be in the same position as if you yourself were present, like Theodoridas, agreeing about some matters and making further inquiries in cases where you had doubts.

The dialogue began something like this: "Diogenes" said Theodoridas, "that the [doctrine laid down] by Epicurus on an infinite number of worlds is true [I am confident] ..., as [if] ... Epicurus ...[26]

---

[25] Cf. Graver 1996.
[26] Transl. by Martin F. Smith 1993, 397-8.

This fragment is preceded by a longer introduction (Fr. 62) which deals with Antipater's positive attitude towards philosophy, Diogenes' planned journeys, and possible encounters. The epistle therefore begins as a rather ordinary letter. In the quoted fragment, Diogenes appears as a fellow Epicurean (cf. the phrase in the funeral letter above: Διογένους ἡμετέρου / "our Diogenes"), discussing one of the issues of Epicurean philosophy – the theory of infinite worlds – with a young student somewhat more argumentatively and authoritatively in the later fragments of the letter (Fr. 64-67). The reason why this fragment deserves particular attention is its striking resemblance to the framed editing of Plato's dialogues. Diskin Clay did not find any special interest in this feature, since he believed that Aristotle's *Protrepticus* was a dialogue embedded in a letter. In fact, all we know for certain is that Aristotle' *Protrepticus* was addressed to one Themison, king of the Cypriots (Stobaeus, *Anthology* IV.32.21).[27] Since we do not have the beginning of the *Protrepticus*, even if Aristotle addressed Themison in an epistle before the dialogue, it is not clear at all whether or not the dialogue itself was embedded in and framed by the letter; this framing, however, does seem to be the case with Diogenes' letter. Clay also plays down this peculiar feature of the fragment by assimilating it to Epicurus' dialogue, the *Symposium*, but the little we have of that dialogue (Plut. *Adv. Col.* 1109E) does not seem to have anything to do with the epistolary genre. Hence Clay's position seems to me rather to reflect a desire to assimilate Diogenes' *Letter to Antipater* to non-extant precedents of the protreptic genre, but there is no real evidence to deny Diogenes his originality in combining two literary genres by embedding a dialogue within an epistle.

Whether or not we regard Diogenes as revolutionizing the ancient epistolary genre, he certainly does not leave much to the imagination concerning the philosophical function of the dialogue form. Although he admits the superiority of a face-to-face discussion, acknowledging that a doctrine under examination can be better articulated when people are present, he also emphasizes that by including his dialogue with Theodoridas in his epistle to Antipater, Antipater has the opportunity to follow the discussion as if he himself had been present. If Antipater were to have any further doubts, Diogenes thus encourages him to make additional inquiries of a kind potentially also available to readers of Diogenes in other parts of the inscription. If that is correct, it also shows that – as opposed to Plato's dialogues, in which the form of representation is directly relevant to the subject-matter – the philosophical function of the dialogue form embedded in Diogenes' epistle served a different purpose: it was simply another means, besides the epistolary genre *per se*, for Diogenes to encourage his readers to make use of the entire inscription by searching on other parts of the wall for those doctrines that the dialogue prompted

---

[27] "The unusual combination of a letter introducing a dialogue is as old as Aristotle's *Protrepticus*, with what must have been its prefatory letter to Themison of Cyprus: Arist. fr. 50 Rose." Clay 1989 /1998, p. 241, n. 34.

them to be more interested in.[28] Therefore, there is no such real interdependence between the dialogue form and the correct understanding of the Epicurean doctrine as we find in the Platonic dialogues. Rather, the dialogue form included in the letter addressed to Antipater is intended to create a connection between the epistle itself and the entire inscription.

If this analysis is correct, then we can also compare it to one of the points Plato brought up in his critique of writing in the *Phaedrus* (275d4-9): a book always says the same thing. If you have some questions about what you read, the only answer you can get is repetition of the wording you have already read. With Diogenes' epistles, however, embedded as they are in the context of other inscriptions, you can seek out the answer on other parts of the wall and find further answers to your questions, which incidentally also will help you deepen your research and your understanding of Epicureanism.[29]

This flexibility, is again, very reminiscent of Seneca's epistolary series. You can start in your reading with any one of his epistles, and your understanding is not hindered if, for example, you start by reading epistle 12. Still, the real, book-by-book structure of the *Epistulae Morales* – or even a deeper understanding of epistle 12 itself – can be attained only if you make the effort to read all the letters of book 1, in order. Only then might you even notice how the first epistle concerning time connects with the twelfth that concerns old age and thus how the two of them frame book 1. Given the introductory section of Diogenes' wall, he certainly had a compositional structure in mind for how to display his writings. And by his innovative application of the epistolary genre, he seems to have achieved a similar effect to Seneca's epistolary series that addresses another worry of Plato's concerning books: the inability of texts to select their audience (*Phdr.* 275e2-3). For Plato, personal selection of the partner in a dialogue was a decisive advantage of oral philosophical inquiry that texts certainly cannot do. Nonetheless, both Seneca's epistolary series and Diogenes' inscriptions, while available to anyone, speak only to those who are not only eager but suited well to learning, or as Diogenes put it in Fr. 2 and Fr. 3, "well constituted".

*
* *

The intellectual richness of Diogenes' apparent use of the epistolary genre thus clearly distinguishes him from the long tradition of Epicurean epistle-writing. Although the *Letter to Mother* may have been originally written by Epicurus, and if it was, to the extent that Diogenes also fits the Epicurean tradition of epistolary

---

[28] Cf. Fr. 30, which asks its reader not to be selective, like passersby.
[29] Cf. Roskam 2007 for the inter-related network of the inscription.

transmission, he certainly had a refreshing relationship with the genre. Diogenes not only stands out by his inventive rhetoric and deep knowledge of Epicureanism in his epistles, but also by his application of his literary skills to a wide erudition that not only brought his Epicureanism carved in stone alive, but also put into effect a new philosophical method of teaching through inscribed texts. Diogenes understood all too well that if his *logos* was to achieve its purpose, it must be displayed "in accordance with art". The philosophical art of letter-writing presupposes not only rhetorical skills but also the knowledge of the nature of the issues dealt with in the epistles and how they ought to be displayed in order to bring salvation.

This innovation within the Epicurean tradition is not without precedents in Hellenistic and Roman philosophy, and some additional textual similarities also betray possible connections I have already hinted at. As Diogenes claims in Fr. 3, the medicines he is publicly advertising in the stoa covering his wall have been fully tested and are also going to help future generations. This claim reminds one not only of the methods but also the very words of Seneca:

> The work that I am doing is for posterity: it is they who can benefit from what I write. I am committing to the page some healthful admonitions, like the recipes for useful salves. I have found these effective on my own sores, which, even if not completely healed, have ceased to spread. (*Ep.* 8.2)[30]

Even though Diogenes' medical metaphor certainly has Epicurean roots – it is enough just to think of the *tetrapharmakos* – I have always wondered whether the stoa covering Diogenes' wall was really only a sign of irony, as has often been noted before, or also a sign of Diogenes' adoption of Seneca's habit of "crossing over even into the other camp, not a deserter, but as a spy" (*Ep.* 2.5).[31]

REFERENCES

Angeli, A., 1988, *Filodemo, Agli amici di scuola. La Scuola di Epicuro* VII. Naples: Bibliopolis.
Bailey, C., 1926, *Epicurus. The Extant Remains*. Oxford: Clarendon Press.
Clay, D., 1973, "Epicurus' Last Will and Testament", *Archiv für Geschichte der Philosophie*: 252-280. Reprinted in: *Paradosis & Survival. Three Chapters in the History of Epicurean Philosophy*. Cambridge 1998: Cambridge University Press: 3-31.
Clay, D., 1989, "A Lost Epicurean Community." *Greek, Roman, and Byzantine Studies* 30, no. 2: 313-35. Reprinted in: *Paradosis & Survival. Three Chapters in the History of Epicurean Philosophy*. Cambridge: Cambridge University Press: 232-56.

---

[30] Transl. from Graver / Long 2015.
[31] I appreciate the invitation to present the first version of this paper at Università Ca' Foscari Venezia by the organizers as well as the many comments from the audience.

Erbì, M. 2020, *Lettere. Frammenti e Testimonianze. Epicuro*. Pisa-Rome: Fabrizio Serra Editore.

Fitzgerald, J. T, 2003, "Last Wills and Testaments in Graeco-Roman Perspective", in J. T. Fitzgerald – T. H. Olbricht – M. L. White (eds.), *Early Christianity and Classical Culture*. Leiden-Boston: Brill: 637-672.

Gordon, P., 1996, *Epicurus in Lycia: The Second-century World of Diogenes of Oenoanda*. Ann Arbor, MI: Michigan University Press.

Gordon, P., 2013, "Epistolary Epicureans", in O. Hodkinson – P. Rosenmeyer (eds.), *Epistolary Narratives*. Leiden-Boston: Brill.

Gordon, P., 2020, "Diogenes of Oenoanda", in P. Mitsis (ed.), *The Oxford Handbook of Epicurus and Epicureanism*. Oxford: Oxford University Press: 531-548.

Graver, M., 1996, *Therapeutic Reading and Seneca's* Moral Epistles. PhD dissertation.

Graver, M. (transl.), – Long, A. A. (ed.), 2015, *Seneca. Letters on Ethics to Lucilius*. Chicago: The University of Chicago Press.

Hall, A. S., 1979, "Who was Diogenes of Oenoanda?" *Journal of Hellenic Studies* 99, 160-63.

Hammerstaedt, J., – Smith, M. F., 2018, "Diogenes of Oinoanda: The New and Unexpected Discoveries of 2017 (NF 214-219) with a Re-edition of Fr. 70-72." *Epigraphica Anatolica* 51, 43-79.

Hammerstaedt, J., – Morel, P-M., – Güremen, R. (eds.), 2007, *Diogenes of Oinoanda. Epicureanism and Philosophical Debates*. Leuven: Leuven University Press.

Inwood, B., 2007 (a), *Seneca. Selected Philosophical letters*. Oxford: Oxford University Press.

Inwood, B., 2007 (b), "The Importance of Form in Seneca's Philosophical Letters." In: Morello, R. & Morrison, A. D. (eds.) 2007, *Ancient Letters. Classical & Late Antique Epistolography*. Oxford: Oxford University Press.

Jones, C. P., 1986, *Culture and Society in Lucian*. Cambridge, MA: Harvard University Press.

Laks, A., 1976, "Édition critique et commentée de la "Vie d'Épicure" dans Diogène Laërce (x 1-34)", in: Bollack, J. and Laks, A. (eds.), *Études sur l'Épicurisme antique*, I, Lille: Publication de L'Université de Lille III, 1-118.

Mensch, P. (transl.) – Miller, J. (ed.), 2018, *Lives of the Eminent Philosophers. Diogenes Laertius*. Oxford: Oxford University Press.

Németh, A., 2017, *Epicurus on the Self*. London-New York: Routledge.

Rosenmeyer, P. A., 2001, *Ancient Epistolary Fiction: The Letter in Greek Literature*. Cambridge: Cambridge University Press.

Rosenmeyer, P. A., 2006, *Ancient Greek Literary Letters. Selections in Translation*. London-New York: Routledge.

Roskam, G., 2007, "Diogenes' Polemical Approach, or How to Refute a Philosophical Opponent in an Epigraphic Context." In: Hammerstaedt, J., Morel, P-M., Güremen, R. (eds.) 2007. *Diogenes of Oinoanda. Epicureanism and Philosophical Debates*. Leuven: Leuven University Press, 241-70.

Smith, M. F., 1993, *Diogenes of Oinoanda: The Epicurean Inscription*. Naples: Bibliopolis

Smith, M. F., 1998, "Excavations at Oinoanda 1997: The New Epicurean Texts." *Anatolian Studies* 48, 125-70.

Usener, H., 1887/2010, *Epicurea*. Cambridge: Cambridge University Press.

Verde, F. (ed.), 2022, *Epicuro: Epistola a Pitocle*. In collaborazione con Mauro Tulli, Dino De Sanctis, Francesca G. Masi. Baden-Baden: Academia.

Part III

Ancient Reception of Epicurean ethics and epistemology

EPICUREAN TRANSLATIONS/INTERPRETATIONS BY CICERO AND SENECA

Stefano Maso

INTRODUCTORY REMARKS

Both Cicero and Seneca had a very accurate knowledge of the Greek language. Cicero is the first to develop a Latin philosophical language, capable of responding to the specific needs of a discipline that only in the first century BC acquired credibility and found consensus among men of culture, rhetoricians, and politicians.

Alongside Cicero there is only one contemporary of his: Lucretius with his *De rerum natura*. This masterpiece is the reference framework for the Latin translation and knowledge of Epicurus' philosophical terminology. As we know, even Lucretius – like Cicero – is not merely a translator, that is, someone limited to rendering original Greek texts in Latin; rather he is a man of letters, a poet, who set out to introduce, collect, and explain to the Romans the fundamental topics of Epicurus' doctrine: those which, in his opinion, could earn the greatest credit in the cultural environment of Rome, and which deserved to be explained and – if necessary – perfected.

As for Seneca: in this case we are faced with an openly Stoic philosopher, able to deepen the theoretical aspects of his school with original openings devoid of any qualms (or reverence) towards tradition. Furthermore, he is – as in the case of Cicero – a personality of the highest political level, able to easily master Latin and Greek.

In this essay, starting from detailed examples taken from the texts of Cicero and Seneca, I will attempt to highlight the characteristics of their approach to Epicurus' Greek thought and language, showing – as far as possible – the peculiarities within a fundamental strategic convergence.

1. CICERO'S STRATEGY IN DEALING WITH THE GREEK LANGUAGE

Cicero, and similarly Lucretius, worked in two directions: on the one hand, they tried to find the Latin equivalents for the technical vocabulary used by Greek philosophers; they proposed, in this way, to make them linguistic 'tools' for the regular use of Roman philosophers. On the other hand, on several occasions they retained the Greek word simply transliterating it into Latin. Lucretius was not satisfied with the *patrii sermonis egestas* (*RN* 1.832), that is, with what the semantic panorama made available to him. Among the most interesting examples: the use of "homoeomerian" (*RN* 1.830-842) in reference to the Anaxagorean doctrine (Cicero will attempt "concentio", in its version from Plato's *Timaeus* 14). Or we can think of "harmonia" (3.98-101) with which he transliterates something that means "verum habitum quendam vitalem corporis".[1]

As we know, the attention to the most effective Latin translation leads Lucretius to the great caution shown in the face of the Greek ἄτομος / ἄτομον, for which he uses: *rerum primordia* / *materies* / *genitalia corpora* / *semina rerum* / *exordia rerum* / *corpora prima* / *corpuscula* / *elementa*.[2] Cicero, on the other hand, will not hesitate to use the transliteration "atomus" (*fato* 23), even if he does not disdain "individuum" (*fin.* 2.75).

The same goes for εἴδωλα, for which in *De rerum natura* there are: *simulacrum* / *imago* / *figurae* / *effigies*. Cicero has *imago*; but he too reproduces, in one case, the Greek directly: εἴδωλα ἀπειρία (*fin.*1.21).

Like Lucretius, Cicero also underlines the limitations that the Latin language presents at his time; however, he lets us understand how he will move towards the obscurities of technical languages. So, he writes:

[1] Cic., *fin.* 3.15
Si enim Zenoni licuit, cum rem aliquam invenisset inusitatam, inauditum quoque ei rei nomen inponere, cur non liceat Catoni? nec tamen exprimi **verbum e verbo** necesse erit ut interpretes indiserti solent, cum sit verbum, quod idem declaret, magis usitatum; equidem soleo etiam quod uno Graeci, si aliter non possum, idem **pluribus verbis** exponere. Et tamen puto concedi nobis oportere ut **Graeco verbo** utamur, si quando minus occurret Latinum, ne hoc 'ephippiis' et 'acratophoris' potius quam 'proegmenis' et 'apoproegmenis' concedatur. Quamquam haec quidem praeposita recte et reiecta dicere licebit.[3]

Thanks to this original and technical 'testament', we understand that Cicero contemplated three possibilities:
   a) use a word that has the same meaning in Greek and in Latin;
   b) render with a circumlocution the concept that in Greek is rendered with a single word;
   c) use the Greek term (transliterated or not).

---

[1] See Powell 1995; Sedley 1998; Warren 2007.

[2] Maso 2016.

[3] "If Zeno was allowed to invent a new term to match the discovery of an unfamiliar idea, then why not Cato? None the less, there is no need for an exact **word-for-word** correspondence when a more familiar term already exists to convey the same meaning. That is the mark of an unskilled translator. My usual practice, where there is no alternative available, is to express **a single Greek word by several Latin ones**. And I still think we should be allowed **to use a Greek word** when there is no Latin equivalent. If 'ephippia' and 'acratophora' are allowed, then 'proêgmena' and 'apoproêgmena' should certainly be allowed too, even though they may correctly be rendered as 'preferred' and 'rejected'", (transl. Woolf; emphasis added. For the translations of the Latin and Greek texts I have consulted the works listed below. I have slightly modified the translations when necessary. The translations for the works not listed here are mine).

Glucker attempted a more analytic classification.⁴ Anyway, the accuracy and critical sensitivity that Cicero demonstrates leads Glucker to conclude that – despite the fact that at the time the idea that works of literature are likely to remain for many generations, or forever, is not all that common among the ancient writers – Cicero had some prospective readership in mind which went beyond his own age and country.⁵

The lucidity with which Cicero becomes aware of his work as interpreter/translator is admirable. Point (a) and point (b) have similar characteristics: it is a question of finding one or more Latin words that allow us to understand the meaning of the original word. For (a) the responsibility for the decision taken is high: any misunderstanding of the translator risks perpetuating itself for a long time. Even with (b) we are in a delicate situation: first, there is the admission that there is no Latin word capable of referring to the original concept denoted by the Greek; however, the proposed circumlocution appears less demanding because it is less definitive: it appears as a suggestion that must help the Latin reader to grasp the true meaning of the original. In the case of point (c) the situation is completely different: the corresponding Latin word is absent, and any substitutive circumlocution approximates the meaning but is not considered successful. Hence the decision to implement the Latin language by proposing a transliteration of the Greek word (in some occurrences even a simple 'cast') with the claim, however, that this 'neologism' becomes the heritage of scientific language.

I point out that for point c) there is no lack of uncertainty on Cicero's part. An example is given by the way in which Cicero intends to translate ἐτυμολογία:

[2] Cic., *Top.* 35
Multa etiam ex notatione⁶ sumuntur. Ea est autem, cum ex vi nominis argumentum elicitur; quam Graeci ἐτυμολογίαν appellant, id est **verbum ex verbo** 'veriloquium'; nos autem novitatem verbi non satis apti fugientes genus hoc notationem appellamus, quia sunt verba rerum notae. Itaque hoc quidem Aristoteles σύμβολον appellat, quod Latine est 'nota'. Sed cum intellegitur quid significetur minus laborandum est de nomine.⁷

---

⁴ Glucker 2012: 37-96; on pp. 52-58, he distinguishes translations *verbum e verbo, verbum pro verbo, verbum quod ideam valeat, verbum ipsum interpretari* ("translations ad sensum"). On the passage of *De finibus* mentioned, see Glucker 2015: 40-41.

⁵ Glucker 2012: 46. The scholar even concludes, "Yet one might say that this philosophical vocabulary may well be regarded as Cicero's abiding contribution to philosophy." Lévy 1992, 92-106, had previously dealt with highlighting Cicero's attitude to the philosophical schools and his attention to the technical language of each. Powell 1995: 291, goes back to underlining Cicero's care in explaining the choices he made, especially in the case in which he had to introduce a neologism.

⁶ With "notatio" Cicero means the signifier or mark evoking the *semantema*.

⁷ "Many elements are derived from *notatio*. It occurs when the argument is deduced from the signifying power of a word. The Greeks call this 'etymology', and this translates in Latin (**word for word**) 'veriloquence'. But we, reluctant as we are to improper neologisms, we call this genus notation, because words are *notae* (tokens) of things. Aristotle moreover uses in this case the term *sumbolon*,

More interesting still, in general, is to try to understand the particular attention that Cicero shows when the philosophical vocabulary appears in all its complexity. Exemplary is the case of *voluntas*, an important word in Stoic philosophy, but not only: it is also connected to the Aristotelian conception of deliberation and choice, in addition to the Epicurean tradition. In the latter case, κατὰ βούλησις constitutes the way in which, something happens by a spontaneous act of will. It is exactly the opposite of what happens with regard to the regular movements that are observed in the agglomerations constituting the celestial bodies (and also the gods who – for the Epicureans – are nothing more than a little agglomerated fire): these one move as needed (τὴν ἀνάγκην), *Hrd.* 77. In § 81, Epicurus reiterates that we must not believe that blessed and immortal creatures can have will (βουλήσεις), perform actions (πράξεις), and be the cause (αἰτίας) of something that is contrary (ὑπεναντίας) to their nature.

We then observe that in *KD* XXXII the verb "to want" is compared to the verb "to be able to": μὴ ἐδύνατο ἢ μὴ ἐβούλετο; as well as in an occurrence from D.L. 10.11: "Send me a cheese casserole so I can (δύνωμαι), when I want (βούλομαι), squander a little (πολυτεύσασθαι)."

Yet here is now the important passage in which Cicero questions himself on the way to translate βούλησις:

[3] Cic., *Tusc.* 4.12
Natura enim omnes ea, quae bona videntur, secuntur fugiuntque contraria; quam ob rem simul obiecta species est cuiuspiam, quod bonum videatur, ad id adipiscendum impellit ipsa natura. Id cum constanter prudenterque fit, eius modi adpetitionem Stoici βούλησιν appellant, nos appellemus **voluntatem**, eam illi putant in solo esse sapiente; quam sic definiunt: voluntas est, quae quid cum ratione desiderat. quae autem ratione adversante incitata est vehementius, ea libido est vel cupiditas effrenata, quae in omnibus stultis invenitur.[8]

It is a particularly intriguing passage for several reasons. First, Cicero declares that he is referring to the Stoics. In fact, what he writes is also influenced by the Epicurean perspective: the juxtaposition of *voluntas* with *adpetitio* and *desiderium* (and the subsequent reference "per differentiam" to *libido* and *cupiditas*) lead directly to the Epicurean theoretical framework and the connected theory of pleasure.

---

which corresponds in Latin *nota*. But when the meaning is understood, the commitment to the word which expresses it is less."

[8] "By nature, all people pursue those things which they think to be good and avoid their opposites. Therefore, as soon as a person receives an impression of something which he thinks is good, nature itself urges him to reach out after it. When this is done prudently and in accordance with consistency, it is the sort of reaching which the Stoics call a *boulēsis*, and which I shall term a 'volition.' They think that a volition, which they define as 'a wish for some object in accordance with reason,' is found only in the wise person. But the sort of reaching which is aroused too vigorously and in a manner opposed to reason is called 'desire' or 'unbridled longing,' and this is what is found in all who are foolish" (transl. Graver).

Also of particular interest is the use of the subjunctive "appellemus", which signals Cicero's uncertainty. This usage is because, according to Cicero, the word *voluntas* has a wider spectrum of meaning than βούλησις.[9] It is not a pure form of tension or *adpetitio* as for the Stoics, though remaining distinguishable from *desiderium*; it is not exclusively dependent on judgment or opinion but not even radically opposed to reason; it should not be perceived as πάθος. In opposition to the Stoic doctrine, βούλησις can be determined as a result of a perfectly thought-out decision or, in any case, deemed convenient: a subjective decision that argues in favour of the thesis of 'free will', undoubtedly supported by the Epicureans.[10]

Yet here is also the case of ἡδονή, the key word of Epicurean ethics, for which certainly Cicero – like Lucretius – has *voluptas* at his disposal and, with this word, he can re-propose the central concept (i.e., the limit of pleasure: the "catastematic pleasure") of the *KD* XIX: cf. *fin.* 1.63; 2.87. I report this last passage alongside an Epicurean sentence:

[4] a) Cic., *fin.* 2.87-88
Negat Epicurus diuturnitatem quidem temporis ad beate vivendum aliquid afferre, nec minorem voluptatem percipi in brevitate temporis, quam si illa sit sempiterna. (...) Cum enim summum bonum in voluptate ponat, negat infinito tempore aetatis voluptatem fieri maiorem quam finito atque modico. (...) Negat enim summo bono afferre incrementum diem.[11]

[4] b) Epic., *KD* XIX
Ὁ ἄπειρος χρόνος ἴσην ἔχει τὴν ἡδονὴν καὶ ὁ πεπερασμένος, ἐάν τις αὐτῆς τὰ πέρατα καταμετρήσῃ τῷ λογισμῷ[12].

In *fin.* 2.12 Cicero gets angry with the Epicurean Torquatus because he does not accept being accused of misunderstanding as to the pleasure of Epicurus. And so, Cicero reflects on the possible translation:

[5] Cic., *fin.* 2.12-13
Itaque hoc frequenter dici solet a vobis, non intellegere nos, quam dicat Epicurus voluptatem. Quod quidem mihi si quando dictum est (est autem dictum non parum

---

[9] See Maso 2021: 73-84.
[10] Cic., *fato* 25: *Ad animorum motus voluntarios non est requirenda externa causa; motus enim voluntarius eam naturam in se ipse continet ut sit in nostra potestate nobisque pareat*, "We don't need to look for an external cause for the voluntary motions of the mind. Since such is the nature of voluntary motion, that it must needs be in our own power and obey us."
[11] "(Epicurus denies) that temporal duration adds nothing to the happiness of a life, and that no less pleasure is enjoyed in a short space of time than in the whole of time. (...) Epicurus holds that pleasure is the supreme good, and yet claims that there is no greater pleasure to be had in an infinite period than in a brief and limited one. (...) Here it is denied that time adds anything to the supreme good" (transl. Woolf).
[12] "Infinite time and finite time contain equal pleasure, if one measure the limits of pleasure with reasoning" (transl. L&S).

saepe), etsi satis clemens sum in disputando, tamen interdum soleo sub irasci. Egone non intellego, quid sit ἡδονήν Graece, Latine voluptas? utram tandem linguam nescio? deinde qui fit, ut ego nesciam, sciant omnes, quicumque Epicurei esse voluerunt? (...) Ut scias me intellegere, primum idem esse dico voluptatem, quod ille ἡδονήν. Et quidem saepe quaerimus verbum Latinum par Graeco et quod idem valeat; hic nihil fuit, quod quaereremus. Nullum inveniri verbum potest quod magis idem declaret Latine, quod Graece, quam declarat voluptas. Huic verbo omnes, qui ubique sunt, qui Latine sciunt, duas res subiciunt, laetitiam in animo, commotionem suavem iucunditatis in corpore.[13]

There is almost a sort of impatience on the part of Cicero towards those who doubt his ability to understand and interpret.[14] His linguistic and philosophical competence is confirmed by the fact that, on other occasions, he has the opportunity to specify further nuances relating to the meaning of ἡδονή.

- See the word *laetitia*: *fin* 2.13-14; and 3.35, which contains a clarification on the translation alluding to "ἡδονή *animi*".
- See *delectatio* opposed to *obscena voluptas* (*fin.* 2.7).
- See the adverb *iucunde* (*fin.* 2.82), where Cicero recalls how friendship cannot be distinguished from pleasure, because, if it is true that without friendship we cannot live safely and without fear, then, without friendship, we could not even live pleasantly (i.e., *iucunde*).
- See *fin.* 2.11: *voluptas* is made corresponding to *indolentia* (= ἀναλγησία).

As far as *voluptas* is concerned, though, Cicero also engages in the direct translation of three Epicurean maxims: [6] *Tusc.* 3.47; [7] *Tusc.* 5.26; [8] *fin.* 1.57-58:

[6] a) Cic., *Tusc.* 3.47
At idem ait non crescere voluptatem dolore detracto, summamque esse voluptatem nihil dolere.[15]

---

[13] "That is why you Epicureans resort so often to saying that the rest of us do not understand what Epicurus meant by pleasure. This is a claim that tends to make my hackles rise whenever it is made (and it is not infrequently made), however good-natured I may be in debate. It is as if I did not know what *hêdonê* is in Greek, or *voluptas* in Latin. Which language is it that I do not understand? And how come that I do not understand it, whereas anyone you like who has chosen to be an Epicurean does?" (...) "Let me show you that I do. Firstly, what I mean by *voluptas* is exactly what he means by *hêdonê*. We often have to search for a Latin equivalent to a Greek word with the same sense. No search is called for in this case. No Latin word can be found which captures a Greek word more exactly than *voluptas* does. Everyone in the world who knows Latin takes this word to convey two notions: elation in the mind, and a delightfully sweet arousal in the body" (transl. Woolf).

[14] An illuminating question is Cicero's *instrumental* use of his own linguistic competence, in order to discredit the ethical conception of Epicureanism. Cicero confirms himself as an excellent reader and translator. However, this facility does not automatically make him a reliable interpreter. See Maso 2017: 25-46.

[15] "But Epicurus also says that once pain is gone, pleasure does not increase; and that the summit of pleasure is to have no pain at all" (transl. Graver).

[6] b) Epic., *KD* XVIII
Οὐκ ἐπαύξεται ἐν τῇ σαρκὶ ἡ ἡδονή, ἐπειδὰν ἅπαξ τὸ κατ ἔνδειαν ἀλγοῦν ἐξαιρεθῇ, [ἀλλὰ μόνον ποικίλλεται.] (κτλ.).[16]

[6] c) Epic., *KD* III
Ὅρος τοῦ μεγέθους τῶν ἡδονῶν ἡ παντὸς τοῦ ἀλγοῦντος ὑπεξαίρεσις.[17]

On this first occurrence we observe that the Ciceronian text only partially translates the 'first' part of *KD* xviii (this maxim continued evoking the theme of the 'limit' of pleasure connected to the mental capacity to recognize its characteristic). The second part of the Ciceronian text seems to come from the initial part of *KD* iii where the incompatibility of pleasure and pain is emphasized – going back once again to the theme of 'limit'.

Cicero knows very well this clear assumption of the alternative 'pleasure *vs* pain'. He clearly illustrates it in *fin.* 1.38, recalling that for Epicurus there is no intermediate state between pleasure and pain: "non placuit Epicuro medium esse quiddam inter dolorem et voluptatem"; hence, "doloris omnis privatio recte nominata est voluptas."

It is precisely against this thesis that Cicero lashes out, recovering the thought of the peripatetic Hieronymus of Rhodes (*fin.* 2.8; 16; 18; 32; 35; 41; 4.49; 5.14; 20; 73) that distinguishes "voluptas" from "do not hurt" and who maintains that the latter is the 'highest good'.

[7] a) Cic., *Tusc.* 5.26
Fortunam exiguam intervenire sapienti.[18]

[7] b) Epic., *KD* XVI
Βραχέα σοφῷ τύχη παρεμπίπτει (...)[19]

[7] c) Cic., *Tusc.* 5.27 (= Metrod. *fr.* 49 Körte)
Occupavi te ... Fortuna, atque cepi omnisque aditus tuos interclusi, ut ad me adspirare non posses.[20]

The translation of *KD* XVI is literal, but even on this occasion Cicero is limited only to the initial part. The original maxim went on to explain that reason (ὁ λογισμός)

---

[16] "The pleasure in the flesh does not increase when once the pain of need has been removed, [but it is only varied]" (transl. L&S).
[17] "The removal of all pain is the limit of the magnitude of pleasures" (transl. L&S).
[18] "Fortune makes little impact on the wise man" (transl. Douglas). See *infra* p. 210, with reference to Seneca's interpretation.
[19] "Fortune is of little importance to the wise." This maxim continues: "Reason (λογισμός) has already preordained (διῴκηκε) the greatest and most important things (μέγιστα καὶ κυριώτατα), and for the whole course of life (κατὰ τὸν συνεχῆ χρόνον) it preorders (διοικεῖ) and will preorder (διοικήσει) them."
[20] "I have beaten you to it, Fortune, and seized and blocked your lines of approach, so that you cannot come near me" (transl. Douglas).

comes into play for really great and important things: it rules now and always. Cicero instead uses the quote from Epicurus to question the seriousness of those scholars who have only pleasure in mind while they speak of "honesty", "wisdom", and "justice". This use of the brief quotation from Epicurus is, in the next § 27, reinforced by a parallel quotation, this time from the Epicurean Metrodorus, in which the wise man's victory over luck is emphasized (*occupavi te, Fortuna*). Then Cicero again warns against pleasure as an end in itself and concludes by denouncing the impossibility of giving credit to those who have put the goods in bowels and marrow: *qui omne bonum in visceribus medullisque condideris.*

[8] a) Cic., *Fin.* 1.57-58
Clamat Epicurus, is quem vos nimis voluptatibus esse deditum dicitis, non posse iucunde vivi, nisi sapienter, honeste iusteque vivatur, nec sapienter, honeste, iuste, nisi iucunde.[21]

[8] b) Epic., *KD* V
Οὐκ ἔστιν ἡδέως ζῆν ἄνευ τοῦ φρονίμως καὶ καλῶς καὶ δικαίως <οὐδὲ φρονίμως καὶ καλῶς καὶ δικαίως> ἄνευ τοῦ ἡδέως· ὅτῳ δὲ τοῦτο μὴ ὑπάρχει, οὐκ ἔστι τοῦτον ἡδέως ζῆν.[22]

Here, in addition to the integration present in Cicero, which Diogenes of Oinoanda will later confirm (fr. 37 Smith, "lower margin"), note how Cicero uses *iucunde* to translate ἡδέως, and that, moreover, he brings everything back to the theme of "voluptas".

As already stated, Cicero is aware of his role as a 'mediator' of Greek culture and philosophical language. As for Epicureanism, Cicero deals with its physical doctrine (*De finibus, De divinatione, De fato*), theological doctrine (*De natura deorum*), and ethical doctrine (*De finibus, Tusculanae disputationes*). He shows that he knows the doctrine's foundations correctly, since he had Phaedrus and then Zeno of Sidon as his masters. He had direct knowledge of Lucretius' *De rerum natura*.[23] Finally, he seems to directly know some texts of Epicurus handed down and evidently circulating at the time. Cicero accurately quotes some works. First he cites the *Ratae sententiae* (Κύριαι δόξαι), in *fin.* 1.16; 2.20; *ND* 1.45; 1.85; 1.113; *off.* 3.116; *fam.* 15.19.2. Then he quotes the *Ep. ad Idomeneum*, in *fin.* 2.99; the *Testamentum*, in *fin.* 2.103;

---

[21] "Epicurus, the man whom you accuse of being excessively devoted to pleasure, in fact proclaims that one cannot live pleasantly unless one lives wisely, honourably and justly; and that one cannot live wisely, honourably and justly without living pleasantly" (transl. Woolf).
[22] "It is not possible to live happily if you do not live a wise and beautiful and just life, nor to live a wise and beautiful and just life without living happily; those who lack this cannot live happily."
[23] See *ad Quint. Fr.* 2.9.3.

De fine (Περὶ τέλους), in *Tusc.* 3.41 and 44;[24] *De voluptate* (Περὶ ἡδονῆς), in *div.* 2.59;[25] *De pietate* (Περὶ εὐσεβείας), in *ND* 1.115; *De sanctitate* (Περὶ ὁσιότητος), in *ND* 1.115 and 122;[26] and *De regula et iudicio* (that probably corresponds to Περὶ κριτηρίου ἢ Κανών), in *ND* 1.43-44. Obviously, we cannot determine whether Cicero knew all these works directly or if he used doxographical collections, subjects, and maxims that were available at the time.[27] The fact remains, though, that these are accurate citations and that they almost always refer to specific works.

The source of a long passage, *ND* 1.49-50, in which Epicurus deals with physics, cannot be identified with certainty.[28] In this passage we find peculiar words of the Epicurean language:

[9] a) Cic., *ND* 1.49-50
Epicurus autem, qui **res occultas et penitus abditas** (i.e. ἄδηλα) non modo **videt animo** (i.e. πρόληψις) sed etiam sic tractet ut manu, docet eam esse vim et naturam deorum, ut primum non sensu sed **mente cernatur** (i.e. λόγῳ θεωρητούς), nec **soliditate** (i.e. στερέμνια) quadam nec **ad numerum** (καθ' ἀριθμόν), ut ea quae ille propter **firmitatem** στερέμνια appellat, sed **imaginibus similitudine et transitione** perceptis (i.e. εἴδωλα and ἀναλογία / ὁμοείδεια and ὑπέρβασις; see μετάβασις καθ' ὁμοιότητα), cum infinita simillumarum imaginum species ex innumerabilibus individuis existat et *ad nos adfluat[29] (i.e. ἐκ τῆς συνεχοῦς ἐπιρρύσεως), cum maximis **voluptatibus** (i.e. ἡδονή) in eas **imagines** (εἴδωλα) mentem intentam infixamque nostram intellegentiam capere quae sit et beata natura et aeterna. Summa vero vis infinitatis et magna ac diligenti contemplatione dignissima est. In qua intellegi necesse est eam esse naturam ut omnia omnibus paribus paria respondeant; hanc ἰσονομίαν appellat Epicurus id est **aequabilem tributionem**.[30]

---

[24] See Usener 1887: 119-23.
[25] It is the only quotation from this book, which, moreover, is not present in the catalog of Diog. Laert., X 27-28. See Usener 1887: 101.
[26] Cic., *ND* 1.115: *At etiam de sanctitate, de pietate adversos deos libros scripsit Epicurus*. In Diog. Laert. X 27 there is a Περὶ ὁσιότητος and a Περὶ θεῶν, but not a Περὶ εὐσεβείας. Similarly in Plutarch., *Non posse suaviter*, 1102c. Pease 1955: I 506-07 believes that in Cicero's case we are dealing with a simple synonymy. According to Pease, *De pietate* would not be among the works Epicurus would have written.
[27] The collection consisting of the Κύριαι δόξαι is but one example. It is difficult to establish when it was compiled. A later collection, as is well known, is made up of the *Gnomologium Vaticanum*. As for secondhand citations, D'Anna 1965: 38 believes that Cicero's knowledge of the *Epistula ad Menoeceum* – given the way he refers to this text in the catalog of desires – in *fin.* 2.26 might constitute such a case.
[28] See Usener [1887]: 232-38.
[29] The manuscript tradition hesitates between *ad deos adfluat* (Leydensis Vossianus 84) and *ad eos adfluat* (Leydensis Vossianus 86). Following Lambinus (ed. 1565-1566), we can assume ad*e [oadn] os* > *ad eos* (Vossianus 86) and therefore the correction *ad nos* which allows not to prejudice the canonical interpretation of the atomic movement. For an update of the debate on this point, see Maso 2017, 98-100.
[30] "Epicurus then, as he not merely **discerns abstruse and recondite things** (ἄδηλα) **with his mind's eye** (πρόληψις), but handles them as tangible realities, teaches that the substance and nature of **the gods** (τοὺς θεούς) is such that, in the first place, it **is perceived** not by the senses but **by the mind** (λόγῳ θεωρητούς); and that not **for their physical solidity or for their singularity** (καθ' ἀριθμόν), as in the case of those bodies, which Epicurus in virtue of their **substantiality** entitles στερέμνια, but, thanks to the perceived **images** (εἴδωλα) according to their **similarities** (ἀναλογία / ὁμοείδεια) and **succession**

The first part of this passage was related to a scholium at *KD* i, see 139 Us. p. 71:

[9] b) Epic., Schol. ad KD i = Fr. 355 Usener (= § 139 p. 71)
ἐν ἄλλοις δέ φησι τοὺς θεοὺς **λόγῳ θεωρητούς** (i.e. *mente cernatur*), οὓς μὲν **κατ' ἀριθμὸν** (*ad numerum*) ὑφεστώτας, οὓς δὲ **κατὰ ὁμοείδειαν** (i.e. *imaginibus similitudine*) ἐκ τῆς συνεχοῦς **ἐπιρρύσεως** (*adfulat*) **τῶν ὁμοίων εἰδώλων** (*simillumarum imaginum*) ἐπὶ τὸ αὐτὸ ἀποτετελεσμένους ἀνθρωποειδεῖς.[31]

The textual comparisons with the Epicurean language are evident and help to understand, in Latin, the interpretative line of Cicero. Some details are worth mentioning:
- *soliditas* / *firmitas* clearly are useful to translate στερέμνια (see *ND* 1.49 = [194] Arrighetti);
- the locution "imaginibus similitudine et transitione perceptis", in addition to including the translation of the words εἴδωλα and ἀναλογία / ὁμοείδεια and ὑπέρβασις, refers to the specific doctrine of μετάβασις καθ' ὁμοιότητα which appears immediately afterwards: the arrival of images made up of atoms, characterized by their extreme similarity (ἀναλογία) and, as such, perceived. If we accept that *transitio* is a technical translation of ὑπέρβασις, we point to a mechanistic interpretation;[32] if it is rather inclined to suggest μετάβασις, the interpretation would be of a logicist type.[33]
- *ex innumerabilibus individuis existat et ad nos adfluat*: in evidence is the reference to the countless number of images that flow from an object. It is so great that Epicurus, in the second book of *Peri phuseos*, speaks of ἀπειρία ("infinite quantity", coll. 101-102), to the point that the "emanations" (ἀποστάσεις) from the bodies (στερέμνια) have unsurpassed speed (ταχυτῆτά τινα ἀνυπέρβλητον, col. 111) and become "continuous effluvium" (συνεχὴς

(ὑπέρβασις) [see μετάβασις καθ' ὁμοιότητα] – since an endless form of similar images arises from the innumerable atoms and **streams** to us [see ἐκ τῆς συνεχοῦς ἐπιρρύσεως]), our mind – concentrated with great **pleasure** (ἡδονή) and having fixed our attention on these **images** (εἴδωλα) – understands what constitutes a blessed and eternal nature. Moreover, there is the supremely potent principle of infinity, which claims the closest and most careful study; we must understand that it has the following property, that in the sum of things everything has its exact match and counterpart. This property is termed by Epicurus ἰσονομίαν, or the principle of **uniform distribution**." For the exegesis of this passage and for Cicero's underlying critique of the Epicurean doctrine, see Maso 2017: 50-52.

[31] "In other (*scil.* works) Epicurus says that the gods are **understandable with reason**: both those subsisting **in their individuality**, and those – who are endowed with human form – produced **by similarity** from the continuous **flow of similar images** to obtain the same object."

[32] See Purinton 2001: 203-09.

[33] See Bailey 1928: 447-49. DeWitt 1942: 46: "Shapes apprehended by method of analogy and inference by induction". According to Bailey, it is essential to remember that *similitudo* is a translation of ἀναλογία, see *Hrd*. 58-59. Philippson 1916: 602, believed instead that it was decisive to recall the expression κατ ὁμοείδιαν.

ἀπόρροια) towards our sense organs and our mind (coll. 94.2-25 and 38-75).[34]

On other occasions, less appreciably contextualized in arguments or insights on Epicurean issues, we can find further examples of the translation of single words, generally attributable to the epistemological scientific side. Here are some examples:
- *simulacrum* / *species* translates εἰκών (*ND* 105; 107 = [194-195] Arr.)
- *anticipatio* / *praenotio* translate πρόληψις (*ND* 1.4-44 = [174-175] Arr.)
- *aequabilis distributio, aequilibritas* translate ἰσονομία (*ND* 1.50; 1.109 = [176] Arr.)
- *morbi* translates νοσήματα (*fin.* 1.59)
- *fortuna* translates τύχη (*fin.* 1.63, see *KD* XVI)

As for σωφροσύνη, Cicero shows great awareness of the importance of this concept. It refers to the four general virtues (justice, wisdom, fortitude, temperance) that Stoics and Epicureans know, but which the Epicureans then lead back to pleasure, not honesty.[35] For translation Cicero evokes *temperantia, moderatio, modestia*; he even proposes *frugalitas*. And so, he explains:

[10] Cic., *Tusc.* 3.16
Haud scio an recte ea virtus frugalitas appellari possit, quod angustius apud Graecos valet, qui frugi homines χρησίμους appellant, id est tantum modo utilis; at illud est latius; omnis enim abstinentia, omnis innocentia (quae apud Graecos usitatum nomen nullum habet, sed habere potest ἀβλάβειαν; nam est innocentia adfectio talis animi quae noceat nemini) ...[36] reliquas etiam virtutes frugalitas continet.[37]

Once again Cicero shows his linguistic sensitivity: can we translate σωφροσύνη also with *frugalitas*? The problem is that, in Greek, the correspondent for *homines frugi* is χρησίμους: a word with a very limited range of meaning compared to "frugi", and which refers precisely to *utilitas*, that is, to the concepts of "useful", "beneficial", more than that of "wisdom", "fairness". *Frugalitas* is a virtue that – like temperance – also includes others: for example, "restraint" (*abstinentia*) and "innocence'" (*innocentia*). Even regarding this latter virtue, Cicero allows a linguistic observation:

---
[34] For the interpretation of the surviving columns of *Peri phuseos*' second book, see the recent critical edition by Giuliana Leone (2015) and the clarifications on the effluvium of images in Leone 2015: 47-49.
[35] See *fin.* 2.48.
[36] The text is incomplete, but the overall meaning is clear.
[37] "It may be, though, that the best term for it is 'frugality.' The corresponding Greek term is too narrow in its application: they call frugal people *chrēsimoi*, that is, merely 'useful.' But *frugalitas* is a broader term, carrying with it not only *abstinentia*, 'restraint' and *innocentia*, 'harmlessness' (for which there is no Greek term in use, though *ablabeia* or 'non-hurtfulness' might serve, since harmlessness is the disposition not to hurt anyone), but all the other virtues as well" (transl. Graver).

in Latin there is a word of active value. *In-nocentia* in fact indicates the disposition of the soul for which one does not harm anyone; in Greek, Cicero does not know a correspondent. It could be ἀβλάβεια, which Cicero coins deriving from ἀβλαβής ("he who does not harm"). It should be noted that the first actual attestation of ἀβλάβεια will only be later, in Plut., *Non posse suaviter vivi secundum Epicurum* 1090b, with passive value.

As a further confirmation of the scrupulousness in interpreting the technical value of the words, we observe Cicero, in *fin.* 3.32, when he defines the effect of something that results posterior and subsequent (*posterum* et *consequens*), using the Greek ἐπιγεννηματικόν. How can we fail to remember, on this occasion, the technical word (ἀπογεγεννημένα)[38] adopted by Epicurus to indicate the products of the mind, in book xxv of the *peri phuseos*?

On the other hand, the interpretations of three key words not only for Stoic philosophy but also for Epicurean philosophy are illuminating: πρόνοια, κατάληψις, and πρόληψις.

As for the first, see among other passages: *ND* 1.18; 2.73; 2.160. In particular:

[11] Cic., *ND* 2.160:
Quid multitudinem suavitatemque piscium dicam, quid avium; ex quibus tanta percipitur voluptas, ut interdum Pronoea nostra Epicurea fuisse videatur.[39]

Obviously, the intention of comparing the Stoic Providence to the Epicurean anti-deterministic perspective is, in this passage, completely ironic; here it is only of interest to consider the linguistic aspect.

As for κατάληψις, remember that this word belongs to the technical language of the Stoa. However, Diogenes Laertius (in his book on Epicureanism, 10.33) evokes κατάληψις[40] in connection with πρόληψις. The latter would be a kind of learning/grasping (κατάληψιν) or right opinion (δόξαν ὀρθήν), or idea (ἔννοιαν), or universal notion (καθολικήν νόησιν) inherent in us. About the Ciceronian translation, see *Luc.* 17; 31; 145. In particular:

---

[38] See Epic. xxv, Laursen 1997: 19-29 (= Arrighetti 34.2-24), and Masi 2006: 82-94.
[39] "Why should I speak of the teeming swarms of delicious fish? or of birds, which afford us so much pleasure that our Stoic Providence appears to have been at times a disciple of Epicurus?" (transl. Rackham). On this occasion Cicero limits himself to transliterating. Usually he translates with *providentia*, see: *ND* 2.58, 73-80, 87, 98, 127, 140; 3.78, 92; *Rep.* 2.5; *Tim.* 10. In partic. *ND* 1.18: "fatidicam Stoicorum Pronoeam, quam Latine licet Providentiam dicere."
[40] Κατάληπτα is most likely to be reconstructed also in *PHerc.* 1148, [29] 26.18 (Arrighetti).

[12] a) Cic., *fin.* 3.17
Rerum autem cognitiones (quas vel comprehensiones vel perceptiones vel si haec verba aut minus placent aut minus intelleguntur, καταλήψεις appellemus licet), eas igitur ipsas propter se adsciscendas arbitramur.[41]

Cicero also proposes the opposite of what understanding implies: ἀκατάληπτον; in *Luc.* 18, referring to Philo's thought, he evokes the impossibility that something can be understood: *negare quicquam esse quod comprehendi posse: id enim volumus esse* ἀκατάληπτον.[42]

Finally, see πρόληψις. This word is fundamental in the technical language of both the Stoa and the Epicurean school. See *ND* 1.37; 1.43-44; 2.7; *Luc.* 30. On these occasions Cicero translates by diversifying; respectively: *notio animi, anticipatio, praenotio, praesensio, notitia rerum*.[43]

In *ND* 1.43-45 the Epicurean Velleius proposes *anticipatio* and *praenotio* as a translation of πρόληψις:

b) Cic., *ND* 1.43-44
quae est enim gens aut quod genus hominum quod non habeat sine doctrina anticipationem quandam deorum, quam appellat πρόληψιν Epicurus id est anteceptam animo rei quandam informationem, sine qua nec intellegi quicquam nec quaeri nec disputari potest. (...) fatemur constare illud etiam, hanc nos habere sive **anticipationem**, ut ante dixi sive **praenotionem** deorum (sunt enim rebus novis nova ponenda nomina, ut Epicurus ipse πρόληψιν appellavit, quam antea nemo eo verbo nominarat).[44]

---

[41] "Now cognitions (which we may call graspings or perceivings, or, if these terms are disagreeable or obscure, 'catalepses' from the Greek) we consider worth attaining in their own right" (transl. Woolf). As for the possible interpretative nuances in the use of these three words proposed by Cicero, cf. Malaspina 2022: 309-323. As for *perceptio* (concerning which we must bear in mind αἴσθησις), we observe its frequent presence in Cicero (in *div.* 2.9 we find: *quid sensibus perciperentur*); Seneca, on the other hand, never uses *perceptio* but only the forms of the verb *percipere*, in particular *perceptus/a* (e.g., *ben.* 1.1.12; 3.5.1; 5.17.7; *ep.* 99.5).

[42] Here undoubtedly Cicero favours the best adequacy of *comprehensio* in the rendering of the Greek concept. See Malaspina 2022: 311-312.

[43] In *Luc.* 30, he specifies that because of mental operations and memory that builds similes, we witness the formation of concepts called sometimes ἔννοιαι other times προλήψεις. See, in the present collection of essays, the contribution by J.-B. Gourinat. As for the implications related to the Stoic context, see Maso 2022: 142-147.

[44] "For what nation or what tribe of men is there but possesses untaught some 'preconception' (*anticipationem quandam*) of the gods? Such notions Epicurus designates by the word πρόληψιν, that is, a sort of preconceived (*anteceptam*) mental picture of a thing, without which nothing can be understood or investigated or discussed. [...] We must admit it as also being an accepted truth that we possess a 'preconception,' (*anticipationem*) as I called it above, or 'prior notion,' (*praenotionem*) of the gods. For we are bound to employ novel terms to denote novel ideas, just as Epicurus himself employed the word *prolepsis* in a sense in which no one had ever used it before" (transl. Rackham 1933/1967).

Anticipatio and *praenotio* are absent in almost all classical Latin literature. We find only one attestation of *anticipatio* in Servius' commentary, *in Verg. Aen.* 6,359.4; *praenotio* is, instead, a real *unicum*.

In Lucretius, 4.1057, we find an interesting *praesagire*: "Namque voluptatem praesagit muta cupido" (Silent craving presages pleasure). Cicero does not disdain this opportunity. So, for example, he writes in *Div.* 1.65: "One who has knowledge of a thing before it happens (*qui ante sagit, quam oblata res est*) is said to 'presage' (*praesagire*), that is, to perceive the future in advance (*futura ante sentire*)." This juxtaposition of *praesagire* and *ante sentire* leads us in the direction of *praesentire* and *praesensio*. *Praesensio* is precisely the technical term that Cicero preferably adopts, probably because the purely logical/functional aspect of *anticipatio* or *praenotio* responds less to the authentic sense of Greek.

Indeed, Epicurus seems to have better specified the role and status of the πρόληψις. Firstly, it must not be confused with feeling or passion. In *Canon*, Epicurus states that there are three criteria of truth: αἱ αἰσθήσεις (sensations), αἱ προλήψεις and τὰ πάθη (passions). We must therefore distinguish its traits and first connect the πρόληψις to the memory of sensation, that is, to the persistence of the physical trace (ἐγκατάλειμμα) of what has happened, and which has been confirmed several times in subsequent experiences.[45] In fact, a very strong relationship will be established between the "notions that derive from an act of the mind" (τὰς φανταστικὰς ἐπιβολὰς τῆς διανοίας)[46] and πρόληψις. This link is essential if we want to connect the experience already acquired with the prefiguration of the future, without the latter being considered a pure and simple "hypothesis", "presupposition" (ὑπόληψις). Προλήψεις are clear and evident by virtue of their anchoring to the original sensation and their being an instrument for the experience and comprehension of the present.

Cicero seems to refer to the scientific πρόληψις. Hence, he prefers the word *praesensio*. He uses *praesensio* mostly in *De natura deorum* and in *De divinatione*. To *praesensio* he attributes a precise scientific value, since on the one hand, with it, it would refer to the different forms and possibilities of divination;[47] on the other, *praesensio* would attest to the existence of the surrounding reality, of its becoming, and of the gods:

[13] Cic., *ND* 2.45
Sed cum talem esse deum certa notione animi praesentiamus, primum ut sit animans, deinde ut in omni natura nihil eo sit praestantius, ad hanc **praesensionem notionemque** nostram nihil video quod potius accommodem quam ut primum

---

[45] On this see Diog. Laert. X 33.
[46] See Diog. Laert. X 3. In L&S 17 A, Epicurus' technical expression is translated as follows: "focusings of thought into an impression".
[47] See *div.* 1.1: *praesensionem et scientiam rerum futurarum*; 1.105: *praesensio aut scientia veritatis futurae*. Because of that: *praesensio divinatio est* (2.14).

hunc ipsum mundum, quo nihil excellentius fieri potest, animantem esse et deum iudicem.[48]

However, Cicero then ends up associating the *praesensio rerum futurarum* indifferently to Stoicism (e.g., to Cleanthes, in *ND* 2.13; 3.16) and to atomism (*Div.* 1.5; 2.31–32); this connection means that the word does not seem to have, for him, any connotation of school. *Praesensio*, therefore, simply but incontrovertibly refers to the opportunity (and necessity) of overcoming the conjectural moment because of a correct interpretation of the signals and their adequate explanation.

I believe that this sample is sufficient to highlight the characteristics, in the phase of translation from the Greek,[49] of the operation theorized and realized by Cicero. Of course I concentrated on the Epicurean translations, but even in this delicate context Cicero's seriousness and correctness as an interpreter did not fail.

2. SENECA: THE TRANSLATION/INTERPRETATION OF AN OPPONENT

In the case of Seneca, we are faced with an openly Stoic philosopher, able to deepen the theoretical aspects of his school with original innovations devoid of any qualms (or reverence) towards tradition and opposing schools, as in the case of Epicureanism. Furthermore, he is – similarly to Cicero – a personality of the highest political level, able to easily master Latin and Greek.

Concerning the way of relating with Greek culture, with the language of Greek philosophy, see A. Setaioli, *Seneca e i Greci*, 1988 (as regards Epicurus, see 171-248). Epicurus is the philosopher most quoted by Seneca; at the centre of this interest are, first, some issues of a moral nature. Probably Seneca directly knew some Epicurean texts, and his knowledge does not depend only on the epitome of Philonides of Laodicea (Syria), a philosopher who lived at the court of Antiochus IV, between 200 and 130 BC, and who during his stays in Athens had access to the Garden's library.[50] Usener considered Philonides to be one of the sources available to Seneca (*contra* Setaioli 1988, 176). Of course, especially in the first 29 letters of the Senecan corre-

---

[48] "Assuming that we have a definite and preconceived idea (*certa notione animi praesentiamus*) of a deity as, first, a living being, and, secondly, a being unsurpassed in excellence by anything else in the whole of nature, I can see nothing that satisfies this preconception or idea (*praesensionem notionemque*) of ours more fully than, first, the judgement that this world, which must necessarily be most excellent of all things, is itself a living being and a god" (transl. Rackham).

[49] I would like to point out a recent book by Aubert-Baillot 2021; in particular, I refer to: *Épicure et les Épicuriens*, part II, chap. 3, 487-532. The scholar emphasizes the precision and subtlety of Cicero's references to classical and Hellenistic philosophy, as well as the variety in use and their function especially in the letters. This collection appears as a sort of laboratory of thought that allows us to see the genesis of bilingualism.

[50] Concerning Philonides, see Snyder 2000: 49-50; see *PHerc.* 1044, *fr.* 30.3-8 (ὑπομνήματα).

spondence, we can assume that the philosopher resorted to a gnomology and that he exploited the rubrics of moral matter: poverty *vs* wealth, life *vs* death, friendship.

However, the in-depth knowledge of some Epicurus' letters seems indubitable: this is true at least for *ep.* 9 where, in the name of the Stoic ideal of self-sufficiency, Seneca argues with the concept of friendship from both the Megaric Stilpo and Epicurus; see then *epp.* 21 and 22 (mentioning the letter to Idomeneus); the *ep.* 18, which refers to a group of letters sent by Epicurus to Polyaenus; *ep.* 52, in which Seneca pauses to examine the different character of his various pupils and, referring to an Epicurean schematization, distinguishes as follows: a) those who without the help of anyone manage to open the way to the truth; b) those who need a guide to trace their path and precede them; c) those who, by accepting to be guided and advised, are nevertheless unable to progress without the impulse of a *coactor*. Finally, *ep.* 79.15 on "celebrity" among posterity.

Ep. 9 is also interesting because Seneca signals the difficulty and the risk of misunderstanding inherent in the translation of ἀπάθεια:

[14] Sen. *ep.* 9.1-3
An merito reprehendat in quadam epistula Epicurus eos qui dicunt sapientem se ipso esse contentum et propter hoc amico non indigere, desideras scire. Hoc obicitur Stilboni ab Epicuro et iis quibus summum bonum visum est animus **inpatiens**. In ambiguitatem incidendum est, si exprimere ἀπάθειαν uno verbo cito voluerimus et **inpatientiam** dicere; poterit enim contrarium ei quod significare volumus intellegi. Nos eum volumus dicere **qui respuat omnis mali sensum**: accipietur is **qui nullum ferre possit malum**. Vide ergo num satius sit aut **invulnerabilem** animum dicere aut animum **extra omnem patientiam positum**. Hoc inter nos et illos interest: noster sapiens vincit quidem incommodum omne **sed sentit**, illorum ne sentit quidem. Illud nobis et illis commune est, sapientem se ipso esse contentum.[51]

As already mentioned, the reference to Epicurus is frequent. However, despite the abundance of citations present in the Senecan correspondence, we have a single text of which we have the Epicurean original:

---

[51] "You are eager to know whether Epicurus was justified in the criticism expressed in one of his letters against those who say that the wise person is self-sufficient and for this reason has no need of a friend. It is a charge made by him against Stilpo and others who say that the highest good is an **impassive** mind. (If we choose to express the Greek word *apatheia* by a single term and say *impatientia*, we cannot help but create ambiguity, for *impatientia* can also be understood in the opposite sense to what we intend: we mean by it **a person who refuses to feel any misfortune**, but it will be taken to refer to **one who cannot bear any misfortune**. Consider, then, whether it might not be better to speak of the **invulnerable** mind or the mind **set beyond all suffering**.) Our position is different from theirs in that our wise person conquers all adversities, **but still feels them**; theirs does not even feel them. That the sage is self-sufficient is a point held in common between us" (transl. Graver).

[15] a) Sen. *ep.* 14.17
Nunc ad cotidianam stipem manum porrigis. Aurea te stipe implebo, et quia facta est auri mentio, accipe quemadmodum usus fructusque eius tibi esse gratior possit. **'Is maxime divitiis fruitur qui minime divitiis indiget.'** 'Ede' inquis 'auctorem.' Ut scias quam benigni simus, propositum est aliena laudare: Epicuri est aut Metrodori aut alicuius ex illa officina.[52]

[15] b) Epic., *Men.* 130
ἥδιστα πολυτελείας ἀπολαύουσιν οἱ ἥκιστα ταύτης δεόμενοι.[53]

Note the translation of πολυτελείας with *divitiis*: the Epicurean context refers to abundance during a banquet (as Saint Ambrose will interpret in taking up, as if it were a maxim, the Epicurean text; see Ambros., *Epist. Classis* I, 63, 19: *quod ii copiis convivii moderate utantur qui non immoderate eas quaerunt*). Seneca instead intends to refer to wealth and the lust for wealth. Is this a signal, perhaps, that the Epicurean maxim was handed down in isolation in a *gnomologium*?

As for the methods of the Seneca's translation, not only in some cases does Seneca provide more than one version or reading of the original;[54] above all we must also remember that he, like Cicero, often uses Epicurus to reinforce the Stoic point of view.

An example – certainly limited, but no less significant for this – is *KD* XVI, which we have already partially addressed:

[16] a) *KD* XVI
Βραχέα σοφῷ τύχη παρεμπίπτει, τὰ δὲ μέγιστα καὶ κυριώτατα ὁ λογισμὸς διῴκηκε καὶ κατὰ τὸν συνεχῆ χρόνον τοῦ βίου διοικεῖ καὶ διοικήσει.[55]

[16] b) Cic., *fin.* 1.63
Optime vero Epicurus, quod **exiguam dixit fortunam intervenire sapienti**, maximasque ab eo et gravissimas res consilio ipsius et ratione administrari.[56]

---

[52] "Now you are stretching out your hand for the daily dole; I will fill you up with a golden one. And since I have mentioned gold, learn how the use and enjoyment of it may be made more pleasant for you: **He enjoys riches most who has least need of riches.** 'Tell me the author,' you say. Just to show you how generous I am, I am determined to praise another's material: it is Epicurus, or Metrodorus, or somebody from that shop" (transl. Graver). Seneca's uncertainty in attributing the translated maxim to Epicurus rather than to Metrodorus is probably due to the *gnomologium* he had in his hands; see Setaioli 1988: 184-189.
[53] "Those who need it less enjoy abundance with greater pleasure."
[54] See, among others, *ep.* 97.13.
[55] "Luck has little importance for the wise, since reason has already preordained the greatest and most important things, and for the whole course of life it preorders and preorders them." Stob. II 8.28 (p. 159, 18-19 Wach.) provides a shorter text: βραχεῖα σοφῷ τύχη παρεμπίπτει, τὰ δὲ μέγιστα καὶ κυριώτατα λογισμὸς διῴκηκε κατὰ τὸν βίου συνεχῆ χρόνον.
[56] "Epicurus made the excellent remark that '**Chance hardly affects the wise**'; the really important and serious things are under the control of their own deliberation and reason" (transl. Woolf).

[16] c) Cic., *fin.* 2.89
Ita fit beatae vitae domina **fortuna**, quam Epicurus ait **exiguam intervenire sapienti**.[57]

[16] d) Cic., *Tusc.* 5.26
Quid melius quam **fortunam exiguam intervenire sapienti**?[58]

[16] e) Sen., *const. sap.* 15.4
Ne putes istam Stoicam esse duritiam, Epicurus, quem uos patronum inertiae uestrae adsumitis putatisque mollia ac desidiosa praecipere et ad uoluptates ducentia, **'raro'** inquit **'sapienti fortuna interuenit'**.[59]

Both Cicero and Seneca exploit only the initial part of the Epicurean maxim. Did this only belong to a gnomology which they both referred to? We do not know. However, clearly the second part of the maxim argues in favour of a rigid determinism that neither Cicero nor Seneca think about. The rationality of *sapiens* (i.e., *consilium* and *ratio*) seems important for Cicero; Seneca, rather, aims to re-evaluate the meaning of pleasure. As for the translation of the maxim: Seneca perfectly retains the order of words; Cicero does not. Cicero keeps the *iunctura* "fortunam exiguam" (i.e., noun and attribute); Seneca uses an adverb: "raro".

Now, however, here is letter 66, which constitutes an interesting example because it is exceptionally not concentrated only on the moral side, but also addresses medical issues and thereby, inevitably, the specialized terminology of medicine. We must first assume that Seneca is able to directly read the letter written by Epicurus, on his deathbed, to Idomeneus. Writing to his friend Claranus, Seneca focuses on the meaning of virtue and a happy life, the role of reason, the tranquility of an honest man. In § 18, Seneca evokes the iconic example of the Phalaris bull and confronts Epicurus. We do not have the original of this reference, but only what is reported by Diog. Laert. X 118: "Even in torture the wise man is happy" (κἂν στρεβλωθῇ δ' ὁ σοφόν, εἶναι αὐτὸν εὐδαίμονα). Well, Seneca reports the exclamation of Epicurus in reference to the Phalaris story: "Dulce est et ad me nihil pertinet ... dulce esse torreri".[60] This is not the case for Seneca and for the Stoic school, which, on the other hand, distinguishes very well between pain and pleasure; thus, as Seneca will specify in the following *letter* 67, evoking the Stoic Attalus:

---

[57] "So the happy life turns out to be at the mercy of chance, despite Epicurus' claim that **chance hardly affects the wise**" (transl. Woolf).
[58] "What is better than to say '**Fortune makes little impact on the wise man?**'" (transl. Douglas).
[59] "Lest you consider it to be a hardness of the Stoics, Epicurus – whom you assume as the patron of your inertia and whom you consider the proponent of soft and lazy precepts and conducive to pleasure – says: '**Fortune is rarely an impediment to the wise.**'"
[60] See Cic., *Tusc.* 2.17: "quam suave est, quam hoc non curo"; *Tusc.* 5.31: "quam hoc suave est"; 5.73: "quam pro nihilo puto"; *fin.* 2.88: "Quam hoc suave"; 5.80: "Quam suave est! Quam nihil curo!"; *Pison.* 42: "... dicturum tamen suave illud esse." According to Setaioli 1988, 234, Seneca may have Cicero present.

[17] Sen., *ep.* 67.15-16
'Malo me fortuna in castris suis quam in delicis habeat. Torqueor, sed fortiter: bene est. Occidor, sed fortiter: bene est.' Audi Epicurum, dicet et 'dulce est'. Ego tam honestae rei ac severae numquam nomen molle inponam. Uror, sed invictus: quidni hoc potabile sit? – non quod urit me ignis, sed quod non vincit.[61]

Returning to *letter* 66, in the concluding part Seneca takes up the Epicurean *Letter to Idomeneus*:

[18] a) Sen., *ep.* 66.47
Dabo apud Epicurum tibi etiamnunc simillimam huic nostrae divisionem bonorum. Alia enim sunt apud illum quae malit contingere sibi, ut corporis quietem ab omni incommodo liberam et animi remissionem bonorum suorum contemplatione gaudentis; alia sunt quae, quamvis nolit accidere, nihilominus laudat et conprobat, tamquam illam quam paulo ante dicebam malae valetudinis et dolorum gravissimorum perpessionem, in qua Epicurus fuit illo **summo ac fortunatissimo die suo**. Ait enim se **vesicae et exulcerati ventris tormenta** tolerare ulteriorem doloris accessionem non recipientia, **esse nihilominus sibi illum beatum diem. Beatum autem diem agere nisi qui est in summo bono non potest**.[62]

[18] b) Sen., *ep.* 92.25
Quid porro? non aeque incredibile videtur aliquem in summis cruciatibus positum dicere 'beatus sum'? Atqui haec vox in ipsa officina voluptatis audita est. **'Beatissimum' inquit 'hunc et ultimum diem ago'** Epicurus, cum illum hinc **urinae difficultas** torqueret, hinc insanabilis exulcerati dolor ventris.[63]

[18] c) Epic., *ad Idom*.
τὴν μακαρίαν ἄγοντες καὶ ἅμα τελευτῶντες ἡμέραν τοῦ βίου ἐγράφομεν ὑμῖν ταυτί· **στραγγουρικά** τε παρηκολούθει καὶ **δυσεντερικὰ πάθη** ὑπερβολὴν οὐκ ἀπολείποντα

---

[61] "'I would rather have fortune keep me in its encampments than in luxury. I am tortured, but courageously; it is well. I am slain, but courageously; it is well.' Listen to Epicurus; he will say also 'It is pleasant.' I, however, will never call such a stern and honorable deed by so soft a name. I am burned, but undefeated: why should this not be desirable? Not because the fire burns me but because it does not defeat me" (transl. Graver).

[62] "I will show you a division of goods in Epicurus that is again very similar to this one of ours. In his works, there are some things which he prefers to have happen to him – such as 'rest for the body, free from every discomfort, and relaxation for the mind as it rejoices in contemplating its own goods' – and other things which, although he prefers them not to happen, he nonetheless praises and regards with favor, including what I was talking about a little while ago: the endurance of ill health and of very severe pain. That is what Epicurus himself went through on that **'last and most blessed day' of his life**. For he said that the torments he was experiencing from **his bladder and from stomach ulcers** were 'such as do not admit of any increase of pain,' **but that all the same that was a 'blessed day' for him. But one cannot spend a blessed day unless he is in possession of the highest good**" (transl. Graver).

[63] "But wait – don't we find it equally incredible that someone undergoing extreme torment should say, 'I am happy'? Yet those words have been heard within the very workshop of pleasure. 'This final day of my life is the happiest,' said Epicurus when he was experiencing the double torture of **urinary blockage** and an incurable ulcer of the stomach" (transl. Graver).

τοῦ ἐν ἑαυτοῖς μεγέθους· ἀντιπαρετάττετο δὲ πᾶσι τούτοις τὸ κατὰ ψυχὴν χαῖρον ἐπὶ τῇ τῶν γεγονότων ἡμῖν διαλογισμῶν μνήμῃ.[64]

[18] d) Cic., fin. 2.96
Audi, ne longe abeam, moriens quid dicat Epicurus, ut intellegas facta eius cum dictis discrepare: 'Epicurus Hermarcho salutem. Cum ageremus', inquit, 'vitae beatum et eundem supremum diem, scribebamus haec. tanti autem aderant **vesicae et torminum morbi**, ut nihil ad eorum magnitudinem posset accedere.' Miserum hominem! Si dolor summum malum est, dici aliter non potest. sed audiamus ipsum: 'Compensabatur', inquit, 'tamen cum his omnibus animi laetitia, quam capiebam memoria rationum inventorumque nostrorum. sed tu, ut dignum est tua erga me et philosophiam voluntate ab adolescentulo suscepta, fac ut Metrodori tueare liberos'.[65]

Note that Seneca does not perform a calque of στραγγουρία but uses *urinae difficultas*. Cicero has *vesicae et torminum morbi*, where *torminum morbi* refers to δυσεντερία; in *Tusc.* 2.45, we find *quamis idem forticulum se in torminibus et in stranguria sua praebeat*, "... although he is strong enough to withstand renal colic"; in *fam.* 7.26.1 Cicero reports the expression: στραγγουρικὰ καὶ δυσεντερικὰ πάθη.

Seneca demonstrates in this as in other cases the intention to also render the technical terminology in an understandable Latin.

The attention for Epicurus is always present in Seneca, as in Cicero. In Seneca it appears not only in the moral field – as can be seen from the quotations reported in the first 29 letters of the *Epistolary* to Lucilius[66] – but also in the scientific field. An example among many is given by the evocation of the Epicurean thesis relating to the doctrine of earthquakes (*nat. q.* 6.20.5), where, among other things, the Senecan method of approaching and comparing different doctrines (Aristotle, Democritus, Metrodorus, Epicurus) corresponds to the way in which Epicurus dealt with the analysis of phenomena that cannot be verified by direct experience (i.e., the method of the plurality of possible causes).[67]

---

[64] "I was spending the blessed day and, at the same time, the last of my life when I was writing you this letter. **The pains of the bladder and of the entrails** were such that they could not be greater than those. Yet all these things were opposed by the joy of the soul for the memory of our past conversations."

[65] "So let me remind you of what Epicurus said on his deathbed, and you will see that his deeds are at odds with his words: 'Epicurus sends Hermarchus his greetings. I am writing on the last day of my life, but a happy one. **My bladder and bowels** are so diseased that they could hardly be worse.' Poor man! If pain really is the greatest evil, that is all one can say. He continues: 'Yet all this is counterbalanced by the joy I feel as I recall my theories and discoveries. If you are to live up to the goodwill you have shown towards me and towards philosophy since your youth, then be sure to take care of Metrodorus' children'" (transl. Woolf).

[66] The characteristics of the quotations from Epicurus in the first part of the Senecan Letters have been the subject of frequent investigations. See in particular: Setaioli 1988: 182-223; Maso 1999: 103-131.

[67] As for the *pleonachos tropos* (the method of the plurality of possible causes), see recently Masi 2022: 259-275.

3. SOME CONCLUSIONS

Cicero and Seneca constitute two exceptional opportunities to focus on the way in which the transmission of philosophy (and the technical philosophical language) from Greece to Rome occurred. Here we have addressed the method and intentions with which they approached the Epicurean doctrine. We are not faced with two professional translators, but with two scholars capable of grasping, interpreting, and transferring the thoughts of an original master of Greek philosophy into their native language. By focusing on some key words, we were able to detect the effort to compare two worldviews, adapting some Greek concepts to a new linguistic context not yet perfectly equipped for the requirements of philosophical reflection. Both Cicero and Seneca are aware of the risks involved in translation: the translator has the responsibility to misunderstand, thus transmitting the outcome of the misunderstanding to disciples and potential new readers. This function is especially evident when translating a single key word. In fact, *transliteration* leaves the door open to the direct appropriation of the original (and the etymological meaning it contains). However, it does not mean that we cannot intervene again at a later stage and suggest a real translation proposal. The same thing happens when a *circumlocution* constitutes the translation: meaning is approached with caution, but in a reliable way; however, the opportunity for future language choice is open. Instead, in the case of *translation with a word* already existing in the Latin language, the translator's responsibility is immediately evident. What he 'chooses' will leave its mark. This circumstance is evident when different words are proposed to translate the same concept present in Greek: think of εἰκών (for which there is *simulacrum, species*), but also of πρόληψις, for which there are: *praesagire* (Lucretius), *praesensio, praenotio, anticipatio* (Cicero), and *praesumptio* (Seneca, *ep.* 117.6, who uses this technical word to indicate the man's knowledge of the gods). In the case of the Epicurean ἐνάργεια, Cicero without hesitation proposes *perspicuitas* or *evidentia* (*Luc.* 17); Seneca never uses these nouns but only the inflected forms of the verb *perspicere* (e.g., *ep.* 109.18; *nat. q.* 3 *pr.* 1), and, on two occasions, the attribute *evidens* (*ep.* 13.12; *nat. q.* 2.32.1).

From what we have been able to ascertain, regarding the Epicurean doctrine, Cicero and Seneca both acted with the intention of not compromising the meaning of the original. Cicero probably did so as motivated by the aim to show in an unequivocal way the limits of the doctrine he opposed; Seneca, with the intent of illuminating its hidden qualities to propose them in a new theoretical context, the Stoic one.[68] We can grasp this intention also from the small details that characterize Seneca's stylistic signature. As a possible example, we can consider the Epicurean

---

[68] This is the well-known thesis expressed in *ep.* 33.6-7, where he compares the simple Epicurean *flosculi* to the substantial harvest of the Stoics.

maxim (unfortunately not available to us in the original) that Seneca, in *ep.* 23.9, translates in two different ways: (a) "molestum est semper vitam inchoare", or, as he explains *si hoc modo magis semper sensus potest exprimi*, (b) "male vivunt qui semper vivere incipiunt". Evidently the meaning of the two translations is the same, but, in the second one, we immediately grasp the mark of the Stoic Seneca in the polyptotus *vivunt / vivere*.[69]

On a more general level, we can think of the way in which Seneca – after Cicero – re-elaborates the doctrine of "living unnoticed" (λάθη βιώσας) and of renouncing the tiring occupations of daily life (ἀσχολία), re-proposing it as the doctrine of *otium*.[70]

REFERENCES

Aubert-Baillot, S., 2021, *Le grec et la philosophie dans la correspondance de Cicéron*, Turnhout: Brepols.
Bailey, C., 1928, *Greek Atomists and Epicurus*, Oxford: Clarendon Press.
D'Anna, G., 1965, *Alcuni aspetti della polemica antiepicurea di Cicerone*, Roma: Edizioni dell'Ateneo.
DeWitt, N. W., 1942, "Gods of Epicurus and the Canon", *Trans. of Royal Soc. of Canada*, 3 ser. 2, vol. 36: 33-49.
Douglas, A. E., 1985, *Cicero. Tusculan disputations* 1 (Edited with Translation and Notes), Warminster: Aris & Phillips.
Douglas, A. E., 1990, *Cicero. Tusculan Disputation* 2. & 5 (Edited with Translation and Notes), Warminster: Aris & Phillips.
Epicurus, 2012, *Sulla natura. Libro II*, a cura di G. Leone, Napoli: Bibliopolis.
Glucker, J., 2012, "Cicero's Remarks on Translating Philosophical Terms – Some General Problems", in J. Glucker – C. Burnett (eds.), *Greek into Latin from Antiquity until the Nineteenth Century*, London-Turin: Warburg Institute-Nino Aragno ed.: 37-96.
Glucker, J., 2015, "Cicero as Translator and Cicero in Translation", in *Philologica* 10: 37-53.
Graver, M., 2002, *Cicero on the Emotions, Tusculan Disputations 3 and 4* (Transl. and with Commentary), Chicago-London: The University of Chicago Press.
Graver, M., – Long, A. A., 2015, *L. Annaeus Seneca. Letters on Ethics: to Lucilius* (Transl. with an Introduction and Commentary), Chicago: The University of Chicago Press.
Laursen, S., 1997, "The Later Parts of Epicurus, On Nature, 25th Book", *Cronache Ercolanesi* 27: 5-82.

---

[69] Setaioli 1988, 199-200, points out this quality and suggests that the Greek original may have contained the obvious: βίου ... ζῶμεν.

[70] Concerning the λάθη βιώσας, for which see Plutarch., *lat. viv.* 1129C, refer to Roskam 2007: 33-41. In the surviving Epicurus' texts, we find only allusions to the topic of engagement and lack of time or leisure (ἀσχολία): *Pyth.* 85; *Sent. Vat.* 14; *ep. fr.* 119 [Arrighetti]. On the relationship between Cicero's and Seneca's interpretation of *otium*, see Maso 2023: 182-187.

Lévy, C., 1992, "Cicéron créateur du vocabulaire latin de la connaissance: essai de synthèse", in *La langue latine, langue de philosophie: Actes du colloque organisé par l'École française de Rome*, Rome: 92-106.

Leone, G., 2015, "Nuovi spunti di riflessione sulla dottrina epicurea degli εἴδωλα dalla rilettura del II libro *Sulla natura*", in F. G. Masi – S. Maso (eds.), *Epicurus 'on eidola'*, Peri phuseos *Book ii. Update, Proposals, and Discussions*, Amsterdam: Hakkert, 35-53.

L&S = Long, A. A. – Sedley, D. 1987, *The Hellenistic Philosophers*, i: *Translation of the Principal Sources with Philosophicals Commentary*; ii: *Greek and Latin Texts with Notes and Bibliography*, Cambridge: Cambridge University Press.

Malaspina, E., 2022, "Noterelle filosofiche e linguistiche sulla resa di κατάληψις negli *Academici libri* di Cicerone", in A. Borgna – M. Lana (eds.), *Epistulae a familiaribus. Per Raffaella Tabacco*, Alessandria: Edizioni dell'Orso: 309-323.

Masi, F. G., 2006, *Epicuro e la filosofia della mente, Il xxv libro dell'opera 'Sulla Natura'*, Sankt Augustin: Academia Verlag.

Masi, F. G., 2022, "L'indeterminatezza ontologica dei *meteora*", in F. Verde (ed.), in collaborazione con M. Tulli, D. De Sanctis, F. G. Masi, *Epicuro: Epistola a Pitocle*, Sankt Augustin: Academia Verlag: 259-275.

Maso, S., 1999, "La question épicurienne", in S. Maso, *Le regard de la vérité. Cinq études sur Sénèque*, Paris: L'Harmattan: 103-131.

Maso, S., 2016, "L'atomo di Lucrezio", *Lexikon philosophicum* 4: 173-182.

Maso, S., 2017, *Grasp and Dissent. Cicero and Epicurean Philosophy*, Turnhout: Brepols.

Maso, S., 2021, "Desiderium voluntas non est", in E. Cattanei – S. Maso (eds.), *Paradeigmata voluntatis. All'origine della concezione moderna di volontà*, Venezia: Edizioni Ca' Foscari: 73-96.

Maso, S., 2022, *Cicero's Philosophy*, Berlin-Boston: De Gruyter.

Maso, S., 2023, "*Romanum otium*: la prospettiva pubblica della ricerca interiore secondo Cicerone e Seneca", *Antiquorum philosophia* 17: 173-189.

Moreschini, C., 1979, "Osservazioni sul lessico filosofico di Cicerone", *Annali della Scuola Normale Superiore di Pisa, Classe di Lettere e Filosofia* 2: 78-178.

Pease, A. S. (ed.), 1955, *M.T. Ciceronis De natura deorum libri III*, Cambridge, MA: The Harvard University Press; repr. Darmstadt: Wissenschaftliche Buchgesellschaft, 1968.

Philippson, R., 1916, "Zur Epikureischen Götterlehre", *Hermes* 51: 568-608.

Powell, J. G. F., 1995, "Cicero's translations from the Greek", in J. G. F. Powell (ed.), *Cicero the Philosopher. Twelve Papers*, Oxford: Clarendon Press: 273-300.

Purinton, J., 2001, "Epicurus on the Nature of the Gods", *Oxford Studies in Ancient Philosophy* 21: 181-231.

Rackham, H., 1979, *Cicero. De natura deorum, Academica* (ed. with an English translation), Cambridge, MA-London: Harvard University Press; London [1933[1]].

Reinhardt, T., 2003, *Cicero. Topica*, Oxford: Oxford University Press.

Roskam, G., 2007, *Live Unnoticed: On the Vicissitudes of an Epicurean Doctrine*, Leiden-Boston: Brill.

Sedley, D., 1998, *Lucretius and the Transformation of Greek Wisdom*, Cambridge: Cambridge University Press.

Setaioli, A., 1988, *Seneca e i Greci. Citazioni e traduzioni nelle opere filosofiche*, Bologna: Pàtron.
Snyder, H. G., 2000, *Teachers and Texts in the Ancient World. Philosophers, Jews and Christians*, London-NewYork: Routledge.
Usener, H. (ed.), 1887, *Epicurea*, Leipzig: Teubner; repr. Stuttgart, 1966.
Warren, J., 2007, "Lucretius and the Greek Philosophy", in *The Cambridge Companion to Lucretius*, S. Gillespie – P. Hardie (eds.), Cambridge: Cambridge University Press: 19-32.
Woolf, R., 2001, in J. Annas – R. Woolf (eds.), *Cicero. On Moral Ends*, Cambridge: Cambridge University Press.

"TO INQUIRE IMPLIES TO KNOW": EPICURUS AND SEXTUS ON THE POSSIBILITY OF KNOWLEDGE

Stéphane Marchand

The relationship between Skepticism and Epicureanism became a classic topic since Marcello Gigante emphasized the multiple links between the two positions from a historical and philosophical point of view.[1] On the one hand, both stances shared a common interest in empiricism and accurate attention to *phainomena*;[2] on the other hand, from a Skeptical point of view, Epicureanism is fully dogmatic, and from an Epicurean point of view, a sceptical attitude towards knowledge is a fundamental error. Although Skepticism and Epicureanism share common concepts, they pursue strictly opposite goals.

However, Sextus makes frequent use of Epicurean arguments, and it seems interesting to wonder to what extent such use entails common views or, on the contrary, is shaped by a misunderstood, a dialectical, or even more complex strategy. In this paper I focus on the argument that to inquire necessarily entails to know or at least to have a notion of the object of such an inquiry (Us. 255). Sextus Empiricus is one of the sources for this fragment; but he mentions this argument in various and seemingly contradictory ways, either to confirm his own Skeptical method (*AM* I 57 and XI 21, which are quoted by Usener), or to employ as an anti-Skeptical argument (*AM* VIII 337). This contradictory use of the argument is intriguing, and the primary aim of this paper is to evaluate the difference between the two stances on two crucial issues at stake in this argument: the nature of inquiry and the function of preconception. Such a comparison, I believe, makes it possible to illuminate a radical opposition on the function of language and concepts between the two stances. To carry out such a programme, it is necessary (part 1) to establish the meaning of such argument in the Epicurean context and (part 2) to analyze Sextus' strategy when using this argument, in order to show that, despite the apparent convergence between the two positions on this argument, this common use is based on a fundamental disagreement on the nature and function of concepts and, more precisely, of *prolepsis* or preconception. This undertaking will lead us to historical questions (part 3) and, in particular, to the importance of the problem of the possibility of knowledge in Epicurus' time.

---

[1] Gigante 1981; see also Marchand and Verde 2013.
[2] Glidden 1986; Marchand 2013.

1. "TO INQUIRE IMPLIES TO KNOW": THE EPICUREAN ARGUMENT

1.1. Us. 255

1.1.1. Prolepsis and the possibility of inquiry

The argument is well summarized by Diogenes Laertius:

> καὶ οὐκ ἂν ἐζητήσαμεν τὸ ζητούμενον εἰ μὴ πρότερον ἐγνώκειμεν αὐτό· οἷον 'τὸ πόρρω ἑστὸς ἵππος ἐστὶν ἢ βοῦς;' δεῖ γὰρ κατὰ πρόληψιν ἐγνωκέναι ποτὲ ἵππου καὶ βοὸς μορφήν· οὐδ' ἂν ὠνομάσαμέν τι μὴ πρότερον αὐτοῦ κατὰ πρόληψιν τὸν τύπον μαθόντες.

> We would not have started any investigation of something if we had no prior cognizance of it. For example, whether the thing standing far away is a horse or an ox; for we must have some prior cognizance of the shape of a horse or ox in line with a preconception. Nor would we have applied any names to something if we had not previously learned its impression in line with a preconception.[3]

Preconception (πρόληψις) appears to be the empirical solution given by Epicurus to *Meno*'s paradox,[4] since it provides a previous minimal understanding of what we are searching for. A *prolepsis* gives us a previous knowledge of the "shape" (μορφή) or "impression" (τύπος) of a thing which allows us to recognize it in the world and in language; it is a kind of first knowledge, or a foreknowledge which allows our subsequent knowledge. The texts that compose Us. 255 do not so much focus on the definition of *prolepsis* or its function as a criterion of truth, but they do point to an effect of such a theory, namely, the fact that preconception is the condition of some epistemic attitudes. These attitudes are not described in Diog. Laert. X 33, but appear in other sources, such as Clement of Alexandria:

> ναὶ μὴν καὶ ὁ Ἐπίκουρος, ὁ μάλιστα τῆς ἀληθείας προτιμήσας τὴν ἡδονήν, πρόληψιν εἶναι διανοίας τὴν πίστιν ὑπολαμβάνει· πρόληψιν δὲ ἀποδίδωσιν ἐπιβολὴν ἐπί τι ἐναργὲς καὶ ἐπὶ τὴν ἐναργῆ τοῦ πράγματος ἐπίνοιαν· μὴ δύνασθαι δὲ μηδένα μήτε ζητῆσαι μήτε ἀπορῆσαι μηδὲ μὴν δοξάσαι, ἀλλ' οὐδὲ ἐλέγξαι χωρὶς προλήψεως. πῶς δ' ἂν μὴ ἔχων τις πρόληψιν οὗ ἐφίεται μάθοι περὶ οὗ ζητεῖ; ὁ μαθὼν δὲ ἤδη κατάληψιν ποιεῖ τὴν πρόληψιν.

> What more, even Epicurus, who most of all appreciates pleasure rather than truth, assumes that πίστις is a preconception of the mind. He defines preconception as a focusing on something evident, namely, on an evident notion of an object, [saying that] no one is able to inquire or be puzzled or have an opinion [about anything], or even refute [anything] without preconception. And how could anyone learn what one inquires about without having a preconception of the desired object? But one who has learnt already changes the preconception into an apprehension.[5]

---

[3] Diog. Laert. X 33: Greek text from Dorandi 2013; translation by White 2021.
[4] See Pease's comment to Cicero's *DND* I 43-45 (Pease 1955); and Obbink 1992: 198 and Tsouna 2016: 172; see *infra* part 1.2.2.
[5] Clement of Alexandria, *Stromata* II 4, 16-17 translation in Havrda 2022.

Even though Clement seems to confuse *prolepsis* with *epibolè* and tries to bridge the former with his own conception of πίστις, his version of the argument interestingly insists on those epistemic attitudes that require preconception, namely, "to inquire", "to be puzzled", "to have an opinion", and "to refute" (μήτε ζητῆσαι μήτε ἀπορῆσαι μηδὲ μὴν δοξάσαι, ἀλλ' οὐδὲ ἐλέγξαι). A similar list can also be found in Cicero's *De natura deorum* when he defines Epicurus' *prolepsis* as "a sort of preconceived mental picture of a thing, without which nothing can be understood or investigated or discussed" (*sine qua nec intellegi quicquam nec quaeri nec disputari potest*).[6] There is no doubt that this list is significant: the need for a *prolepsis* is linked not only to the specific attitude of inquiry but to any attempt as well to judge or to have a *doxa*, that is, to wonder or decide or demonstrate if a proposition is true or false.[7] From this list and from the presence of such central terms as δοξάσαι and *intellegi*, we must conclude that the argument goes beyond the problem of the possibility of inquiry and concerns the general possibility of knowledge: no cognition at all is possible without a *prolepsis* to recognize, judge, and understand the empirical information we receive from sensation.

1.1.2. *Sextus' case*
The same argument is used by Sextus Empiricus with an abbreviated list of these epistemic attitudes:

> Ἐπεὶ οὔτε ζητεῖν οὔτε ἀπορεῖν ἔστι κατὰ τὸν σοφὸν Ἐπίκουρον ἄνευ προλήψεως, εὖ ἂν ἔχοι πρὸ τῶν ὅλων σκέψασθαι τί τ' ἐστὶν ἡ γραμματική, καὶ εἰ κατὰ τὴν ἀποδιδομένην ὑπὸ τῶν γραμματικῶν ἔννοιαν δύναται συστατόν τι καὶ ὑπαρκτὸν νοεῖσθαι μάθημα.

> Since it is not possible either to investigate or to reach an impasse according to the wise Epicurus, without a preconception, it would be a good idea before anything else to inquire what grammar is, and whether, according to the conception delivered by the grammarians, any consistent and real disciplines can be conceived.[8]

As it is usual in his methodology, Sextus mentions this argument to show the necessity of beginning with an inquiry into the notion of a thing beforehand, rather than into its existence.[9] Although Sextus sometimes amalgamates the conception-question with the existence-question,[10] many passages in his extant work follow this path, with or without reference to Epicurus, as in *AM* II 1:

---

[6] Cic. *DND* I xvi 43, translation by Rackham 1951.
[7] See Morel 2008: 47
[8] Sextus Emp. *AM* I 57; translation by Bett 2018.
[9] See also *AM* XI 21.
[10] See Bett 1997: 62-65. See also Bett forthcoming part 3.

ἀλλ' ἐπεὶ κοινὸν ὑπάρξεως τε καὶ ἀνυπαρξίας ἐστὶν ἡ ἔννοια, καὶ οὐδὲν τούτων ἕτερον οἷόν τέ ἐστι ζητεῖν μὴ προλαβόντας ὅ ἐστι τὸ ζητούμενον, φέρε πρῶτον σκεψώμεθα τί ἂν εἴη ῥητορική, τὰς ἐπιφανεστάτας εἰς τοῦτο τῶν φιλοσόφων ἀποδόσεις παρατιθέμενοι.

But since the conception is common to existence and non-existence, and it is not possible to do any investigation of either of these without having formed a preconception of what it is that is being investigated, let us first inquire into what rhetoric is, setting out the most prominent accounts of this given by the philosophers.[11]

Even if Epicurus is not mentioned, this is the same *prolepsis*-argument as Bett's translation of μὴ προλαβόντας by "without having formed a preconception" shows. Before we inquire into the existence or the non-existence of something, we should investigate its notion. According to Sextus, his method is justified by the fact that we can have a notion of things that exist as well as of things that do not exist (such as unicorns or hippocentaur).[12] This position is, roughly, the meaning of κοινὸν ὑπάρξεως τε καὶ ἀνυπαρξίας ἐστὶν ἡ ἔννοια in the previous text *AM* II 1.

In those cases where Sextus mentions this argument,[13] he is not directly arguing against Epicurus, but introducing his own methodology. Two features in Epicurus' quotation are appealing to the Skeptical stance: first, Sextus emphasizes that he shares notions also used by Epicurus (such as ἀπορεῖν, ζητεῖν, and πρόληψις) to show that Epicurus himself could agree with some of the main Skeptical features; secondly, it introduces the possibility of discussing and inquiring about a notion without implying the existence of the reference of such a notion, which since the Sophistic movement has been one of the main difficulties of an anti-realist approach to language. With this reference, Sextus polemically pretends to find in Epicurus an ally for an anti-realistic view of concepts, such a view being crucial for his own conception of skepticism (see *infra*, part 2.1.1).

1.2. Epicurus' conception of *zetesis*
To see how problematic this strategy is, we should begin by asking how Epicurus connected *zetesis* to *prolepsis*.

1.2.1. Us. 255 as a development of Hrdt. 37-38
Both the reference to the function of *prolepsis* and the list of epistemic attitudes can be linked with *Hrdt.* 37-38:[14]

πρῶτον μὲν οὖν τὰ ὑποτεταγμένα τοῖς φθόγγοις, ὦ Ἡρόδοτε, δεῖ εἰληφέναι, ὅπως ἂν τὰ δοξαζόμενα ἢ ζητούμενα ἢ ἀπορούμενα ἔχωμεν εἰς ταῦτα ἀναγόντες ἐπικρίνειν, καὶ

---
[11] Translation from Bett 2018.
[12] See Sextus Emp. *PH* II 10.
[13] See also, e.g., *AM* VII 27 and IX 12.
[14] Asmis 1984: 20 f.

μὴ ἄκριτα πάντα ἡμῖν <ἴῃ> εἰς ἄπειρον ἀποδεικνύουσιν ἢ κενοὺς φθόγγους ἔχωμεν. [38] ἀνάγκη γὰρ τὸ πρῶτον ἐννόημα καθ' ἕκαστον φθόγγον βλέπεσθαι καὶ μηθὲν ἀποδείξεως προσδεῖσθαι, εἴπερ ἕξομεν τὸ ζητούμενον ἢ ἀπορούμενον καὶ δοξαζόμενον ἐφ' ὃ ἀνάξομεν.

Now first of all, Herodotus, we must have a firm grip on what our expressions denote, so that we are able to assess any points of doctrine that are either under investigation or perplexing by referring back to those things, and so that everything won't end up undecided for us as we go on in an endless string of proofs – in which case our expressions turn out empty. [38] For every expression we must look at the first concept and not demand any proof in addition, if at least we're going to have anything to which to refer the point of doctrine that is under investigation or perplexing.

Although πρόληψις is not mentioned, τὰ ὑποτεταγμένα τοῖς φθόγγοις and τὸ πρῶτον ἐννόημα denote *prolepsis*.[15] The point is to show that, before we can judge (ἐπικρίνειν) whether a proposition or judgment at stake in the letter (τὰ δοξαζόμενα) is true or false, we must make sure that the words we use to judge refer to reality. In order to grant that Epicurus' discourse can be scientifically (i.e., empirically) controlled, we must make sure that the reasoning follows empirical conclusions (which is the point of § 38, introduced by ἔτι, l. 482). Yet first of all (πρῶτον, l. 474), we must guarantee that our primary concepts are the results of an empirical process that guarantees their validity. If all our concepts were the results of our decision, all our discussion would remain undecided (ἄκριτα), since they would be more a matter of words than of things, of *pragmata*.[16] The point of *Hrdt.* 37-38 seems to be that we cannot demonstrate the veracity of our primary concepts; the truth of such an inquiry would depend on demonstrating the truth-value of our concepts, which would depend on demonstrating the truth-value of the concepts used for that demonstration, and so on *ad infinitum*.[17] Epicurus seems to shape the notion of *prolepsis* in order to stop this indefinite process, since, as the result of an empirical process, a *prolepsis* is evident (it does not require any demonstration) and is true (it has a propositional content that corresponds to external reality).[18] For this reason, *prolepsis* is one of the

---

[15] Glidden 1983a: 195-196, 1985: 179 has challenged this view. For the discussion of Glidden's position, see Hammerstaedt 1996. According to Sedley 1973: 21 τὸ πρῶτον ἐννόημα is "an embryonic concept which Epicurus later elaborated into that of πρόληψις".

[16] For the disqualification of word's discussion, see Diog. Laert. X 34: τῶν τε ζητήσεων εἶναι τὰς μὲν περὶ πραγμάτων, τὰς δὲ περὶ ψιλὴν τὴν φωνήν; see also *Peri Phuseôs* book XXVIII fgt 12, col.V and book 25, as well as Laursen 1997: 39.

[17] See Barnes 1996: 211-212.

[18] Barnes 1996: 213 makes an interesting reference to *Peri Phuseôs* book XXVIII (fr.6 col. I, l.11 and fr.13 col. VII sup, l.4-5) where Epicurus also uses ὑποτάττειν: "it is explicitly stated that what is 'collected under' an utterance is a belief, a δόξα, and this usefully confirms my earlier claim that concepts and preconceptions which lie behind our beliefs and inquiries are propositional items – indeed, are themselves beliefs". We should specify that if preconceptions are propositional, they are, however, a special kind of δόξαι since they cannot be false.

truth-*criteria*.[19] As David Sedley has said, beyond the conventionalist meaning of words, there is a natural first meaning or a *prolepsis* which can serve as a yardstick to escape useless discussion about words.[20]

Thus, *Hrdt*. 37-38 is related to Us. 255 because it explains in what sense *prolepsis* is a kind of foreknowledge or a preliminary knowledge that is a condition for further knowledge, and it explains the reference to various epistemic attitudes. Not only inquiry requires a *prolepsis*, but also all the processes involved in judging the truth of an opinion. We cannot decide if an opinion about reality is true or false without referring to a *prolepsis*. The δοξαζόμενα that are ζητούμενα or ἀπορούμενα[21] refer mainly[22] to the invisible objects at stake in the *Letter of Herodotus* and are judged with reference to "what our expressions denote" (τὰ ὑποτεταγμένα τοῖς φθόγγοις) or to "a first concept" (τὸ πρῶτον ἐννόημα), or to "an impression" (τύπος) "in line with a preconception" (κατὰ πρόληψιν, Diog. Laert. X 33). These objects of opinion are "under investigation or perplexing" because a *prolepsis* is necessary even to deny the truth of some propositions. Thus, of all the objects discussed in the letter (which are τὰ δοξαζόμενα), some of them will receive confirmation that they are the case, some of them will be denied, and some of them will remain in *aporia*.[23]

---

[19] Diog. Laert. X 31; cf. Long 1971: 120: "The position about the criteria, as I understand it, is that προλήψεις are necessary for the formation and testing of all assertions and objective judgments. Sensations and feelings provide us with data for making judgments. But the test of whether a judgment about such data is true requires a check, under optimum sensory conditions, that the data match or are not inconsistent with our preconceptions of what they are data of." For an inquiry on Lucretius use of *prolepsis* (*notitia*), see Rover 2022, 2023.

[20] Sedley 1973: 23. *Peri Phuseôs* Book XXV and XXVIII provide various examples of that appeal to *prolepsis*. See, e.g., Book XXVIII, fgt. 12, col. III l.5-12, according to which human error has "the form that arises in relation to preconceptions and appearances because of the manifold conventions of language" (ἡ ἀμ[α]ρτία ἐστὶν τῶν ἀνθρώπων οὐδὲν ἕτερον ἔχουσα σχῆμα ἢ τὸ ἐπὶ τῶμ προλήψεων γιγν[ό-]μενον καὶ τῶμ φαιγ[ομ]ένων διὰ τοὺς πολυτρόπους ἐ[θι-]σμοὺς τῶν λέξεων).

[21] The absence of the article τὰ before ζητούμενα and ἀπορούμενα is a sign that we are not dealing with three different kinds of objects. However, since the three terms are not equivalent, I take ζητούμενα or ἀπορούμενα as two species of the general category τὰ δοξαζόμενα, as White translates it; perhaps Epicurus should have written τὰ δοξαζόμενα τὰ ἢ ζητούμενα ἢ ἀπορούμενα. Diog. Laert. X 38 mentions τὸ ζητούμενον ἢ ἀπορούμενον καὶ δοξαζόμενον, reinforcing the idea that the first two terms describe two species of the same genus δοξαζόμενον, introduced by the epexegetical καί. I thank F. Bakker for the discussion of this point.

[22] Yet not uniquely, cf. Hammerstaedt 1996: 233 "Tuttavia le opinioni, i problemi e le difficoltà non si estendono solo a ciò che è oscuroa ai sensi oppure non ancora confermato, ma anche a φαινόμενα e συμπτώματα e a problemi etici come quelli menzionati nell'*Epistula ad Menoeceum*."

[23] According to Bailey 1926: 176, "ζητούμενα are problems concerned with the investigation of external things; ἀπορούμενα problems raised in mind apart from immediate sense-impression," but I don't see the evidence for such a claim. I am inclined to think that the division between ζητούμενα / ἀπορούμενα could refer to the difference between objects for which we have to decide or judge if something is the case and objects for which we cannot, which could be the case of multiple explications or avowals of ignorance. Besnier 1994: 119 refers, however, to another explanation according to which the terms refer to the three goals of a dialectical discussion: to judge an opinion, to decide between two options that are presented either positively (*a* or *b*), either negatively (neither *a* nor *b*). Such hypothesis, in my opinion, does not fit with the reference to ζήτησις in Us. 255.

Thus, the inquiry here refers to the general task of the *phusiologia* which will begin after these preliminary remarks on the reliability of our tools of knowledge. Once we agree that our primary concepts and sensations are true, we can decide, by means of empirical reasoning, which of our opinions are true or false, when under investigation or perplexing. These preliminary remarks of §§ 37-38 are crucial: if we do not grant that our primary concepts are true, we cannot decide whether our empirical reasoning is true or false, since the decision will depend not only on the reality of our proposition but also on the veracity of our primary concepts.

1.2.2. Prolepsis' theory as a solution to a platonic issue

The presentation of *prolepsis* as a condition of inquiry is also clearly determined by the Platonic context of the question of the possibility of inquiry from the *Meno*. The connection with Meno's paradox is emphasized by Plutarch in a fragment quoted by Damascius in his *Commentary of Plato's* Phaedo:

> οἱ δὲ Ἐπικούρειοι τὰς προλήψεις.— ἃς εἰ μὲν διηρθρωμένας φασί, περιττὴ ἡ ζήτησις· εἰ δὲ ἀδιαρθρώτους, πῶς ἄλλο τι παρὰ τὰς προλήψεις ἐπιζητοῦμεν, ὅ γε οὐδὲ προειλήφαμεν.

> The Epicureans, finally, appeal to 'preconceptions' – if, by this, they mean fully developed notions, seeking is superfluous; if undeveloped ones, what motive do we have to search for something else in addition to those preconceptions, something of which we do not have a preconception at all?[24]

Plutarch's presentation emphasizes that Epicurus does not solve Meno's dilemma since it can be applied to the solution itself: if *prolepsis* is knowledge in itself, it needs no addition; if it is not full knowledge and is partially unknown, how are we to know what is lacking and what must be sought in order to attain knowledge? Plutarch denies the central feature of the Epicurean *prolepsis*, which is to be a preparatory and anticipatory knowledge: not a full knowledge, but a first knowledge condition for real knowledge.

As is well known in *Meno* 80d-e, Meno shows that Socrates' avowal of ignorance contradicts his task of searching the truth, since to search, it is necessary to have at least some knowledge of the object of inquiry. To escape such an "eristic argument", we need an intermediate position between full-knowledge and ignorance. According to Epicurus, research is possible because our empirical relation with reality gives us such minimal knowledge, which takes the form of *prolepsis*. As the result of an empirical process, such a solution has the advantage of avoiding both

---

[24] I 280, transl. Westerink 1977, who shows that the text is from Damascius and not Olympiodorus as Usener thought (I owe the philological explanation to Marc-Antoine Gavray). In his fragment (also edited by Sandbach in Plutarch's *Moralia* VII fgt. 215), Plutarch had previously discussed Aristotle and the Stoic solution to *Meno*'s puzzle, see Bonazzi 2017: 123 f.

the mythological and the innate aspect of the *anamnesis* solution proposed by Socrates in the *Meno*.

Epicurus probably shaped his answer as a direct reference to *Meno*'s puzzle and, more generally, to the Platonic discussion.[25] E. Asmis has already hypothesized that "Epicurus' coinage of the word πρόληψις was inspired by Plato", more precisely by the passage in the *Phaedo* on *anamnesis*, when Plato insists on the necessity of a prior knowledge (προειδέναι) in order to have and recognize a sensation.[26] The difference, of course, is that for Epicurus, *prolepsis* comes directly from sense-perceptions; for that reason, *prolepsis* is an empirical (and thus non-Platonic) answer to a Platonic question.

Two other texts not cited by Usener provide evidence that Epicurus did associate inquiry with a Platonic context.[27] The first one is a testimony on Diotimus – in this context he could be either a Democritean or a Stoic – which attributes to Democritus positions of Epicurean origin:

> Διότιμος δὲ τρία κατ' αὐτὸν ἔλεγεν εἶναι κριτήρια, τῆς μὲν τῶν ἀδήλων καταλήψεως τὰ φαινόμενα— ὄψις γὰρ τῶν ἀδήλων τὰ φαινόμενα, ὥς φησιν Ἀναξαγόρας, ὃν ἐπὶ τούτῳ Δημόκριτος ἐπαινεῖ—, ζητήσεως δὲ τὴν ἔννοιαν—περὶ παντὸς γάρ, ὦ παῖ, μία ἀρχὴ τὸ εἰδέναι περὶ ὅτου ἔστιν ἡ ζήτησις—, αἱρέσεως δὲ καὶ φυγῆς τὰ πάθη· τὸ μὲν γὰρ ᾧ προσοικειούμεθα, τοῦτο αἱρετόν ἐστιν, τὸ δὲ ᾧ προσαλλοτριούμεθα, τοῦτο φευκτόν ἐστιν.

> But Diotimus said that according to him there are three criteria: for the apprehension of unclear things, apparent ones (for apparent things are a sight of things that are unclear, as Anaxagoras said, and Democritus praised him for this); for investigation, the conception ("for in every case, my boy, the only starting-point is knowing what the investigation is about"); and for choice and avoidance, effects on us.[28]

Sedley has shown that the strategy of Diotimus – whom he considers to be Diotimus the Stoic – is to attribute to Democritus the Epicurean innovations of the *Canon*.[29] The second criterion, even though it replaces *prolepsis* with *ennoia*, is closely related to our question. The interesting point here is the reference to *Phaedrus* 237b-c,[30]

---

[25] One cannot avoid to mention here the Aristotelian response of *An. Post.* II 19 (99b15 f.), which Epicurus probably knows. The originality of Epicurus' response seems to show that pure empirical knowledge shaped on perception and memory of the particulars is sufficient to solve *Meno*'s puzzle, whereas for Aristotle sensation is "of universals" (100b1).

[26] Asmis 1984: 49-50.

[27] Asmis 1984: 35; Brunschwig 1988: 148-149.

[28] *AM* VII 140-141.

[29] Sedley 1992: 44.

[30] περὶ παντός, ὦ παῖ, μία ἀρχὴ τοῖς μέλλουσι καλῶς [237E] βουλεύσεσθαι· εἰδέναι δεῖ περὶ οὗ ἂν ᾖ ἡ βουλή, ἢ παντὸς ἁμαρτάνειν ἀνάγκη. τοὺς δὲ πολλοὺς λέληθεν ὅτι οὐκ ἴσασι τὴν οὐσίαν ἑκάστου. "There is only one way, dear boy, for those to begin who [237c] are to take counsel wisely about anything. One must know what the counsel is about, or it is sure to be utterly futile, but most people are ignorant of the fact that they do not know the nature of things" (transl. Harold N. Fowler).

which is also found in Cicero *De finibus* in the context of the discussion of Epicurus' methodology:

> *Omnis autem in quaerendo quae via quadam et ratione habetur oratio praescribere primum debet, ut quibusdam in formulis: ea res agetur, ut inter quos disseritur conveniat quid sit id de quo disseratur. Hoc positum in* Phaedro *a Platone probavit Epicurus sensitque in omni disputatione id fieri oportere.*

> However, in philosophical investigation a methodical and systematic discourse must always begin by formulating a preamble like that which occurs in certain forms of process at law, 'The issue shall be as follows'; so that the parties to the debate may be agreed as to what the subject is about which they are debating. This rule is laid down by Plato in the *Phaedrus* and it was approved by Epicurus, who realized that it ought to be followed in every discussion.[31]

Cicero's aim is to show that Epicurus contradicts himself, when, on the one hand, he demands an agreement on the terms of the discussion before any discussion and, on the other hand, he refuses to give a definition precisely because a *prolepsis* is sufficient to understand what we are talking about. The Platonic quotation refers to the passage in which Socrates explains the necessity of first agreeing on a definition (ὅρον) of love "and then keeping this definition in view and making constant reference to it, let us inquire whether love brings advantage or harm" (τὴν σκέψιν ποιώμεθα εἴτε ὠφελίαν εἴτε βλάβην παρέχει) (237d). Without such agreement at the beginning of the inquiry (ἐν ἀρχῇ τῆς σκέψεως), the inquirers will "agree neither with themselves nor with each other" (237c).

Leaving aside the polemical aspect of both *testimonia*, it seems that Epicurus was interested in the idea of a first knowledge and agreement as a condition for further inquiry (emphasized by Sextus with μία ἀρχή, *oratio praescribere primum debet* in Cicero). He could have used this passage in the same context that Meno's puzzle in order to show that any inquiry or judgment must be preceded by the foreknowledge of the object of the inquiry (τὸ εἰδέναι περὶ ὅτου ἔστιν ἡ ζήτησις / *quid sit id de quo disseratur*; the shift from the Platonic reference to σκέψις to ζήτησις in Diotimus' testimony is another sign of the adaptation of the Platonic injunction to the Epicurean context). If it so, Cicero probably missed the connection between the Epicurean refusal of definition and the necessity of agreement on the object of the inquiry.[32]

Hence, the fragment Us. 255 appears as a central piece of Epicurus' epistemology: starting from the Platonic issue expressed by Meno's dilemma, it emphasizes that, in order to grant the validity of the empirical inference that leads from the visible to the invisible, one should begin to ensure that one has access to a real preconception of the *pragmata*, in order to avoid sterile discussion about words.

---

[31] Us. 264, Cic. *De Finibus* II 1-11, 3-4 (transl. Rackham).
[32] Us. 258, see Asmis 1984: 39 f.; Besnier 1994; Giovacchini 2003.

2. SEXTUS AND "CONCEPTUAL PIRACY"

It is time to analyze Sextus' strategy. Despite the apparent agreement on the argument, a philosophical analysis of the nature and function of the *prolepsis* will show that we are dealing a typical case of 'conceptual piracy' by Sextus Empiricus, who borrows arguments and concepts from dogmatic positions in order to serve his own purpose. Certainly, the fact that Sextus borrows his concepts from dogmatic philosophy is not a big news; however, it seems worthwhile to understand precisely to what extent Sextus' contention on language depends on the Epicurean conception of *prolepsis*, that is, to define precisely for what reasons he chose this terminology, what was his interest in it, and what remains incompatible in both stances as regards their conception of language.

2.1. The gap between Sextus and Epicurus on the inquiry argument

When Sextus quotes Epicurus in *AM* I 57 or XI 21, his intention is not to refute Epicurus, nor to make a dialectical move that could lead to an opposition of arguments. Yet his use of the argument is far from being without polemical intention. It has an obvious ironic side by claiming that even the 'wise' Epicurus could agree with his method of inquiry. However, more profoundly, Sextus' move expresses a radical disagreement about the nature of philosophical inquiry and of *prolepsis*. Indeed, by using a realistic Epicurean argument in an anti-realist context, Sextus contradicts a fundamental feature of Epicureanism.

2.1.1. Two conceptions of prolepsis

The first difference is related to the conception and function of *prolepsis*. Such concept is also a key-concept for Sextus, allowing him to elude from the *apraxia* objection and to demonstrate the possibility of the Skeptical inquiry.[33] Sextus' use of the term is not systematic: he often uses *prolepsis*, *ennoia*, and *epinoia* interchangeably, sometimes as a dogmatic concept.[34] Leaving aside passages in which Sextus refers to a dogmatic conception (as in *AM* XI 44, 68, and 129) or specifically to the Epicurean conception of *prolepsis*,[35] the Skeptical conception of *prolepsis* refers to (1) the fact that we do have concepts, in a purely passive way, without assuming the reality of the object of such concept, and (2) the fact that these concepts can be common if they are based on common conditions of experience. Thanks to *prolepsis* we can live and make choices "following the preconception which accords with his ancestral laws and customs" *(AM* XI 152); we can follow common rules; we can live "by experience and without opinions, in accordance with the common observations

---

[33] e.g. *AM* XI 152.
[34] For a comprehensive study of Sextus' use of the term, see Bett forthcoming part 1.
[35] E.g., *AM* VIII 337 and 331 a; on those passages, see Fine 2014: 354 and *infra*.

and preconceptions, and to suspend judgment about what is said with dogmatic superfluity and far beyond the needs of ordinary life" (*PH* II 246; see also *PH* I 23-24). Hence, Skeptical *prolepsis* is to be considered as a subclass of *phainomena* related to the possession of some concepts or views that can be empirically abstracted from our milieu.

The feature (1) – the passive feature – is the guarantee that *prolepsis*, although it is a thought, is formed on a set of information-data received on empirical grounds, which we can consider without making any commitment to their truth or rightness. Sextus gives a description of this process in *PH* II 10-11, which, while not using the vocabulary of *prolepsis*, accurately describes it. Here, Sextus addresses the objection of the impossibility of inquiry made by anonymous philosophers, which I believe to be Epicureans:[36]

εἰ δὲ φήσουσι μὴ τοιαύτην [λέγειν] κατάληψιν ἡγεῖσθαι ζητήσεως προσήκειν, νόησιν δὲ ἁπλῶς, οὐκ ἔστιν ἀδύνατον [ἐν] τοῖς ἐπέχουσι περὶ τῆς ὑπάρξεως τῶν ἀδήλων ζητεῖν. νοήσεως γὰρ οὐκ ἀπείργεται ὁ σκεπτικός, οἶμαι, ἀπό τε τῶν παθητικῶς ὑποπιπτόντων <καὶ> κατ' ἐνάργειαν φαινομένων αὐτῷ λόγων γινομένης καὶ μὴ πάντως εἰσαγούσης τὴν ὕπαρξιν τῶν νοουμένων· οὐ γὰρ μόνον τὰ ὑπάρχοντα νοοῦμεν, ὥς φασιν, ἀλλ' ἤδη καὶ τὰ ἀνύπαρκτα. ὅθεν καὶ ζητῶν καὶ νοῶν ἐν τῇ σκεπτικῇ διαθέσει μένει ὁ ἐφεκτικός· ὅτι γὰρ τοῖς κατὰ φαντασίαν παθητικὴν ὑποπίπτουσιν αὐτῷ, καθὸ φαίνεται αὐτῷ, συγκατατίθεται, δεδήλωται.

If they say they mean that it is not apprehension of this sort but rather mere thinking which ought to precede investigation, then investigation is not impossible for those who suspend judgment about the reality of what is unclear. For a sceptic is not, I think, barred from having thoughts, if they arise from things which give him a passive impression and appear evidently to him and do not at all imply the reality of what is being thought of – for we can think, as they say, not only of real things but also of unreal things. Hence someone who suspends judgment maintains his sceptical condition while investigating and thinking; for it has been clear that he assents to any impression given by way of a passive appearance insofar as it appears to him.[37]

As for the Epicurean *prolepsis*, Skeptical pre-notions are the result of a passive process that guarantees that we do not add any *doxa* to an impression. Such a theory makes it possible to explain both how Skeptics can make inquiries and how they can think and use language. Hence Skeptical *prolepsis* is linked to 'reality' as a mere empirical and phenomenological fact, as a *phainomenon*: it includes natural facts

---

[36] My arguments for believing that this version of the argument is Epicurean are that Sextus previously addressed a Stoic version of the argument from II 1 to 9 (to inquire entails to grasp the thing – καταλαμβάνειν), then the same argument appears with a less restrictive comprehension of καταλαμβάνειν as mere νόησιν δὲ ἁπλῶς (II 10), which can be considered as Epicurean (*pace* Fine 2014: 322 f., which considers it as a whole Stoic argument).
[37] Transl. Annas and Barnes 1994.

(such as the contradiction of appearances),[38] laws, and customs. Sextus' contextualist approach to language can also be considered under the same label. We speak and argue with words that we understand by a purely empirical process, and we can adapt to the context of language use, as well as we can speak several languages.[39] The difference with the Epicureans here is the fact that a Skeptical *prolepsis* does not guarantee that things are as the *prolepsis* presents them. The fact that we can investigate, speak and act on the basis of a *prolepsis* is not an argument for its veracity.

This point brings us to the second characteristic: community. If Skeptics follow some *prolepseis* to act, it is not because those *prolepseis* have some special feature *per se* that would give them authority. If they do so, it is because they find some of them common to a group of people whom they believe act without making additional judgment, that is, *common people* as opposed to *philosophers*.[40] For this reason, Sextus explains that Skeptics "are not in conflict with common preconceptions of humanity" (οὐδὲ μαχόμεθα ταῖς κοιναῖς τῶν ἀνθρώπων προλήψεσιν), since they "do in fact posit the recollective sign, which is used in ordinary life" (*AM* VIII 157-158).

The semantic status of *prolepsis* is thus different in the two stances, since Sextus clearly rejects its main function for Epicureans, namely, the idea that a *prolepsis* could be used as a self-evident criterion of what a thing really is. For Sextus, nothing grants that a thing is really as a *prolepsis* describes it. According to him, the *prolepsis*-approach is a means to show that he can use all the common concepts – even dogmatic concepts – without any problem, since he uses them as empirical facts. This is precisely the reason why he does not discuss the words and uses the language loosely (καταχρηστικῶς).[41] His approach to language is completely contextualist: he does not think that any word can be the sign of what a thing really is; words are only empirical tools.[42]

As we have seen, the function of Epicurean *prolepsis* is precisely the opposite. For, from an Epicurean perspective, the linguistic theory that grounds the conception of *prolepsis* is that our primary concepts are true results of a natural process.[43] Epicurean' *prolepsis* is a subclass of concepts which entails a commitment to their

---

[38] *PH* I 211: "the contraries appear to hold of the same thing is not a belief of the Skeptics but a fact which makes an impression not only on the Skeptics but on other philosophers too – and indeed on everyone."

[39] See Desbordes 1982; Glidden 1983b; Spinelli 1991; Glidden 1994; Corti 2009; Spinelli 2014.

[40] See Marchand 2015: 98 ff.

[41] *PH* III 119; *AM* VI 2.

[42] It seems, then, that a Skeptical *prolepsis* is a mere notion, from which we can make the distinction between the dogmatic *prolepsis* (which involves a judgment on the nature and the existence of a thing) and the Skeptical *prolepsis* (which has the peculiarity to be common and purely empirical). See Spinelli 1995: 329: "Sesto la [sc. la pre-concezione radicata in lui] chiama a ragione πρόληψις, tenendola tuttavia ben distinta dalle prenozioni dogmatiche, perché prodotta non dalla riflessione teorica, ma dalla consuetudine delle norme tradizionali e delle leggi patrie."

[43] For Epicurean texts against conventionalism, see Epicurus *Hrdt.* 75-76; Lucret. *DRN* V 1028 f.; Diogenes of Oinoanda Fgt 12, col.II-V.

truth. Even though Sextus seems to concede that they are common phenomena that can ground our activity and empirical reasoning, he never considers that we can infer that the nature of the reality can be known from these phenomena. One of the reasons for this inability is the lack of *consensus omnium*. Even if we experience common phenomenon, we could experience the disagreement between different *prolepseis*.[44]

As regards Epicurus, there is a scholarly debate as to know whether he uses the *consensus omnium* argument to grant the truth of *prolepsis*.[45] It should be noted that the empirical status of *prolepsis* makes it impossible to grant that there could ever be a real consensus on all our *prolepseis*, since their formation is conditioned by contingent circumstances. For example, we can hardly claim that all people do have the *prolepsis* of a rhinoceros without living in a word where they can see images of such an animal. In order to understand the crucial difference between Sextus' and Epicurus' stance, we must emphasize, as Voula Tsouna has done, that Epicurean's *prolepsis* is linked to a "disposition to acquire such concepts and this disposition is activated by the appropriate empirical stimuli".[46] This means that for Epicurus all men who are in the same disposition and in the same condition should develop the same preconception of natural things and the same general conception, and that is the reason why we have the same preconception of what, for example, a man or a horse is, and also of justice, virtue, atom and void; for this reason, we can debate about these objects without having to define or demonstrate what we mean by these names. Admittedly, some objects are more common than others, but with respect to fundamental concepts such as justice, virtue, atom, void, we can assume that everyone, through his experience has access to their preconception.[47]

Thus, for Epicurus, a *prolepsis* grants that we have one and only one *prolepsis* corresponding to a given empirical situation.[48] If we experience conflicting conceptions, it must be for the reason that we have added some opinion to the empirical preconception, as in the case with divergent conceptions of gods in *Men.* 123-124.[49] For that reason, *prolepsis* is a kind of universal knowledge or, according

---

[44]   *AM* VIII 333a quoted *infra*.
[45]   In Cic. *DND*, Velleius refers to such argument for the *prolepsis* of God, but Tsouna 2016: 180 sq. suggests that it was not Epicurus' own argument, because of the lack of other sources. Epicur. *Men.* 123 mentions κοινὴ τοῦ θεοῦ νόησις but according to Obbink 1992: 200-201 "the term has the force, not of, 'common' in the sense of 'universally shared' belief, but rather of a 'basic' or 'underlying' idea". There is discussion in order to know if god's *prolepsis* has a special status, being the only one which is natural and innate, and shared by all men – cf. Tsouna 2016: 165.
[46]   Tsouna 2016: 184.
[47]   See the example of the void in Epicurus, *Peri Phuseôs* Book XXVIII, Fr.8, col. IV-V.
[48]   As emphasized by Betegh and Tsouna forthcoming part. 1 "having the preconception of F means that I have access to *the* concept of F, which truly captures what it takes to be F, as opposed to merely having *a* concept of F".
[49]   οὐ γὰρ προλήψεις εἰσὶν ἀλλ' ὑπολήψεις ψευδεῖς αἱ τῶν πολλῶν ὑπὲρ θεῶν ἀποφάσεις – "For the claims most people make about gods are not preconceptions but false misconception." See also

to Diog. Laert. X 33, "a cognition, or a correct belief, or a mental idea, or universal insight stored within us – κατάληψιν ἢ δόξαν ὀρθὴν ἢ ἔννοιαν ἢ καθολικὴν νόησιν ἐναποκειμένην (l. 33)".[50]

For Sextus, rather, a *diaphonia* between *prolepseis* is always possible, while for Epicurus such a *diaphonia* would be the sign that these conceptions are not *prolepseis* but mere opinions.[51] Thus, Sextus' conception of *prolepsis* would not realize the realistic or existential function of Epicurus' *prolepsis*, since such a conception is precisely the guarantee that we can rely on their indubitable nature and a kind of universality. Sextus' conception of *prolepsis* is precisely shaped by the denial that a true concept could ever be possible, even if common concepts are possible. Thus, even if Sextus' conception of *prolepsis* shares a common feature with Epicureanism as a passive, common and empirical concept,[52] Sextus' use of Epicurus' argument is based on a completely different function.

2.1.2. *Difference on inquiry*

The second difference that emerges from the comparison between Sextus and Epicurus is related to their conception of inquiry. It seems obvious that Sextus chose this argument precisely because it introduces to his own conception of *skepsis*. In fact, Epicurus' reference to *aporein* and *zetein* made this argument very appealing to the Skeptics, who refer to these terms as constitutive of their attitude (cf. *PH* I 7 and Diog. Laert. IX 70). In Us. 255, Sextus wants to show that, *volens nolens*, even the founder of the Garden legitimates his own practice of skepticism.

Indeed, this appropriation is not very fair: as we have seen, Epicurus does not describe a method of inquiry in *Hrdt.* 37-38, but rather the condition of possibility of any inquiry and any judgment thanks to the realistic function of *prolepsis*. Sextus' use of the argument does not at all point to this realistic aspect. Instead, he makes a deviant use of Epicurus' argument by judging that if Epicurus can discuss the truth-value of his δοξαζόμενα on the basis of a *prolepsis*, it implies that he can discuss a belief without having to commit himself to the existence of the object to

---

Men. 123 and the disputed text: οὐ γὰρ φυλάττουσιν αὐτοὺς οἵους νομίζουσιν: I take νομίζουσιν as referring to the *prolepsis* of gods.

[50] This difference on *prolepsis* between both stances is the reason why I see important limits in the alleged proximity between Epicureanism and Pyrrhonism in language. Admittedly, as Giovacchini 2023: 26 pointed out, there is a common interest on a pragmatic conception of language, but roughly speaking the Epicurean position is shaped on the very assumption that words grasp reality.

[51] This explains the fact that Epicurus could say both that there is a common or universal conception of God and that many people are wrong in their representation of gods; cf. Obbink 1992: 202 "the point is that actual universality is not the point. 'Consensus' for Epicurus, in so far as it plays a criterial role, cannot mean 'what everybody actually (now) believes'."

[52] See Glidden 1990: 416-418 who points out that the term *prolepsis* had a colloquial use at Sextus' time that could not be Stoic (since Stoic *prolepsis* involves a cataleptic impression) and "had more to do with the original Epicurean use of the term as an habituated form of pattern recognition, the familiar apprehension of something typically perceived rather than the clear conception of thing". For the Stoic account of *prolepsis*, see Gourinat's paper in the present volume

which the *prolepsis* refers. For this reason he mentions the fact that a notion can refer to something that exists or not (*AM* II 1 and *PH* II 10 cited *supra*) and pretends to believe that he can get support from Epicurus for distinguishing concept from existence. In the end, though, the Skeptical *skepsis* is a discussion of a concept in order to show that no concept at all – hence no *prolepsis* – can ever grant that anything exists as the concept describes it. The discrepancy here is obvious: since, even if Epicurus admitted that some inquiries could end in a negative conclusion, it is not his intention in *Hrdt.* 37-38 or in the other texts of Us. 255 to show that every inquiry will end negatively.[53] Rather, his aim seems to be to point out that *even if* we can discuss whether an impression can be considered as a case to be subsumed under a concept, we cannot discuss the empirical validity and meaning of such a concept as far as *prolepsis* is concerned. Thus, Sextus' seemingly neutral or bona fide use of Epicurus' argument does exactly the opposite of what Epicurus intended!

2.2. Later *variatio* on a Meno's theme
2.2.1. The anti-Skeptical use of the argument
Sextus was well aware that his convergence with Epicurus was only occasional since he also mentions uses of this argument against his own position to show the contradiction of the Skeptical position:

> Παρεστακότες καὶ τὸ ἐκ τίνος ὕλης ἐστὶν ἡ ἀπόδειξις, ἀκολούθως πειρασόμεθα καὶ τοὺς σαλεύοντας αὐτὴν λόγους προχειρίσασθαι, σκεπτόμενοι, πότερον ἀκολουθεῖ τῇ ἐπινοίᾳ καὶ προλήψει ταύτης ἡ ὕπαρξις ἢ οὐδαμῶς. Καίτοι τινὲς εἰώθασιν ἡμῖν, καὶ μάλιστα οἱ ἀπὸ τῆς Ἐπικούρου αἱρέσεως, ἀγροικότερον ἐνίστασθαι, λέγοντες "ἤτοι νοεῖτε, τί ἐστιν ἡ ἀπόδειξις, ἢ οὐ νοεῖτε. καὶ εἰ μὲν νοεῖτε καὶ ἔχετε ἔννοιαν αὐτῆς, ἔστιν ἀπόδειξις· εἰ δὲ οὐ νοεῖτε, πῶς ζητεῖτε τὸ μηδ' ἀρχὴν νοούμενον ὑμῖν;"

> Having described what demonstration is made of, we will follow this by trying to get a grip on the arguments that make it shaky, inquiring whether its reality follows from its conception and prior notion or not. Indeed some people, especially those of the Epicurean school, tend to resist us in a rather crude way, saying "Either you understand what demonstration is, or you do not. And if you understand it and have a conception of it, there is demonstration; but if you do not understand it, how can you investigate what you have not the slightest understanding of?"[54]

One may wonder if Sextus' formula οἱ ἀπὸ τῆς Ἐπικούρου αἱρέσεως is not a sign that he was aware that the objection was shaped by later Epicureans and not by Epicurus himself. He will later mention Demetrius of Laconia (145-75 B.C.E) in

---
[53] There is, however, a scholarly discussion about the extent to which Sextus' inquiry is aimed at finding truth; for an interpretation more favourable than mine (Marchand 2010) to the idea that the Skeptic searches the truth, see, e.g., Perin 2010; Machuca 2021. An interesting overview of use of *zetesis* in Sextus can be found in Smith 2022: 63-66.
[54] *AM* VIII 337, translation by Bett 2005.

AM VIII 348, who may be the source of the objection in this context.[55] Accordingly, the text shifts from *prolepsis* to *noesis*, but Sextus mentions *prolepsis* just before quoting the objection when he introduces the argument as a kind of "ontological implication".[56] And the formula ὁ μηδ' ἀρχὴν νοούμενον ὑμῖν ("what you have not the slightest understanding of") implies that the argument points not only to the absence of a notion, but also to the absence of a pre-notion. In order to discuss and doubt the notion of demonstration, we should at least have a minimal notion or a pre-notion of what a demonstration is. Here comes the "ontological implication": in the case of Epicurean *prolepsis*, the very fact of having a pre-notion of something implies the existence of such a thing as a cause of the formation of the *prolepsis*,[57] which leads to a contradiction for the Skeptical stance.

2.2.2. The Skeptic reply

Sextus responds from 331a to 336a by articulating two arguments that focus on the nature of *prolepsis*. The first one is related to the plurality of *prolepsis* (332a-333a):

εἰ μὲν γὰρ μίαν εἴχομεν τοῦ ζητουμένου πράγματος πρόληψιν, κἂν ταύτῃ συνεξακολουθήσαντες τοιοῦτ' ἐπιστεύομεν ὑπάρχειν, ὁποῖον κατὰ μίαν προσέπιπτεν ἔννοιαν· νῦν δ' ἐπεὶ πολλὰς ἔχομεν τοῦ ἑνὸς ἐννοίας καὶ πολυτρόπους καὶ μαχομένας καὶ ἐπ' ἴσης πιστὰς διά τε τὴν ἐν αὐταῖς πιθανότητα καὶ διὰ τὴν τῶν προϊσταμένων ἀνδρῶν ἀξιοπιστίαν, μήτε πάσαις πιστεῦσαι δυνάμενοι διὰ τὴν μάχην, μήτε πάσαις ἀπιστῆσαι τῷ μηδεμίαν ἄλλην ἔχειν αὐτῶν πιστοτέραν, μήτε τινὶ μὲν πιστεῦσαι, τινὶ δὲ ἀπιστεῖν διὰ τὴν ἰσότητα, κατ' ἀνάγκην ἤλθομεν εἰς τὸ ἐπέχειν.

For if we had just one preconception of the object being investigated, then sticking closely to this we would believe that the matter was such as it struck us in virtue of that one conception; but in fact, since we have many conceptions of this one thing, which are also varied and conflicting and equally trustworthy (both on account of their own persuasiveness and on account of the trustworthiness of the men who support them), being unable either to trust all of them because of the conflict, or to distrust all of them because of having none other that is more trustworthy than them, or to trust one and distrust another because of their equality, we necessarily arrive at suspension of judgment.[58]

---

[55] However, Spinelli 2013: 158 noted that Demetrius is the only Epicurean (apart from Epicurus himself) mentioned by Sextus, so for him the formula refers to other Epicureans than Demetrius.

[56] Brunschwig 1988.

[57] *Pace* Fine 2014: 353, this argument cannot be labelled as an "ontological argument". It is not by chance that Brunschwig speaks of an "ontological implication", for if the Epicurean *prolepsis* entails the existence of a material cause, this cause must refer to something empirical. This argument is much more a 'proof by effect' or *a posteriori* rather than an ontological one. The connection between *prolepsis* and ontological propositions is not established by the way of existence as a predicate, but rather by the fact that having a *prolepsis* of something entails the existence of a material, hence existent, cause of the thing.

[58] *AM* VIII 333a, translation by Bett 2005.

Whereas Epicurean *prolepsis* should be unique with respect to a given community of perceivers in the same condition, Skeptical *prolepsis* is plural even if it would be produced by the same object. These points were involved in the analysis devoted to *PH* II 10-11: even though Sextus explained the possibility for a Skeptic to act and think on the basis of a *prolepsis*, his own conception of *prolepsis* as a passive process could not impeach the disagreement between *prolepseis* since the contrariety of appearances is a fact which is common to all men.[59] Therefore, the commonality of *prolepsis* cannot be taken as a sign that every reality is shaped as the *prolepsis* describes it, since we can always find counter-examples or examples of a deviant conception. This difference appears, for example, in the conception of the gods. On the one hand, Sextus assumes that "for all humans, on the contrary, have a common preconception (κοινὴν πρόληψιν) about God, according to which god is a blessed and imperishable animal, perfect in in happiness and not receptive of anything bad" (*AM* IX 33); or that "most of the dogmatists, and the common preconception of ordinary life (ἡ κοινὴ τοῦ βίου πρόληψις) say that there is [sc. a god]" (*AM* IX 50); or that "according to the common conceptions and prior notions (κατὰ τὰς κοινὰς ἐννοίας καὶ προλήψεις) of all humans there *is* holiness" (*AM* IX 124). On the other hand, he mentions several disagreements about the gods, including about their existence (*AM* IX 51). Therefore, commonality cannot be the sign of the existence of a reality, since this commonality is not universal. Admittedly, if something could really appear to all men in the same way, we could accept it as the sign of a reality.[60] This, though, is never the case, and for this reason the commonality can only be something like a criterion of action, but not, in any case, a criterion of truth.[61]

The second argument is related to the problem of error. If to have a *prolepsis* of something is to grasp a thing (VIII 334a), then the Epicurean must admit that every object of his inquiry exist, which is absurd and not at all what Epicurus meant to say in *Hrdt*. 37-38. A subtler version of this argument appears in reference to Epicurus' theory of error:

ἀλλ' οἶμαι ὅτι ἀπολογούμενοι φήσουσιν, ὡς ἐπινοεῖ μὲν Ἐπίκουρος τὰ τέσσαρα στοιχεῖα, οὐ κατείληφε δὲ πάντως· ψιλὸν γὰρ κίνημά ἐστι τῆς διανοίας ἡ ἐπίνοια, ἧς ἐχόμενος ἀντιλέγει τῷ εἶναι τέσσαρα στοιχεῖα. τοίνυν καὶ ἡμεῖς ἔχομεν ἐπίνοιαν τῆς ἀποδείξεως,

---

[59] One may wonder if this principle might not be the unique universal *prolepsis* for a Skeptic, which Sextus calls a "fact" in *PH* I 221.

[60] This principle appears frequently in Sextus, and probably comes from Aenesidemus. Sextus himself draws a parallel between Aenesidemus and Epicurus on this principle, cf. *AM* VII, 8. See Marchand 2019. Bett forthcoming (part 4) points out that this argument on conception appears only in *AM* VIII and "is not typical of Sextus' approach".

[61] Cf. Brunschwig 1988: 149 who claims that this argument accepts the "ontological implication". It seems to me, however, that the argument makes the distinction between the *de jure* validity of such an implication and the *de facto* observation that an unambiguous *prolepsis* is impossible.

καὶ ἀπὸ ταύτης ἐξετάσομεν, εἴτε ἔστιν εἴτε καὶ μή, ταύτην δὲ ἔχοντες οὐχὶ καὶ τὴν κατάληψιν ὁμολογήσομεν.[62]

But I think that they will say in defense that Epicurus does conceive the four elements, but has absolutely not apprehended them; for conception is a mere movement of thought, which he holds onto in his opposition to there being four elements. So we too have a conception of demonstration, and on the basis of this we will examine whether or not it is; but in having this we do not also agree to the apprehension.

Obviously, Epicurus does not claim that every concept refers to existing things;[63] he does not even say that the reference to a *prolepsis* is the sign that the object denoted by the *prolepsis* actually exists. The example of "the prior notion and conception of the four elements" (*AM* VIII 335a: πρόληψιν καὶ ἐπίνοιαν Ἐπίκουρος τῶν τεττάρων στοιχείων) is something that Epicurus supposedly did not accept as existent as mere elements. The concept of air, water, and the like as elements must have arisen from a false reasoning by analogy with the only elements that are real for the Epicureans: atoms. Therefore, if we refer to *Hrdt.* 37-38, we should say that the thesis that air, water, and the like are elements is precisely an object of opinion that we could judge to be false on the basis of our sensation and our *prolepsis* of what an element is. The expression "a mere movement of thought" refers to Epicurus theory of error in *Hrdt.* 51 as "some other change within ourselves that is connected (*sc.* to the presentational application) but has some divergence".[64] According to Sextus, the mere fact of recognizing that we can discuss on the basis of false conceptions – which are in any case real movements of thought within us – is sufficient to give an answer to the Epicurean attack. From a Skeptical point of view, no difference can be made between these false conceptions and the *prolepsis* which is necessarily true. Sextus' second argument thus interprets Epicurus' definition of error in a deviant way, since the term has a different meaning from an Epicurean and Skeptical point of view. From the latter point of view, it means that all our concepts could be, after all, ψιλὸν κίνημά τῆς διανοίας, such internal movements are sufficient to live, to speak, and to act.[65] From the former, it follows that such a movement is an empty concept that does not correspond to reality, although it is constructed on true and natural concepts such as an element.

The confrontation between the use of the same argument in different contexts reveals that Sextus was well aware that the proximity between the two stances on this argument was purely occasional. As in the case of Us. 255, it also seems that

---

[62] *AM* VIII 336a.
[63] Asmis 1984: 29
[64] *Hrdt.* 37-38: ἄλλην τινὰ κίνησιν ἐν ἡμῖν αὐτοῖς συνημμένην μὲν διάληψιν δὲ ἔχουσαν; as Usener I supplied <τῇ φανταστικῇ ἐπιβολῇ> to precise συνημμένην.
[65] For this reason Machuca 2013 points out that the Skeptical discussion of the Epicurean criterium of truth implies (at least from a logical point of view) external world skepticism.

Epicurus' *prolepsis* has an ontological and foundational function that is completely denied by Sextus' use of *prolepsis*. Despite the apparent proximity of the two stances on the nature of *prolepsis*, a major difference emerges that is related to the fact that, although both stances are empirical, Epicurus' empiricism is strictly connected to the refusal of gnoselogical skepticism and an anti-realistic approach of language.

3. CONCLUSIVE REMARKS ON SKEPTICISM IN THE FOURTH CENTURY BCE.

To conclude, I wish to make some remarks on that confrontation from an historical point of view. This confrontation confirms that Epicurus did not know or face any 'Skeptical' position in his extant work, if by 'Skeptical' we refer to the two schools that have promoted *epoche* as a goal and understood their method as a systematic and endless search for truth. The analysis of Sextus' version of Us. 255 showed that he was aware that the inquiry-argument was not designed to refute skepticism. The analysis of *Hrdt.* 37-38 confirmed that fact: *prolepsis* theory is not an anti-Skeptical theory,[66] even though this theory was later used to refute Skeptics. Moreover, Sextus' careful distinction between Epicurus and later Epicureans in *AM* VIII 337 give reasons to think that he was aware that the anti-Skeptical use of this theory was developed later, probably under the pressure of the New Academy or the spread of Timon's mockery, early after Epicurus' death since Colotes (born 320 BCE) and perhaps also Polystratus (third century) seem to have formulated anti-Skeptical arguments.[67]

However, the fact that Skeptical schools appeared after Epicurus does not mean that he did not address the problem of the possibility of knowledge. Instead, an analysis of Us. 255 and *Hrdt.* 37-38 showed that Epicurus was primarily concerned with by this problem.[68] It is very significant that in the *Canon* Epicurus invented both the notion of *prolepsis* and the criterion of truth;[69] the sequence of *Hrdt.* 37-38 confirms that the two are firmly connected. In order to establish a firm foundation for knowledge, Epicurus has to admit that sense-perceptions and our first concepts are undoubtedly true. The question now is why Epicurus needed to produce such a ground. Why did Epicurus address the so-called Skeptical challenge when he did

---

[66] The same analysis could be provided for *KD* XXIII and XXIV which are sometimes presented as an anti-Skeptical argument.
[67] See Polystratus 21-22 (Indelli), commented by Svavarsson 2004: 282-283; Plutarch, *Adv. Col.*, 1120, 1121E-1124B.
[68] Cf. Barigazzi 1969: 289: "Épicure eut la constante préoccupation de combattre le scepticisme. (...) l'épicurisme est né d'une lutte non seulement contre le platonisme, mais aussi contre le scepticisme". By 'skepticism' the author refers to the position of Pyrrho inspired by "plusieurs éléments sceptiques qui remontent jusqu'aux temps les plus reculés et qui, à travers la Sophistique, l'école éléoérétrienne, celle de Mégare et celle de Démocrite, ont abouti à Pyrrhon dans la seconde moitié du IVe siècle".
[69] See Diog. Laert. X 33 and Cic. *DND* XVI 43.

not know and could not know any Skeptical philosophers in the proper sense of the term? G. Striker described the shift from the question "What is knowledge?" to "Is there knowledge?" which, according to her, began with Epicurus.[70] In conclusion, I would like to add some remarks on 'proto-Skepticism' or – to avoid the overdetermined term 'skepticism' – on such 'gnoseological pessimism' which seems to be the target of Epicurus' theory of *prolepsis*.

How can such a 'gnoseological pessimism' be characterized? According to Epicurus' argument from Diog. Laert. X 37, it seems to be a move that denies the possibility of any knowledge by pointing out that if we want to judge a belief to be true or false, we need to produce a demonstration of the correctness of our own concepts. If we do not have such a demonstration, then our concepts must be empty (κενοὺς φθόγγους ἔχωμεν) and everything should be undecidable or unjudgeable for us (ἄκριτα πάντα ἡμῖν <ἴῃ>). Therefore, this gnoseological pessimism is not an ephectic position, since it shows that no judgment can ever be based on our *doxazomena*, our concepts being uncertain and non-demonstrable. This pessimism is neither primarily 'metaphysical' nor 'ontological'; it is rather a 'gnoseological pessimism' and more precisely a linguistic or a semantic pessimism, based on the inability to secure the truth of our concepts, considering them to be mere matters of convention and in need of justification.

Even if we have few and scarce data on this pessimism, some scholars have made hypotheses upon which we can try to give a description of this movement. Once acknowledged that Pyrrho was not a Skeptic and was not concerned with *epoche*,[71] there is no reason to believe that he was not a part of such a pessimism.[72] Epicurus knew of Pyrrho's existence and even praised his way of life (T28DC); he was also a pupil of Nausiphanes, who was himself related to Pyrrho. Even if it is impossible to prove directly that Epicurus was responding to Pyrrho in *Hrdt.* 37-38, my main hypothesis is that a debate between these two philosophers was possible. More precisely, such hypothesis could explain some features of Pyrrho's main testimony (T53DC), where Timon said that in particular that "<Pyrrho> declared that things are equally undifferentiated, unstable and unjudgeable" (ἐπ' ἴσης ἀδιάφορα καὶ ἀστάθμητα καὶ ἀνεπίκριτα), and that "for this reason neither our sensations nor our opinions are true or false".[73] Here there is, if not a textual parallel, at least a philosophical one. Pyrrho describes things as ἀνεπίκιρτα; Epicurus wants to avoid that all things are ἄκριτα. The latter provided the theory of *prolepsis* to enable to judge the truth of our opinions about things, while Pyrrho concludes that it is impossible

---

[70] Striker 1996: 143.
[71] Brochard 2002; Couissin 1929; Bett 2000.
[72] Spinelli 2020: 100 pointed out that Epicurus qualification of Pyrrho as "ignorant and uneducated" (T30DC *apud* Diog. Laert. X 8) could have the meaning of denouncing "un pensatore incapace di dare una soluzione positiva (e dogmaticamente indiscutibile) alla domanda su 'come sono fatte le cose'".
[73] Translation by M. Bonazzi in the second edition of *Pirrone. Testimonianze* Decleva Caizzi 2020.

to make such a judgment. *Hrdt.* 37-38 could be a valid answer to Pyrrho's negative view. The experience of sense-perception analyzed on atomic grounds gives reason to think that *pragmata* are precisely determined and differentiated, and the experience of linguistic minimal understanding gives reason to think that we have common concepts which can be explained by our empirical nature. Thus Epicurus' epistemology could be an answer to Pyrrho's phrase "neither our sensations nor our opinions are true or false": our sensations are always true, and given this position and the empirical origin of our primary concepts, we can decide whether our opinions are true or false.[74] Even if the evidence is not sufficient to prove that Pyrrho is precisely Epicurus' target,[75] we can remark at least that Pyrrho was part of the same wave of pessimistic views at the end of the fourth century BCE that Epicurus was indeed targeting.

Due to the lack of testimony or Pyrrho's scant interest in theoretical problems, we do not know what exactly the reasons for Pyrrho's position were. In this conclusion, I would like to stress the fact that Epicurus' theory of *prolepsis* could give some clues to understand the philosophical state of mind – which I call 'gnoseological pessimism' – which can explain Pyrrho's contention and give an insight on his reasons. Two directions seem pertinent both to explain Pyrrho's claim and Epicurus' reaction: Democritean and Megarian circles may indeed instantiate such a pessimistic wave.[76]

It is well known that later Democriteans such as Metrodorus of Chios, Anaxarchus, and Nausiphanus conclude from Democritus' principles to the impossibility of knowledge (at least the impossibility of knowledge without making the hypothesis of atoms and void).[77] The pessimistic interpretation of Democritus is related to his position on the conventionality of sense-perception as opposed to the true reality of atoms and void, and the assertion that no knowledge of this convention is possible.[78] Thus, although Democritus was neither a Skeptic,[79] nor did he deny the possibility of knowledge, his critical position against the veracity of sense-perception and more generally the difficulty of having an accurate and complete understanding of nature

---

[74] According to my interpretation the distinction between ontological and gnoseological interpretation of T53DC which divides the scholars is not useful; my position on this point is convergent with Svavarsson 2004.

[75] However, this is the position of Barigazzi 1969: 290. See also Gigante 1981chap. 2.

[76] On this problem, scholars are broadly divided between those who interpret Epicurus' reaction as a development of a discussion with Aristotle's view (especially his arguments against Democritus) and those who interpret Epicurus' contention as a direct response to Democritus or Democriteans – and, more generally, philosophers who express doubts about the possibility of knowledge; see Sedley 1983: 15.

[77] See the interpretation of Metrodorus' *incipit* (DK70B1) by Brunschwig 1996; for Anaxarchus, see *AM* VII 87-88; for Nausiphanes, see Seneca, *Ep.* 88, 46; cf. Warren 2002; Burnyeat 2017.

[78] For this interpretation of DK 68B9, see Sextus Emp. *AM* VII 135-139, VIII 6, DL IX, 72 (=DK 68B117), Plutarch, *Adv. Col.* 1110 E-F (=DK 68A57) and Diogenes of Oinoanda (fgt. 7 II 2-14 Smith).

[79] For a comprehensive approach to the problem, see Morel 1998; Curd 2001; see also Piergiacomi 2017 for arguments related to Democritus conventionalist approach to language.

seems to give rise to a more pessimistic view in later Democritean circles. It is not the place here to determine to what extent these circles are a source for Pyrrho's assertion.[80] As far as *Hrdt.* 37-38 is concerned, though, Epicurus' position seems to be a clear response to a pessimistic interpretation of Democritus' principles by granting the veracity of truth-sensation. *Prolepsis*-theory – by claiming that certain of our concepts are related to a natural experience and that the sensation is always true – provides an argument to escape to such an interpretation of Democritus' position. For that reason, I am inclined to think that Pyrrho could be an accurate represent of this pessimistic gnoseology surfing on a pessimistic interpretation of Democritus.[81]

Another source of this epistemic pessimism may be found in the Megarians and their conventionalist conception of language, against whom Epicurus produced a response with the theory of *prolepsis* (notably in *Peri Phuseôs* Book XXVIII).[82] Diodorus has a subjective theory of meaning claiming that the meaning of a term is constituted only by the intention of the speaker. For him, a word has no meaning by itself, and he notably called one of his slaves Ἄλλα μὴν to show his pure conventionalist approach to language.[83] Such an approach – and the overall Megarians approach to language and criticism of sense-knowledge[84] – involves a gnoseological question that must be resolved before any other kind of inquiry.[85] We saw that ambiguity and equivocality were real issues for Epicurus: the *Letter to Herodotus* mentions the *amphiboliai* that can arise in the initial development of language and give birth to peculiar enhancement of languages;[86] he engaged in a discussion against philosophers who play with ambiguity,[87] against whom his *Peri Amphibolias* – quoted in *Book* 28 – was probably written. It is probable – as Sedley has already pointed out – that Diodorus' circle constituted a key-target of this conception of the truth of *prolepsis* and linguistic demonstration of the possibility of knowledge.

---

[80] R. Bett points out the difference between Democritus' and Pyrrho's position and criticizes the hypothesis that Democritus was a source for Pyrrho's metaphysical position (Bett 2000: 152-160); in my opinion, his interpretation relies on a strict distinction between epistemology and metaphysics which may not have been accurate in Pyrrho's time.

[81] On this interpretation, see Decleva Caizzi 1984.

[82] Especially Epicurus' *Peri Phuseôs* Book XXVIII, fr. 13 col. V, inf.

[83] See Fgt 111 and 112 Döring 1972, cf. also Muller 1985. Thus, Diodorus could fit perfectly with the description of "certain people taking words in various ridiculous senses, and indeed in every sense in preference to their actual linguistic meaning", *Peri Phuseôs* book XXVIII fr. 13 col. V sup., Sedley 1973: 48.

[84] Cf. Fgt. 27 Döring.

[85] We know that Epicurus wrote a treatise *Against the Megarians* quoted in Diog. Laert. X 27. Gigante 1981: 94; Leone 2003 emphasized that the linguistic arguments against Megarians in *Peri Phuseôs* Book XXVIII are aimed at answering the question of the possibility of knowledge of physical world.

[86] *Hrdt.* 76, from which we must recognize that "first meaning" does not mean the first original meaning that appeared to the first men, but the first natural or logical meaning. See also Sedley 1973: 20-21.

[87] See Masi 2023 who makes interesting parallel with *Peri Phuseôs* Book XIV. See also Tepedino Guerra 1990; Leone 2002.

His conventionalist view was so radical that he even argued that there is no real ambiguity but only obscurity, since meaning depends only on the psychological intention of the utterer.[88] Such a position entails an epistemic pessimism or at least a linguistic pessimism based on the impossibility of building knowledge on our natural and empirical conception.[89] Epicurus' solution to cases of ambiguity, as we have seen, is quite different; according to him ambiguity – and the infinite discussion of meanings – can be avoided by referring to a "first meaning", which is precisely the function of *prolepsis*. Admittedly, Epicurus is directly answering to Diodorus' circle without any necessity to refer to Pyrrho; and the controversial presentation of Pyrrho as a disciple of Bryson, himself a disciple of Stilpon the Megarian (T1A = Diog. Laert. IX 61) cannot be considered as an evidence of such inspiration.[90] Still, my point here is to point out the very existence of such a pessimistic wave which creates the intellectual conditions to understand the contention in T53DC by Pyrrho, according to whom "things are equally undifferentiated, unstable and unjudgeable" and "neither our sensations nor our opinions are true or false".[91] Pyrrho seems to be aware that a lot of arguments have been given in its time against the possibility of knowledge. And his practice of *antilogia* leads to negative and pessimistic conclusion which can be compared to the later Democritean conclusions as well as to that of the Megarians.[92] Admittedly, Pyrrho's goal was *aphasia*, and he showed no attempt to write or describe the nature – even the paradoxical nature – of things. Yet the practice of *antilogia* by itself denotes the ability to articulate contradictory discourses about everything,[93] as well as a pessimistic approach to language and reasoning. The possibility of a pessimistic interpretation of Democritus' stance, the Megarians anti-naturalist contention on language, as well as Pyrrho's pessimistic views on knowledge and language constitute according to me a pessimistic wave that explains Epicurus' invention of *prolepsis*.

*
* *

---

[88] Fr. 111 Döring (=Gellius XI 12, 1-3). Diodorus probable solution of the veiled paradox is that it is sufficient to show that in the paradox "to know" is pronounced with different intentions, hence different meanings, so that there is no contradiction between the two propositions "I know my father" and "I don't know my father".

[89] See Sedley 1973: 72 who interprets Diodorus' use of the paradox of the Veiled man "to back up the Eleatic thesis that there can be no true knowledge of the physical world". Although there is a disagreement about the dependence on the Parmenides tradition (see Muller 1988: 71-75), scholars seem to agree that position is based on the denial of the possibility of knowledge of the physical world.

[90] There are various doubts on this succession, see Decleva Caizzi 1981: 132-135.

[91] Translation in *Testimonianze* Decleva Caizzi 2020.

[92] Aenesidemus said that "Pyrrho did not determine anything dogmatically because of the conflict of arguments" (διὰ τὴν ἀντιλογίαν) (T8 DC).

[93] *Phaedo* 89d-90c and *Respublica* 479a-c, two texts in which Plato uses the *ou mallon* formula to describe the possibility of attributing contradictory predicates to sensible objects.

In sum, the Epicurean theory of knowledge can be interpreted as a powerful response to the wave of epistemic pessimism that emerged in the end of the fourth century. The argument of Us. 255 which bridges between *zetesis* and *prolepsis* can be interpreted a key element of this empirical response. The fact that Sextus uses this argument to support his position should not be interpreted as evidence of dialogue or convergence between the two schools. Rather, Sextus' use of the argument clearly shows that the linguistic and epistemic status of *prolepsis* is one of the main philosophical disagreements between Epicureanism and Skepticism.[94]

REFERENCES

Annas, J., – Barnes, J., 1994, *Sextus Empiricus: Outlines of Scepticism*, Cambridge-New York: Cambridge University Press.

Asmis, E., 1984, *Epicurus' scientific method*, Ithaca: Cornell University Press.

Bailey, C. (ed.), 1926, *Epicurus: The Extant Remains*, Oxford: Clarendon Press.

Barigazzi, A., 1969, "Épicure et le scepticisme", in *Actes du VIIIe Congrès Paris, 5-10 avril 1968*, Paris: Les Belles Lettres: 286-293.

Barnes, J., 1996, "Epicurus: Meaning and Thinking", in M. Gigante – G. Giannantoni (eds.), *Epicurismo Greco e Romano: Atti del Congresso Internazionale Napoli, 19-26 Maggio 1993*, Naples: Bibliopolis: 197-220.

Besnier, B., 1994, "Épicure et la définition", in L. Jerphagnon – J. Lagrée – D. Delattre (eds.), *In honorem Jean-Paul Dumont. Ainsi parlaient les Anciens*, Lille: Presses Universitaires du Septentrion: 117-130.

Betegh, G., – Tsouna, V., forthcoming, "Epicureans on Preconceptions and Other Concepts", in G. Betegh – V. Tsouna (eds.), *Conceptualising Concepts in Greek Philosophy*. Cambridge: Cambridge University Press.

Bett, R. (ed.), 1997, *Sextus Empiricus. Against the Ethicists (Adversus Mathematicos XI)*, Oxford: Clarendon Press.

Bett, R., 2000, *Pyrrho, His Antecedents, and His Legacy*, Oxford-New York: Oxford University Press.

Bett, R. (ed.), 2005, *Sextus Empiricus. Against the Logicians*, Cambridge: Cambridge University Press.

Bett, R. (transl.), 2018, *Sextus Empiricus: Against Those in the Disciplines*, Oxford: Oxford University Press.

---

[94] Parts of this paper were presented in 2022, at the Venezia Spider conference; in the *Prolepsis* program I organized at the Université Paris 1 Panthéon-Sorbonne; and in Prague's Institute of Philosophy. I would like to thank all the organizers and participants at these events – especially Frederik Bakker, Gábor Betegh, Mauro Bonazzi, Marc-Antoine Gavray, Alain Gigandet, Matyáš Hvradas, Francesca Masi, Stefano Maso, Vladimír Mikeš, Pierre-Marie Morel, Attila Németh, Voula Tsouna, Francesco Verde, Diego Zucca – for their comments and questions. I am also grateful to André Laks and Plinio Junqueira Smith for their comments and in-depth discussion of this paper.

Bett, R., forthcoming, "Doing Things with Concepts in Sextus Empiricus", in G. Betegh – V. Tsouna (eds.), *Conceptualising Concepts in Greek Philosophy*, Cambridge: Cambridge University Press.
Bonazzi, M., 2017, "The Platonist Appropriation of Stoic Epistemology", in T. Engberg-Pedersen (ed.), *From Stoicism to Platonism: The Development of Philosophy, 100 BCE–100 CE*, Cambridge: Cambridge University Press: 120-141.
Brochard, V., 2002, *Les sceptiques grecs*, 4th ed., Paris: Le Livre de poche.
Brunschwig, J., 1988, "Sextus Empiricus on the kriterion: the skeptic as conceptual legatee", in J. M. Dillon – A. A. Long (eds.), *The Question of 'Eclecticism'. Studies in Later Greek Philosophy*, Berkeley: University of California Press: 145-175.
Brunschwig, J., 1996, "Le fragment DK 70 B 1 de Métrodore de Chio", in K. Algra – P. van der Horst – D. Runia (eds.), *Studies in the History & Historiography of Ancient Philosophy*, Leiden-New York-Cologne: Brill: 21-38.
Burnyeat, M. F., 2017, "'All the World's a Stage-Painting': Scenery, Optics, and Greek Epistemology", in *Oxford Studies in Ancient Philosophy* 52: 33-76.
Corti, L., 2009, *Scepticisme et langage*, Paris: Vrin.
Couissin, P., 1929, "L'origine et l'évolution de l'*épochè*", *Revue des études grecques* 42: 373-397.
Curd, P., 2001, "Why Democritus was not a Skeptic", in A. Preus (ed.), *Before Plato*, Albany: State University of New York Press: 149-169.
Decleva Caizzi, F. (ed.), 1981, *Pirrone. Testimonianze*, Naples: Bibliopolis.
Decleva Caizzi, F., 1984, "Pirrone e Democrito: Gli atomi: un 'mito'?", *Elenchos* 5: 5-23.
Decleva Caizzi, F. (ed.), 2020, *Pirrone. Testimonianze*, 2nd ed., Milan: LED.
Desbordes, F., 1982, "Le langage sceptique. Notes sur le *Contre les grammairiens* de Sextus Empiricus", *Langages* 65: 47-74.
Dorandi, T. (ed.), 2013, *Diogenes Laertius. Lives of Eminent Philosophers*, Cambridge: Cambridge University Press.
Döring, K., 1972, *Die Megariker: Kommentierte Sammlung der Testimonien*, Amsterdam: B. R. Grüner.
Fine, G., 2014, *The possibility of inquiry: Meno's paradox from Socrates to Sextus*, Oxford: Oxford University Press.
Gigante, M., 1981, *Scetticismo e epicureismo: per l'avviamento di un discorso storiografico*, Naples: Bibliopolis.
Giovacchini, J., 2003, "Le refus épicurien de la définition", *Cahiers Philosophiques de Strasbourg* 15: 71-90.
Giovacchini, J., 2023, "Thinking or Speaking: the Paradoxes of the Epicurean Theory of Language", in F. G. Masi – P.-M. Morel – F. Verde (eds.), *Epicureanism and Scientific Debates: Antiquity and Late Reception*, Leuven: Leuven University Press: 15-37.
Glidden, D. K., 1985, "Epicurean prolepsis", *Oxford Studies in Ancient Philosophy* 3: 175-217.
Glidden, D. K., 1983a, "Epicurean semantics", in ΣΥΖΗΤΗΣΙΣ. *Studi sull' epicureismo greco e latino offerti a Marcello Gigante*, Naples: Macchiaroli: 185-226.
Glidden, D. K., 1983b, "Skeptic Semiotics", *Phronesis* 28: 213-255.
Glidden, D. K., 1986, "Marcello Gigante and the Sceptical Epicurean", *Ancient Philosophy* 6: 169-176.

Glidden, D. K., 1990, "Colloquium 11: Epicurean Thought", *Proceedings of the Boston Area Colloquium in Ancient Philosophy* 6: 413-446.

Glidden, D. K., 1994, "Parrots, Pyrrhonists and Native Speakers", in S. Everson (ed.), *Language*, New York: Cambridge University Press: 129-148.

Hammerstaedt, J., 1996, "Il ruolo della πρόληψις epicurea nell'interpretazione di Epicuro, Epistula ad Herodotum 37sg", in G. Giannantoni – M. Gigante (eds.), *Epicurismo Greco e Romano : Atti del Congresso internazionale Napoli, 19-26 maggio 1993*, Naples: Bibliopolis: 221-237.

Havrda, M., 2022, "Fragments of Greek Epistemology in *Stromateis* II", *Adamantius* 28: 208-221.

Laursen, S., 1997, "The later parts of Epicurus, *On Nature*, 25th Book", *Cronache Ercolanesi* 27: 5-82.

Leone, G., 2002, "Epicuro, *Della natura*, libro XXXIV (PHerc. 1431)", *Cronache ercolanesi* 32: 7-135.

Leone, G., 2003, "Rileggendo il XXVIII libro *Della natura* di Epicuro: riflessioni e proposte", *Cronache Ercolanesi* 33: 159-64.

Long, A. A., 1971, "*Aisthesis, prolepsis* and linguistic theory in Epicurus", *Bulletin of the Institute of Classical Studies* 18: 114-133.

Machuca, D. E., 2013, "La critique du critère de vérité épicurien chez Sextus Empiricus: Un scepticisme sur le monde extérieur ?", in S. Marchand – S. Verde (eds.), *Épicurisme et scepticisme*, Rome: Sapienza Università Editrice: 105-127.

Machuca, D. E., 2021, "Can the Skeptic Search for Truth?", *Elenchos* 42: 321-349.

Marchand, S., 2010, "Le sceptique cherche-t-il vraiment la vérité ?", *Revue de Métaphysique et de Morale* 65: 125-141.

Marchand, S., 2013, "Le statut particulier de l'épicurisme dans le néo-pyrrhonisme", in S. Marchand – S. Verde (eds.), *Épicurisme et Scepticisme*, Rome: Sapienza Università Editrice: 63-82.

Marchand, S., 2015, "Sextus Empiricus, scepticisme et philosophie de la vie quotidienne", *Philosophie Antique* 15: 91-119.

Marchand, S., 2019, "Énésidème et le phénomène commun. Relativisme, empirisme et scepticisme", in S. Marchand – D. Machuca (eds.), *Les Raisons du doute : Études sur le scepticisme antique*, Paris: Classiques Garnier: 241-270.

Marchand, S., – Verde, F. (eds.), 2013, *Épicurisme et scepticisme*. Rome: Sapienza Università Editrice.

Masi, F. G., 2023, "Language Theory, Scientific Terminology and Linguistic Controversies in Epicurus' On Nature", in F. G. Masi, – P.-M. Morel – F. Verde (eds.), *Epicureanism and Scientific Debates: Antiquity and Late Reception*, Leuven: Leuven University Press: 39-63.

Morel, P.-M., 1998, "Démocrite. Connaissance et apories", *Revue Philosophique de la France et de l'Étranger* 188: 145-163.

Morel, P.-M., 2008, "Method and evidence: on the epicurean preconception", *Proceedings of the Boston Area Colloquium in Ancient Philosophy* 23: 25-48.

Muller, R., 1985, *Les Mégariques : fragments et témoignages*, Paris: Vrin.

Muller, R., 1988, *Introduction à la pensée des Mégariques*, Paris: Vrin.

Obbink, D., 1992, "What all men believe must be true: Common conceptions and *consensio omnium* in Aristotle and Hellenistic philosophy", *Oxford Studies in Ancient Philosophy* 10: 193-231.

Pease, A. S. (ed.), 1955, Cicero. *De natura deorum* (2 vols.), Cambridge, MA: Harvard University Press.

Perin, C., 2010, *The Demands of Reason: An Essay on Pyrrhonian Scepticism*. Oxford: Oxford University Press.

Piergiacomi, E., 2017, "Naming the Principles in Democritus: An Epistemological Problem", *Apeiron* 50: 435-448.

Rackham, H. (transl.), 1951, Cicero. *De natura deorum ; Academica*. London-Cambridge, MA: W. Heinemann-Harvard University Press (Loeb Classical Library).

Rover, C., 2022, "Lucretius' prolepsis", *Elenchos* 43: 279-314.

Rover, C., 2023, "Lucretius' Epistemological Language", in F. G. Masi – P.-M. Morel – F. Verde (eds.), *Epicureanism and Scientific Debates: Antiquity and Late Reception*. Leuven: Leuven University Press: 105-135.

Sedley, D. N., 1973, "Epicurus *On nature* book 28", *Cronache ercolanesi* 3: 5-79.

Sedley, D. N., 1983, "Epicurus' refutation of determinism", in ΣΥΖΗΤΗΣΙΣ: *studi sull' epicureismo greco e romano offerti a Marcello Gigante*, Naples: Bibliopolis: 11-51.

Sedley, D. N., 1992, "Sextus Empiricus and the atomist criteria of truth", *Elenchos* 13: 21-56.

Smith, P. J., 2022, *Sextus Empiricus' neo-Pyrrhonism: Skepticism as a rationally ordered experience*, Cham: Springer.

Spinelli, E., 1991, "Sceptics and Language : *phōnaí* and *lógoi* in Sextus Empiricus", *Histoire, épistémologie, langage* XIII (2): 57-70.

Spinelli, E., 1995, *Sextus Empiricus. Contro gli etici*, Naples: Bibliopolis.

Spinelli, E., 2013, "Sextus Empiricus et le τέλος épicurien: le plaisir est-il par nature digne d'être choisi ?", in S. Marchand – F. Verde (eds.), *Épicurisme et Scepticisme*, Rome: Sapienza Università Editrice: 151-166.

Spinelli, E., 2014, "Contre la rhétorique: langage pyrrhonien et « usage commun de la vie » selon Sextus Empiricus", in J.-M. Counet (ed.), *Philosophie et langage ordinaire de l'antiquité à la renaissance*, Paris/Louvain: Peeters: 97-111.

Spinelli, E., 2020, "Un ginepraio scettico nel XXXIV libro Sulla natura di Epicuro? Fra ipotesi esegetiche e polemica filosofica", in G. Leone – F. G. Masi – F. Verde (eds.), *Vedere l'invisibile. Rileggendo il XXXIV libro Sulla natura di Epicuro (PHerc. 1431)*, Naples: Centro Internazionale per lo Studio dei Papiri Ercolanesi Editore: 95-105.

Striker, G., 1996, "The Problem of the Criterion", in *Essays in Hellenistic Epistemology and Ethics*, Cambridge: Cambridge University Press: 150-165.

Svavarsson, S. H., 2004, "Pyrrho's Undecidable Nature", *Oxford Studies in Ancient Philosophy* 27: 249-295.

Tepedino Guerra, A., 1990, "Il contributo di Metrodoro di Lampsaco alla formazione della teoria epicurea del linguaggio", *Cronache Ercolanesi* 20: 17-25.

Tsouna, V., 2016, "Epicurean Preconceptions", *Phronesis* 61: 160-221.

Warren, J., 2002, *Epicurus and Democritean Ethics: an Archaeology of* Ataraxia. New York-Cambridge: Cambridge University Press.

Westerink, L.G. (ed.), 1977, *[Damascius] The Greek Commentaries on Plato's* Phaedo, Amsterdam: North-Holland Publishing Co.

White, S. (transl.), 2021, *Diogenes Laertius: Lives of Eminent Philosophers: An Edited Translation*, Cambridge: Cambridge University Press.

ALEXANDER OF APHRODISIAS AND THE NATURALNESS OF JUSTICE (*MANTISSA* 19): AN ATTACK AGAINST EPICURUS?

Maddalena Bonelli

Mantissa 19[1] deals with a canonical theme of the reflection of Hellenistic philosophy – Stoic but also Epicurean, that of the existence or non-existence of natural justice.[2] As is often the case, here, too, 'Alexander' of Aphrodisias[3] tackles a crucial issue of that time by moving within strictly Aristotelian coordinates.[4] Generally the polemic is against the Stoics, who share with Aristotle the thesis according to which justice is by nature, maintaining though that positive laws derive force and efficacy (*vis*) from a single eternal law, which is identified with divine rationality itself.[5] However, as I will try to show, a part of *Mantissa* 19 seems instead to attack the Epicurean thesis of social coexistence as conventional. At the same time, we seem to be able to detect an Epicurean influence in Alexander's own treatment of justice.

1. JUSTICE IS BY NATURE

In the first lines of *Mantissa* 19 (156, 28-30), Alexander proposes an argument that will be repeated and defended later in the text:

[T1]
That what is just [is so] by nature.
That what is just [is so] by nature is shown by the fact that <human beings> are communal by nature, but community cannot survive without justice.[6] (transl. Sharples 2004)

---

[1] Alexander of Aphrodisias, *De animi liber Mantissa* (from now Alexander, *Mantissa*). I would like to thank the participants at the Venice symposium for their helpful comments.
[2] Yet as Sharples 2005: 280 rightly points out, the question of whether justice is a matter of nature or convention is a central one from the time of the Sophists.
[3] Talking of 'Alexander' regarding the *Mantissa*, as with other collections of *Quaestiones*, is a delicate matter. Indeed, it is not certain that Alexander is the author, but it is certainly material from his school. See in this regard Sharples 2005: 282-283.
[4] This is what Accattino states (2015: 44), and he is certainly right. His claim, however, needs to be nuanced, because Alexander makes use also of Platonic, Stoic, and probably Epicurean material, as I will try to show.
[5] On this topic see for example Cicero, *De legibus* II 8-10 (= *SVF* III 316).
[6] Alex. *Mantissa* 19,156, 28-30: Ὅτι φύσει τὸ δίκαιον. Ὅτι φύσει τὸ δίκαιον, δείκνυται ἐκ τοῦ φύσει κοινωνικόν <μὲν> εἶναι [30] <τὸν ἄνθρωπον>, μὴ δύνασθαι δὲ κοινωνίαν διαμένειν χωρὶς δικαιοσύνης.

The argument proposed by Alexander is the following one:
1) human beings are communal by nature;
2) community cannot survive without justice;
3) therefore, justice is by nature.

In order to work, the argument must be transformed as follows, and one premise must be added:[7]
1*) the human community is by nature;
2*) the human community cannot survive without justice;
3*) if X is necessary for Y to survive, and Y exists by nature, then X exists by nature;[8]
4*) therefore, justice is by nature.

However, the first part of *Mantissa* 19 (156, 31-157, 18) aims to demonstrate just that human beings are communal by nature. Elsewhere, Alexander states, "that community is worthy to be chosen by man on its own account, is clearly recognisable from the fact that community is natural for them".[9] Later (see below, note 11) Alexander will show that he considers 1) and 1*) as equivalent. In any case, from the argument of *Mantissa* 19,156, 28-30 it emerges that, more modestly than for the Stoics, the origin of natural justice is found in the community, and the community in the natural impulse of men to live together. I will not dwell on this part: I am interested in moving on to the next section, where perhaps we can find an attack on the Epicureans and at the same time an Epicurean influence.[10]

2. IF JUSTICE IS BY CONVENTION, JUSTICE IS BY NATURE (*MANTISSA* 19, 157, 18-159, 9)

2.1. The argument

Next, in *Mantissa* 19 (157, 18-159, 14) Alexander tries to prove that justice is by nature (see *supra*, 156, 28-30 and note 6), starting from the opposite thesis, according to which justice is by convention, or stipulation:

---

[7] Thanks to Giulia Mingucci for drawing my attention to the formalization of the argument, as well as to my anonymous reviewers for pointing out the need for an additional premise.

[8] Alexander asserts precisely this sort of premise in *Mantissa* 19,157, 18-3 (see *infra*, and note 13).

[9] Alexander, *Ethical Problems*, 147, 24-26: ἀλλὰ μὴν ὅτι δι᾿ αὑτὸ τοῖς ἀνθρώποις αἱρετὸν ἡ κοινωνία, γνῶναι πρόχειρον ἀπό τε τοῦ κατὰ φύσιν αὐτοῖς εἶναι τὴν κοινωνίαν. Perhaps Alexander is thinking here to the passage in the *Politics* (1252a25-1253a1) in which Aristotle, through the description of the genesis and development of human communities, thinks to show that the human community (namely, the *polis*) is by nature. A recent article on this topic is Rapp 2021.

[10] For the *Mantissa*'s first part, see Sharples 2005: 283-287; Accattino 2015: 43-45.

[T2]
Even from the same statement, that what is just is [so] by stipulation, one could attest that human beings are communal by nature. For if all human beings need [20] what is just and this agreement naturally – for [it is] not that some do and some do not – and they adopt this as something that preserves community, then [being] communal will belong to all human beings by nature. And if community is by nature,[11] then it is necessary for what is just, too, to belong to them by nature. For it is not possible to say that [they] need what is just, without also [saying] that what is just is by nature[12] [25]. For that, without which it is impossible for some one of the things that belong to us by nature to be, must necessarily also [itself] be by nature. For example: it is impossible to see without eyes; and for this reason, since seeing is by nature, so too are the eyes by nature. Similarly ears are by nature, for it is not possible to hear without these, and hearing is by nature; and in general the sense organs [belong] to us [30] by nature, since the activities performed through them, too, belong to us by nature. If then we are communal by nature, but community is impossible without justice, it is necessary for what is just, too, to exist by nature.[13] (transl. Sharples 2004 slightly modified)

According to Alexander, even starting from the thesis that justice is [so] by stipulation, we attest that human beings are communal by nature. Yet if so, then justice too is by nature.

The argument goes like this:
1°) if justice is by stipulation, human beings are communal by nature;
2°) if community is by nature,[14] it is necessary that justice is by nature;
3°) conclusion: justice is by nature.

Justification of 1°): if human beings naturally need to agree on rules in order to live together – namely, if they need justice by stipulation – then they cannot but live together, that is, they are by nature inclined to live together.

Justification of 2°): if human beings are by nature inclined to live together, the rules which govern living together will also be by nature. Here Alexander considers

---

[11] In these lines it seems clear to me that for Alexander 1) "human beings are communal by nature" is equivalent to 1*) "the human community is by nature".
[12] 157, 25 φύσει: this is an addition suggested by Bruns.
[13] Alex. *Mantissa* 19, 157, 18-3: καὶ ἐξ αὐτοῦ τοῦ θέσει λέγειν τὸ δίκαιον εἶναι μαρτυροῖτ' ἂν τὸ φύσει κοινωνικὸν εἶναι τὸν ἄνθρωπον. εἰ γὰρ δέονται [20] μὲν τοῦ δικαίου καὶ τῆς συνθήκης ταύτης φυσικῶς πάντες ἄνθρωποι (οὐ γὰρ οἱ μέν, οἱ δὲ οὔ), τοῦτο δὲ ὡς τῆς κοινωνίας ὂν σωστικὸν παραλαμβάνουσιν, εἴη ἂν πᾶσιν ἀνθρώποις τὸ κοινωνικὸν ὑπάρχον φύσει. φύσει δὲ οὔσης τῆς κοινωνίας ἀνάγκη καὶ τὸ δίκαιον αὐτοῖς ὑπάρχειν φύσει. οὐ γὰρ οἷόν τε λέγειν τοῦ δεῖσθαι δικαίου, μηκέτι δὲ εἶναι τὸ δίκαιον φύσει. [25] οὐ γὰρ χωρὶς ἀδύνατον εἶναί τι τῶν ὑπαρχόντων ἡμῖν <φύσει>, ἀνάγκη καὶ τοῦτο εἶναι φύσει. οἷον ἀδύνατον ὁρᾶν χωρὶς ὀφθαλμῶν. διό, καὶ τοῦ ὁρᾶν ὄντος φύσει, καὶ οἱ ὀφθαλμοὶ φύσει. ὁμοίως καὶ τὰ ὦτα φύσει (οὔτε γὰρ χωρὶς τούτων ἀκούειν οἷόν τε, καὶ τὸ ἀκούειν φύσει), καὶ καθόλου τὰ αἰσθητήρια ἡμῖν φύσει τῷ καὶ τὰς ἐνεργείας τὰς δι' αὐτῶν ὑπάρχειν ἡμῖν [30] φύσει. εἰ δὴ καὶ κοινωνικοὶ μέν ἐσμεν φύσει, ἀδύνατος δ' ἡ κοινωνία χωρὶς δικαιοσύνης, ἀνάγκη καὶ τὸ δίκαιον εἶναι φύσει.
[14] See *supra*, note 11.

"by nature" conventional rules: i) by comparing eye/vision, ear/hearing, and in general sense organs/perception with the pair justice/community; and ii) by defining justice as a rule, or set of rules, for living together (lines 25-30).

So, even if justice is by stipulation, justice is by nature. For if rules are by stipulation, their foundation is natural, since all humans are forced to give themselves rules. Furthermore, if humans are by nature inclined to live in society, then the rules that regulate living-together, namely justice, will also be by nature. Indeed, that without which it is impossible to have something that belongs to man by nature, must itself be by nature.

2.2. The Aristotelian component of the argument

[T3]
If, because different things are just among different peoples, for this reason they[15] say that [what is just does] not [exist] by nature, it is clear that they will say that that which is the same among all [does exist] by nature. And if they will say that what is written down is based on an agreement, and not by nature, for the reason that it is written down, it is clear that it is necessary for these people [35] to say that what does not have its force depending on writing is by nature and is not based on an agreement. But there are many things like this, <which>[16] we are accustomed to call, from the very [feature] that applies to them, "unwritten laws", which are common to all human beings, at any rate those that are not incapacitated[17] [158]. Respecting one's elders and revering the divine and honouring one's parents and betters are unwritten and common [elements of] justice observed by nature among all human beings. For they neither make agreements with one another about these things nor write them down, but taking these as agreed and confirmed [5] by nature as being so, they make laws about the manner of the honour, some in this way, some in that, and some thinking that they will do these things through [actions] of this sort, others through those of that sort, those in which each person is previously habituated; it is concerning these that, from this point on, justice based on an agreement has its force. For it is justice and legality based on an agreement that tells us to revere the divine or honour our parents in this way or that. And for this [10] reason each of these things [is done] in different ways among different peoples at different times; but honouring [parents] and revering the divine is established in the nature of human beings always and among all. And for this reason [it does not apply] at one time but not at another, or among some people but not among others.[18] (transl. Sharples 2004, slightly modified)

---

[15] Who? See *infra*, in the conclusion.
[16] 157, 36: <ἃ> this is an addition suggested by Bruns.
[17] Sharples 2004: 170, note 575, remarks that this observation is not found in the Aristotelian text that underlies this passage, namely, *NE* V. There is not even a reference in *NE* V to unwritten laws.
[18] Alex. *Mantissa* 19,157, 31-158, 17: εἰ δ', ὅτι παρ' ἄλλοις ἄλλο τι δίκαιον, διὰ τοῦτο οὐ φύσει φήσουσιν αὐτό, δῆλον, ὡς φύσει τοῦτ' ἐροῦσιν, ὃ παρὰ πᾶσίν ἐστιν ταὐτό. καὶ εἰ τὸ ἔγγραφον ἐροῦσιν, διότι ἐστὶν ἔγγραφον, κατὰ συνθήκην καὶ οὐ φύσει, δῆλον ὡς ἀνάγκη τούτοις [35] φύσει καὶ μὴ κατὰ συνθήκην λέγειν τὸ τὴν ἰσχὺν οὐκ ἐν τοῖς γράμμασιν ἔχον. ἔστι δὲ τοιαῦτα πολλὰ <ἃ> καὶ προσαγορεύειν εἰώθαμεν ἀπ'αὐτοῦ τοῦ πάθους ἄγραφα νόμιμα, κοινὰ πᾶσιν ἀνθρώποις ὄντα, τοῖς γε μὴ πεπηρωμένοις [158]. τό τε γὰρ αἰδεῖσθαι

Here, Alexander tries to show that there is no contrast between justice by nature and justice by convention. The arguments presented in these lines are based on certain Aristotelian theories found in various texts, which Alexander combines following the well-known exegetical criterion of explaining Aristotle by Aristotle.[19]
Here are the arguments:

1) lines 157, 30-31: those who deny that there is a natural justice rely on the observation that the norms of justice vary from place to place; but if they say that, they have to admit that norms identical for everyone are by nature;
2) lines 157, 31-158, 3: those who deny natural justice remark that laws have force insofar as they are in written form; but if they say that, they must admit that if there are rules that have force regardless of the fact that they have been written, then these are natural. These, Alexander states, are the unwritten laws (respect the elders, worship the divine, honour parents and those who are better);
3) lines 158, 3-10: in all rules of justice sanctioned by men, a natural component and a conventional component coexist, the latter consisting in the way in which the natural component (i.e., the unwritten laws) is formalized.

As Accattino rightly observes,[20] the criterion of the variability of laws to establish their conventionality is the old argument of the Sophists, along with the thesis that laws established and written by humans are conventional. Yet those who say that, Alexander remarks, have to accept that there are natural laws, that is, those laws that have force regardless of the fact that they have been agreed upon and written down. Here, Alexander mentions unwritten laws, which Aristotle had identified as "common natural right" in *Rhetoric*.[21] Now, if there are unwritten laws, there are laws by nature. If anything, they will vary in the way in which they are expressed.

It is complicated to establish the debt to Aristotle in what Alexander says in lines 158, 3-10, namely, that laws are natural – they are in fact those that are unwritten and accepted by all humans – but that the arbitrariness of humans merely intervenes in determining how they are applied, which can indeed vary. Alexander is certainly

---

τοὺς πρεσβυτέρους καὶ τὸ σέβειν τὸ θεῖον καὶ τὸ τιμᾶν τοὺς γονέας καὶ τοὺς βελτίονας, ἄγραφα καὶ κοινὰ δίκαια παρὰ πᾶσιν ἀνθρώποις φύσει τηρούμενα. οὐ γὰρ περὶ τούτων οὔτε συντίθενται πρὸς ἀλλήλους οὔτε γράφουσιν, ἀλλ' ὡς ὁμολογουμένων καὶ κεκυρωμένων [5] ὑπὸ τῆς φύσεως οὕτως ἔχειν, περὶ τοῦ τρόπου τῆς τιμῆς νομοθετοῦσιν, οἱ μὲν οὕτως, οἱ δὲ οὕτως, καὶ οἱ μὲν διὰ τοιῶνδε, οἱ δὲ διὰ τοιῶνδε ταῦτα ποιήσειν ἡγούμενοι, ἐν οἷς ἂν ἕκαστος ᾖ προειθισμένος, περὶ ἃ λοιπὸν τὸ κατὰ συνθήκην δίκαιον ἰσχὺν ἔχει. ὧδε μὲν γὰρ ἢ ὧδε σέβειν τὸ θεῖον ἢ τιμᾶν τοὺς γονεῖς τὸ κατὰ συνθήκην δίκαιόν τε καὶ [10] νόμιμον λέγει. διὸ καὶ ἄλλοτε ἄλλως παρ' ἄλλοις τούτων ἕκαστον. ἀεὶ δὲ καὶ παρὰ πᾶσίν ἐστι τὸ τιμᾶν τε καὶ σέβειν τὸ θεῖον ἐν τῇ τῶν ἀνθρώπων ἐνιδρυμένον φύσει. διὸ καὶ οὐχ ὁτὲ μέν, ὁτὲ δ' οὔ, οὐδὲ παρ' οἷς μέν, παρ' οἷς δ' οὔ.

[19] On Alexander's exegetical strategies, see, for example, Donini 1995: 107-129.
[20] Accattino 2015: 47.
[21] See Aristotle, *Rhetoric* I 13, 1374a24-b4ss; I 15 (about that see Sharples 2005: 286).

indebted to *Nicomachean Ethics* V 10, 1334b18-1335a5 (= *EE* IV 10)[22] – a very difficult passage of which Alexander retains only the central thesis and little else, namely:
  i) some examples of conventional law that seem conventional ways of realizing unwritten laws (*NE* V 10, 1334b21-22: "paying a ransom of the one mina or sacrificing a goat rather than two sheep");
  ii) the criticism of the criterion of variability as characteristic of conventional laws (*NE* V 10, 1334b24-27: "Some people think that all (justice) is like this, because they see that what is natural is unvarying and has the same force everywhere, just as fire burns both here and in Persia, but what is just changes (from one place to another)");
  iii) the thesis which governs the entire passage, according to which natural and conventional components coexist in all rules of justice sanctioned by men.

Aristotle in fact says little about natural justice,[23] which is perhaps the reason why Alexander, following the exegetical criterion already mentioned,[24] tries to fill the

---

[22] Aristotle, *EN* V 10, 1334b15-1335a5: Τοῦ δὲ πολιτικοῦ δικαίου τὸ μὲν φυσικόν ἐστι τὸ δὲ νομικόν, φυσικὸν μὲν τὸ πανταχοῦ τὴν αὐτὴν ἔχον δύναμιν, καὶ οὐ τῷ δοκεῖν ἢ μή, νομικὸν δὲ ὃ ἐξ ἀρχῆς μὲν οὐδὲν διαφέρει οὕτως ἢ ἄλλως, ὅταν δὲ θῶνται, διαφέρει, οἷον τὸ μνᾶς λυτροῦσθαι, ἢ τὸ αἶγα θύειν ἀλλὰ μὴ δύο πρόβατα, ἔτι ὅσα ἐπὶ τῶν καθ' ἕκαστα νομοθετοῦσιν, οἷον τὸ θύειν Βρασίδᾳ, καὶ τὰ ψηφισματώδη. δοκεῖ δ' ἐνίοις εἶναι πάντα τοιαῦτα, ὅτι τὸ μὲν φύσει ἀκίνητον καὶ πανταχοῦ τὴν αὐτὴν ἔχει δύναμιν, ὥσπερ τὸ πῦρ καὶ ἐνθάδε καὶ ἐν Πέρσαις καίει,τὰ δὲ δίκαια κινούμενα ὁρῶσιν. τοῦτο δ' οὐκ ἔστιν οὕτως ἔχον, ἀλλ' ἔστιν ὥς· καίτοι παρά γε τοῖς θεοῖς ἴσως οὐδαμῶς, παρ' ἡμῖν δ' ἔστι μέν τι καὶ φύσει, κινητὸν μέντοι πᾶν, ἀλλ' ὅμως ἐστὶ τὸ μὲν φύσει. τὸ δ' οὐ φύσει. ποῖον δὲ φύσει τῶν ἐνδεχομένων καὶ ἄλλως ἔχειν, καὶ ποῖον οὒ ἀλλὰ νομικὸν καὶ συνθήκῃ, εἴπερ ἄμφω κινητὰ ὁμοίως, δῆλον. καὶ ἐπὶ τῶν ἄλλων ὁ αὐτὸς ἁρμόσει διορισμός· φύσει γὰρ ἡ δεξιὰ κρείττων, καίτοι ἐνδέχεται πάντας ἀμφιδεξίους γενέσθαι. τὰ δὲ κατὰ συνθήκην καὶ τὸ συμφέρον τῶν [1135a] δικαίων ὅμοιά ἐστι τοῖς μέτροις· οὐ γὰρ πανταχοῦ ἴσα τὰ οἰνηρὰ καὶ σιτηρὰ μέτρα, ἀλλ' οὗ μὲν ὠνοῦνται, μείζω, οὐδὲ πωλοῦσιν, ἐλάττω. ὁμοίως δὲ καὶ τὰ μὴ φυσικὰ ἀλλ'ἀνθρώπινα δίκαια οὐ ταὐτὰ πανταχοῦ, ἐπεὶ οὐδ' αἱ πολιτεῖαι, ἀλλὰ μία μόνον πανταχοῦ κατὰ φύσιν ἡ ἀρίστη ("Of justice in a city-state part is natural and part is conventional; natural that which has the same force everywhere, and not according to what people decide, conventional that where at the start it makes no difference whether it is this way or that, but when they make the law it does, like paying a ransom of the one mina or sacrificing a goat rather than two sheep, and also all laws made about individuals, as in the case of sacrificing to Brasidas, and decrees that are voted on. Some people think that all (justice) is like this, because they see that what is natural is unvarying and has the same force everywhere, just as fire burns both here and in Persia, but what is just changes (from one place to another). This is not so, however, though it is so in a way. Among the gods, perhaps, it is not so at all; among us there is some (justice) that is by nature, even though all is variable – nevertheless, there is some that is by nature and some that is not. What of sort of thing among these that can also be otherwise is by nature, and what sort is not but conventional and by agreement, [even] if both are similarly changeable, is clear. And the same distinction will fit the other cases too: by nature the right [hand] is stronger, but it is possible for all become ambidextrous. Justice that is according to an agreement and to what is advantageous (συμφέρον) is similar to measures; for the measures for wine and corn are not equivalent everywhere, but bigger where they are buying and smaller where they are selling. Similarly justice that is not natural but man-made is not the same everywhere; for neither are the constitutions of states, but (nevertheless) there is one which is in accordance with nature everywhere, (namely) the best" (transl. Sharples 2005)). For the analysis of this passage, see Sharples 2005: 280-283; Accattino 2015: 47-53.

[23] See on that Sharples 2005: 280; Morel 2021, 197-223.

[24] See *supra*, note 19.

gap by referring to the unwritten laws in the *Rhetoric*. Alexander in fact feels the need to mention universal rules, not least because, as Sharples points out,[25] the horizon of his discussion is no longer the *polis*, but the human community in general. Here we can perhaps see the influence of Hellenistic philosophies (Stoic and Epicurean) on Alexander's way of thinking about natural law.

2.3 The Platonic component of the argument

[T4]
That it is justice that holds community together is clear from those who are thought to be most unjust. These are robbers, whose community with one another is preserved by [their] justice towards one another. [20] For it is on account of [their] not taking advantage of one another and not defrauding [one another], and [their] respecting what seems to be superior and preserving what has been agreed, and assisting the weaker, that their community with one another endures, [though] they do altogether the opposite of these things to those whom they wrong. The greatest sign that these things are just by nature is that, if they agreed the opposite things to these with one another as being just [25], their community could not endure, although it would have followed [sc. if justice were purely a matter of agreement] that everything that came about in [the context of] an agreement would preserve community in a similar way. But if certain things preserve community whether people make an agreement or not, and the opposites of these destroy it, then the things that preserve those who make an agreement are by nature, even if they come about in accordance with an agreement. For the agreement seems [30] to be a certain seeking for what is just by nature, and common agreement on what has been found [...].
Moreover, those who decide to act unjustly and engage in robbery do not examine the established laws and engage in robbery and evil-doing through contravening these, but, on the basis that the [actions] through which robbing [takes place] are clearly injustices, [35] they go to it. But if certain things are unjust by nature, and not [unjust merely] through contravening the things that have been agreed on as just, it is also necessary to say that the things opposite to these are just by nature. And that there are things that are unjust by nature is clear from the fact that among all peoples [159], even those who have laws most opposite, there are certain things in common which those who choose to act unjustly do to those that they wrong. For almost all the things that robbers do to those they wrong are the same among all [peoples]. But if so, it is clear that the things opposite to these which are unjust by nature, are just by nature. [5] For acting unjustly is nothing other than contravention of what is just. So, if there is by nature something that is contravention of what is just, it is clear that much sooner will what is just, contravention of which is unjust, be by nature. For contravention of something is posterior to that of which it is contravention. And what is unjust by nature is nothing other than contravention of and contrariety to what is just by nature.[26] (transl. Sharples 2004, slightly modified)

---

[25] Sharples 2005: 287.
[26] Alex. *Mantissa* 19, 158, 17-159, 9: ὅτι γὰρ τὸ δίκαιον συνέχει τὴν κοινωνίαν δῆλόν ἐστιν ἐπὶ τῶν ἀδικωτάτων εἶναι δοκούντων. οὗτοι δέ εἰσιν οἱ λῃσταί, οἷς ἡ πρὸς ἀλλήλους κοινωνία ὑπὸ δικαιοσύνης

This passage starts from the case of the band of brigands, first put forward by Plato in the *Republic*:

[T5]
Suppose a city, or an army, or robbers, or thieves, or any other group of people, are jointly setting about some unjust venture. Do you think they'd be able to get anywhere if they treated one another unjustly? – Of course not. – What if they didn't treat one another unjustly? Wouldn't they stand a much better chance? – They certainly would. – Yes, because the injustice, I imagine, Thrasymachus, produces faction and hatred and fights among them, whereas justice produces co-operation and friendship, doesn't it? – Let's say it does, he said, I don't want to disagree with you. – Thank you, my friend. Now, another question. If it is the function of injustice to produce hatred wherever it goes, then when it makes his appearance among free men and slaves, won't it make them hate one another, and quarrel with one another, and be incapable of any joint enterprise? – Yes, it will.[27] (transl. Griffith 2000, slightly modified)

The passage is located in the Socratic refutation of Thrasymachus' second thesis that "justice is the good of others" (*Rep.* I, 343C), that is, that justice consists in the observance of laws enacted in the interests of the powerful and not of their subjects.[28] The objection to this argument,[29] which is found in the passage under

σώζεται τῆς πρὸς ἀλλήλους. [20] διά τε γὰρ τὸ μὴ πλεονεκτεῖν ἀλλήλους καὶ διὰ τὸ μὴ ψεύδεσθαι, καὶ διὰ τὸ τιμᾶν τὸ κρεῖττον δοκοῦν καὶ τὸ τὰ συγκείμενα φυλάττειν, καὶ διὰ τὸ βοηθεῖν τοῖς ἀσθενεστέροις, διὰ ταῦτα ἡ πρὸς ἀλλήλους αὐτοῖς κοινωνία συμμένει, ὧν πᾶν τοὐναντίον εἰς οὓς ἀδικοῦσιν ποιοῦσιν. ὅτι γὰρ φύσει ταῦτά ἐστι δίκαια, σημεῖον μέγιστον τὸ μηδ', ἂν συνθῶνται [25] τὰ ἀντικείμενα τούτων πρὸς ἀλλήλους ὡς δίκαια, δύνασθαι συμμένειν αὐτῶν τὴν κοινωνίαν, καίτοι γε ἦν ἂν ἀκόλουθον πᾶν ὁμοίως τῆς κοινωνίας εἶναι σωστικὸν ἐν συνθήκῃ γενόμενον. εἰ δὲ τὰ μὲν συνθεμένων καὶ μὴ συνθεμένων τηρεῖ τὴν κοινωνίαν, τὰ δ' ἀντικείμενα τούτων φθείρει, ἃ συνθεμένους σώζει, φύσει ταῦτά ἐστιν, κἂν κατὰ συνθήκην γένηται. ἔοικεν γὰρ [30] ἡ συνθήκη ζήτησίς τις εἶναι τοῦ φύσει δικαίου καὶ ὁμολογία κοινὴ τῶν εὑρημένων […] ἔτι οἱ διεγνωκότες ἀδικεῖν τε καὶ λῃστεύειν οὐκ ἐξετάσαντες τὰ κείμενα νόμιμα διὰ τοῦ ταῦτα παραβαίνειν λῃστεύουσίν [35] τε καὶ κακουργοῦσιν, ἀλλ' ὡς ὄντων φανερῶν ἀδικημάτων, δι' ὧν τὸ λῃστεύειν, ἄγουσιν ἐπ' αὐτό. εἰ δ' ἔστιν ἄδικά τινα φύσει, καὶ οὐ τῇ τῶν συγκειμένων δικαίων παραβάσει, ἀνάγκη καὶ δίκαια φύσει λέγειν εἶναι τὰ τούτοις ἐναντία. ὅτι δέ ἐστιν ἄδικα φύσει, δῆλον ἐκ τοῦ παρὰ πᾶσιν καὶ [159] τοῖς ὑπεναντιωτάτους ἔχουσι νόμους εἶναί τινα κοινά, ἃ οἱ τὸ ἀδικεῖν προαιρούμενοι πράττουσιν, εἰς οὓς ἀδικοῦσιν. πάντα γὰρ σχεδὸν οἱ λῃστεύοντες παρὰ πᾶσιν τὰ αὐτὰ ποιοῦσιν, εἰς οὓς ἀδικοῦσιν. εἰ δὲ τοῦτο, δῆλον ὡς καὶ τὰ τούτοις ἀντικείμενα, οὖσιν ἀδίκοις φύσει, δίκαιά ἐστι φύσει. καὶ [5] γὰρ οὐδ' ἄλλο τί ἐστιν τὸ ἀδικεῖν ἢ παράβασις τοῦ δικαίου. ὥστε εἰ παράβασις δικαίου ἐστίν τις φύσει, δῆλον ὡς καὶ τὸ δίκαιον πολὺ πρότερον, οὗ ἡ παράβασις ἄδικός ἐστι, φύσει. ὕστερον γὰρ ἡ παράβασις τινος ἐκείνου, οὗ ἐστιν παράβασις. οὐδὲν γὰρ ἄλλο ἄδικόν ἐστι τὸ φύσει, ἢ παράβασις καὶ ἐναντίως τοῦ φύσει δικαίου.

[27] Plato, *Republic* I 351c-e: δοκεῖς ἂν ἢ πόλιν ἢ στρατόπεδον ἢ λῃστὰς ἢ κλέπτας ἢ ἄλλο τι ἔθνος, ὅσα κοινῇ ἐπί τι ἔρχεται ἀδίκως, πρᾶξαι ἄν τι δύνασθαι, εἰ ἀδικοῖεν ἀλλήλους; – Οὐ δῆτα, ἦ δ' ὅς. – Τί δ' εἰ μὴ ἀδικοῖεν; οὐ μᾶλλον; – Πάνυ γε. – Στάσεις γάρ που, ὦ Θρασύμαχε, ἥ γε ἀδικία καὶ μίση καὶ μάχας ἐν ἀλλήλοις παρέχει, ἡ δὲ δικαιοσύνη ὁμόνοιαν καὶ φιλίαν· ἦ γάρ; – Ἔστω, ἦ δ' ὅς, ἵνα σοι μὴ διαφέρωμαι. – Ἀλλ' εὖ γε σὺ ποιῶν, ὦ ἄριστε. τόδε δέ μοι λέγε· ἆρα εἰ τοῦτο ἔργον ἀδικίας, μῖσος ἐμποιεῖν ὅπου ἂν ἐνῇ, οὐ καὶ ἐν ἐλευθέροις τε καὶ δούλοις ἐγγιγνομένη μισεῖν ποιήσει ἀλλήλους καὶ στασιάζειν καὶ ἀδυνάτους εἶναι κοινῇ μετ' ἀλλήλων πράττειν; – Πάνυ γε. The example of the band of brigands returns in Cicero *De officiis* II 40, a sign that it must have become a *topos*.
[28] On this passage and on the figure of Thrasymachus in general, see Vegetti 1998: 233-256.
[29] The only really valid Socratic objection, according to Vegetti 1998: 255.

analysis, is that between perfectly unjust individuals – i.e., dedicated to exercising the famous *pleonexia* on both subjects and fellows – no form of cooperation would be possible. The point of the passage is that, according to Socrates, any human association (be it a city, an army, a band of robbers or thieves) that wants to carry out an unjust deed could not achieve any result if the members did injustice to each other. This position allows Socrates to conclude that injustice, by producing hatred and conflict wherever it is found, would render humans incapable of agreeing on any common action.

At first sight, Alexander's passage under analysis would seem to be based exclusively on the Platonic one, at least in the first lines, where the commentator explicates Socrates' argument by stating, as proof that the just holds any human community together, that even the community of robbers is guaranteed by mutual justice (lines 158, 17-20). Alexander suggests that insofar as the robbers do form a band, they have a sense of justice at least to one another, even though they reject same standards of conduct towards people not in their group. Further, Alexander says, it is possible to use the cooperating robbers as an argument in favour of the naturalness of justice since the robbers are acting in contravention of norms that are universal (and knowingly so). Since contraventions are posterior to that which they contravene, then there are prior and universal norms of justice.[30]

In the continuation of the text, however, Alexander presents some interesting insights that go beyond the Platonic text based not only on Aristotelian, but also Hellenistic influences, with particular reference to the Epicureans.

2.4 The Epicurean component of the argument

The first interesting point of *Mantissa* 19, 158, 20-159, 9 is that the justice that holds the community of robbers together consists precisely in that set of unwritten laws (such as not prevaricating and not deceiving one another, honouring the one who appears to be the strongest, keeping pacts, helping the weakest, etc.), which keep all human communities together, including those that outwardly behave in the opposite way, that is, unjustly (lines 158, 20-23). Here the reference is, as we have seen, to Aristotle' *Rhetoric*. The point, central to the whole passage,[31] is a kind of demonstration of the naturalness of unwritten laws. For if justice were only a matter of stipulation, one could stipulate as just the opposite of unwritten laws and, even then, the community would be safeguarded. Yet this situation does not happen, for in the absence of unwritten laws the community dissolves, which is a manifest sign (if not a demonstration) that unwritten laws are laws by nature. If therefore some rules – whether by stipulation or not – preserve the community and others destroy it, those that preserve the community will be by nature (lines 24-29); for, as

---

[30] I would like to thank one of my anonymous reviewers for making these aspects explicit.
[31] See Sharples 2005: 289.

Alexander pointed out,[32] that without which a thing by nature cannot exist, it is also by nature. In lines 29-31, then, Alexander presents a kind of interesting definition of conventionality as a search for what is right by nature and an agreement on what has been found.

The last part of the text (158, 33-159, 9), which is also extremely brilliant, shows that robbers are such not simply because they transgress agreed laws, but because they behave in a way that is patently unjust and recognized as such by all human communities. Still, if there is behaviour that is unjust by nature (that of robbers, recognized by all as unjust), there will also, and previously, be behaviour that is just by nature.

For some scholars, *Mantissa* 19, 158, 17-159, 9 does not merely take up the Platonic *topos*, but indirectly polemicizes against the 'conventionalists' of his time, namely, the Epicureans.[33] It seems to me that in Alexander's text under analysis there is not only an attack on a contractualist position that could be attributable to the Epicureans, but also an influence that the Epicureans themselves exerted on Alexander's theory of legal justice.

Contrary to the commonplace that portrays the Epicurean sage as disinterested in and almost horrified by the political dimension,[34] we find a group of the *Capital Maxims* (*Kyriai Doxai* XXXI-XXXVIII, *apud* DL X, 150-153) attributed to Epicurus concerning legal justice, in which Epicurus speaks of the just by nature, justice, and community (κοινωνία).

In *KD* XXXI[35] Epicurus speaks of the just by nature, closely subordinated to the human community,[36] which he identifies with the advantageous of not wronging each other. The text is problematic[37] and has led scholars to emphasize either the naturalistic or the conventional element.[38] Certainly, in the passage, conventionalism is there, especially because of the use of σύμβολον; but there is also a kind of naturalism, because justice is by nature an inseparable quality of the human community. Indeed, justice expresses the useful, which for the Epicurus coincides

---

[32] See *supra*, note 13.
[33] Striker 1996: 266; Accattino 2015: 54-57. More cautious Sharples 2005: 287-291.
[34] See on this subject Morel 2007: 167-170.
[35] *KD* XXXI: Τὸ τῆς φύσεως δίκαιόν ἐστι σύμβολον τοῦ συμφέροντος εἰς τὸ μὴ βλάπτειν ἀλλήλους μηδὲ βλάπτεσθαι ("Natural justice is a symbol or expression of expediency, to prevent one man from harming or being harmed by another" [transl. Hicks]).
[36] The insistence on human community as origin and goal of the just by nature is also found in Hermarchus, Epicurus' successor at the head of his Garden, according to a long quotation from Porphyry in his *De abstinentia* I, 7-12; see on this subject Morel 2007: 170-172.
[37] On the problematic nature of the text, and particularly the interpretation of the term σύμβολον, see Morel 2007: 176-178; Morel 2015: 580-582. In my opinion we can use here the sense of σύμβολον that we find in the first chapter of Aristotle's *De interpretatione*, namely, "expression".
[38] For an overview of the scholarly positions, see Morel 2000: 393-411 (especially 396) and Morel 2007: 167-186.

with the satisfaction of vital needs.[39] The strict dependence of the just by nature on the human community is also well emphasized by Alexander. However, it is well known that for the Epicureans, humans do not necessarily tend to associate,[40] which certainly weakens the link of consequentiality between human κοινωνία and natural laws. Instead, Alexander emphasizes this link, probably in polemic against the Epicureans. It is reasonable to think that not harming each other is for Alexander an unwritten natural law, which is variously articulated.

Interesting, then, is the Epicurean assertion that the just, conceived as the useful in relation to mutual κοινωνία, is equal for all.[41] Here, Alexander and Epicurus seem to agree, with the difference that for Epicurus mutual coexistence is a social pact,[42] whereas for Alexander it is a natural impulse of men to associate. For both Epicurus and Alexander, then, the application of this general right varies from country to country or for other reasons. Indeed, the fact that what is just is the same for everyone does not detract from the fact that laws may vary from place to place and age to age – in other words, they are or should be modifiable.

In short, the Epicurean position is more complex than simple conventionalism since Epicurus will agree that what is just in general is what contributes best to human communities living well, but that the specific *nomoi* which best contribute to that aim will vary depending on circumstance.[43] Alexander shares this view. On the other and, Epicurus says that, when they no longer serve the common good, which is just by nature, laws can be replaced by others that are functional.[44] It is not certain that the same thesis can be attributed to Alexander, insofar as conventional

---

[39] Morel 2015: 580-581: "se l'utile, essendo definito dalla soddisfazione dei bisogni vitali, è il referente naturale del giusto, allora il giusto conforme all'utile è allo stesso tempo conforme alla natura. In tal modo, la formula può avere un senso naturalista, senza con ciò escludere che la giustizia dipenda da un accordo." See also Morel 2007: 177-178.

[40] This is the meaning of *KD* XXXII and XXXIII, in which it appears that coexistence with others is neither spontaneous nor natural, but the result of a decision. Significant, however, is *KD* XXXIII (Οὐκ ἦν τι καθ'ἑαυτὸ δικαιοσύνη, ἀλλ'ἐν ταῖς μετ'ἀλλήλων συστροφαῖς καθ'ὁπηλίκους δήποτε ἀεὶ τόπους συνθήκη τις ὑπὲρ τοῦ μὴ βλάπτειν ἢ βλαπτεσθαι: "there never was an absolute justice, but only an agreement made in reciprocal intercourse in whatever localities now and again from time to time, providing against the infliction or suffering of harm" [transl. Hicks]), in which, according to Morel 2015, Epicurus denies justice *per se* of the Platonic kind, arguing instead that "il criterio del giusto è fornito dalla comunità, nella quale e a tutela della quale questa o quella legge viene istituita. È dunque nell'ambito di un patto, e in nessun altro luogo, che il giusto deve essere definito" (p. 579). Once again, the close dependence of legal justice on the human community is highlighted.

[41] Epicurus, *KD* XXXVI: Κατὰ μὲν <τὸ> κοινὸν πᾶσι τὸ δίκαιον τὸ αὐτό· συμφέρον γάρ τι ἦν ἐν τῇ πρὸς ἀλλήλους κοινωνίᾳ· κατὰ δὲ τὸ ἴδιον χώρας καὶ ὅσων δήποτε αἰτίων οὐ πᾶσι συνέπεται τὸ αὐτὸ δίκαιον εἶναι ("taken generally, justice is the same for all, to wit, something found expedient in mutual intercourse; but in its application to particular cases of locality or conditions of whatever kind, it varies under different circumstances" [transl. Hicks]).

[42] Such a pact, however, seems to have a natural origin: see Morel 2007: 177, which presents a useful association of the origin and development of the human community with the phenomenon of the origin of language (natural) and its development (conventional) found in Epicur. *Hrdt*, 75-76.

[43] Thanks to one of my anonymous reviewers for making these aspects explicit.

[44] Epicurus, *KD* XXXVII e XXXVIII.

laws are ways of exercising unwritten laws, which Alexander has the air of holding immutable.

*
* *

To conclude, I would like to try to answer two crucial questions raised by the second part of *Mantissa* 19: What is the theory attacked by Alexander of Aphrodisias? Who are the conventionalists that Alexander is targeting?

Regarding the first question, it seems to me that we can either identify two conventionalist theses or a single thesis supported by two types of arguments, ones older and dating back to the Sophists, the others more modern and of Epicurean origin.

The first thesis, or alternatively ancient arguments in support of a single thesis, is Sophistic in origin, and bases the conventionality of justice on two arguments: 1) the variability of laws, which change from place to place; 2) the force of laws, based on their being enshrined and written. Against this thesis, Alexander opposes the existence of unwritten, universally valid laws, the conventional component of which only concerns the way in which different countries apply these unwritten laws. The reference is clearly Aristotle, who, however, as will be noted, is not expressly mentioned. We have also noted that the theory proposed by Alexander about the coexistence of a natural and a conventional element in laws is only partly traceable to Aristotle.

The second thesis, or alternatively more modern arguments in support of a single thesis, starts from a Platonic observation (found in the passage from the *Republic* that we have read) and is articulated through arguments that seem to me of Epicurean origin, as attested by *Capital Maxims* XXXI-XXXVIII. According to the Platonic example – again, it will be noted that Plato is not explicitly mentioned here, although the example of the robbers makes us immediately think of *Republic* I 351c-e – any human association, even one formed to operate according to injustice, must be based on just rules, especially that of not prevaricating and not using mutual deception. We find a similar thesis, albeit more detailed, in Epicurus, according to which just by nature, strictly dependent on the human community (κοινωνία), is identified with the advantage of not being mutually wronged. This just, conceived as the useful in relation to mutual κοινωνία, for Epicurus is equal for all. It is a thesis largely shared by Alexander, a thesis that he nevertheless attacks on two fundamental points. For Epicurus, in fact, human association is not natural, in the sense that one can also decide not to associate; moreover, for Epicurus, rules that allow coexistence are the result of agreements and are all, it seems to me, declinations of the fundamental rule of not harming one another. Regarding this last, fundamental rule, scholars are divided between those who believe it is natural and those who believe it is conventional. If this rule is conventional, then Alexander's attack is strong, but if it is somewhat natural, then Alexander's criticism is toned down and his position may have been influenced by the Epicurean one. Indeed for Alexander, human beings tend by nature to associate, and the fundamental rules on which conventional laws are based are unwritten, universal and immutable laws. Proof of this basis is that if laws contrary to those recognized by Alexander as natural – such as not prevaricating and not deceiving one another; honouring the one who appears to be the strongest; keeping pacts; helping the weakest, etc. – were stipulated as just, no human association could survive. Alexander argues that if conventional rules safeguard the community, they will be natural. The concept of conventionality is greatly attenuated by Alexander since he characterizes it as a search for the natural right and an agreement to recognize it as such. Yet perhaps a similar position could also be attributed to Epicurus, albeit with due caution.

Let us now turn to the second important question, namely: Who are the conventionalists that Alexander attacks?

It has already been noted that no author is cited, although we can identify Platonic, Aristotelian, and Sophistic arguments (against which, in fact, both the Platonic example and Aristotelian arguments seem to go). As far as the 'more modern' conventionalists are concerned, it must honestly be acknowledged that the reference to Epicurus is not so obvious, although I have tried to show that there are some plausible arguments for bringing him up. Perhaps then we simply must ask ourselves whether these arguments would have any strength against the Epicurean position, whether or not they had it as a primary target.[45] Yet arguments that seem to go against the Epicurean position in *Mantissa* 19 are refuted, especially because Alexander never finds answers that do not come from his Aristotelian armoury. On the other hand, that Epicurus is not mentioned proves nothing: we have the well-known case of the *De fato*, in which Alexander never mentions the authors of the theory he attacks, who are identifiable with the Stoics. Nor is the fact that the theory presented by Alexander is not clearly recognizable as Epicurean a proof: after all, we do not know what version of Epicurean theory Alexander had at his disposal. Once again, the parallel with *De fato* is clear, because here Alexander attacks a Stoic version of determinism so unrecognizable that it has been assumed either that he produced an obviously erroneous version in order to criticize it more easily, or that it was the version of a Stoic of his time. Moreover, in other Alexander's works there are passages in which the Commentator *par excellence* polemicizes with Epicurus (see Sharples 1990), which leads us to conclude that in the second part of *Mantissa* 19 Epicurus and/or Epicureans could reasonably be his interlocutors.

---

[45] Thanks to one of my anonymous reviewers for this suggestion.

References

Accattino, P., 2015, "Una difesa aristotelica del giusto per natura: Alessandro di Afrodisia, Mantissa 19", in M. Bonelli (ed.), *Aristotele e Alessandro di Afrodisia (*Questioni etiche e Mantissa*). Metodo e oggetto dell'etica peripatetica*, Naples: Bibliopolis: 43-57.

Alexander of Aphrodisias, 1882, *Alexander Aphrodisiensis Praeter commentaria scripta minora, Commentaria in Aristotelem Graeca*, in I. Bruns (ed.), *Commentaria in Aristotelem Graeca*, Suppl. 2.2, Berlin: Academia litterarum Regiae Borussicae.

Alexander of Aphrodisias,1887, *De animi liber Mantissa*, in *Alexandri Aphrodisiensis praeter commentaria scripta minora, Commentaria in Aristotelem Graeca*, in I. Bruns (ed.), *Commentaria in Aristotelem Graeca*, Suppl. 2.1, Berlin: Academia litterarum Regiae Borussicae.

Diogenes Laertius, 1925, *Lives of Eminent Philosophers* II, R. D. Hicks (ed.), London: Loeb.

Donini, P.-L., 1995, "Alessandro di Afrodisia e i metodi dell'esegesi filosofica", in C. Moreschini (ed.), *Esegesi, parafrasi e compilazione in età tardoantica*, Naples: D'Auria: 107-129.

Epicurus, 1887, *Epikourou Kuriai Doxai*, in H. Usener (ed.), *Epicurea*, Leipzig: Teubner.

Morel, P.-M., 2000, "Épicure, l'histoire et le droit", *Revue des Études anciennes* 102: 393-411.

Morel, P.-M., 2007, "Les communautés humaines", in A. Girandet, – P.-M. Morel (eds.), *Lire Épicure et les épicuriens*, Paris: PUF: 167-186.

Morel, P.-M., 2015, "Alle origini del contrattualismo. La concezione epicurea del giusto tra natura e convenzione", *Iride* 28: 571-582.

Morel, P.-M., 2021, *La Nature et le bien. Aristote et la question naturaliste*, Louvain-la-Neuve: Peeters

Plato, 2000, *The Republic*, G. R. F Ferrari (ed.), T. Griffith (transl.), Cambridge: Cambridge University Press.

Rapp, Ch., 2021, "Whose State? Whose Nature? How Aristotle's polis is 'Natural'", in P. Adamson – Ch. Rapp (eds.), *State and Nature – Studies in Ancient and Medieval Philosophy*, Berlin: De Gruyter: 81-118.

Sharples, R. W., 1990, "The School of Alexander?", in R. Sorabji (ed.), *Aristotle Transformed*, London: Duckworth: 83-111.

Sharples, R. W., 2004, *Alexander of Aphrodisias, Supplement On the Soul*, transl. by R.W. Sharples, London: Bloomsbury.

Sharples, R. W., 2005, "An Aristotelian Commentator on the Naturalness of Justice", in C. Gill (ed.), *Virtue, Norms and Objectivity: Issues in Ancient and Modern Ethics*, Oxford: Clarendon Press, 279-293.

Striker, G., 1996, *Essays on Hellenistic Epistemology and Ethics*, Cambridge: Cambridge University Press.

Vegetti, M., 1998, "Trasimaco", in Plato, *La repubblica* I, M. Vegetti (ed.), Naples: Bibliopolis, 233-256.

ABOUT THE CONTRIBUTORS

Mauro Bonazzi is Professor of Ancient Philosophy at the University of Bologna. He is the author of several books and articles on the Sophists, Plato and Platonism. Among his recents publications: *En quête des Idées. Platonisme et philosophie hellénistique d'Antiochus à Plotin*, Paris, Vrin («Histoire des doctrines de l'antiquité classique») 2015; *The Sophists*, Cambridge, Cambridge University Press 2021; *Platonism: A Concise History from the Early Academy to Late Antiquity*, Cambridge, Cambridge University Press 2023.

Maddalena Bonelli is Associate Professor of Ancient Philosophy at the University of Bergamo. She is the author of three books and several articles on Plato, Aristotle, Alexander of Aphrodisia, the Peripatetic tradition, and on women philosophers of the Antiquity. Among her books: *Alessandro di Afrodisia e la metafisica come scienza dimostrativa* (2001), Timée le Sophiste: *lexique platonicien* (2007), *Leggere il* Fedone *di Platone* (2015). She has also edited *Filosofe, Maestre, Imperatrici. Per un nuovo canone della storia della filosofia antica* (2020).

Jean-Baptiste Gourinat is Directeur de recherche (Senior Researcher) at the CNRS and currently Director of the "Centre de recherches sur la pensée antique Léon Robin", a CNRS research unit at Sorbonne Université, in Paris. His research in ancient philosophy focuses on Stoicism, Aristotle and the Neoplatonic tradition. His main publications include *Les stoïciens et l'âme* (1996, 2nd ed. 2017), *La dialectique des stoïciens* (2000), *Le stoïcisme* (2007, 6th ed. 2023), Plotin, *Traité 20, Qu'est-ce que la dialectique ? traduction et commentaire* (2016). He is also the editor of several volumes including *L'éthique du stoïcien Hiéroclès* (*Philosophie antique* Hors-Série 2016) and (with J. Lemaire), *Logique et dialectique dans l'Antiquité* (2016).

Giuliana Leone is Professor of Papyrology at the University of Naples Federico II. Her main interest are Herculaneum papyri and in particular those containing books of Epicurus' *On Nature*. She published critical editions of Books 2 (2012, La scuola di Epicuro, vol. 18), 14 (1984, Cronache Ercolanesi), and 34 (2002, Cronache Ercolanesi), and studies on many others (especially Books 3 and 11). She is the author of several articles on the digitalization of ancient inventories of Herculaneum Papyri and on the history of the studies of Papyrology. She has also edited, with Francesca Masi and Francesco Verde, *'Vedere l'invisibile'. Rileggendo il XXXIV libro Sulla natura di Epicuro* (2020).

Stéphane Marchand is an Assistant Professor (Maître de conférences) at the University Paris 1 Panthéon Sorbonne (Gramata – SPHERE UMR 7219). He specializes in the History of Ancient Skepticism and has published several papers on this topic, along with co-authoring collective books (with F. Verde, *Epicurisme et Scepticisme*, Sapienza Università Editrice, 2013; with D. Machuca, *Les raisons du doute*, Garnier, 2018) and a monograph (*Le Scepticisme*, Vrin, 2018). Additionally, he has translated Plato's *Gorgias* and Gorgias' *Encomium of Helen* (with Pierre Ponchon).

Stefano Maso is Full Professor of Ancient Philosophy at the Università Ca' Foscari, Venezia. He studies mainly the thought of the Sophists, Stoicism, Epicureanism and philosophy in Rome. He has translated into Italian *Dissoi logoi* and Cicero's *De fato*. Among his recent books: *Grasp and Dissent. Cicero and Epicurean Philosophy* (2017); *Dissoi logoi*, Edizione criticamente rivista (2018); *Cicero's Philosophy* (2023). He has also edited, with Iker Martínez Fernández, *Diez estudios sobre filosofía helenística y romana. La escuela italiana contemporánea* (2022).

Phillip Mitsis is the Alexander S. Onassis Professor of Hellenic Culture and Civilization at New York University and Academic Director of the American Institute for Verdi Studies. He writes on ancient philosophy and its influence on early modern philosophers, and on Greek and Roman literature. Recent publications include *Natura Aut Voluntas. Recherches sur la pensée politique et éthique hellénistique et romaine et son influence* (Brepols, 2020) and, as editor, *The Oxford Handbook of Epicurus and Epicureanism* (Oxford University Press, 2020).

Pierre-Marie Morel is Professor of Ancient Philosophy at the University Paris 1 – Panthéon-Sorbonne (Gramata – SPHERE UMR 7219) and member of the Institut Universitaire de France. He is the author of several books and articles on Aristotle, Democritus and the Epicurean tradition. He has translated into French Epicurus'*Letters* and *Maxims* and the fragments of Diogenes of Oinoanda. Among his recent books: *La nature et le bien. L'éthique d'Aristote et la question naturaliste* (2021) and *Le plaisir et la nécessité. Philosophie naturelle et anthropologie chez Démocrite et Épicure* (2021). He has also edited, with Francesca Masi and Francesco Verde, *Epicureanism and Scientific Debates. Antiquity and Late Reception*, vol. 1 (2023).

Attila Németh is Senior Research Fellow at the Institute of Philosophy, The Research Centre for the Humanities, HUN-REN, Budapest. He is the author of Epicurus on the Self, London: Routledge (2017/2020), and published several papers on ancient atomism, Hellenistic philosophy and Seneca. He has edited with Dániel Schmal, *The Self in Ancient and Early Modern Philosophy*, London: Bloomsbury

(2025), and with Andreas Blank, *Esteem and the Self in the History of Philosophy*, London: Routledge (2025).

Wim Nijs received his PhD in Classical Studies and in Philosophy from KU Leuven and Sapienza Università di Roma in 2022. He is a Postdoctoral Researcher in Greek Studies at KU Leuven, where he specializes in the intellectual culture and philosophy of the Hellenistic and Roman periods. He was recently awarded a Junior Research Fellowship from the Research Foundation – Flanders (FWO) to investigate the pathology of interpersonal aggression in Early Imperial culture. He has recently published a monograph on *The Epicurean Sage in the Ethics of Philodemus* (Brill, Leiden-Boston 2024), and has written several articles and papers, both on the ancient Epicureans and on non-Epicurean authors such as Plutarch and Lucian.

Geert Roskam is Professor of ancient Greek literature at the KU Leuven. He is the author of several books and articles on Hellenistic philosophy (esp. Epicureanism) and Middle-Platonism (esp. Plutarch). He has published commentaries on several of Plutarch's works (2007 and 2009) and is also the author of *On the Path to Virtue. The Stoic Doctrine of Moral Progress and its Reception in (Middle-)Platonism* (Leuven 2005), *'Live Unnoticed' (Λάθε βιώσας). On the Vicissitudes of an Epicurean Doctrine* (Leiden-Boston 2007) and *Plutarch* (Cambridge 2021).

Francesco Verde is an Associate Professor of the History of Ancient Philosophy at Sapienza University of Rome. His research interests focus mainly on Hellenistic philosophies, including Epicureanism, Peripatos, Sceptical Academy, and Stoicism. Some of his recent publications include F. Verde (ed.), *Epicuro: Epistola a Pitocle*, In collaborazione con M. Tulli-D. De Sanctis-F. G. Masi, Academia, Baden-Baden 2022 and *Peripatetic Philosophy in Context: Knowledge, Time, and Soul from Theophrastus to Cratippus*, De Gruyter, Berlin-Boston 2022.

INDEX OF ANCIENT NAMES

Aegyptus (son of Zeus) 155 and n.
Alexander of Aphrodisias 7, 108, 245-247 and n., 249-251 and n., 253-257, 259
Alexinus of Elis 180
Amynomachus 182
Anaxagoras 21, 224
Anaxarchus 237 and n.
Anaximenes 15, 21
Antiochus IV Epiphanes 207
Antipater (Epicurean) 183, 186-188
Apelles (addressee of Epicurus' *Letter to Apelles*) 52, 56
Aphrodite 62
Apollodorus (Epicurean) 47n.
Arcesilaus 86-87, 100, 182
Archelaus (mentioned in Diog. Oen. NF 215) 184-185
Archimedes 57-58
Ariadne 148n.
Aristo of Chios 85
Aristobulus of Cassandreia 63
Aristotle 5, 7, 15, 21, 27, 29, 32-34 and n., 41-42, 43n., 44, 48, 50, 67, 78 and n., 79n., 93-94 and n., 113 n., 115n., 119-120, 134, 137, 150n., 167-168, 187 and n., 195 and n., 212, 223n., 224n., 237n., 245, 246n., 249-250, 253, 254n., 256, 259-260
Athenaeus 48, 167 and n., 181
Attalus (Stoic) 210
Aulus Gellius 84
Balbus (Stoic) 102
Batis (Epicurean) 181
Boethus (Epicurean) 144n., 145n.
Brasidas 250n.
Bryson 239
Carneades 79
Cato (the Younger) 194 and n.

Chrysippus 4, 79, 83-89, 99, 101-102, 105-111, 116, 181
Cicero 6, 53-54, 76n., 85-88 and n., 90-93 and n., 95-96, 99-104, 106-107, 109, 112-115, 127, 150n., 177, 182-183, 193-207 and n., 209-210 and n., 212-214 and n., 219, 225, 260
Claranus (Senecas' addressee) 210
Cleanthes 84-85, 87-89, 97, 102-105, 109, 207
Clement of Alexandria 218-219
Colotes of Lampsacus 172, 174 and n., 235
Damascius 233 and n.
Danaus 155 and n.
Demeter 104
Demetrius Laco 16, 50, 144-146 and n., 156, 157n., 160 and n., 177, 231, 232n.
Democritus 16, 21, 27n., 86, 119, 145n., 171-173 and n., 212, 244, 237-239 and n., 260
Diodorus Cronus 238-239 and n.
Diodotus (Athenian orator) 27n.
Diogenes (mentioned in Arcesilaus' will) 182
Diogenes Laertius 5, 11, 52n., 68-73 and n., 75, 85, 88-95 and n., 98, 113-114, 123n., 179-181 and n., 204, 218
Diogenes of Oinoanda 1, 4, 6-7, 27-28, 30n., 36, 39, 141n., 147n., 156, 177-178 and n., 182-189, 200, 260
Diogenes (of Tarsus, Epicurean) 63
Diomedes 62
Dion (mentioned in Diog. Oen. NF 215) 184-185
Dionysus 104
Dioscuri 104
Diotimus (Democritean or Stoic philosopher) 181, 224-225

Epictetus 110-111, 116n.
Euclid 49, 57-58, 63
Euripides 61
Florus 168
Galen 88
Gorgias 260
Hector 52, 57
Hera 104
Heracles 155 and n.
Heraclitus 52, 61-62
Hermarchus 126, 129-130, 179-180, 182-183, 212 and n., 254n.
Hermes 104
Herodotus (addressee of Epicurus' *Letter to Herodotus*) 25, 179, 220-221
Hesiod 47
Hieronymus of Rhodes 199
Homer 52, 55, 57, 62, 119, 167n.
Idomeneus 129, 156, 179, 181-183, 208, 210
Lactantius 148
Leonteus 155-156, 181
Leontion 155n., 158-159
Lucian 261
Lucilius (Senecas' addressee) 212
Lucretius 2, 12, 18-20, 22, 61, 78n., 120, 126, 128, 130-135 and n., 144-146 and n., 150, 156-158 and n., 159n., 160 and n., 177, 184n., 193-194, 197, 200, 206, 213
Lyco 182
Lysias 126-127
Mammarion 56, 58
Medea 148n.
Meno 223, 225, 231
Metrodorus of Chios 237 and n.
Metrodorus of Lampsacus 50n., 52, 56-57, 148 and n., 153, 155 and n., 156, 158-160, 179-182, 200, 209 and n., 212 and n.
Mys 56

Nausiphanes 48 and n., 50 and n., 236-237 and n.
Numenius 87, 100n.
Odysseus 61, 63
Oenomaus 85
Olympiodorus 29, 223n.
Pantheia 63
Parmenides 239n.
Pelias 148n.
Persaeus (Stoic) 104
Phaedrus (Epicurean) 177, 200
Phalaris 210
Philip of Opus 57
Philo of Larissa 205
Philodemus of Gadara 29, 36 and n., 50, 54-55, 56n., 59n., 60, 62, 92 n., 135n., 141n., 143n., 148n., 149-156 and n., 177, 179-180
Philonides of Laodicea 180, 207 and n.
Plato 5, 29, 32-34, 41, 44, 48, 50, 53, 54n., 67, 71, 76-77, 79, 86-87 and n., 94, 99, 100n., 107, 110-111, 113n., 115n., 167 and n., 169-172, 182, 186-188, 194, 224-225, 239n., 252, 256, 259-260
Plutarch 3-5, 19, 54, 56-60, 62-63 and n., 75, 83, 85, 107, 110-111 and n., 129, 144n., 148n., 150n., 156n., 167-174 and n., 235 and n., 261
Polyaenus 85, 148n., 155-156, 160, 167-168, 179, 181, 208
Polystratus 173n., 235
Porphyry 254n.
Posidonius 85, 103n.
Prodicus 104
Protagoras 86, 87n., 168, 170, 172
Protarchus of Bargylia 180
Pyrrho of Elis 48, 168, 172, 235n., 236-239 and n.
Pythagoras 57, 145n.
Pythocles (addressee of Epicurus' *Letter to Pythocles*) 52, 55-58, 179-180

INDEX OF ANCIENT NAMES

Saint Ambrose 209
Seneca 6, 113-115, 180, 186, 188-189, 193, 199n., 205n., 207-214 and n., 260
Servius (commentator) 206
Sextus Empiricus 7, 48-50, 53, 60, 71, 75-77, 85-86, 95-100, 112, 170, 217, 219-220, 225-235 and n., 240
Siro (Epicurean) 177
Socrates 32n., 77, 86, 91n., 113, 171, 223-225, 253
Speusippus 115n.
Stilpo of Megara 208 and n., 239
Thaumasias (relative of Arcesilaus) 182
Themison of Cyprus 187 and n.
Theodoridas of Lindos (Epicurean) 185-187
Theon (Aelius) 62n., 181n.
Theopheides (Hermarchus' addressee) 180

Theophrastus 16
Theopompus 63
Theotimus (imitator of Epicurus)
Thrasymachus 252 and n.
Timocleia 63
Timocrates 148
Timon of Phlius 48, 78n., 235-236
Tityos 113
Torquatus (Epicurean) 53-54, 58, 60, 62, 177, 197
Triarius 53
Varro 101
Velleius (Epicurean) 102, 104, 205, 229n.
Xenophon 63, 167n.
Zeno of Citium 83-89 and n., 98-102 and n., 104-105 and n., 109-110, 115n., 194 and n.
Zeno of Sidon 50n., 143n., 177, 181, 200
Zeus 49, 104, 129

INDEX OF MODERN NAMES

Accattino, P. 245n., 246n., 249 and n., 250n., 254n.
Adam, H. 57n.
Albini, F. 57n.
Alesse, F. 100n., 110n., 148n.
Angeli, A. 27n., 29-30 and n., 33n., 83n., 85 and n., 143n., 179
Annas, J. 159n., 227n.
Arenson, K. E. 159n.
Arkins, B. 159n.
Armstrong, D. 36n., 149n.
Arrighetti, G. 12n., 16n., 17-21 and n., 61n., 73, 75
Asmis, E. 51n., 54n., 59 and n., 74n., 75n., 78n., 119n., 131n., 220n., 224 and n., 225n., 234n.
Assante, M. G. 157n.
Aubert-Baillot, S. 207n.
Babut, D. 111n.
Bailey, C. 14 and n., 71 and n., 73, 180, 202n., 222n.
Bakker, F. A. 2, 21 and n., 67n., 73n., 142n., 153n., 222n., 240n.
Barigazzi, A. 17-21 and n., 235n., 237n.
Barnes, J. 93n., 221n., 227n.
Bénatouïl, T. 29n., 37n., 43n., 50n., 142n.
Bendlin, A. 144n.
Berti, E. 78n.
Besnier, B. 222n., 225n.
Betegh, G. 229n., 240n.
Bett, R. 219n., 220 and n., 226n., 231n., 232n., 233n., 236n., 238n.
Bignone, E. 15 and n., 73, 78n.
Blank, A. 260n.
Blank, D. 48n., 55n., 56n., 59n., 68n.
Bollack, J. 13 and n.
Bollack, M. 13 and n.
Bonazzi, M. 2, 5, 167, 169n., 223n., 236n., 240n., 259

Bonelli, M. 7, 25n., 245, 259
Bown, A. 25n., 76n., 125-127 and n.
Brennan, T. 143n., 159n.
Brochard, V. 236n.
Brown, E. 149n.
Brown, R. D. 141n., 144n., 145n., 146n., 159n.
Brunschwig, J. 3, 21 and n., 224n., 232n., 233n., 237n.
Burnyeat, M. F. 237n.
Cacciabaudo, F. 2
Casevitz, M. 111n.
Cassan, M. 2
Castagnoli, L. 25n., 172n.
Cavalli, R. 68n.
Cavallo, G. 144n.
Celkyte, A. 59n.
Chandler, C. 55n.
Chantraine, P. 119n.
Chilton, C. W. 143n.
Clay, D. 48n., 52n., 55n., 144n., 178 and n., 182 and n., 183n., 187 and n.
Colaizzo, M. 143n.
Collette-Dučić, B. 111n.
Collingwood, R. G. 129 and n.
Comparetti, D. 114n.
Corradi, M. 78n.
Corsi, F. G. 2, 142n.
Corti, A. 14n., 144n., 146n., 157n.
Corti, L. 228n.
Couissin, P. 236n.
Curd, P. 237n.
D'Anna, G. 201n.
De Lacy, Ph. 132-133 and n., 135n., 174n.
De Sanctis, D. 2, 12n., 261n.
Decleva Caizzi, F. 170n., 236n., 238n., 239n.
Delattre, D. 13 and n., 31 and n., 155n.
Desbordes, F. 228n.

DeWitt, N. W. 202n.
Di Fabio, T. 51n., 161n.
Diano, C. 4, 5, 119-120 and n., 123, 125-126, 128-129, 131-132
Dixon, S. 153n.
Donini, P.-L. 249n.
Dorandi, T. 2, 5, 67n., 72-73 and n., 122, 123n.
Duvernoy, J.-F. 141n.
Dyson, H. 84n., 88n., 108n.
Erbì, M. 2, 55n., 67n., 179-180 and n., 181n., 182n.
Erler, M. 2, 36n., 48n., 54n., 55n., 59n., 167n.
Eshleman, K. 62n.
Evans, M. 149n.
Ferrari, G. R. F. 145n.
Fine, G. 57n.
Fitzgerald, J. T. 183n.
Flamigni, G. 116n.
Flemming, R. 141n., 160n.
Flores, E. 12, 18 and n.
Forcignanò, F. 2
Fowler, D. P. 131n., 132
Fratantuono, L. 158n.
Frede, D. 149n.
Freeman, K. 48n.
Furley, D. 171n.
Gale, M. R. 20n.
Gargiulo, T. 49n.
Gassendi, P. 8, 71, 73n.
Gavray, M.-A. 240n.
Giannantoni, G. 119n.
Gigandet, A. 240n.
Gigante, M. 11, 75, 141n., 143n., 146n., 217 and n., 237n., 238n.
Giorgianni, F. 144n., 146n., 157n.
Giovacchini, J. 2, 37n., 141n., 225n., 230n.
Glad, C. E. 150n.
Gladhill, C. W. 131n.

Glidden, D. K. 217n., 221n., 228n., 230n.
Glucker, J. 195 and n.
Goldschmidt, V. 84n.
Gomperz, T. 17 and n.
Gordon, P. 51n., 144n., 159n., 161n., 177n., 178n., 179 and n., 181n.
Goulet, R. 84n.
Gourinat, J.-B. 2, 4, 35n., 83, 84n., 87n., 88n., 99n., 110n., 111n., 116n., 205n., 230n., 259
Graff Fara, D. 127n.
Graver, M. 186n.
Güremen, R. 177n.
Hadot, I. 83n.
Hahmann A. 3-4, 67-71 and n., 72n., 77, 78n.
Hall, A. S. 183n.
Hammerstaedt, J. 2, 30n., 147n., 177n., 183-184 and n., 185n., 221n., 222n.
Hankinson, R. J. 142n.
Havrda, M. 218n.
Hvradas, M. 240n.
Hershbell, J. P. 172n.
Heßler, J. E. 2, 55n., 121-122 and n., 124n.
Inwood, B. 180 and n.
Ioppolo, A. M. 78n., 79n., 85n.
Iovine, G. 21 and n.
Irwin, T. 25n.
Isnardi Parente, M. 20n., 21 and n., 73
Jackson-McCabe, M. 115n.
Jones, C. P. 184n.
Kechagia, E. 85 and n., 169n., 172n., 174 and n.
Konstan, D. 2, 92n., 116n., 119n., 127-128 and n., 141n.
Kurz, D. 27n., 29
Laks, A. 48n., 182n., 240n.
Lambinus, D. 201n.
Lapini, W. 12 and n., 14n.
Leiwo, M. 152n.
Lentricchia, M. 154n.

INDEX OF MODERN NAMES

Leone, G. 2-3, 11 and n., 12n., 14n., 15n., 16n., 19n., 20n., 142n., 203n., 238n., 259
Lesher, J. H. 33n., 34n.
Lévy, C. 195n.
Lloyd, G. E. 27n.
Long, A. A. 69n., 72n., 73 and n., 74n., 75, 87n., 121 and n., 124n., 125-129 and n., 131 and n., 173n., 222n.
Longo Auricchio, F. 48n., 160n.
Machuca, D. E. 231n., 234n., 260
Malaspina, E. 205n.
Manfredi, M. 20 and n.
Mansfeld, J. 103n.
Marchand, S. 2, 7, 25n., 217 and n., 228n., 231n., 233n., 260
Marmodoro, A. 25n.
Martínez Fernández, I. 260
Masi, F. G. 1-2 and n., 8, 14n., 16 and n., 17n., 32n., 67n., 70n., 142n., 204n., 212n., 238n., 240n., 259-261
Maso, S. 2, 6, 193, 194n., 197n., 198n., 201n., 202n., 205n., 212n., 214n., 240n., 260
McOsker, M. 36n., 59n., 61n.
Mensch, P. 34n., 78n.
Mikeš, V. 240n.
Miller, J. 78n.
Mingucci, G. 2, 246n.
Mitsis, F. 2, 4-5, 25n., 119, 149n., 260
Monet, A. 3, 21 and n.
Morel, P.-M. 1-3, 8, 13 and n., 25, 29n., 35n., 67n., 75n., 89n., 91n., 92n., 94n., 120n., 130n., 132n., 135n., 136n., 159n., 172n., 177n., 185n., 219n., 237n., 240n., 250n., 254n., 255n., 260
Movia, G. 78n.
Muller, R. 238n., 239n.
Natorp, P. 72n.
Németh A. 2, 6, 69n., 177, 184n., 240n., 260

Netz, R. 55n.
Nijs, W. 2, 5, 25n., 36n., 141, 143n., 144n., 146n., 149n., 150n., 261
Nussbaum, M. C. 141n., 159n.
O'Connor, D. K. 149n.
O'Keefe, T. 56n., 149n., 173n.
Obbink, D. 218n., 229n., 230n.
Opsomer, J. 171n.
Parisi, A. 47n., 50n., 54n.
Pease, A. S. 201n., 218n.
Peralta, A. 2
Perin, C. 231n.
Philippson, R. 202n.
Piergiacomi, E. 2, 16n., 119n., 120 and n., 144n., 237n.
Podolak, P. 56n.
Ponchon, P. 260
Pope, M. 145n.
Purinton, J. 202n.
Powell, J. G. F. 194n., 195n.
Pucci, P. 119n.
Puglia, E. 144n.
Ranocchia, G. 144n., 146n., 157n.
Rapp, Ch. 246n.
Remes, P. 152n.
Rist, J. M. 149n.
Robitzsch, J. M. 3-4, 67-71 and n., 72n., 77, 78n., 89n.
Rosenmeyer, P. A. 178n., 183n.
Rosini, C. M. 12, 17
Roskam, G. 2-3, 47, 50n., 51n., 57n., 143n., 148n., 160n., 188n., 214n., 261
Rover, C. 2, 8n., 222n.
Runia, D. 103n.
Santoro, M. 16n.
Schiesaro, A. 131n.
Schmal, D. 260
Schneider, J. G. 72 and n.
Scott, D. 32n., 34n., 115n.

Sedley, D. N. 3, 21 and n., 72n., 73-75 and n., 83n., 91n., 92n., 93n., 95n., 96, 97n., 99n., 115n., 116, 121 and n., 124n., 125, 128, 153n., 171n., 173n., 194n., 221n., 222 and n., 224 and n., 237n., 238 and n., 239n.
Senkova, M. 160n.
Setaioli, A. 207, 209n., 210n., 212n., 214n.
Sharples, R. W. 245n., 246n., 248n., 249n., 250n., 251 and n., 253n., 254n., 257
Sider, D. 51n.
Smith, M. F. 30n., 147n., 177n., 182-183 and n., 184n., 185 and n., 186n.
Smith, P. J. 231n., 240n.
Snyder, H. G. 207n.
Spinelli, E. 2, 25n., 27n., 76n., 78n., 228n., 232n., 236n.
Striker, G. 70n., 78n., 93n., 94, 99n., 129n., 236 and n., 254n.
Suits, D. B. 152n.
Svavarsson, S. H. 235n., 237n.
Taub, L. C. 142n.
Tepedino Guerra, A. 48n., 238n.
Todd, R. B. 15n.
Togni, P. 94 and n.
Trabattoni, F. 2, 25n., 71n., 78n.

Tsouna, V. 2, 25n., 37n., 43n., 56n., 70n., 91n., 92n., 97n., 116n., 142n., 149n., 152n., 218n., 229 and n., 240n.
Tulli, M. 261
Tutrone, F. 141n., 143n., 144n., 153n.
Usener, H. 11 and n., 14, 72-74, 121 and n., 144n., 179, 201n., 207, 217, 223n., 224, 234n.
Vamvouri Ruffy, M. 62n.
van Beethoven, L. 60-61, 63
Van der Stockt, L. 150n.
Vassallo C. 104n.
Vegetti, M. 252n.
Verde, F. 1-4 and n., 8, 12n., 13n., 14 and n., 15n., 16n., 25n., 27n., 37n., 48n., 50n., 55n., 59n., 67, 68n., 77n., 79n., 89n., 91n., 93n., 119n., 127n., 142n., 145n., 170-171 and n., 179 and n., 217n., 240n., 259-261
Vogliano, A. 17 and n., 19-20 and n.
von Arnim, H. 100
von der Mühll, P. 73-75, 121
Warren, J. 58n., 144n., 152n., 154n., 194n., 237n.
Westerink, L. G. 224n.
White, M. J. 50n.
White, S. 73, 74n., 75, 222n.
Wismann, H. 43 and n.
Zacher, K.-D. 57n.
Zucca, D. 2, 240n.

Milton Keynes UK
Ingram Content Group UK Ltd.
UKHW022025041124
450718UK00008B/98